20th Century Anecdotes

ALSO BY FRANK PEPPER IN SPHERE BOOKS:

20th Century Quotations
Dictionary of Biographical Quotations

20th Century Anecdotes

Compiled by

Frank S. Pepper

SPHERE BOOKS LIMITED

A SPHERE BOOK

First published in Great Britain 1990 by
Sphere Books Ltd

Typeset by Selectmove Ltd, London
Printed and bound in Great Britain by
Cox & Wyman Ltd, Reading

ISBN 0 7474 0022 9

Sphere Books Ltd
A Division of
Macdonald & Co (Publishers) Ltd
Orbit House
1 New Fetter Lane
London EC4A 1AR
A member of Maxwell Pergamon Publishing Corporation plc

Contents

This book reflects the varied life and mind of its compiler. Frank Pepper was the creator of Roy of the Rovers, Rookfist Rogan, Captain Condor and many other heroes from children's comics over the past fifty years. Under different pen-names he also wrote adventure stories and educational books. Even after he retired from full-time writing, he produced a series of reference books which is completed by *Twentieth Century Anecdotes*.

Fans of his comic-strip heroes were enthalled by Frank Pepper's appreciation of the bizarre but telling situation around which each week's instalment was spun. In this collection of anecdotes that appreciation of the bizarre is transferred to the events of real life.

As a freelance journalist Frank Pepper saw the twentieth century develop and he gathered together a vast reference library of newspaper cuttings, each one recording an extraordinary situation or thought-provoking story. This book is drawn from them and paints a portrait of the century through its witty episodes and remarkable characters.

Frank Pepper died at the end of 1988 soon after completing this collection. Its publication will add still more to the many amusing stories he told.

ABDICATION

In the evening we dined at the Stanleys' cheerless, characterless house, and at ten o'clock turned on the wireless to hear "His Royal Highness Prince Edward" speaking his farewell words in his unmistakable slightly Long Island voice. It was a manly, sincere farewell, saying that he could not carry on the responsibilities of Kingship without the support of the woman he loved. There was stillness in the Stanleys' room. I wept, and murmured a prayer for he who had once been Edward VIII.

Then we played bridge.

Sir Henry Channon, DIARY 11 *Dec* 1963

Lord Louis Mountbatten was with the new George VI on the sad evening in December 1936 when the two men had stood in Fort Belvedere together watching the ex-king pack his bags.

"Dickie, this is absolutely terrible," Mountbatten remembers the new king saying. "I'm only a naval officer. It's the only thing I know about."

"This is a very curious coincidence," Lord Mountbatten replied, for my father once told me that when the Duke of Clarence died your father came to him and said almost the same things that you have said to me now and my father answered: "George, you're wrong. There is no more fitting preparation for a king than to have been trained in the navy."

Robert Lacey, MAJESTY 1977

ABORTION

Students at the University of California were asked by Mr L. Agnew of the department of Medical History for their reaction to the following:

"The father has syphilis, the mother tuberculosis. They have had four children – the first blind, the second died, the third was deaf and dumb, the fourth had tuberculosis. The mother is pregnant with her fifth child. The parents are willing to have an abortion. You have to make the decision."

Most of the students voted in favour of abortion. Mr Agnew's comment to them: "Congratulations. You have just murdered Beethoven."

Revd Michael Stagg, OUTLOOK

ABSENTMINDEDNESS

William Cecil, bishop of Exeter, was travelling by train to a confirmation when he mislaid his ticket and was unable to produce it for an inspector who assured him, "It's quite all right, my Lord. We know who you are." "That's all very well," replied the bishop, "but without my ticket how do I know where I am going?"

John Train, TRULY REMARKABLE OCCURRENCES 1978 (*Versions of this story are told of other notoriously absentminded people including G. K. Chesterton and Dwight Morrow*)

The absentminded G. K. Chesterton was devoted to his mother. When he became engaged to be married he was so eager to share the happy event with her that he went straight home and wrote her a long letter. Mrs Chesterton was delighted with her son's news, although she was not at all surprised to receive his letter. She was in the room with him when he wrote it.

J. Braude, SPEAKERS' AND TOASTMASTERS' HANDBOOK 1971

On rising this morning I carefully washed my boots in hot water and blacked my face, poured coffee on the sardines and put my hat on the fire to boil. These activities will give you some idea of my state of mind.

G. K. Chesterton, letter to a friend, reporting his engagement, quoted Maisie Ward, GILBERT KEITH CHESTERTON 1944

Out of Chesterton's absentmindedness grew the individual garb. In days when great attention was paid to wearing clothes to suit the occasion he would turn up to a lecture in plus fours and a tail coat accidentally taken from a friend half his size – and talk wonderingly about the miracle that had either shrunk his coat or increased his girth. Despairing of making him tidy, Frances determined instead to make him picturesque. She covered his disorder with the flowing cloak and broadbrimmed hat – a style he happily adopted as his trademark.

John Ennis, Reader's Digest, The Man Who Was G.K.C. May 1974

In the years before the Great War a huge shambling man, six feet four inches tall, with long chestnut hair and weight 20 stone, could often be seen wandering down Fleet Street. Dressed in a black cloak and a sombrero hat, with pince-nez perched incongruously on his nose, he carried a swordstick and his pockets bulged with "penny dreadfuls". From time to time he stopped to read a book or write something down, or paused in the middle of the road while the traffic whirled about him, apparently struck by a most important thought. Most of the time he seemed to be chuckling over secret jokes of his own. This was G. K. Chesterton.

Richard Ingrams, Telegraph Magazine 24 *May* 1974

Lady Diana Cooper was chronically unable to recognise faces (including, now and then, her son's). In the interval of a Covent Garden gala in honour of the 100th birthday of Sir Robert Mayer, the musical benefactor, she was approached by "an extremely pleasant lady" who seemed vaguely familiar. Trying desperately to find a name to match the face she struggled through some general conversation. Then the awful truth dawned. "I sank into a curtsey and said 'I am terribly sorry Ma'am. I didn't recognise you without your crown on.' The Queen, not batting a royal eyelid said, 'Well, I thought it should be Sir Robert's evening.'"

Nigel Ryan, Daily Telegraph 21 *Jun* 1986

"Peking, Alec. Peking, Peking." Sir Alec Douglas-Home's devoted wife Elizabeth would constantly repeat to him while walking behind him down the steps of the aeroplane, when he was Foreign Secretary. "Peking, Peking" in order to prevent him saying to his hosts as he stood before the microphone, "I am very happy to be back in Montreal" (or Rome, or Washington, or Moscow).

William Douglas-Home, MR HOME PRONOUNCED HUME 1979

Professor Irwin Edman's absentmindedness was his trade mark and the source of much humour at Columbia University. One day he stopped a student on Riverside Drive and asked "Pardon me, am I walking north or south?" The student answered, "North, Professor." "Ah," replied Edman, "then I have had my lunch."

Bennett Cerf, TRY AND STOP ME 1946

Professor Irwin Edman spent an evening with a colleague and his wife and the conversation was spirited until about two o'clock in the morning when, after several elaborate yawns had been ignored the colleague said, "Irwin, I hate to put you out, but I have a nine o'clock class in the morning." "Good lord!" said Irwin, blushing violently, "I thought *you* were in *my* house."

Ibid.

Roger Fry was dreamy, vague, incapable of noticing anything but spiritual discomfort. I was lunching at his home after a sitting. His slippers could not be found anywhere, and a game of hunt-the-slipper ensued. In the midst of the fun a loud crash was heard, and a voice said, "Coal, sir." "Put it, my good man –" said Fry, whirling round and round like a kitten chasing its tail, losing his spectacles and speaking in a voice weak from fatigue "– Oh well, put it on the bed." At this point I found the slippers in the milk jug, and the fun stopped.

Edith Sitwell, TAKEN CARE OF 1965

At a party at the home of the German mathematician David Hilbert his wife noticed that he had neglected to put on a clean shirt. She ordered him to do so. He went upstairs; ten minutes passed, Hilbert did not return. Mrs Hilbert went upstairs to find Hilbert lying peacefully in bed. It was the natural sequence of things. He took off his coat, then his tie, then his shirt and so on, and went to sleep.

George Polya, SOME MATHEMATICIANS I HAVE MET

My tutor at Eton, Mr Arthur James, had a brilliant brain for classics, but not for other things. After he retired he went to live near Paignton, in Devonshire. One day he was bicycling home when he met a friend who stopped him and in the course of conversation remarked that James had got a new bicycle. "Dear me," said James, "I must have taken the postmaster's by mistake." He thereupon returned to the post office, some seven miles, leaned the bicycle against the wall, went inside, apologised to the postmaster, mounted the same bicycle and rode home on it.

Cyril P. Foley, AUTUMN FOLIAGE 1935

William James was walking along a Cambridge, Massachusetts, street accompanied by a pair of his students, a boy and a girl. A large, imposing figure, white-bearded, swinging his cane, talking to himself, oblivious to others, approached them. Remarked the girl, "Whoever he is, he is the epitome of the absent-minded professor.". "What you really mean," said James, "is that he is present-minded somewhere else."

Jacques Barzun, A STROLL WITH WILLIAM JAMES 1983

As he was not due to appear in the opening scenes of *Peer Gynt* at the Old Vic Wilfred Lawson decided to view them from the dress circle, and amazed a woman sitting next to him by leaning across during an unexpected lull in the action and whispering, "This is where I come in."

Sheridan Morley, Radio Times 27 *Jul–2 Aug* 1985

The Greek dictator, General George Metaxas, inspecting a Mediterranean air base, was invited to try out a new flying boat. He undertook to pilot it himself and all went well until the commander, his host, observed that they were about to make a landing on an aerodrome. "Excuse me, General, but it would be better to come down on the sea. This is a flying boat." "Of course, Commander, what was I thinking of," said Metaxas, suddenly recollecting himself and making a safe landing on the water. Rising from the controls he said, "Commander, I greatly appreciate the tact with which you drew my attention to the incredible blunder which I nearly made." Saying which he opened the door and stepped into the sea.

Edmund Fuller, ANECDOTES 1942

Michael Ramsey, Archbishop of Canterbury, was even as a curate renowned for his absentmindedness. His landlady was tidying his room one day when there came a knock at the door. "Mr Ramsey's not here," she called, "he's gone out." "Oh yes, of course," came the reply. "Thank you very much." Recognising the voice as that of her young lodger the landlady opened the door in time to see Ramsey disappearing round the corner.

Clifton Fadiman, LITTLE, BROWN BOOK OF ANECDOTES 1985

See also **FORGETFULNESS**

ABSTINENCE

After a month on the wagon Don Marquis came up to the bar at the Player's Club, and ordered a double martini. "I've conquered my goddam will-power," he announced to the assembled company.

B. A. Botkin, A TREASURY OF AMERICAN ANECDOTES 1957

ABUSE

Henry James was complaining to us that Ellen Terry had asked him to write a play for her, and now that he had done so, and read it to her, had refused it. My wife, desiring to placate, asked, "Perhaps she did not think the part suited to her?" H.J. turned to both of us, and with resonance and uplifted voice replied, "Think? *Think*? How should the poor chattering hag THINK?"

Edmund Gosse, letter to John Bailey 14 *Apr* 1920

Amy Lowell, the American poet, was lecturing and reading some of her own poems when, at a certain spot, the audience tittered. She stopped, eyed them sternly, and waited for silence. When it came she began again; but again they tittered in the same place. This time she stopped longer and looked at them more sternly. Finally, when she reached the passage a third time and they once more tittered, she closed the book with a snap, said savagely but precisely to them, "You unregenerate sons of bitches," and walked off the platform.

Eunice Tietjens, THE WORLD AT MY SHOULDER 1938

When H. W. Nevinson was literary editor of the *Daily Chronicle*, G. B. Shaw, who reviewed for the paper, declined to work except on special terms and wrote threatening the paper with all the powers of the Author's Society. Nevinson replied, "Dear Sir, I am directed by the editor to inform you that he will see you damned before he gives you more than five pounds for the article in question."

Not to be out-abused Shaw replied, "Dear Sir, please inform the editor that I will see him and you and the whole *Chronicle* staff boiled in Hell before I do it for that money."

Cecil Roberts, HALF WAY 1931

I was walking through the bazaars of Cairo when an Arab cafe idler called out "God curse your father, O Englishman." I could not refrain from answering in Arabic that I would also curse his father – if he were able to inform me which of his mother's nine and ninety admirers his father had been. In a few seconds I heard footsteps behind me and felt a hand on each arm. "My brother," said the Arab, "return I pray you and drink coffee with us, and smoke. I did not think your worship knew Arabic, still less correct Arabic abuse, and we would fain benefit from your important thoughts."

Sir Ronald Storrs, ORIENTATIONS

ACCIDENT

I was once involved in a bad train smash in America. I was shaving when it happened and crawled out of the window still clutching my towel. The towel came in useful, for the first man I came across had his leg almost severed and I looked round for something to make a tourniquet. About me was the Utah desert – not a bush from which to pull a branch. Then my eye caught sight of something grey on the sand. I reached over and got it. It was the wind-and-sun-dried skeleton of a coyote. I broke off two of the ribs, placed them beneath the towel and twisted until the blood-flow stopped.

Dr William E. Aughinbaugh, I SWEAR BY APOLLO 1939

As a young don at University College, Oxford, I became Lord Beveridge's research assistant and shared a holiday cottage with him and his wife Jessy. When Beveridge took off his jacket one hot day in the garden Jessy's petrol-driven lawn mower got out of control, ran into the rough, and hooked itself on to the jacket. When this was extracted from the machine the whole of one side consisted of one-and-a-half inch strips of Cotswold worsted. Beveridge insisted on wearing it, ribbons and all, for the rest of the afternoon and even at dinner.

Harold Wilson, THE MAKING OF A PRIME MINISTER *1916–1964* 1986

A bullet, probably fired 25 years ago, injured an Exeter man yesterday. Mr Wallace Bridle, of Red Cow Village, was planing some timber at the Rawle Gammon and Baker works at Alphington when the bullet flew out and grazed his arm. The bullet, a .303, had been embedded in the timber, which was imported from Finland. And it was thought the bullet might have been fired during the Russian-Finnish War of 1940.

Western Morning News 25 *Sep* 1965

St John Brodrick, the Secretary of State for India, made excuses so that there was no official reception for Lord Curzon, the Viceroy, when he arrived at Charing Cross. The following day the roof of the station fell in. "How like St John," said Lady Curzon, "to bring it off a day late."

David Dilks, CURZON IN INDIA VOL 2 1970

Lisbon. For 20 years a shell case has stood with a number of others inside the entrance to the Artillery Museum here. Every morning at five minutes to eight the 20 employees have filed in ready for the opening at eight o'clock. The shells, which at first they noticed, had by now become unnoticed, and in any case they were "duds". Today the 20 employees, led by Domingos Costa, walked in. Domingos Costa took a last puff at his cigarette and flipped the stub into the shell case. There was a violent explosion. Costa and two others were killed. Three more were gravely injured.

News Chronicle 3 *Aug* 1947

In 1925 Isadora Duncan insisted on being taken for a drive from a studio at Nice by a young Italian. As she went out of the studio she called out, "Adieu, mes amis, je vais à la gloire." As the car started Isadora was seen to throw the long fringed end of her shawl over her left shoulder. The car started forward at full speed, and the shawl seemed to trail on the ground beside the wheel. Mary Destri screamed, "Ton châle, Isadora! Ramasse ton châle!"

The car stopped. The watchers thought it was to allow Isadora to pick up the end of her shawl. They walked towards it and saw that Isadora's head had fallen forward. They ran. The driver was out of the car gesticulating, howling in Italian, "I have killed the Madonna! I have killed the Madonna!"

Irma Duncan, ISADORA DUNCAN'S LAST DAYS 1929

I am in bed with aches and bruises. Two days ago Thunderbird [Ian Fleming] thundered into an ice-cream van. My head broke the windscreen.

We were collected by two schoolmistresses. Clearly their only pleasure in life is the frequent crashes at their front door. "We put the kettle on when we heard the horn screaming," they told us while forcing strong tea upon us and enjoying the yelps of pain as they poured Jeyes Fluid on my broken knees. They were very disappointed at our minor abrasions.

Ann Fleming, letter to Evelyn Waugh 16 *Jul* 1960

During the making of *The Ladykillers*, directed by Sandy Mackendrick, I had to stand on the edge of a 60-foot-high wall and I took hold of what looked like a solid iron rail for support. "Is this secure?" I called down when I realised the rail was in fact only wood. "Perfectly!" they called from below. Whereupon it snapped, and I had the good fortune to fall backwards.

Sir Alec Guinness, BLESSINGS IN DISGUISE 1985

I have just come across a note from our trip to Nigeria in January. A bus that had run off the road and into a wall had "God is our leader" as its motto.

Cecil King, DIARY 21 *Jul* 1970

After Sinclair Lewis's death in Rome from alcoholism his body was cremated and the urn containing his ashes sent to the U.S. Embassy for safe keeping until their final disposal. A caller was surprised to find one of the consular staff on his knees, busy with a brush and pan, an overturned urn beside him. "Whatever are you doing?" he asked. "Sweeping up Sinclair Lewis," was the response.

Barnaby Conrad, FUN WHILE IT LASTED 1969

Liu Ming-Hui, a Taiwanese farmer, was knocked over by a car while taking his favourite pig to stud. The anxious porker ran all the way home to lead Liu's wife back to the spot, thus saving Liu's bacon.

Sunday Telegraph, 21 *Apr* 1985

In September 1937 Bessie Smith, the American black jazz singer, travelling with her white business manager near Clarksdale, Mississippi, was seriously injured in a car accident. The doctor who arrived on the scene directed that the manager, who was suffering from concussion, should be sent to the nearby hospital but that the singer should go to a "blacks only" hospital many miles away. She bled to death before she got there.

David Frost, THE WORLD'S WORST DECISIONS 1983

J. C. Squire was accident-prone. Once a pheasant he had shot landed on his head and knocked him out.

Alan Pryce-Jones, THE BONUS OF LAUGHTER 1987

"We try not to be surprised in this business," said the factory inspector, "but the shop assistant who cut her *toe* off with a bacon slicer shows what we are up against. She stood on it to close a window."

Observer, quoted Denys Parsons, FUNNY AMUSING, FUNNY AMAZING 1969

Professor Lodge and some other people were sitting in the common room at the University of East Anglia when someone told the story of a friend of his who had been about to leave for a family holiday when, looking out of her bedroom window, she saw her husband drive off at great speed. A few minutes later she looked out of her back bedroom window and was surprised to see her husband, digging furiously in the garden. What had happened was that driving off to buy some last-minute cat food he had discovered on his return that he had run over the cat and had to bury it.

Auberon Waugh, Sunday Telegraph 14 *Jun* 1981

ACHIEVEMENT

When sculptor Auguste Rodin was reaching the end of his long and brilliant life a friend came to his studio and found him weeping over a statue he had just completed. The visitor was at a loss to understand the old man's grief and looking at the statue remarked, "But it's perfect."

"I think so too, and that is why I am weeping," Rodin replied. He had come to the moment of truth, the realization that he had gone as far as his imagination and craftsmanship could take him.

Cyril Smith, DUET FOR THREE HANDS 1982

ACQUAINTANCE

Lytton Strachey wasted no words in conversation. A young and robust friend of ours, Constant Lambert, meeting him at a party said, "You don't remember me, Mr Strachey? We met four years ago." "Quite a nice interval I think, don't you?" remarked Mr Strachey pleasantly, and passed on.

Edith Sitwell, TAKEN CARE OF 1965

ACTING

At the Savage Club, Eric Linklater wanted to know about Gerald Ames; we'd been hailed by him. "An actor who talks about only one subject – acting," said James Agate. "He also talks about his pedigree," I said. "That's acting, too," said James.

Reginald Pound, THEIR MOODS AND MINE 1937

Jean-Louis Barrault's first part was that of Dullin's servant in Ben Jonson's *Volpone*. To overcome his stage-fright, Barrault had recourse to a weird exercise; he hid one night among the props, and when the building was empty slipped into Volpone's bed on the stage and spent the night there, with the curtains drawn apart in front of an imaginary audience, breathing in the air and mystery of the theatre.

Observer, Profile 23 *Sep* 1951

When Owen Nares and I were engaged for the leading parts in the revival of *Diplomacy* in 1913 the choice was at first severely criticised. At the rehearsals Sir Squire Bancroft and Sir Gerald Du Maurier sat watching day by day. One afternoon the rest of the company were dismissed, and we were terrified when we were asked to go through the big scene on the empty stage with only Sir Squire and Du Maurier in the stalls. At the end not a word.

For what seemed a very long time we stood on the stage waiting for someone to say something – to tell us that we were wrong and would not do – or were right. Then, very slowly, Old B and Gerald came on to the stage and said that we had made them cry so much that they were not able to face us sooner. I think that was one of the most marvellous moments of my life. *Diplomacy* ran at Wyndhams for eighteen months.

Gladys Cooper, GLADYS COOPER 1931

Noel Coward's first London appearance was in *The Goldfish* at the Little Theatre in 1911. A boy with elfin ears and a bad temper, he slapped June Howard-Tripp with a ballet shoe, and subsequently proved his professional aplomb by stealing her one and only line when she became crucially immobilised by a chocolate eclair.

Sheridan Morley, A TALENT TO AMUSE 1969

I offered an old actor named Dieudonné a part in one of my plays. He merely had to be on the stage a few seconds, and had to lisp a few lines, but he came to me and said, "Is it absolutely necessary that this character lisp?". "Not absolutely, why?" "Because I thought, if it didn't make any difference, instead of lisping I could stutter. That would stretch out the part."

Sacha Guitry, IF I REMEMBER RIGHT 1935

It was not necessary for Ruth Draper to suffer through a sketch in order to suggest agony – she was not at all a method actor. Sometimes she would come off stage and say she had been thinking about what she would have for supper later. I was once in the wings, at the Haymarket, and Ruth was doing a dramatic episode in a sketch. I was so lost in the story, and her performance, that I forgot it was Ruth acting out there in the lights, and I was startled, in a brief pause between episodes when she ran off-stage and said to me in a rush, "I'm starving. Get someone to fetch me a ham sandwich. Get two." Before she turned to walk back into the lights she was instantly the next character.

Joyce Grenfell, JOYCE GRENFELL REQUESTS THE PLEASURE 1976

Noel Coward, despairing of ever getting Edith Evans to learn his *Hay Fever* accurately, finally murmured, "Edith, the line is 'On a clear day you can see Marlow' not 'On a *very* clear day you can see Marlow.' On a *very* clear day you can see Marlow and Beaumont and Fletcher as well."

Sheridan Morley, Radio Times 27 *Jul* 1985

Edith Evans once said if she could not think what to do with a line she spoke it as if it was obscene. One has only to think of the intonation on "A handbag!" in *The Importance of Being Ernest* to know what she meant. I once asked her if she had ever worked on eighteenth-century plays. "No, my dear," she said. "I don't like eighteenth-century plays. Give me Restoration plays. I'm always game for a bit of bawdy."

Donald Sinden, A TOUCH OF THE MEMOIRS 1982

In one of the plays in which they co-starred Lynn Fontanne had to hit Alfred Lunt across the face. A devoted wife, she tried for some time without bringing herself to do it. Everyone became exasperated as the scene stuck at that point. Finally Lunt burst out, "For God's sake, you're the lousiest actress I've ever played opposite." Miss Fontanne, her hang-up overcome, struck him sharply. Thereafter at every performance Lunt used to whisper, "Don't be lousy, dear."

Edmund Fuller, ANECDOTES 1942

John Gilbert was once called upon at short notice to play the role of the heroine's father in a Chicago production. He learned his lines in record time but was still struggling to remember the name of the character he was playing, Numitorious, when the play opened. A colleague having helpfully suggested the Book of Numbers as a mnemonic, Gilbert rushed on the stage with renewed confidence that evening and delivered his opening line, "Hold! 'Tis I – her father, Deuteronomy!"

Gyles Brandreth, GREAT THEATRICAL DISASTERS 1982

During Alan Bennett's play *Forty Years On*, in which Sir John Gielgud played a headmaster, he would leave the stage with an ad-libbed line to one of the schoolboys, such as, "So glad Green House did so well in the swimming cup, Jenkins," or "Got to beat Swain in the cross-country, haven't we, Jenkins?" One night he went off saying, "I've got the most terrible trouble with my income tax."

John Mortimer, IN CHARACTER 1983

When speaking a line while drinking iced tea, if I bring the glass up too soon I sound like a man hollering into a barrel. If I hold it up in front of my mouth I spoil my expression. If I put it down too hard I kill a couple of words on the sound track. If I don't, I make it sound unreal. I have to hold the glass at a slight angle to keep the reflections out of the lens. It has to be absolutely still to keep the ice from tinkling. And, finally, I have to remember to keep my head up because I have a double chin.

Cary Grant, quoted Walter Winchell, Reader's Digest Oct 1965

Many great actors have been famous for their powers of observation. Lucien Guitry was no exception. Given the role of Rostand's Chanticleer, he studied farmyard cocks in Normandy. "Have you ever observed that a rooster runs with his hands in his pockets?"

Cornelia Otis Skinner, ELEGANT WITS AND GRAND HORIZONTALS 1962

As the aged queen in *Victoria Regina*, Helen Hayes' imitation of an old woman's laugh was a masterpiece of accuracy. Miss Hayes knew that laughter in the very old is a strong surge of merriment in a body too frail to express it, but she was dissatisfied with her version of Victoria's laugh at 70. The second night she noticed an old lady having a fine time in the front row. Her laughter came in short, hard chuckles from the deep folds of her black silk dress, and after each spasm she gasped, wiped her eyes with her handkerchief, and settled back in her seat, sighing pleasurably. Miss Hayes made a careful study of this laugh. From then on, Victoria's laugh was that of the elderly playgoer and as such was perfectly true to life.

Margaret Case Harriman, New Yorker 1942

My husband W. H. Kendal had the peculiar gift of being able to turn pale whenever he wished. In *The Queen's Shilling* he had a scene in which, playing the part of a soldier who had been wounded in the arm, he had an acrimonious passage of words with his colonel. The latter gripped him by the wounded place so harshly that my husband's face actually blanched. He became so white that women in the audience used to faint.

Dame Madge Kendal, AUTOBIOGRAPHY 1933

Charles Laughton was adept at getting the audience to applaud even his ailments. During the run of *The Party* in London he was sometimes afflicted by a fit of coughing. He would signal apologetically for the curtain to be brought down, then after a pause he would appear in front of it, still coughing and wheezing, and get a round of applause. When the coughing fit subsided he made humble apologies to the audience and then announced he would continue with the play. More applause. When the curtain rose again there was further clapping – and the show went on.

Gordon Snell, THE THEATRE BOOK OF QUOTES AND ANECDOTES 1982

When performing at a Birmingham repertory theatre Hugh Manning found himself stranded on stage with a piano and a vase of daffodils, a fellow actor having failed to enter on cue. He strolled across to the piano and fingered one of the daffodils, looking anxiously towards the wings. The actor still did not appear. Manning picked up the flower, sniffed it, and finally in desperation ate it. The audience roared with laughter. The improvisation was such a success, in fact, that Manning found himself expected to eat a daffodil at every subsequent performance.

Gyles Brandreth, GREAT THEATRICAL DISASTERS 1982

Arthur Bourchier gave Robert Morley his first job as an elderly, lineless pirate. It was only a pound a week, but it was the professional theatre, and as Robert walked down Jermyn Street after securing the job he was approached by a lady of the streets who inquired professionally, "Doing anything, love?" To which Robert, at least two feet off the ground replied, "Yes, I'm a pirate at the Strand Theatre."

Margaret Morley, LARGER THAN LIFE

The American actor Dustin Hoffman, playing a victim of imprisonment and torture in the *The Marathon Man* prepared himself for the role by keeping himself awake for two days and nights. He arrived at the studio dishevelled and drawn, to be met by his co-star Laurence Olivier. "Dear boy you look absolutely awful," exclaimed the First Lord of the Theatre. "Why don't you try acting? It's so much easier."

Alan Hamilton, The Times 17 May 1982

I got my first part at the age of seven; an elf in a school play. I had one line, something like, "Come on brothers, for it is cold." I put on a terrific shivering act in rehearsal, shuttering "C-c-c-come on b-b-brothers f-f-for it is c-c-c-cold." The result was that they took the line away from me. I think I've been trying to get that line back ever since.

Jonathan Pryce, Observer Magazine 9 *Nov* 1986

Shirley Temple's mother used to bring the necessary cinematic tears to the child star's eyes by telling her that her pet dog had had an accident. After the successful shot, Mummy would explain that the accident was not serious and the pet would recover.

Sheilah Graham, MY HOLLYWOOD 1984

At the first rehearsal of Dame May Whitty's first entrance in *The Madras House* Harley Granville-Barker told her, "From the moment you come on you must make the audience understand that you live in a small town in the provinces and visit a great deal with the local clergy; you make slippers for the curate and go to dreary tea-parties." She realised the value of these admonitions. But she was used to working through the lines, and the line in this case was "How do you do?"

Eric Salmon, GRANVILLE BARKER, A SECRET LIFE 1982

Some of Beerbohm Tree's defects were useful on the stage. He was so completely preoccupied with himself that he was always surprised when someone else spoke; and this delighted Bernard Shaw, one of whose hardest tasks as a producer was to induce actors to speak as if they had never heard their cues before, instead of betraying that they knew all about it beforehand.

Hesketh Pearson, BERNARD SHAW 1942

Guns can be awkward on the stage, especially when they fail to go off at the right dramatic moment. It is a situation that requires quick thinking, as in the case where one actor pulled the trigger with a shout of murderous triumph. There was no sound. The victim obligingly however fell to the ground. The killer looked admiringly at the gun and said, "These silencers are really amazing."

Gordon Snell, THE BOOK OF THEATRICAL QUOTES AND ANECDOTES 1982

An amateur dramatic group staged a full-length Shakespearian production which was acclaimed by all their friends and families and praised by the loçal press also. Not long afterwards they arranged a coach trip to Stratford-on-Avon to see the same play. When they got back someone asked the leading man if the production had been anything like their own.

"It wasn't bad," he replied. "Laurence Olivier played my part."

Ibid.

See also **CINEMA, RADIO, TELEVISION, THEATRE.**

ADDICTION

W. C. Fields always kept a thermos of martini at hand when he was filming, maintaining that it contained nothing but pineapple juice. One day someone tampered with the flask and Field's anguished cry rang out across the set. "Someone has put pineapple juice in my pineapple juice."

Clifton Fadiman and Charles Van Doren, THE AMERICAN TREASURY 1953

Elizabeth Bowen, the novelist, and I were invited to tea by Mrs Guy Cary who, as a Roche by birth, was delighted to entertain another Anglo-Irishwoman. The customary routine had been organised; the purring kettle, the cucumber sandwiches, the chocolate cake. Suddenly Mrs Cary, then well past 80, announced that she had left her handkerchief upstairs and disappeared for a few minutes. Very shortly after, she found that in fetching her handkerchief she had left her glasses. Up the stairs she vanished once more. After the third or fourth climb I noticed that she had a little difficulty in negotiating the steps. I put this down to age. But, trained to Irish ways, Elizabeth was on to the facts in a flash and, when we left the house, turned to me in indignation.

"I, too, like martinis," she said, "and all *we* were offered was tea, which I detest."

Alan Pryce-Jones, THE BONUS OF LAUGHTER 1987

Spencer Tracy gave me a jarring insight into his great personal problem. "What's this?" he asked, pointing to the dessert. "It looks like trifle," I said. He sniffed at a spoonful like a bird-dog. "There's something in it. What is it?" "A touch of rum I think," I said. He pushed his plate away. "That's all I need," he said. "One mouthful of that and I'd be gone for a week. I'm not kidding. I have to fight it all the time. I'm a real alcoholic, and that little bit would start me off."

David Niven, BRING ON THE EMPTY HORSES 1975

The French artist Maurice Utrillo began life with his unmarried mother and unmarried grandmother in a Paris garret. His mother took up art. The Glaxo age had not arrived. When his mother was busy and her baby boy bawled, grandmother soothed him with strong red wine. By the time he was 10 he had a thirst like a rowing blue's and a liver like a sponge.

Stephen and Ethel Longhurst, MAN OF MONTMARTRE 1959

After Maurice Utrillo had had an alcoholic breakdown at 18, his mother, Suzanne Valadon, taught him to paint as an effort to save his sanity. His reputation and wealth soon grew. But still he drank – fuel alcohol, eau-de-cologne, anything, and his pathetic life was a succession of internments in asylums and prisons with Valadon in distraught pursuit.

Wendy Roche, Observer 11 *Dec* 1983

A strange case of addiction occurred in an African regiment when some soldiers from a particularly primitive tribe were put on a charge for eating dubbin. Their Company Commander took what seemed an unnecessarily strong line until he explained, "I thought I'd nip it in the bud before they drank their rifle oil."

The Field, quoted English Digest Mar 1965

See also **INTOXICATION**

ADMIRATION

Isidore Philipp offered to introduce Bela Bartok to Saint-Saens, at that time a great celebrity. Bartok declined. Philipp then offered him Charles-Marie Widor. Bartok again declined. "If you won't meet them, who is there you would like to know?" "Debussy," said Bartok. "But he is a horrid man," said Philipp. "He hates everybody and will certainly be rude to you. Do you want to be insulted by Debussy?" "Yes," said Bartok.

Virgil Thomson, A VIRGIL THOMSON READER 1981

A lady approached Stravinsky and said, "Of all your works I like *Scheherazade* the best." "But madame," he protested, "I did not compose *Scheherazade*." "Oh come now," said his admirer, "don't be modest."

Paul Horgan, ENCOUNTERS WITH STRAVINSKY 1972

ADULTERY

The moment Nancy Astor heard the rumour that Lloyd George lived with his secretary, Frances Stevenson, she went straight to the great little man. "L. G. what is this I hear about you and Frances?" Lloyd George, not the least perturbed, retorted, "And what about you and Philip Lothian?" Nancy replied hotly, "Everyone knows that my relations with Philip are completely innocent." L. G., his spectacles gleaming with mischief, "Then you should be ashamed of yourself." End of interview.

A. L. Rowse, MEMORIES OF MEN AND WOMEN 1980

The actress Zsa-Zsa Gabor was asked by an interviewer how many husbands she had had. A little puzzled she replied, "You mean apart from my own?"

Kenneth Edwards, I WISH I'D SAID THAT 1976

Ibn Saud expressed surprise to Belhaven, a member of the British Mission, that in enlightened England, adultery should go unpunished, whereas in the desert the punishment was death by stoning. Belhaven piqued, retaliated, "How many women have you had?" "I have four wives, as the prophet allows," replied Ibn Saud. "But how many have you had, and how many have you divorced?" "I have married and divorced a hundred, and if God wills I shall marry and divorce many more."

H. G. Armstrong, LORD OF ARABIA 1934

Nancy Astor sat with Bernard Shaw at his death-bed. The old boy woke up suddenly from a coma and said, "Nancy, did you ever hear the story of Adela Patti's husband?" It appears that the *prima donna* and her (foreign) husband arranged a country-house party after what they supposed to be the English fashion. The guests were assembled, the music struck up, when the husband appeared running down the staircase. "You must all go away. I have found a man in bed with my wife."

Consternated, the guests hardly knew what to do and were preparing to leave when the husband appeared again: "You must all come back. It is quite all right. He has apologised."

Apparently this was Shaw's last communication to the world. He thereupon relapsed into coma.

A. L. Rowse, MEMORIES OF MEN AND WOMEN 1980

ADVERTISING

At the time he took up thriller-writing Eric Ambler worked in advertising. He had been given the Exlax account, at a time when the slogan for the laxative chocolate was: Exlax for Incomplete Elimination. The theory was that an inefficient excretory system caused a poisoning of the body. Exlax made sure you got rid of everything. But Mr Ambler's researches revealed that people were buying the stuff under a misapprehension. They thought Incomplete Elimination was a sexual dysfunction which could be cured with chocolate.

James Fenton, The Times 13 *Jun* 1985

Max Beerbohm once told S. N. Behrman, "If I was endowed with wealth I should start a great advertising campaign in all the principal newspapers. The advertisement would consist of one short sentence, printed in huge block letters – a sentence that I once heard spoken by a husband to a wife. 'My dear, nothing in the world is worth buying.'"

David Ogilvy, CONFESSIONS OF AN ADVERTISING MAN 1964

Frank Benson was a splendid athlete. He believed that an actor should be as alert physically as mentally and within his company he organised a cricket and hockey team. It is said that he once advertised, "Wanted. A good fast bowler able to play Laertes."

Donald Sinden, A TOUCH OF THE MEMOIRS 1982

Now and then E. C. Bentley worked as an advertising man. His best campaign, he thinks, was for Eno's Fruit Salts. "The whole story was about constipation, and I invented Mr Can and Mr Can't. Both characters were based on friends of mine."

Philip Oakes, Sunday Times 14 *May* 1972

Whenever Salvador Dali was in town the lobbies of the St Regis in New York or the Hotel Meurice on the rue de Rivoli in Paris would be full of anonymous-looking businessmen with attaché cases and absorbed expressions. Several hundred contracts would be proposed in any one particular year and of these about 50 would come to fruition. They included, in 1970, a 15-second commercial on French television during which Dali rolled his eyes roguishly and said; "I am mad, I am completely mad – over Lanvin chocolates." He was paid 10,000 dollars.

Meryle Secrest, SALVADOR DALI: THE SURREALIST JESTER 1986

Samuel Goldwyn disdained publicity. When a harassed publicist devised a campaign that began "The directing skill of Reuben Mamoulien, the radiance of Anna Stern and the genius of Samuel Goldwyn have combined to bring you the world's greatest entertainment – " Goldwyn nodded approval. "That's the kind of advertising I like. Just the facts. No exaggeration."

Leslie Halliwell, FILMGOER'S BOOK OF QUOTES 1978

When John F. Kennedy was first persuaded to enter politics his father orchestrated the campaign that took him to Congress. Joseph Kennedy declared, "We're going to sell Jack like soap flakes," and did so.

Alden Whitman, COME TO JUDGMENT 1980

Haslam Mills, chief reporter on the *Manchester Guardian*, went into advertising as a star copywriter with the old London Press Exchange. He insisted on, and was given, a room with a view of the church of St Martin-in-the-Fields in Trafalgar Square so that he could, each evening, draw inspiration from the flock of starlings gathering round the spire. This helped him to immortalise the claims of manufacturers of armchairs, pots and pans in copy which is esteemed by romantically minded advertising men.

James Harding, AGATE: A BIOGRAPHY 1986

The best headline I ever wrote contained eighteen words. *At Sixty Miles an Hour the Loudest Noise in the New Rolls Royce Comes from the*

Electric Clock. When the chief engineer at the Rolls Royce factory read this he shook his head sadly and said, "It is time we did something about that damned clock."

Ibid.

Will Rogers was asked by a firm of piano manufacturers to write a short testimonial for their instruments. Unwilling to endorse any product that he could not put to the test he simply replied, "Dear sirs, I guess your pianos are the best I ever leaned against. Yours truly, Will Rogers."

Clifton Fadiman, LITTLE, BROWN BOOK OF ANECDOTES 1985

John Snagge has been against commercial broadcasting ever since he heard a Toscanini radio concert in New York interrupted by the sponsor's slogan "It may be December outside, ladies, but it is always August under your armpits."

Evening Standard, quoted News Review 13 *Nov* 1947

MPs are protesting about a Gas Board advertisement urging couples to share a bath to save fuel. The South Eastern Gas Board advertisement shows a couple sharing a bath, with this comment. "Put a bit of romance into your bath by sharing the water." Mr John Stokes, Conservative MP for Oldbury said, "It is deplorably vulgar and in the worst possible taste. I find it extraordinary coming from a nationalised industry from whom we ought to be able to expect the highest standards."

The slogan was suggested by Mrs Ida Jones, of East Molesley, who won £10 for it in a competition. Interviewed, she said, "I cannot understand what all the fuss is about." Neighbours supported her. One of them said, "People have been sharing a bath for years. There's nothing wrong in it. It's better than a rubber duck."

The Times 29 *Jan* 1974

Edgar Wallace used regularly to insert advertisements in his stories, accepting payment from the interested firms. "I get £25 for a story like that," he would say, indicating his name on the cover of a magazine "but" – pointing to some ingenious clue in the text – "that happens to be worth £200."

Margaret Lane, EDGAR WALLACE 1938

In the lower left corner of a page of the *Cleveland News* was a two-column patent medicine testimonial, from a Mr Alexander Kellough, of 2508 Morris Black Place, who rejoiced to find himself now rid of backache, insomnia, sour stomach and gas pains, and enthusiastically concluded, "Giljan is a wonderful medicine. Any person with trouble such as mine should lose no time in taking it."

In column seven of the same page appeared a brief notice. "Kellough, Alexander. Passed away at his late residence 2508 Morris Black Place."

Time Magazine Nov 1944

A compositor on the *Daily Mail* suggested the idea of increasing the number of advertising columns on the front page from seven to eight by reducing their width by a quarter of an inch, charging the same rates per column, and thus swelling the advertising revenue from it by one seventh. He was paid £100 for this simple idea, and it was responsible for bringing in hundreds of thousands of pounds additional revenue.

Wareham Smith, SPILT INK 1932

A daily newspaper in Nice recently contained the following advertisement: "Millionaire, young, good-looking, wishes to meet, with a view to marriage, a girl like the heroine in M——'s novel." Within 24 hours the novel in question was sold out.

Daily Mail Jan 1930

The advertising department of Lever Bros has received a letter which begins as follows: Sir, ref. your advertisement which says "If it's safe in water, it's safe in Lux". Now about my goldfish –

The Times, Diary

ADVICE

James Agate was fond of giving advice to the young, and would begin by asking a question. "Now if I asked you for a match for my cigar what would you do? The aristocracy would throw me a box; the middle class would pass me a box; the lower class would take out a match and light it for me."

Donald Sinden, A TOUCH OF THE MEMOIRS 1982

While producing one of his own plays J. M. Barrie was approached by an inexperienced member of the cast. Although his part was a very minor one the young actor, anxious to give it the right interpretation, sought Barrie's advice. Sir James gave it some thought. "I am glad you have asked me," he said finally, "I should like you to convey that the man you portray has a brother in Shropshire who drinks port."

John Aye, HUMOUR IN THE THEATRE 1932

A woman confided to Sir Thomas Beecham that her son wanted to learn an instrument, but she couldn't bear the purgatory of his practising in the early stages. "What is the best instrument?" she asked. "I have no hesitation, madam," he said, "in saying the bagpipes. They sound exactly the same when you have finished learning them as when you start learning them."

Harold Atkins and Archie Newman, BEECHAM STORIES 1978

Sir Thomas Beecham said to the orchestra at the rehearsal of Sibelius's *Lamminkainen*: "In this piece you may find it a matter of some difficulty to keep your places. I think you may do well to imagine yourselves disporting on some form of hair-raising locomotion such as Brooklands, or a switchback railway. My advice to you is merely: hold tight and do not let yourselves fall off. I cannot guarantee to help you on again."

Ibid.

A firm of art dealers, rivals of Joseph Duveen's, had sent an Old Master religious painting to one of their clients, a rather strait-laced duke. The duke, not sure whether to buy, asked Duveen for an opinion. Duveen examined the painting and pronounced it very nice. "But," he added, "I presume you are aware that cherubs are homosexual?" The duke did not buy the painting.

Miriam Ringo, NOBODY SAID IT BETTER 1980

An American arriving in England in 1961 for postgraduate study went to visit T. S. Eliot. As he was leaving he noticed that the poet was apparently searching for the right remark with which to bid him farewell. "Forty years ago I went from Harvard to Oxford," Eliot began, "Now what advice can I give you?" There was a prolonged pause while the young man waited for the poet's words of wisdom. Finally Eliot said, "Do you have any long underwear?"

Stanley Weintrub, THE LONDON YANKEE 1974

Zsa Zsa Gabor appeared on a television programme in which guest celebrities attempted to solve viewers' conjugal problems. A young lady asked: "I'm breaking my engagement to a very wealthy man who has already given me a sable coat, diamonds, a stove and a Rolls-Royce. What should I do?" "Give back the stove," advised Zsa-Zsa.

Clifton Fadiman, LITTLE, BROWN BOOK OF ANECDOTES 1985

Ernest Hemingway's son Patrick asked his father to edit a story he had written. Hemingway went through the manuscript carefully then returned it to his son. "But Papa," cried Patrick in dismay, "you've changed only one word." "If it's the right word," said Hemingway, "that's a lot."

A. E. Hotchner, CHOICE PEOPLE 1984

As a young pianist Vladimir Horowitz was shocked by the advice given him by Artur Schnabel; "When a piece gets difficult, make faces."

Oscar Levant, THE UNIMPORTANCE OF BEING OSCAR 1968

A revealing scene took place in a Mainz wine cellar some years ago when Helmut Kohl was prime minister of the Rhineland-Palatinate and gearing up for a leap into federal politics. Advisers had suggested that he should develop a more national appeal, so he gathered his aides round a table and ordered them to attack him with all the criticisms they could muster, so that he could know his weaknesses. "You are provincial, you can't express yourself incisively, you don't seem to stand for anything definite, you have petit-bourgeois prejudices against anything intellectual and you don't look right," they said.

Not one shaft pierced his hide. At the end he said happily, "I thought you were going to tell me there is something wrong," and passed round the wine.

The Independent 17 *Jan* 1987

Just before leaving for a hunting trip in Africa, Theodore Roosevelt invited a famous English big-game hunter to give him some pointers for his trip. After a two-hour conversation at the White House, during which the two were not disturbed, the Englishman came out. "What did you tell the President?" asked a reporter. "I told him my name," said the wearied visitor.

Emily Bax, MISS BAX OF THE EMBASSY 1943

John Gielgud asked Fred Terry for advice when he was constantly being upstaged in a scene by a crafty actor. Terry replied, "Walk in front of him while he's speaking, old boy. He'll have to come down level with you then, otherwise the audience won't be able to see him."

The advice worked.

Ronald Hayman, GIELGUD 1971

In 1937 Frank Lloyd Wright built a house in Wisconsin for the industrialist Hibbard Johnson and his family. One rainy evening Johnson was entertaining some distinguished guests when the roof began to leak, dripping steadily on the top of Johnson's bald head. Irate, he put through a call to Wright in Phoenix, Arizona,

"Frank," he said, "you built this beautiful house for me and we enjoy it very much. But the roof leaks and right now I am with some friends and it is leaking on top of my head." Wright's reply was heard by all. "Well, Hib," he said, "why don't you move your chair?"

Samuel C. Johnson, quoted Clifton Fadiman, LITTLE, BROWN BOOK OF ANECDOTES 1985

Elizabeth II's apparently inexhaustible bladder capacity and ability to stand for ever are techniques developed early in life. The Duke of Windsor used to say that two of the best pieces of advice his father ever gave him were never to refuse an invitation to take the weight off his feet and to seize every opportunity he could to relieve himself.

Robert Lacey, MAJESTY 1977

AGGRESSION

Aboard SS *Moshulu*, 4 Jan 1939. Someone put a lump of shit in my bunk. Thought it was Hermansonn, who has been an absolute bastard to me. So when dinner came I picked up a bowl of custard and threw it in his face. Then we went on deck and fought. It took some time but I won. The captain stopped the fight. It turned out it was Holmberg who did it and I wanted to fight him too, but I was dissuaded. Anyway, it didn't matter. The important thing was to wallop someone. The next time, I'll do it first day on board.

Eric Newby, quoting letter to his parents. A TRAVELLER'S LIFE 1982

AMBIGUITY

One of Bertrand Russell's favourite stories was of the doctor who, when asked by the proud father whether it was a boy or a girl, replied "Yes".

Rupert Crawshaw-Williams, RUSSELL REMEMBERED 1970

Bill Coldstream and Wystan Auden worked together with John Grierson on the Post Office Film Unit. Grierson was a tremendous admirer of the proletariat and used to do films in which workers appeared undressed to the waist, covered in sweat, while the voice of a background narrator described in heroic terms what they were doing. The best effect was produced if an enormous white-hot steel girder was shedding its light on their upturned faces. Wystan and Bill were intensely irritated by the pieties of Grierson. In a run-through of a film on a factory they heard the voice of the narrator say "Ever on the alert, the worker lubricates his tool with soap." Grierson was furious when they told him he ought to cut this line. Bill said it was a pity it had not been left in. It would have been greatly appreciated in the North of England.

Stephen Spender, JOURNAL 26 Feb 1975

Following his address the bishop said to the young reporter who was covering the event, "When you write this up I would appreciate your not mentioning the several anecdotes I related. I may want to use them in other speeches." The newsman obligingly wrote, "The bishop told several stories that cannot be repeated here."

Tom Stuckley, Reader's Digest Jun 1982

AMBITION

The work in Ted Heath's Office increased rapidly around that time (1968) and we decided we needed a second private secretary. One of those interviewed was Jeffrey Archer, who was very disappointed not to get the job. In breaking the news to him I asked him what he was going to do. "I haven't decided yet," he replied, "but either become an MP or make a million." It seemed a bumptious reply at the time, but Jeffrey was in the House within a year, and he has certainly made more than a million.

Jim Prior, A BALANCE OF POWER 1986

In 1944 Alan Brooke, Chief of Imperial Staff, and later Viscount Alanbrooke, remarked to George VI, "Montgomery is a very good soldier, but I think he is after my job." "I thought he was after mine," replied the King.

Richard Collier, THE FREEDOM ROAD 1944–5 1984

Arnold Bennett, having won a prize for a short story in *Tit-Bits* had decided to take up journalism. After a visit to Eden Phillpotts and his family at Torquay he turned his thoughts to novel writing. While the two friends were tramping Dartmoor together Bennett exclaimed "You are dedicated to Devon's Table-lands and River-Cradle. I will dedicate myself to the Five Towns." He left Torquay with three ambitions – to become like Phillpotts a regional novelist, to possess a house in the country and to buy a yacht. He achieved all three.

Edith Wheeler, Western Morning News 6 Jul 1967

It was in the Cherbourg Peninsula, in 1944, while Ian Fleming was sitting by the roadside eating his K ration with Robert Harling, that he said, when asked what he intended to do when the war was over, "Why, write the spy story to end all spy stories." It seemed a bit steep to Harling, himself to become a novelist. "I almost choked on my Spam," he said.

John Pearson, LIFE OF IAN FLEMING 1966

At the end of his elected term of office President Coolidge issued his famous "I do not chose to run" statement. Anxious reporters pressed persistently for more details. "Exactly why don't you want to be president again," asked one, barring his way. "Because", answered Coolidge, brushing him aside, "there is no chance of advancement."

Jacob Braude, SPEAKER'S AND TOASTMASTER'S HANDBOOK 1971

C. B. Fry was not only a first-class athlete but a first-class scholar. "I always wanted to be a minor poet," he explained to James Agate. "I remember when I did my record long jump saying to myself as I was in mid-air half way, 'This may be pretty good jumping. It's dashed poor minor poetry.'" Man's universal desire to shine at something else did not, however, persuade him to accept the Crown of Albania when that nation, impressed like the rest of the world by his brains and his personality, offered him the throne.

James Harding, AGATE: A BIOGRAPHY 1986

New York. Oct 27. The first birth in an aeroplane ever recorded in America occurred yesterday when a seven-and-a-half-pound girl was born to Mrs M. D. Evans while circling in a Fokker aeroplane 1200 feet above Miami, Florida. In the aeroplane at the time, besides Mrs Evans, were her husband Dr M. D. Evans, the baby's godmother, two nurses, two attendants of the local hospital service and an attending physician as well as the two pilots. It had been the ambition of Mrs Evans to be the first woman to give birth to a child in mid-air.

Daily Express 28 *Oct* 1929

"How much do you earn?" Lord Northcliffe asked one of his reporters on the *Daily Mail.* "Eight pounds a week," was the reply. "Are you satisfied?" "Quite." "Then you'd better go. Anyone who thinks he is earning enough is no good here."

Hannen Swaffer, World's Press News 25 *Jun* 1931

I once asked a leading member of the Democratic Party of the United States, who must be nameless, whether Franklin Roosevelt ever had any deep sense of purpose about anything. He hesitated and then said, "Only one. To remain in office."

Lord Boothby, RECOLLECTIONS OF A REBEL 1978

I was an embarrassing child. "What are you going to be when you grow up, little Edith?" Rita asked me. "A genius," I replied. I was promptly removed from the drawing room and put to bed. But my disgrace was not forgotten, and was frequently referred to in after years in a disgusted whisper.

Edith Sitwell, TAKEN CARE OF 1965

ANAGRAM

In the 1936 American Presidential election Roosevelt was running against Alfred Landon. The incumbent president had a campaign slogan consisting of three words: Franklin Delano Roosevelt. But one of his opponent's supporters discovered an exact anagram to this slogan: Vote For Landon Ere All Sink.

Adrian Berry, Daily Telegraph 15 *Oct* 1984

ANCESTRY

At a dinner party in San Francisco in 1966 Princess Margaret was introduced to Barnaby Conrad. "You have a very English name," she said. "Are you English?" "No ma'am," Conrad replied, "but my sixth great-grandmother was. Then she married a lieutenant-colonel and soon after became an American. His name was George Washington."

Clifton Fadiman, LITTLE, BROWN BOOK OF ANECDOTES 1985

When I was in India I met the Maharajah of Udaipur who told me he had recently been staying in country houses in England and had been amused to hear his hosts talking somewhat grandly about tracing their ancestry for three or four hundred years. "I thought," he said, "it might seem a little tactless if I told them I could trace mine with complete precision for 1500 years."

John Boyd-Carpenter, WAY OF LIFE 1980

A white youth in Hawaii, seeking the advice of an old Japanese man as to his courtship of a Japanese woman asked, "Will she object to my colour?" "Not your colour," was the reply, "but perhaps your ancestry." "Why, what's wrong with my ancestry?" "Well, according to your traditions you are descended from a monkey, while according to her traditions she is descended from a sun-goddess."

Clifford Gessler, HAWAII: ISLES OF ENCHANTMENT 1938

ANGLING

The Queen Mother was fishing in Highland waters one afternoon and had waded some way beyond her patch. She was doing no harm to anyone but, when rounding a bend of the river, she was spotted by a vigorous Highland landlady who was also standing in the water, rod in hand. She was spotted, not as a royal personage, but as a possible intruder.

"Private waters!" bawled the hearty sportswoman. There was no response. "Private waters!" Still no response.

In a state of now high indignation the fisherlady waded nearer to the Queen Mother, who turned to smile but also to indicate the delicate state of play. She was recognised and threw the accuser into the most terrible state of confusion. Her first response in the presence of such majesty was to crook the hinges of her knees. She dropped the deepest and most apologetic of curtseys and the private waters flowed into her waders and pegged her to the river bed. She remained there, in the position of postulant, as Britain's best loved grandmama passed by.

Russell Harty, Sunday Times 24 May 1987

There was nobody to meet us at the little station; our telegram had somehow gone astray. So we trudged along the dusty road with our overnight bags. At the Ysayë home we learned that Eugene had gone fishing. We were told where we would find him. Sure enough, there he sat in the broiling sun, with a large sombrero on his head, seeming half asleep. We watched him for quite a while. He did not catch a single fish during that time. Now and then, nevertheless, he pulled in one of his lines. It wasn't fish that he was hauling in. He had fastened beer bottles to his line, which he kept on the bottom for cooling purposes.

Harriet Kreisler, quoted Louis P. Lochner, FRITZ KREISLER 1971

A ghillie took a guest out fishing on an exceptionally wet day. The guest flogged the river for hours on end and took frequent recourse to a bottle of whisky but never offered a dram to his patient companion. Finally, trying to light his pipe, he found his matchbox wet, and nowhere dry enough to strike a match. "Isn't there a single dry spot on the whole of this goddam river?" he complained angrily. "You could try the back of my throat," suggested the ghillie, poker-faced.

Donald Sutherland, THE ENGLISH GENTLEMAN 1978

Travelling by train, my five-year-old son and I were joined by a "compleat angler", fully equipped from fly-studded hat to thigh-length waders. My son watched spellbound as he settled himself, his nets, baskets and rods over two seats. "Where is that man going, mummy?" he asked. "Fishing," I replied. Then he asked in perplexity, "Where is his jam-jar?"

Mrs Elsie Paul, Reader's Digest Jul 1980

ANNIVERSARY

I go this evening to a Fourth of June dinner. I send General Alexander a telegram running as follows: "Many congratulations on the successful development of your battle, and all good wishes for its exploitation. It was most thoughtful of you, as an Old Harrovian, to capture Rome on the Fourth of June."

General Alexander replied, "Thank you. What is the Fourth of June?"

Harold Macmillan, WAR DIARIES: POLITICS AND WAR IN THE MEDITERRANEAN 1943–5 1983

While attending Timbertops School in Australia Prince Charles paid an unexpected visit to the local church for morning service. Apologising for the scanty congregation the rector remarked that most of his parishioners were away because of the holiday weekend. "Not another bank holiday!" exclaimed the Prince. "What's this one in aid of?" There was a slight pause. "Well," said the rector gently, "over here we call it the Queen's Birthday."

J. Esser, Reader's Digest Jan 1974

Alexander Woollcott was terrifically sentimental about birthdays and Christmas. He sent telegrams and letters to many of his friends on their birthdays, and was deeply hurt unless he received similar remembrances in return. To ensure a good haul he sometimes sent out the following letter to selected friends: "Another milestone in American literature is approaching. January 19 is my birthday, in case a sudden flood of sentiment should seek expression in gifts of cash or certified cheques."

Samuel Hopkins Adams, Reader's Digest, The World of A. Woollcott May 1943

In Coventry a man called at the Citizen's Advice Bureau and asked how to have his wife traced. It transpired that they had parted three days after their wedding nearly 25 years earlier, and hadn't seen each other since. Asked whether he was thinking of a divorce the man replied, "Oh no, I just thought it would be nice to get together to celebrate our silver wedding anniversary."

Weekly News, quoted Reader's Digest Oct 1965

ANTHROPOLOGY

A zoologist member of the Athenaeum club was asked if he was acquainted with a very old member. He replied, "No, but give me one of his bones and I'll tell you all about him."

C. Patrick Thompson, World's Press News 9 Jan 1930

APOLOGY

Maurice Baring used to be well known (and liked to be well known) for his ability to balance a glass of champagne on top of his head. Once I asked him, at a party, to perform this trick for the benefit of my wife, who had never seen him do it. He took the glass from my hand, placed it on the top of his head and immediately spilled it all over the wife of a cabinet minister. He sniffed delicately at the disaster and said, in grave and perfectly successful apology, "I ought to have known I could never do it with whisky."

Edward Shanks, John o'London's Weekly 24 Nov 1939

Noel Coward could arrive (late) in an ordinary suit at a Bloomsbury party when everyone else wore evening clothes, call for silence and announce magnanimously, "I don't want anyone to feel embarrassed –."

Sheridan Morley, A TALENT TO AMUSE 1969

One snowy, stormy night Lord Balfour and his brother Gerald struggled forth on foot with their younger relatives to attend a lecture on some improving subject at the Parish Hall. The brothers were at that time respectively Prime Minister and President of the Board of Trade. The family found itself composing the greater part of the listeners, and the chairman apologised profusely to the lecturer for "the miserable quality of the audience".

Blanche E. C. Dugdale, LIFE OF LORD BALFOUR 1938

R. A. Butler sent a letter, in 1975, to an MP explaining why, to his great regret, he would not be able to be present at the formal gathering to mark the retirement from politics of Michael Fraser, former head of the Conservative Research Department. It was a model letter of its kind, apart from its first sentence. That read, either through misfortune or design, "There is no one I would rather attend a farewell meeting for than Michael." To this day no one is certain whether that was intentional or some sort of *double entendre*.

Anthony Howard, RAB: THE LIFE OF R. A. BUTLER 1987

During his daily visits back stage Sir Charles Cochran noticed a certain coolness on Noel Coward's part. After three days Noel came out with it. "I sent you a letter explaining why I have to leave you, and you're pretending you didn't get it." Cochran swore he hadn't seen it, and that night searched his house for it. He found the letter in pieces in a corner where his dog had been chewing it up. He pasted it together and sent it to Coward. Next day he got a reply which said, "Now I understand." It, too, had been torn into pieces.

News Review 11 *Nov* 1948

Uncle Crewe [Lord Crewe] had one weak spot. A canon who tripped up in his drawing room was never allowed in the house again. Even when his brother and sisters visited Crewe Hall the canon had to remain outside.

When an elderly lady from Devonshire later slipped and fell down an entire flight of great stairs at the Hall, her sycophantic husband – perhaps remembering the affair of the canon – hurried forward while his aged wife was still lying stunned and said, "Oh, Lord Crewe, I am so sorry! I do hope my wife hasn't injured your beautiful staircase."

Lady Cynthia Colville, CROWDED LIFE 1963

Edward VII was once riding in a state carriage with the Kaiser, his nephew. They heartily disliked each other but had to keep up a show of friendly conversation. Suddenly one of the horses committed a misdemeanour which unpleasantly contaminated the air of the Mall. Both monarchs ignored it, then it happened again and King Edward, as host, felt forced to apologise. "My dear Uncle Bertie," the Kaiser replied, "please don't mention it – I really thought it was one of the horses."

Peter Coats, OF KINGS AND CABBAGES 1984

At a private view at the Academy, Lord Leighton happened to be standing in front of his picture *And The Sea Gave Up Its Dead* – now in the Tate Gallery – when a lady who had just been introduced to him and who had expressed her admiration for his work, drew his attention to the picture in question by remarking, "Isn't that a horrid picture?" "I'm sorry you don't like it," said Leighton, "because it is mine." "You don't mean to say that you have bought it?" "No, I painted it." "Oh," gasped the lady, "but you really mustn't take any notice of what I say. I know nothing about art. I am only repeating what everyone else is saying."

Gladys Storey, ALL SORTS OF PEOPLE 1929

APPETITE

Lord Astor, by now [1919] 71 years old, had given himself sombrely to the pleasures of food and wine. Always an eater of classical appetite, the old American viscount was now putting away prodigious quantities of food, starting every morning before breakfast with dishes of artichokes and prawns. He gave orders to his chef one month in advance, taking pleasure in meals planned to perfection. Early in October 1919 he entered in the menu book a dinner which was to include, among other things, pheasants and fried oysters, but he did not live to taste it. On October 18 he sat down to a dinner of roast mutton and macaroni, with a bucket of Beaune. He over-ate, burst and died.

Geoffrey Bocca, Sunday Express 22 *Jan* 1956

Having ordered a pizza, Lawrence Berra, the American baseball player, was asked whether he would like it cut in four or eight pieces. "Better make it four," he said. "I don't think I can eat eight."

Clifton Fadiman, LITTLE, BROWN BOOK OF ANECDOTES 1985

Diamond Jim Brady must have been one of the world's greatest gourmands. His heyday was also the heyday of the great new hotels which were springing up all over New York. Diamond Jim knew them all and they knew him. Not only did he eat the fourteen-course dinner, but he managed to put away three and sometimes four helpings of the main dishes. And then, because he touched no drinks throughout the meal, he finished things off by eating the greater part of a box of chocolates.

Parker Morell, DIAMOND JIM: THE LIFE AND TIMES OF JAMES BUCHANAN BRADY 1935

At lunch one day at Cheam School, where Prince Charles was then a pupil, a master was mystified to find him poking at his college pudding after everyone else had finished. "What's wrong, Charles?" he asked. "Have you lost your appetite?" Charles looked up. "To tell you the truth," he said, "I'm not used to such rich food."

Jack Aitken, Sunday Express 5 *Apr* 1964

Churchill liked to conduct the business of Britain over dinner, and Harold Macmillan, then his Minister of Housing, was amazed to see him wash down a dozen oysters, cream soup, chicken pie and vanilla and strawberry ice cream with liberal quantities of Moselle and brandy in Buck's Club.

Robert Lacey, MAJESTY 1975

Aleister Crowley demanded triple absinthes in his high quacking voice, then devoured snails, wild duck, venison and Camembert washed down with torrents of Burgundy, topped off with grappa and Mexican cigars strong as fireworks. He had, as I believe is not unusual with heroin addicts, a hearty appetite.

Maurice Richardson, Observer 26 *Oct* 1969

Tam Dalyell has a passion for eggs, which he carries around with him. In the BBC's Glasgow canteen he was offered a cup of tea. "Thank you," said Tam, producing two fresh eggs from his pocket, "and I'll have these lightly boiled, please."

Observer, Profile 26 *Aug* 1984

Edward VII led a greedy and frivolous social life, mostly at other people's houses. After a dinner of some 10 courses when all the other guests were groaning he exclaimed, "What, no cheese?"

A.J.P. TAYLOR, Observer, reviewing Giles St Aubyn, EDWARD VII: PRINCE AND KING 25 Feb 1979

Until the last Frank Harris kept a ruddy interest in the flesh, as well as the spirit. He insisted, when I marvelled at his long life and hearty appetite, "I can eat anything. At 70-odd, too." There was roast duck and *pommes soufflés*, Chablis with the *hors-d'oeuvres*, and a good solid Chateauneuf du Pape with the duck. Afterwards there were ices and coffee, and then armagnac and cognac. I think Frank took Calvados which is stronger and more decisive as a drink than any apogee of apple-jack. It is a lovely, clearing drink. It is the white-hot poker of the spirits.

"Do you know how I do it?" asked Mr Harris. I confessed I did not. "Every night," said Mr Harris, "at ten o'clock, I take an enema."

Whit Burnett, THE LITERARY LIFE AND THE HELL WITH IT 1936

Max Reger's appetites were enormous and certainly contributed to his early death. He would order a waiter to bring him "two hours worth" of beefsteak and his liquid consumption was of a similar dimension. Before inviting Reger to lunch in London Sir Henry Wood, a considerate host, called the German Club to ascertain his guest's preferences. He was told to provide at least two dozen bottles of beer. "Although the good Reger had lived up to his reputation and had consumed most of the beer without the slightest inconvenience to himself," recalled Wood, "I thought the poor fellow might be thirsty so I offered him a whisky and soda. He was so pleased with the first that he had three more. He did not, however, stay to tea."

Norman Lebrecht, THE BOOK OF MUSICAL ANECDOTES 1985

Madame Clara Schumann had a fondness for good things to eat.

Some friends invited her to lunch with them, which resulted in her feeling ill next day. On an anxious friend enquiring what was wrong, she replied without mincing matters that it was due to the luncheon. "The oyster he was old, the champagne he was cork, and consequently a great disturbance to my inner."

Mathilde Verne, CHORDS OF REMEMBRANCE 1936

APPLAUSE

In the evening I distributed the prizes at the Prendergast School in Lewisham. I distributed a number of prizes to black girls and asked the headmistress why they seemed to be especially applauded. Did the other girls feel sorry for them? No, I was told, it is because they are such good athletes. I am not an observant person but I had noticed their long, graceful limbs. "The athletes and the naughty ones are always cheered loudest."

Lord Longford, DIARY OF A YEAR 1981

ARCHBISHOP

A great-aunt of mine looked up from the correspondence columns of your paper and enquired, "Who is this tiresome man Cantuar who is always interfering in religious matters?"

Arthur Harrison, letter to The Times 23 *Feb* 1987

ARCHITECTURE

When A. J. Balfour's American host pointed out a huge skyscraper, telling him enthusiastically that it was fireproof, Balfour replied, "What a pity."

Gerald Moore, AM I TOO LOUD 1962

Edwin Lutyens was asked to suggest what could be done with the Crystal Palace (before it was burned down). He suggested it might very well be put into a glass case.

Peter Coats, OF KINGS AND CABBAGES 1984

When Sir Edwin Lutyens went to India as architect of the Government buildings at New Delhi he had a difference of opinion with Lord

Hardinge, the Viceroy, over questions of style. Lord Hardinge wanted to adopt the pointed arch and said that the greatest benefactor that India had ever known was Rajah So-and-so, who had always adopted the pointed arch in all the great buildings of his time. Lutyens' reply to this was that the greatest benefactor of India in his opinion was God, and that he had not given the pointed arch when he gave the rainbow.

Sir Lionel Earle, TURN OVER THE PAGE 1934

After a visit to Osterley an American woman whose name, unfortunately, I cannot remember after nearly half a century, was enthusing about the beauty of the rooms. "What decorator had they employed?" she asked. When told that most of the rooms were the work of Adam, she replied firmly, "It may be old, but it's not as old as all that."

Peter Coats, OF KINGS AND CABBAGES 1984

Leo Pavia was driving through Hastings with James Agate. Leo stared at the buildings and remarked, "They could be divided into two styles. Early Wedding Cake and Late Water Closet."

James Harding, AGATE: A BIOGRAPHY 1986

ARMY

Sometimes Nancy Astor's enthusiasm for the soldiers' spiritual welfare bordered on the subversive and during World War I she was actually responsible for one being arrested. She took a convalescing soldier to London to attend a meeting of the First Church of Christian Science in Sloane Street, after which she packed him off in a taxi to Paddington where he would catch a train back. At the station he was stopped and picked up for not having a pass, and Nancy was obliged to appear in court on his behalf.

Geoffrey Bocca, Sunday Express 22 *Jan* 1956

The regimental sergeant-major had a battery of degrading insults at his disposal. One day on RSM's muster parade I was second man, front rank, first platoon. Having just finished five years as an apprentice joiner working at a bench I was a bit round-shouldered. We formed up. All of a sudden a voice rent the air. "Sergeant Mills, second man, front rank, looks like a vulture about to shit." I almost died on the spot.

R. H. Burford, quoted Brian Jackman, Sunday Times Magazine. REMEMBER NATIONAL SERVICE? 28 *Sep* 1986

It was 1940 and a group of raw recruits were studying the barrack-room notice-board in horror. "Reveille at 6.30," groaned one incredulous conscript. "Great," chipped in a farm lad from Devon. "I'll get a lie in then. I'm usually up at five milking the cows."

F. Garwood, Reader's Digest Sep 1978

A reluctant conscript was asked by an army oculist to read a chart. "What chart?" asked the draftee. "Just sit down in that chair and I'll show you." "What chair?" asked the man. Deferred because of his eyesight, the draftee went to a nearby movie. When the lights came on he was horrified to find the oculist in the next seat. "Excuse me," said the conscript as calmly as he could, "Does this bus go to Shipley?"

Newsweek 1942

On my second day in the army, at Fort George, they lined us up and asked us what religion we belonged to. Most of us said Presbyterian. We noticed, however, that anyone who said he was an atheist or an agnostic or that he had no religion was automatically registered Church of England. That satisfied our Scottish souls. But there was a Canadian who wanted to dodge all church parades; so he said he was a Mohammedan. The sergeant just asked him how to spell it and put him down without a murmur. But at half past three the following morning there was a tremendous clatter which woke us all up. It was the sergeant with a little mat in his hand, dragging the Canadian out to do his devotions.

Never was their such a quick conversion. By noon that Canadian was as devout a churchman as the Archbishop of Canterbury himself.

Ian Mackay, News Chronicle 7 Apr 1947

There was a private soldier who went on sick parade. "What's the trouble then?" asked the MO. "I've got a pain in my abdomen, sir." "Now listen soldier," said the MO. "Officers have abdomens. NCOs have stomachs. What you've got is bellyache."

Frank Muir and Simon Brett, FRANK MUIR GOES INTO – 1979

A man who was terrified of being called up asked a rather bright friend how he could get out of it. "Easy," said the friend. "Do what I did. Buy a truss and say you've been wearing it for years. They'll never call you up." So the scared young man did as he was advised. At the army medical the examiner looked at the truss and asked "How long have you been wearing that?" "Oh, several years." "OK," said the MO. "I'll put you down for the Camel Corps." "What!" "Oh come now. If you've been wearing a truss upside down for years you shouldn't have any trouble riding a camel."

Frank Muir and Simon Brett, THE SECOND FRANK MUIR GOES INTO – 1980

When David Niven rejoined the army during the last war he became involved in one of those tedious military exercises carried out as rehearsals for the real thing. On this occasion the general commanding our side thought it would be a good idea to try out the merits of homing pigeons as message carriers and rashly selected Niven for the task. Accordingly he found himself ensconced comfortably enough in a pub well behind the "enemy" lines, from which he was supposed to send back information about troop movements. However, as the hours slipped past nothing whatever happened, and the pigeons cooed away happily in their baskets. Finally, feeling he must justify himself in some way, Niven encoded a message, attached it to a bird's leg, and released it.

Perhaps surprisingly, it duly arrived and everyone, including the general clustered round the signals officer while he decoded the message. It read, "I have been sent home for pissing in my basket."

Douglas Sutherland, THE ENGLISH GENTLEMAN 1978

Sent to our school to explain the benefits of an army career, a recruiting officer enthusiastically listed the opportunities available. "We have immediate openings," he began, "in the computer field, the transport field, the communications field and the research field." Losing his place in his notes, he thought out loud, "Now what field did I leave out?" One alert pupil solicitously murmured, "The battlefield?"

Jerry O'Brien, Reader's Digest Dec 1973

At Mons barracks, Aldershot, cadets were welcomed by an enormous Irish Guards RSM. "Good morning, gentlemen," he said. "While you are here you will call me 'Sir' and I shall call you 'Sir'. The only difference will be that you will mean it."

Alan Road, Observer 1 *May* 1983

In January 1942 I received my call-up papers. At my selection board interview I was asked if I had any preference as to the arm I wished to serve in. I told the officer I was interested in tanks. His eyes blazed with enthusiasm. "Why tanks?" he asked keenly. I replied that I preferred to go into battle sitting down. His sparkle faded abruptly, and I shortly afterwards received a letter ordering me to report to an infantry regiment.

Peter Ustinov, DEAR ME 1977

After listening to the rhythmic but incomprehensible orders issued by the drill sergeant at my camp's open day the mother of one recruit was moved to say. "The parade looked impeccable, sergeant. But I'm afraid I didn't catch a word you said." "I don't know the words either," he said, "but I know the tune."

P. Griffin, Reader's Digest Jul 1978

ART

Alma-Tadema was a lively visitor at the Royal Academy School. Sometimes he was bawdy. In his esteem beauty was what a student should seek. In a drawing of mine of a nude woman sitting on a stool he saw very clearly that beauty had escaped me. Grasping a stick of carbon he made a few rapid lines on the paper. "Look," he cried, "I put in the chain and the toilet roll and she sits on the WC."

Roland Pertwee, MASTER OF NONE 1940

Margot Asquith, presented with an impressionistic, very slight water-colour sketch remarked, "It is like a mouse's sneeze."

Lord David Cecil, Observer, Staying With Margot 20 *Dec* 1981

Out walking with a friend one day Dame Edith Evans paused at the window of a London art gallery. After studying a rather drab water-colour she gave her critical assessment of the picture. "I couldn't have that in my house," she said. "It would be like living with a gas leak."

Clifton Fadiman, LITTLE, BROWN BOOK OF ANECDOTES 1985

During one of his infrequent visits to the Tate Gallery, King George V called out to Queen Mary in quarterdeck tones: "Come here, Mary. This will make you laugh." And he pointed to a row of French Impressionists.

Kenneth Rose, Sunday Telegraph 18 *Apr* 1987

When the Mona Lisa was stolen from the Louvre in 1911 and was missing for two years more people went to stare at the blank space than had gone to look at the masterpiece in 12 years.

Barbara Cartland, BOOK OF USELESS INFORMATION

Matisse's painting *Le Bâteau* hung upside down in the Museum of Modern Art, New York for forty-seven days before anyone noticed. (October 18 – December 4 1961). In that period 116,000 people had visited the gallery.

David Wallenchinsky and Irving Wallace, THE PEOPLE'S ALMANAC 1975

An American called on chance at Sir William Orpen's studio last summer and wanted his portrait done at Orpen's usual price of three thousand guineas. "I'm booked up for six months," said Orpen, doing his stuff as they say. "Too bad," said the American, "because I'm sailing Friday week." "Oh no you're not," said Orpen, pushing the man into a chair. "Just you sit there and don't you bloody well move until I say so."

Reginald Pound, THEIR MOODS AND MINE 1937

Three graduates in fine arts who were given an Arts Council grant of £400 to walk around East Anglia with a 10-foot yellow pole tied on their heads have denied that it was a waste of money. Mr Kenneth Weete, MP for Ipswich, has asked Mr Hugh Jenkins, minister with responsibility for the arts, to investigate why they were given the grant. Mr Raymond Richards, one of the men, says, "The MP's reaction is narrow-minded. It is an attempt to tread new ground in the art world." The three men, graduates from Leeds Polytechnic, who walked 150 miles attached to the pole, call the project "living sculpture".

The Times 13 *Mar* 1976

My parents, though proud of my ability, never took art seriously as a possible career; they regarded it, quite rightly, as a shaky profession and wanted me to have a proper job. "Draw an advertisement for Ingersoll watches and win a grand prize," said the competition. I did, and won first prize – a sweater, a shirt, a Dan Dare watch, a boomerang, etc. All useful stuff. I wanted to carry on winning grand prizes. It felt good.

Gerald Scarfe, SCARFE ON SCARFE. 1986

Sacheverell Sitwell was up at Oxford at the same time as myself. He hung his rooms with drawings by Picasso and Matisse, which were the subject of lewd comment among the more athletic members of the college. There was one drawing by – I believe – Picasso called "Salomé", which represented a skinny and exceedingly revolting old lady prancing in a loathsome attitude before certain generously paunched old men who looked like the sort of people you might meet at a Turkish bath when your luck is out. One day a certain charming don – (an ardent Roman Catholic) – strolled into Sacheverell's rooms, saw the picture, paled slightly and then asked him what it was all about.

Sacheverell said something about "line". And then the don let go. "Line", he said, was the excuse for every rotten piece of work produced by modern artists. If a leg was out of proportion or a face obviously impossible, if the whole design was grotesque and ridiculouss, the excuse was always "line". And he stamped out of the room leaving untouched the excellent lunch that Sacheverell had prepared for him.

Beverley Nichols, TWENTY-FIVE 1926

Once in a shop in the Clichy quarter I saw four still-life paintings by Vincent Van Gogh, each marked "2 francs" with white chalk in one corner. One of them, a few apples in a basket, attracted me especially. I noted that he appeared to have squeezed out a whole tube of vert veronese in streaks for each apple, just touched with a few flecks of the brush and, lo, there were the most wonderful green apples I have ever seen! My hotel was far away on the other side of the river and I was seeing sights. The trouble of carrying a canvas of that size, so loaded with paint that it could not be rolled, was too much for me. I hesitated, and was lost. So vanished my one chance of owning a masterpiece.

A. S. Hartrick, A PAINTER'S PILGRIMAGE 1939

See also **PAINTING, PORTRAIT, SCULPTURE, SURREALISM**

ASSASSINATION

I had kidney trouble during World War I. The eminent, and indeed brilliant, surgeon who eventually removed my kidney was almost the double of King George of Greece, then an exile living at Brown's Hotel in Dover Street. Shortly after he had operated on me he was walking down Dover Street when a Greek republican fanatic, mistaking him for the king, leaped upon him and drove a stiletto into his back.

Lady Cynthia Colville, CROWDED LIFE 1963

I was doing my best to secure an interview with Rasputin. A curious character, a Dobrudjian, rich, stingy and dirty, but influential, promised to produce him. "Get several bottles of the best brandy you can beg or steal," he said. "I will tell him you have it. He will come." The bottles were accumulated in the office of Walter Whiffen, correspondent of the Associated Press, and the Dobrudjian made an appointment with Rasputin for the next afternoon. That evening Rasputin accepted an invitation from Prince Youssoupoff. Youssoupoff killed him.

Arno Dosch-Fleurot, THROUGH WAR TO REVOLUTION 1931

ASTROLOGY

Interviewing Ronald Reagan, and unable to extract anything but bland platitudes, I asked in desperation under what sign of the Zodiac he had been born. The answer was Sagittarius. "And what do Sagittarians do?" I said, not through any curiosity but because having started it, it seemed impossible to abandon the unlikely dialogue. The smile widened still further. For Reagan it was equivalent to being presented with a one-foot putt to win the match. Expertly he stroked the ball into the cup. "I guess you could say they go around doing good to people." Only later did I realise that in fact his sign was Aquarius.

Frank Giles, Sunday Times 1986

A court official has told me that an astrologer wrote to the Prince of Wales [afterwards Duke of Windsor] forecasting the date of his wedding, and the initials of the lady who will be his bride. The date of the wedding was given as May 5 or 6 1934, and the initials of his bride as L. R. P.

J. C. Cannell, WHEN FLEET STREET CALLS 1932

I don't know how it is done these days, but when I was on *Home Notes* there was a girl called Chrissie who went round saying, "What's your sign, dear?" and when you told her, "What would you like to have happen to you this week?"

Katherine Whitehorn, VIEW FROM A COLUMN 1983

ASTRONOMY

Albert Einstein's wife was particularly impressed by the giant telescope at Mount Wilson Observatory. "What do they use it for?" she asked. Her host explained that one of its chief uses was to find out the shape of the universe. "Oh," said Mrs Einstein, "my husband does that on the back of an old envelope."

Bennett Cerf, TRY AND STOP ME 1947

ATHLETICS

Lord Burghley, the Olympic hurdler, never held his powers in such solemn esteem that he disdained to use them light-heartedly. On the maiden voyage of the *Queen Elizabeth*, for the gratification of H.G.Wells, Lord Camrose and A.E.W.Mason, he ran 400 yards after dinner, in evening dress, in 58 seconds. Another athlete who thereafter changed into singlet and shorts to beat the record conceivably missed the point.

Observer, Profile 1 *Oct* 1948

AUDIENCE

Among George Antheil's early avant-garde pieces none caused a greater sensation than his *Ballet mécanique,* scored for automobile horns, aeroplane propeller, fire siren, ten grand pianos and other instruments. When it was performed at Carnegie Hall in 1924 a concert-goer near the orchestra could stand no more than a few minutes of the racket. Tying his handkerchief to his cane, he raised the white flag.

Scott Beach, MUSICDOTES 1977

We were giving a concert in a hotel. After the last strains of Handel's *Largo* floated out, a fat, motherly woman near me leaned out and asked, "Won't you please play Handel's *Largo*?" "But we've just finished it," I said. The fat lady sank back in her chair. "Oh, I wish I'd known," she said. "It's my favourite piece."

May Browne, Reader's Digest Oct 1942

Relaxing in her dressing room after a concert Amelita Galli-Curci heard a knock at the door. Quite accustomed to receiving visits from aspiring young singers seeking free advice and encouragement, she sighed wearily and opened the door. There stood a rather timid young girl clutching a bunch of roses. Galli-Curci invited her in, taking the flowers from her admirer's trembling hand. "Do you sing?" she asked. "Oh no," exclaimed the girl, a little taken aback by the question. "Well then, do you play?" asked the soprano, gesturing towards the piano. "No," replied her visitor, adding somewhat apologetically, "I just listen." Galli-Curci smiled impulsively and embraced the girl. "I had quite forgotten," she said, "that there were people left who *only* listen."

Clifton Fadiman, LITTLE, BROWN BOOK OF ANECDOTES 1985

Oscar Levant described his reprisals against a woman who arrived late for one of his recitals and distracted the audience as she walked along the centre aisle. "I stopped my performance of a Poulenc piece and began choreographing her walk by playing in time with her steps. She hesitated and slowed down – I slowed down. She stopped – I stopped. She hurried – I hurried. By the time she reached her seat the audience was in a state of hysterics and the matron in a state of wild confusion."

Dorothy Herrman, WITH MALICE TOWARDS ALL 1982

In the little Philip Theatre in Sydney where I played for thirteen weeks in 1959 I could see a long way back into the auditorium; on matinee days the ladies came in wearing hats, usually white, and when they laughed they bent forward from the waist and looked like a field of dog daisies bowing in the wind.

Joyce Grenfell, JOYCE GRENFELL REQUESTS THE PLEASURE 1976

By his strange pranks Vladimir di Pachmann made himself more popular than men who were greater musicians. His favourite trick was to put a visiting card under the leg of his piano stool to make it higher. He would play a few bars, then break off and take the card out again. I asked him once why he did these weird things. He laughed and said, "I play to English public on Sunday afternoons. On Sunday English people eat splendid luncheon. They are like lions. They like to sleep when they are full. I don't like to play to people who fall asleep. So I invent my own technique. I play foolish tricks. I make them laugh at Crazy Old Pachmann until I am sure they are awake. Then I begin my concert."

Patrick Murphy, Daily Express 8 Jan 1933

Pianist Artur Rubinstein used to fix his attention on one person in the concert hall in order to establish contact with the audience. This habit did not usually lead to any tangible consequence but once a woman came up to him after a concert in Palermo and said, "I am deeply touched, maestro. During the whole concert I had a feeling that you were playing especially for me. The evening belonged to us alone, and I want to thank you." She shook his hand and left.

Janik Press Service, quoted, Reader's Digest Jul 1977

I established a certain standard of behaviour that, during my playing, there must be no conversation. When they began to talk, I would stop. I would say, "I am sorry to interrupt your conversation. I deeply regret that I am obliged to disturb you, so I am going to stop playing for a while to allow you to continue talking." You can imagine the effect it had. However, it did some good. Many of them said afterwards, "What a change in the audience now at the At Homes. No more talking, thank God."

Ignace Jan Paderewski, MEMOIRS 1939

AUDITION

As an 18-year-old novice, released from RADA to gain practical experience I was tremendously thrilled to be offered my first part as the young stoker in Noel Coward's film *In Which We Serve*. Coward, of course, was a god to anyone with acting ambitions and I turned up for the audition in fear and trembling. Dressed in my sailor's uniform I was left standing in the middle of a vast sound stage at Shepherd's Bush studios, growing more and more nervous every second. Soon the Master arrived, complete with entourage. He saw my small, quaking figure and instantly put the situation to rights. "You won't know me, but I'm Noel Coward," he said, clipping each word like a bus ticket. "*You*, of course, are Richard Attenborough." I felt 10 feet tall and immensely grateful.

Richard Attenborough, Sunday Telegraph 22 *Aug* 1965

When we were composing the second act of *The Rape of Lucretia* Benjamin Britten asked me to audition a girl with him. She came in looking like a provincial schoolteacher. She was so terrified she could only whisper. We wondered how she could possibly sing. I was not impressed. I could see no sign of Lucretia there. I remember she had a particularly ugly hat. Ben and I both felt almost as embarrassed as she. He handed her the score. She read it through once, and then went to the piano and sang part of the Spinning Aria. We were both so moved by the quality of her voice that neither of us spoke.

The poor girl waited, not knowing why we were silent. Thinking she had made a mess of her audition she burst into tears. We then had a job to reassure her, and the more we did it the more she thought we were just being kind. Though Ben and I spent the next few months repeating to Kathleen Ferrier that we adored her voice, we never managed to convince her after that first audition.

Ronald Duncan, HOW TO MAKE ENEMIES 1968

A story is told of an actress who, after months of unsuccessful auditioning, was finally offered a job. She stammered, "I don't think I can accept – I only do auditions."

Donald Sinden, A TOUCH OF THE MEMOIRS 1982

AUTHOR

My last novel *Gemel in London* was my twentieth book. And the proudest achievement of my career is that I have inveigled eleven publishers into publishing me, all of whom have lost money thereby. For I possess this unique distinction, that of all writers with twenty books to their credit I am the worst seller. Nobody has ever read me in book form. A few old ladies residing in boarding houses in Tunbridge Wells occasionally borrow me, and that is all.

James Agate, T.P's Weekly 12 *May* 1928

Vicky Baum's first marriage was to a witty writer. In fact the writer talked more than he wrote. She helped him out by fees earned by harp-playing until the day she found her husband red-eyed, surrounded by discarded paper and groaning for inspiration. He had a commission for six well-paid stories. His deadline had expired and he still hadn't written a word. Shyly Vicky searched out some tales which she had written, but which her father would not allow her to publish. Her husband, overjoyed, sent them off in his own name. It was Vicki Baum's first venture as a professional writer.

Robert Pitman, Sunday Express, reviewing Vicki Baum, I KNOW WHAT I'M WORTH 1961

During the 1930s in a railway carriage Hilaire Belloc noticed a man in front of him reading his *History of England*. He leaned forward asked him how much he had paid for it, was informed of the price, took a corresponding sum out of his pocket, gave it to the man, snatched the book from his pocket and tossed it out of the window.

A.N.Wilson, LIFE OF HILAIRE BELLOC 1982

I observed while dining in Paris at a Duval restaurant a fat, repulsive, cross-grained woman, full of complaint. No one could like or sympathise with her. But I thought – she has been young and slim once. And I immediately thought of a long ten or fifteen thousand word short story "The History of Two Old Women" [eventually the novel *The Old Wives' Tale*]. I gave this woman a sister as fat as herself. And the first chapter would be in the restaurant, both sisters rather like tonight, and written rather cruelly. Then I would go back to the infancy of these two, and sketch it all. One should have lived ordinarily, married prosaically, and become a widow. The other "guilty splendour" and all that. Both are overtaken by fat. And they live together in old age, not too rich, a nuisance to themselves and others. Neither has any imagination. The two lives would have to intertwine. I saw the whole work quite clearly and hope to do it.

Arnold Bennett, Journal 18 *Nov* 1903

Joseph Conrad told me that during the War, being dreadfully pressed for money, he had sold some of his MSS to a bidder who had offered him very large sums. But he said the MSS were not really manuscripts – not what books were printed from. They were passages he had copied out by hand in order to make a little money. He had his family to think of. It was dreadful for a man like Conrad to have to descend to that.

Ford Madox Ford, IT WAS THE NIGHTINGALE 1934

Conrad's relief at finishing a story was always clouded by the thought that soon another would have to be begun. "When I think of it," he said once, leaping from his chair and going over to his writing table, over which he stood as if pleading with some inhuman taskmaster to spare his slave so many more hours of toil and anguish. And then he threw up both arms and apostrophized the inkstand: "To think that all my future, my livelihood, my very life, lies there, in that little black pool."

William Maas, John o'London's Weekly 15 *Sep* 1939

André Gide, French Nobel Prize winner, moved into a new house in Normandy with a study containing every possible convenience. His cousin visiting him there found Gide working at a folding table in the hall. He explained, "The new study is much too comfortable. I simply can't work there."

News Review 30 *Dec* 1948

A magazine had run a competition for the best parody of Graham Greene's work. A week after the prize-winning entry was published a letter appeared from Greene himself. He was delighted that Mr John Smith had won the contest, although he felt that two other competitors, Mr John Doakes and Mr William Jones also deserved prizes. He had sent all three entries himself – they were not parodies, but passages from some of his early novels that he had not considered fit for publication.

Book-of-the-Month Club News Oct 1949

Once or twice James Joyce dictated a bit of *Finnegan's Wake* to Samuel Beckett, though dictation did not work very well for him. In the middle of one such session there was a knock at the door which Beckett did not hear. Joyce said, "Come in," and Beckett wrote it down. Afterwards he read back what he had written and Joyce said, "What's that 'Come in'?" "Yes, you said that," said Beckett. Joyce thought for a moment and then said, "Let it stand."

Richard Ellman, JAMES JOYCE 1959

About a year after *The Town and The City* was published Jack Kerouac arrived in Robert Giroux's editorial office at Harcourt Brace with the famous continuous roll of teletype paper on which he had written a draft of *On The Road*. Kerouac announced that the book was divinely inspired, touched by the Holy Ghost. Giroux looked at the manuscript, as thick as a roll of paper towels, which had come uncorrected from the typewriter. Giroux suggested that "even after you have been inspired by the Holy Ghost you have to sit down and read your manuscript". Then he suggested that the novel might need revision. In an outrage Kerouac swore that nobody was going to change a single word and, denouncing Giroux as a crass idiot, he left the office.

Donald Hall, New York Times Book Review Jan 1980

Crossing the Atlantic, Sinclair Lewis saw a lady on deck reading his latest book, about which there had been some hot discussion. By the place of her finger in the book he judged that she was approaching the passage which had caused the most trouble, and he thought he would keep an eye on her. Presently the lady rose up, walked firmly to the rail and flung the book far into the ocean. But such public verdicts are rare.

A.P.Herbert, APH. HIS LIFE AND TIMES 1970

At his luxurious villa on Cap Ferrat Somerset Maugham has been having trouble with the scenery. His study window, which looks out on the Mediterranean has been blocked up. "Now," says Maugham, "I will write and not look out at the sea all the morning."

News Review 30 *Dec* 1948

In 1918, when he was fifty and working on *Six Characters in Search of an Author*, Luigi Pirandello found himself both a prisoner and an outcast in life. Like an obsessive presence, only his characters peopled his solitude; splinters of a broken dream that had sprung back fully armed to threaten and cajole him. Shut in his study he conversed with them, waving his arms wildly, flashing his eyes and making the strangest faces in the world.

Gaspar Giudice, PIRANDELLO 1975

Vita [Sackville-West] is writing a short story and is furious at having to come across to dinner. The difficulty with her is that if she is interrupted she can never start again. So instead of going to her tower after dinner she retires to bed at 9.15. I never know what to do about these things.

Harold Nicolson, DIARY 4 *Dec* 1955

Edith Wharton mentioned to Henry James that the car in which they were riding had been bought with the proceeds of her latest novel. "With the proceeds of *my* latest novel," said Henry meditatively, "I purchased a small go-cart, or hand-barrow, on which my guests' luggage is wheeled from the station to my house. It needs a coat of paint. With the proceeds of my next novel I shall have it painted."

Percy Lubbock, PORTRAIT OF EDITH WHARTON 1947

See also **PUBLISHING, WRITING**

AUTOGRAPH

Arnold Bennett was autographing copies of his latest book at a literary luncheon. One young man had arrived clutching three copies but was too embarrassed to ask Bennett to sign all three copies at once. Having received his first autograph he returned to the end of the line, hoping Bennett would not recognise him when his turn came again. The author signed the second book without comment and the young man patiently repeated the procedure. Presented with the third copy Bennett paused for a moment and then wrote on the fly-leaf "To — who is fast becoming an old friend."

Clifton Fadiman, LITTLE, BROWN BOOK OF ANECDOTES 1985

Eddie Cantor, leaving the theatre after a show, stopped to sign autographs for a group of children gathered round the stage door. One small boy was standing apart from the others. "Don't you want my autograph too?" asked Eddie. "Hell no," replied the boy scornfully. "I was waiting for you to get through your act so I can see Donald Duck."

Patrick Mahoney, BARBED WIT AND MALICIOUS HUMOUR 1956

The old lady looked indignantly at the book I had just autographed for her. "But usen't you to be J.B.Priestley?" she demanded. "That was a long time ago," I said. "I've been all sorts of things since then."

Gerald Priestland, SOMETHING UNDERSTOOD 1986

After a concert in Leeds Town Hall Sir Malcolm Sargent swept off the podium and whisked his elegant form to the dressing room. His valet timed the pop of the champagne cork to coincide with the opening of the door. Sir Malcolm sank into one chair and propped his ankles on another. One hand held the thin stem of the glass. The other mopped a brow with a silk square. After some minutes there was a gentle tapping at the door.

"Oh God," exhaled the weary performer. There were a few gentle whispers between the valet and the outside world. The door was left ajar as the inevitable question was asked: "Sir Malcolm, shall you be signing autographs?" Another sigh was offered to the Deity. "Oh God, I'll do the first six." "There are only three, Sir Malcolm."

Russell Harty, OBSERVER 18 *Jul* 1978

Travelling by train over the plains of the American Mid-West, two women stopped diffidently at the door of Albert Schweitzer's compartment and asked, "Have we the honour of speaking to Professor Einstein?"

"No, unfortunately not," he replied, "though I can quite understand your mistake, for he has the same kind of hair as I have (rumpling his up). But inside, my head is altogether different. However, he is a very old friend of mine – would you like me to give you his autograph?" And he wrote, "Albert Einstein, by way of his friend, Albert Schweitzer."

T.D.Williams, Reader's Digest Sep 1980

AWARD

In November 1903 a letter announced to Pierre and Marie Curie that the Royal Society of London had bestowed on them one of its highest awards – the Davy Medal.

Marie, who was ill, let her husband go to the ceremony without her. Pierre brought back from England a heavy gold medal, on which their names were engraved. He looked for a place for the medal in their house in the Boulevard Kellermann. He handled it awkwardly. He lost it and found it again.

Finally he confided it to his daughter Irene, who had never had such a gala day in her six years. When his friends came to see him the scientist showed them the child amusing herself with her new toy. "Irene adores her big new penny," he said.

Eve Curie, Sunday Express 17 *Oct* 1937

This year's runner-up in the *Cosmopolitan* New Journalist of the Year competition, Jane White, was a real hit with editor Linda Kelsey. She loved Jane's sensitive feature on pre-marital terror and adored her incisive piece on today's ideal man. All in all she "epitomised the quintessential *Cosmo* woman" – intelligent, witty and feminine. So it was a shock to Ms Kelsey when Jane arrived to claim her prize and revealed her true identity: Liverpool van driver Kevin Sampson.

The Times 7 *Mar* 1986

BABY

J.M. Barrie had only to take a bawling infant in his arms for it to become peaceful and contented. I have seen him do so after a baptismal service with magical effect. He carried the baby from the church to its home without it uttering the faintest cry. Someone asked him how he had succeeded in making it so quiet. "It was easy. I just told it the story of Little Red Riding Hood."

Robert Lynd, News Chronicle 21 *Jun* 1937

John Mortimer tells how he and his wife went to dinner at a house where John Gielgud was a guest. Their young daughter had been put to sleep in a spare bedroom and creeping out with her in a carry-cot they met Gielgud who, peering under the pink plastic hood enquired: "Why on earth did you bring your baby with you? Is it because you're afraid of burglars?"

Philip Oakes, The Times 22 *Mar* 1984

BALDNESS

The *maître d'hôtel* once stopped Groucho Marx as he was entering the dining room of a posh Los Angeles restaurant. "I'm sorry, sir, but you have no necktie." "That's all right," said Groucho, "don't be sorry. I can remember a time when I had no pants." "I'm sorry, sir," repeated the waiter, "you cannot enter the dining room without a necktie." Groucho caught sight of a bald man eating his lunch and yelled across the room, "Look at him! You won't let me in without a necktie, but you let him in without his hair."

Philip Howard, The Times 11 *May* 1987

When I was a child staying in Scotland with my grandfather Lord Lamington I was watering the flowers in the garden when I happened to notice his bald head gleaming in the sun as he was sleeping in the garden. A brilliant idea struck me. I climbed quietly on to a chair behind him, with the watering can in my hand. I lifted it up and watered his head. The effect astonished me. He leapt to his feet and shouted furiously for my nurse whilst mopping the water off with his handkerchief. Nanny came running across the lawn. "Take this child in," he thundered. I was swept up, carried off under her arm like a doll, back to the house. I kicked and screamed. "I wanted to make his hair grow like the flowers," I cried.

Marchesa Stella Vitelleschi, OUT OF MY COFFIN 1937

BALLET

In the twenties in Paris, when Diaghilev was triumphing with his Ballets Russes, his problem was to continue to surprise a sophisticated public. Jean Cocteau, who had undertaken to provide a scenario for a new ballet, asked the great impresario for some direction. Diaghilev replied only, "*Etonne-moi*" (Astonish me).

Bernard Taper, BALANCHINE: A BIOGRAPHY 1984

Like many artists, Nijinsky had a weakness for clever toys. I discovered in Chelsea a jointed wooden duck which was capable of assuming extraordinary expressive attitudes. I procured one for him and he was delighted with it. The following year after *The Rite of Spring* had been produced with his angular choreography one of his first questions to me was, "Well, do you recognise it?" "What?" "Why, the duck of course," and he told me the most effective angular poses in the ballet originated with the duck.

Lydia Lopokova, Radio Times 23 *Jun* 1937

London. Palace Theatre. Pavlova dancing the dying swan. Feather falls off her dress. Two silent Englishmen. One says, "Moulting." That's all they say.

Arnold Bennett, Journal 21 *Apr* 1911

BALLOON

A veteran continental balloonist departed from his wedding reception with his bride in a large hydrogen balloon. Romantically engaged in the bottom of the basket they eventually returned, metaphorically, to earth to find themselves in cloud. The coutryside was flat and the air was still, so they gingerly descended until the pilot could hear dogs barking, clocks striking, and people talking below, but he could neither see nor be seen. He picked out the voices of two women, leant out of the basket and shouted down to them, "What town is this?" The reply was a terrified scream.

Ronald Faux, The Times 4 Jun 1983

I talked to the long-suffering wife of a pilot who had put their balloon down in a field that was newly sprayed with pungent manure. "The basked tipped on to its side and became a large shovel. The balloon dragged us across the full length of the field like some hideous stinking chariot. The inside filled with fresh pig slurry and we were covered from head to foot by the time we stopped. I began to wonder if we ever would. We had a good laugh," she said.

Ibid

When you are there with no wind it's completely silent and you just drift along in a small world of your own. It is so quiet that you can even hear the people below swearing when you throw sand out on their washing.

Christine Turnbull, Daily Telegraph 1 Feb 1969

BATH

My father loved Scotland and took houses there from time to time, transporting the household together with some of his unusual habits. One of these was the setting up of a Turkish bath in empty dog kennels near the front door. One kennel was heated with hot bricks. When hot enough in went Father. Later he emerged to be drenched with buckets of cold water thrown from the roof by the butler. Callers were astounded.

Mrs J.D.Bailey, The Times 26 Jul 1933

During the Government's campaign to economise on electricity in the severe winter of 1947 Hugh Gaitskell, in a speech at Hastings said, "This means getting up and going to bed in cold bedrooms. It may mean fewer baths. Personally I have never had a great many baths myself, and I can assure those who are in the habit of having a great many baths that it does not make a great deal of difference to their health if they have fewer. And as far as appearance is concerned, most of that is underneath and nobody sees it."

As he wrote later, it was meant to be taken as a joke. But Winston Churchill could not resist the opportunity. He said in the Commons, "When Ministers of the Crown speak like this they should not wonder why they are getting into bad odour. I have even asked myself, Mr Speaker, whether you would admit the word 'lousy' as a parliamentary expression in referring to the Administration, purely as one of factual narrative."

Philip M Williams, HUGH GAITSKELL 1979

Anatole France, instead of using his bath for the normal purpose, threw complimentary copies of books sent to him into it, then sold them when the bath was full.

Anthony Powell, Daily Telegraph 14 *Sep* 1967

Complaints were made to the Office of Works (known in the Admiralty as "Works") about the unsatisfactory water supply at the Admiralty. The curious colour of the water was mentioned by Winston Churchill when he wrote to Sir Oswyn Murray, Secretary of the Admiralty, that he "dyed daily in his bath". Murray in reply regretted the inconvenience, and added that "apparently salvation would have to be in faith as 'Works' were unable to help him".

Lady Murray, THE MAKING OF A CIVIL SERVANT 1940

BEARD

Maurice Baring surprised me by saying that at one time he grew a beard, but it was not a success. I said that beards must want a lot of drying after the morning's ablutions. "It is impossible to dry a beard," said Maurice, "mine was damp all day long." I asked what they are like at night. "At night,' he said, shuddering, "they are at their worst. They tickle one's chest, you know, and keep one awake. I used to wake up under the impression that I had fallen asleep in some undergrowth in the forest. It was after one such night that I arose and shaved off my beard."

Sir Harry Preston, LEAVES FROM MY UNWRITTEN DIARY 1936

Natalie Bauer-Lechner coquettishly urged Gustav Mahler to grow again the beard he had sported as a young man. "What are you thinking of?" exclaimed Mahler. "Do you think I go clean-shaven as a matter of personal vanity? There is a very good reason for it. When I conduct I communicate with singers and orchestra not only with my hands and eyes, but with facial expressions, through the mouth and lips. I could not do that if my face was hidden by a beard. I must be quite free."

Norman Lebrecht, THE BOOK OF MUSICAL ANECDOTES 1985

Thomas Richard Shaw grew his goatee beard after his first appointment as an Ambassador, to Upper Volta and Dahomey. "To Africans all white faces look alike, and when I went to functions the guards always ignored me, because they couldn't recognise my face. So I grew a beard and it worked like a charm."

Michael Bateman, Sunday Times 28 Sep 1971

In the Sultanate of Muscat and Oman the forcible cutting of a beard is a severe punishment and indignity. One Sheikh fell into the hands of an enemy, a Wali of slave extraction, who thought it would be an excellent thing to make an example of the prisoner. He accordingly had one side of the sheikh's hairy face shaved completely – one eyebrow, one moustache, and shame of shame, half the beard. Two slaves were then commanded to assault him in public, finally he was led through the streets on an ass, and set free. His tribe had been dishonoured.

Bertram Thomas, ALARMS AND EXCURSIONS IN ARABIA 1931

BEAUTY

I once slammed a door behind me, not knowing that my wife, Gladys Cooper, was standing there, and it fractured her nose. However, I afterwards told her that she ought to be very grateful to me, as it improved her looks vastly. Before her accident she had no bridge to her nose; after it she had a lovely nose. I always maintained I am entirely responsible for her extraordinary beauty.

Herbert Buckmaster, BUCK'S BOOK 1933

BED

The first request of the rather grim and celibate Lord Kitchener, on his appointment as Minister for War in 1914 was for a bed at the War Office, so that he could sleep near his work. "Have you a bed here?" he demanded. "No, my lord," replied the WO messenger. "Then get one." "Y-yes my lord," stammered the man, nervous but anxious to oblige. "S-s-single or double?"

J.B.Booth, LIFE, LAUGHTER AND BRASS HATS 1939

BEE

Honey bees find life easier as marmalade spivs. At Acton, on the outskirts of London, there are bees which steal marmalade by the hundredweight from a preserve factory and deliver it to their embarrassed owner, Mr William Huntley, in his basement flat garden. Last year Mr Huntley had 240 pounds of marmalade in his six hives. Nothing can be done about it. No court can order an apiarist to keep a bee under control.

H. de Winton Wigley, News Chronicle 20 *Mar* 1948

BEGGING

In 1957 *Fortune* magazine made a list of the richest men in America. The name of Paul Getty, until then comparatively unknown, was at the top. After that the stream of begging letters became a torrent. In one record mail delivery came requests for 15 million dollars.

Russell Lewis, Daily Telegraph 5 *Sep* 1960

BIOGRAPHY

I was complaining to George Balanchine about the scarcity of materials pertaining to his life. He had never journalised, and had written perhaps fewer letters than the number of ballets he had choreographed, and had kept no scrapbook. Balanchine listened to my complaint and then replied, "You should think of your task as if you were writing the biography of a racehorse. A racehorse doesn't keep a diary."

Bernard Taper, GEORGE BALANCHINE: A BIOGRAPHY 1984

During his later years, when he was famous, John Steinbeck's wife, Elaine, brought home a paperback book entitled *John Steinbeck* by Frank

William Watt. Steinbeck, who often felt he had been misinterpreted by many of the commentators on his life and work, read it with great interest. Finished, he remarked, "This book doesn't seem to be about me, but it's pretty interesting about somebody."

Jackson Benson, THE TRUE ADVENTURES OF JOHN STEINBECK: WRITER 1984

BIRTH

Joseph Conrad announced the birth of our child in these words: "The house is in a state of disorganisation on account of the arrival of a child of the male persuasion. However, the fuss is over, thank God." When he saw the child he exclaimed: "Why, it's just like a human being."

Mrs Joseph Conrad, CONRAD AS I KNEW HIM 1927

My first public appearance was not a success. Leaning forward expectantly, my mother opened her eyes to look at her first-born. When she saw me hanging upside-down with limbs outstretched, she clutched her bosom and fell back on the pillows in horror. "My God," she cried, "it's a frog," and fainted dead away.

Leslie Mitchell, LESLIE MITCHELL REPORTING 1981

I was born in a small hospital in Tokyo. Mama says she remembers two things: a mouse ran across the floor, which she took as a sign of good luck, and a nurse bending down and whispering apologetically: "I'm afraid it's a girl. Would you prefer to inform your husband yourself?"

Liv Ullmann, CHANGING 1976

Soon after George V came to the throne No. 10 telephoned the Palace on Thomas Hardy's birthday to suggest that the King might care to send a telegram to "Old Hardy". A few hours later Mr Hardy of Alnwick, the much esteemed maker of fishing rods, received the King's congratulations on attaining an age he had not attained, on a day that was an anniversary of nothing.

Kenneth Rose, Sunday Telegraph 26 *Jul* 1987

BIRTHRATE

Nancy Astor got her biggest laugh in the House of Commons, unintentionally, when in one of her speeches she announced that "despite the efforts of Mussolini and the Pope the birthrate in Italy continues to decline".

John Beevers, Sunday Referee 10 *Feb* 1939

BISHOP

I can put on record why so many Anglican bishops are Westcott House men, product of one small Cambridge Theological College. It seems that 30 years ago an incoming Patronage Secretary took over the famous card index containing all the coded information about rising men. Many cards were marked W.H.M. He mistakenly read this as Wife Has Means, and was thus led to suppose that these had the highest qualification for preferment. So began a flood of Westcott House men which still continues, with very happy results.

Don Cupitt, Sunday Telegraph 12 *Oct* 1986

The Sandringham gamekeeper, who had taken Bishop Herbert of Norwich out shooting, said of him, "He was just like any other gentleman, except that he said 'Bother' when he missed."

Colin Stephenson, MERRILY ON HIGH 1965

Geoffrey Rippon is MP for Hexham, and they have a bishop who was formerly Bishop of the Gilbert and Ellice Islands, and treats his parishioners including Rippon, as if they were Gilbert islanders. He is apt to read out the number of a hymn and say, "Now don't mumble, but there is no necessity to shout."

Cecil King, DIARY 29 *Jul* 1970

The Government was to be grateful for an obscure House of Lords ruling about suitable attire for bishops which narrowly helped to overcome religious opposition and win an important division on the Shops Bill earlier this week.

The bishops, who are strongly opposed to the Bill, are bound by a custom from 1800 when the right of the Bishop of Lincoln to vote was disputed because he was not wearing his lawn sleeves.

Before the vote a number of bishops were planning to visit the Archbishop of Canterbury, who had recently undergone an operation. They packed away their robes and changed into "civvies". When the division bell began to ring they found they were improperly dressed to vote. The Government thus avoided its first major defeat on the Bill by just six vital votes.

Daily Telegraph 23 Jan 1986

BLINDNESS

Aldous Huxley's cousin commiserated with him on his near blindness. "But it is not without compensations," replied Huxley. "Being able to read Braille, I can read in bed with a book beneath the blankets. So my hands are kept warm on the coldest nights."

Ronald W. Clark, THE HUXLEYS 1980

In the railway terminus of an eastern city an old lady and a small girl sat knitting side by side. The needles moved swiftly between the old lady's worn fingers, while the little girl, biting her tongue in concentration, was trying to pick up a dropped stitch. Finally with tears in her eyes, she handed her knitting to the old lady. "I'm in a mess again, Grandma. Please fix it for me." In no time the knitting was returned to her, all damage repaired. The little girl sighed in admiration. "You know, Grandma," she said, "sometimes I wish I was blind, too."

Christine Nelson, Reader's Digest Dec 1944

BOASTING

Irritated by heavyweight boxing champion Mohammad Ali's boasts of "I'm the greatest" a colleague asked him what he was like at golf. "I'm the best," said Ali. "I just haven't played yet."

Richard L. Crouser, IT'S UNLUCKY TO BE BEHIND AT THE END OF THE GAME 1984

When I was Governor of the Straits Settlements, Clemenceau was among the visitors to Singapore. He was going on from there to Java and I told him about a certain native rajah who, whenever he met a European, always asked him how many children he had. When the visitor owned up to three or four, as the case might be, the rajah would say, "I have eighty-five."

But Clemenceau was ready for him. When he passed through Singapore he said to me, "I went to see your philoprogenitive rajah. As you prophesied, he asked me how many children I had." "What did you say?" "I told him I had a hundred and twenty-three. There was no spirit left in him."

Sir Laurence Guillemard, TRIVIAL FOND RECORDS 1937

BOOK

John Betjeman had agreed to judge the entries in the children's book category for the Arts Council National Book Awards. He was receiving a large fee for his services, but had agreed to act if he did not have to read too many books. Eventually about 20 were delivered at his house, where he proceeded to judge them, supping champagne the while, by a curious process of osmosis, holding them one by one on his hand as if weighing them and occasionally sniffing a volume. "The smell is important," he giggled.

Charles Osborne, GIVING IT AWAY 1986

The latest acquisition to Cilla Black's library is *Ulysses*. "It cost me thirty-five shillings and I got stuck on the first page. I think that's disgusting, don't you? No, not the content. I mean writing a book so that people can't understand it."

Russell Twisk, Radio Times 25 *Jan* 1968

My grandfather left me the foreign rights of *A History of the English Speaking Peoples* in his will. I remember him sending me a proof copy of the book bound in brown paper when I was at Eton. The housemaster asked me if I'd got a dirty book.

Winston Churchill Jnr, Sunday Times 6 *Aug* 1967

At Wells we went to the Palace where he lunched with the bishop. Much talk of Barchester. "There is nothing I like better than to lie on my bed with my favourite Trollope," the Bishop said to everyone's consternation.

Sir Henry Channon, DIARY 4 *Apr* 1942

A friend who wished to check some point on aeronautics asked in his library for books on Metropolitan Vickers. He was handed Crockford's Clerical Dictionary.

The Times, Diary 7 *Jan* 1987

BORE

A bore once blundered uninvited into a literary gathering hosted by Mark Van Doren, Professor of English at Columbia University, and immediately spread a pall of dullness over the whole party. After his departure the interloper became the topic of discussion. Someone observed that it must be heartbreaking for someone like him to see the face of everyone to whom he spoke freeze with distaste and boredom. "You forget that a person like that has never seen any other kind of expression," said Van Doren.

Bennett Cerf, SHAKE WELL BEFORE USING 1948

BOREDOM

Warren Robinson Austin, American delegate to the United Nations, was asked whether he did not become tired during the apparently interminable debates. "Yes, I do," he replied, "but it is better for aged diplomats to be bored than for young men to die."

Clifton Fadiman and Charles Van Doren, THE AMERICAN TREASURY 1955

Lord Beaverbrook never stuck at anything for very long. In politics he never fought a controversy through to a finish. He was constantly announcing that he was giving up control of his newspapers. At the dinner table he often lost interest in the middle of a conversation and fell asleep, or appeared to do so. Even when composing his works of history – the things he cared for most – he sometimes said, "Aw, the hell with it," and laid aside his dictation for the day, or for a couple of months. He understood himself. He said, "I am always excited at the beginning of a journey and bored after the first few miles."

A.J.P. Taylor, BEAVERBROOK 1972

At a dinner given on some fairly grim PEN Club Conference occasion Cyril Connolly was sitting opposite me and I noticed the tears start in his eyes, then trickle down his cheeks. Suddenly he got up from the table, came over to me and insisted on changing places. Intense boredom with the lady journalist on his left had driven him to this extreme course of action.

Stephen Spender, Times Literary Supplement 6 *Dec* 1974

BORROWING

Nancy Astor is always direct. If people borrow books from her and forget to return them they must not be surprised to read in the "agony" columns of newspaper advertisements asking for them back.

John Beevers, Sunday Referee 19 *Feb* 1939

BOXING

It was one thing to knock down old-time boxer Stanley Ketchel. It was quite another thing to keep him down. On those rare occasions when he did suffer the indignity of being decked he usually came off the canvas in a rage. An incredulous friend, hearing of Ketchel's death, offered a suggestion. "Stand over him and start counting. He'll get up at nine."

Richard L. Crouser, IT' S UNLUCKY TO BE BEHIND AT THE END OF THE GAME 1983

In 1946 Joe Louis was preparing to defend his title against Billy Conn. He was warned to watch out for Conn's great speed and his tactic of darting in to the attack and then moving quickly out of his opponent's range. In a famous display of justified confidence Louis replied, "He can run, but he can't hide."

Miriam Ringo, NOBODY SAID IT BETTER 1980

The expression "the real McCoy" originated in a bar-room brawl when a drunk insisted that Kid McCoy, the welterweight champion, was not who he claimed to be. McCoy flattened his opponent, who struggled back to his feet and said, "It's the real McCoy."

H. Allen Smith, THE LIFE AND LEGEND OF GENE FOWLER 1977

When Dempsey was training for his first fight with Gene Tunney he sent a spy to watch Tunney work out, and pick up tips on his opponent's style. The spy returned in great good humour. "It's a set-up," he said. "I seen the lug readin' a book."

Bennett Cerf, TRY TO STOP ME 1944

BROADCASTING *see* **RADIO, TELEVISION**

BROTHER

Mr Justice Avory was listening to the argument of a barrister who said that the prisoner and his victim were so friendly in their relations that in effect they were brothers. "So were Cain and Abel," drily commented the judge.

Daily Telegraph, Obituary 14 *Jun* 1935

BUREAUCRACY

Once when our units were operationally very busy, there came a signal from some ass at the War Office demanding a return of the number of ATS girls in our formation who had suffered from chilblains during their most recent winter in civil life. According to the rules of the system, I should have signalled such a request to each of our brigades, which would in turn have harried their units large and small for figures. I could imagine what they would say when they got it. So instead I put the signal in my pending tray, waited a week or so, thought of a number, or rather two numbers and signalled it back. I shall never know what grave decisions were taken on the basis of these statistics. But it taught me the good lesson as an administrator that if you bother busy people with silly questions you are likely to get silly answers.

John Boyd-Carpenter, WAY OF LIFE 1980

A north-east of Scotland farmer, who received a letter from a Government department instructing him to go on with his ploughing, as he had not ploughed his quota, replied that his staff was depleted and that the lambing season had come upon him, so that ploughing would have to be suspended for a short period.

He has received a reply instructing him to suspend lambing for a month.

Reynolds News, quoted Michael Bateman, THIS ENGLAND

Good luck to the ratepayers of Harrow, Middlesex. One of them recently found an official note on his dustbin explaining why his rubbish had not been collected – a tick was put next to the box which said that the bin was "not fit for use". Underneath the official note was a further handwritten one which explained that the reason why the bin was damaged was that it had been run over by the dustcart.

Daily Telegraph 30 *Jul* 1985

The Bursar of Moor Park College for adult education at Farnham, Surrey, has just received from Southern Gas by post six identical postcards to announce the opening in Aldershot of a new servicing department.

They were addressed to him respectively at the Student's Room, Clock Tower Lodge, Farm Lodge, the Flat, the Cellar and the Potting Shed. These are the places where the meters are.

Peterborough, Daily Telegraph

BURGLAR

My grandmother was reading in the drawing room one evening when she heard a step outside. "Who's that?" she called. "Only me, darling," came the reply. Whereupon she re-immersed herself in Trollope and the burglar sauntered upstairs and removed all her jewellery.

Jilly Cooper, Sunday Times 27 *Nov* 1977

See also **CRIME**

BURIAL

The most curious visitor I ever had at the Foreign Office was probably "Vice-Consul Puffkins" who was announced one day in the usual way by the office-keeper who informed me that he was below in a taxi.

"Show him up," I said. The office-keeper hesitated and then made a surprising remark. "I can't, sir." "Why not?" "He's dead, sir." "Dead! But you said he was below in a taxi." "So he is, sir."

I sent someone to investigate and to explain that we did not keep a mortuary chapel at the Foreign Office.

The next day he was again announced, accompanied by a young lady who turned out not to be Mrs Vice-Consul Puffkins, but who had accompanied the defunct Vice-Consul all the way from his post in the South Seas in the hope that a benevolent Government would grant her the wherewithal to remove him from their joint taxi and place him in a decent burial ground.

Unfortunately only Mrs Vice-Consul was entitled to burial fees and she had not been seen or heard of for years. So to this day I have no idea what happened to Vice-Consul Puffkins; whether he is still circulating round Whitehall in a ghostly taxi, or whether his one-time admirer successfully mislaid him in a railway cloakroom, or whether he was taken back by her to the South Seas, or whether he is reposing securely in a corner of Kensal Green.

J.D.Gregory, ON THE EDGE OF DIPLOMACY 1929

BUSINESS

I bought my first oil lot by bluff. I hired a local bank executive to bid for me at a land auction. This unnerved the other bidders who assumed the banker was acting for a big oil company. They decided it was futile to bid at all. The lot was knocked down to me for £180. Four months later I sold it for £14,000.

J. Paul Getty, MY LIFE AND FORTUNES 1964

Bernard Berenson, in the days when he wasn't so powerful, said to Bauer the antique dealer, "A man as scholarly as you shouldn't be a dealer. It's horrible to be a dealer." To which Bauer replied, "Between you and me there is really no great difference. I'm an intellectual dealer, and you are a dealing intellectual." Berenson never forgave him.

Rene Gimpel, DIARY OF AN ART DEALER 1966.

Whatever the business occasion, Salvador Dali and his wife Gala had practical ways of dealing with it. Lionel Poilane, owner of a famous Paris bakery, who collaborated with Dali on several sculptures made out of bread, had received no payment for his services. Finally Dali presented him with one of his paintings. When Gala heard of that she said, "Yes, I know he gave it to you, but give it back to me." So he did, to his eternal regret.

Meryle Secrest, SALVADOR DALI: THE SURREALIST JESTER 1986

Samuel Goldwyn made his first dent in the wall of prejudice against the movies in 1913. On Columbus Day he telephoned Arthur Friend to meet him at the Hoffman House. "I've found a backer," said Sam. "He wants us to meet him with a prospectus. What's a prospectus?"

Alvin Johnson, THE GREAT GOLDWYN 1937

Denis Healey does not reduce everyone to quivering wrecks with his notorious penchant for the use of expletives. While holidaying in the Highlands he appeared at the village shop to buy six bottles of tonic water. When he found he had left his money in the hotel he offered to return and pay later. The assistant whisked the bottles away, fixed him with a look –

the sort, I am told which would outface a rutting stag at 50 paces – and said, "Sorry, we don't give credit to people with no fixed address."

The Times, Diary 28 *Aug* 1985

Mr Selfridge told me that for years he had asked to buy a small shop that impeded the progress of his business. He offered nine thousand pounds but the owner wanted thirteen thousand. At last, in desperation, Mr Selfridge said, "Look here, will you toss for it? If you win, I'll pay your price; if I win, you accept mine."

The owner, a little dazed by this unorthodox approach, agreed. Mr Selfridge tossed a penny and won, and was immediately contrite. He wanted to increase his offer, but the owner said no.

Sir Harry Preston, LEAVES FROM MY UNWRITTEN DIARY 1936

Lord Weinstock employed builders on the roof of his Wiltshire home, with the proviso that there should be no smoking on site, to avoid fag-ends on the drive. On the Sunday he went out and picked up cigarette butts and chewing gum wrappers, putting them in a neat pile outside the site foreman's hut. Then he wrote to the firm, threatening to bill them for this time spent collecting the litter.

The Independent, Profile: Lord Weinstock 20 *Dec* 1986

A reader recently in New York spotted the sign "English Dollars gladly Exchanged" in a souvenir shop window and entered to point out the mistake. The jovial proprietor thanked her profusely for being so observant. Later, while she was paying for a Statue of Liberty model he confided to her that Britishers who came in to correct the error were responsible for more than 20 per cent of his trade during the tourist season.

Daily Telegraph 19 *May* 1979

BUTLER

James Ainslie, butler to King George VI, was a man of imposing presence and engaging phrase. After being lightly admonished by the Master of the Household he replied, "Let me assure you, Sir Piers, that my sole object is to obey the orders of the Master of the Household and give pleasure to the ladies-in-waiting.

Kenneth Rose, KINGS, QUEENS AND COURTIERS 1985

At a house party in Bognor in September 1916 Mr Asquith's butler Yeo was made to stand up in the room and do his really excellent stunts. He barked like a lion, made a noise like sawing wood, followed by very good imitations of various prominent guests at Downing Street, their voices and walks – McKenna, Haldane, Lord Morley and so on. It was a very pungent scene, the PM lolling in glee, chuckling away at his butler ridiculing his colleagues. I had a rare luxury of being *shocked to the core.*

Lady Cynthia Asquith, DIARIES 1915–18 1968

The Astors knew how to keep their servants. Edwin Lee, their butler, was with them for 50 years. Only once did Mr Lee threaten to leave, owing to some unreasonable demands by her ladyship. Lady Astor, quick as a flash, replied, "In that case, Lee, tell me where you are going because I am coming with you," and they ended up laughing.

Rosina Harrison, ROSE: MY LIFE IN SERVICE 1975

Once, when I needed John Christie for something, and could not find him I asked Childs, his butler, where he was, and Childs told me. It was some entirely unexpected, out-of-the-way place. "Childs," I said, "how do you know he is *there*? Did you ask him before he left?" Childs said, "A good butler never asks his master where he is going, but always knows."

Rudolf Bing, 5000 NIGHTS AT THE OPERA 1972

When I was sharing rooms with William Douglas-Home in South Eaton Place before the war there was a retired butler who was a mixture of Jeeves and Robertson Hare. He used to put on a powdered wig and wait on us when we had supper parties. And we would ask the guests, "Anyone know of a good butler? We're thinking of making a few changes here," and he'd drop the dish. It was all the most marvellous fun.

Brian Johnston, quoted Mark Amory, Sunday Times Magazine 17 *Apr* 1977

I went to give an entertainment at a famous New York house. After going upstairs to leave my wrap I noticed the beautifully carved banisters. "If I don't slide down that," I told myself, "I'll die." There was nobody in sight. I took a deep breath and landed in a heap at the foot of the stairs. Imagine my horror when I saw bearing down upon me the butler, whose frosty hauteur had frozen my soul when I arrived. He picked me up and dusted me off without a flicker of expression on his correct countenance, meanwhile murmuring cordially, "Very good, miss. Very good indeed. I've always wanted to take a go at it myself."

Marie Dressler, MY OWN STORY 1935

Dunsany Castle, the home of Lord Dunsany in County Meath, Ireland, was sacked by the Black and Tans. As the soldiers departed, leaving a trail of destruction in their wake, Lord Dunsany's butler politely enquired, "Who shall I say called?"

Simon Winchester, THEIR NOBLE LORDSHIPS: THE HEREDITARY PEERAGE 1978

As he was driving back to his mansion, Pickfair, Douglas Fairbanks saw an Englishman of aristocratic mien and familiar face trudging along the road in the heat. He stopped to offer him a ride, which the stranger accepted. Still unable to remember the man's name, Fairbanks invited him for a drink and in the course of conversation attempted to elicit some clues as to his visitor's identity. The visitor seemed to know many of Fairbanks' friends and was evidently well acquainted with the estate, for he made approving comments on some recent changes. Fairbanks eventually managed a whispered aside to his secretary who had just come in. "Who is this Englishman? I know he's Lord somebody, but I can't remember his name." "That", replied the secretary, "is the English butler you fired last month for getting drunk."

Viscount Castlerosse VALENTINE'S DAYS

Mr Froode, my grandfather's butler, once a week, when the housekeeper was bending into the linen cupboard, would push her in and lock the door. She regularly gave notice to my grandmother, who gravely turned it down, knowing that for the housekeeper to leave would be to admit defeat, which she would rather die than do.

Lord Home, THE WAY THE WIND BLOWS 1976

On an evening in 1921, at Polsden Lacey, the home of Tory hostess Mrs Ronnie Greville, the food was good and the wine well chosen. It was Sunday night, the dining table was laden with sparkling glass and shining silver. Pyramids of fruit and sweets scattered here and there in reach of everybody. Only one detail was going wrong. The butler was obviously tight.

Austen Chamberlain was the most important and impressive guest. He carried on with an interesting and informative monologue on Ireland and had reached the story of the momentous decision of the Unionist group in 1886 when Mrs Greville's attention wavered.

On a scribbling pad she was busy writing. Summoning her butler, well known for his intemperate habits, she handed him the written message. The butler placed the note on a big and beautiful salver and, walking unsteadily to Austen Chamberlain, with a deep bow presented the message. Austen paused in his admirable exposition of the intransigence of the Irish race. He slowly fixed his monocle and read the startling message: "You are drunk. Leave the room."

Lord Beaverbrook, THE DECLINE AND FALL OF LLOYD GEORGE 1963

Somerset Maugham was attending a dinner party. The Chinese butler remarked pleasantly, "Good evening, Mr Maugham. I think it only fair to tell you I didn't much care for your last book." An hour later Mr Maugham was missing from among the assembled guests. A scouting party found him in the kitchen, hotly defending his literary style to the butler.

Bennett Cerf, SHAKE WELL BEFORE USING 1948

My uncle, Lord Northbrook was Viceroy of India and later became First Lord of the Admiralty when he invited some Parsees to dinner at eight o'clock. As no one had turned up by 8.20 my uncle rang for the butler and asked if anyone had arrived. The butler said no. "But", said my uncle, "I thought I heard the front door bell ring about eight as I was coming downstairs." "Oh yes my lord," said the butler, "some nigger minstrels called about that hour but I sent them about their business." It is impossible to imagine a more regrettable incident, for they did not venture to ring again.

Cyril P. Foley, AUTUMN FOLIAGE 1935

CALAMITY

During the last war a young subaltern had the misfortune to have his reproductive organs removed by a shell which had passed neatly through his legs. "Good gracious," he said, "whatever will mummy say?"

Douglas Sutherland, THE ENGLISH GENTLEMAN 1978

CANDOUR

Margot Asquith's candour knew no bounds. On one occasion she unwisely agreed to present at court a lady of doubtful reputation. The application was refused and Margot received a furious letter of protest from her acquaintance. Her reply was in her best vein. "I am sure that what you say is quite true, and that many people just as, if not even more, immoral have been presented at Court."

Mark Bonham Carter, Sunday Times 23 *Sep* 1962

Haldane is one of the very first figures that I can remember in my childhood. He was an extraordinary character. I've never seen anyone at all like him. When he first came to our house in Hampstead my father [H.H. Asquith] told me to shake hands with him. I greeted him as a friend and said, "I've seen you before, Mr Haldane." Haldane said with surprise, "But where did you see me before?" I said, "In the Nonsense Book, of course." His kind of pneumatic bulk, spheroid outline and twinkling benignity was exactly like the old men in Edward Lear's book.

Lady Asquith of Yarnbury (Violet Bonham Carter), quoted Norman St John Stevas, The Times 22 *Nov* 1969

CANNIBAL

I once talked to an old cannibal who, hearing of the Great War raging in Europe, was most curious to know how we Europeans managed to eat such huge quantities of human flesh. When I told him the Europeans did not eat their slain foes he looked at me with shocked horror and asked what sort of barbarians we were, to kill without any real object.

Bronislaw Malinowski, Reader's Digest Mar 1938

CARD GAMES. *See* **PASTIME**

CAT

Vice-Admiral Grenfell kept several Siamese cats as pets on his flagship. One of them was called "Queen Alexandra" and when the real queen came with King Edward VII to have lunch aboard she was told about her namesake. During lunch a sailor entered and, going up to the admiral, whispered something in his ear. When at intervals the man appeared a second and a third time to do the same thing the queen asked the admiral what all the whispering was about.

"Well, your Majesty," the admiral replied, "if you really want to know, I must tell you. This man has just told me that Queen Alexandra has given birth to her third baby."

Admiral Sir Frederic William Fisher, NAVAL REMINISCENCES 1938

A.L. Rowse is the only person I know who used to ring up his cat from the United States. They apparently had lively interchanges.

Roy Strong, The Times 5 *Nov* 1983

Jean Peters [who married Howard Hughes in 1957] formed an attachment to a rather mangy-looking tomcat. One day it went missing. Hughes mounted a vast operation to look for it. He directed proceedings from his home, insisting on progress reports every hour. The creature was finally run to earth in a derelict barn. Hughes examined it and finding it an unsuitable addition to his household, interviewed several couples prepared to take it in. None were found acceptable. It went, instead, to a luxurious cattery, where it was installed in an individually decorated room, complete with television. As one of the rules of this establishment required that former owners write to their pets once a month Hughes hired an Australian named Harry to relieve him of the chore. Harry was still on the payroll at Hughes death.

Peter Bushell, GREAT ECCENTRICS 1984

CAUTION

President Hoover's caution in public speaking was sometimes attributed to his Quaker upbringing. On a train journey a travelling companion remarked to Hoover that sheep in a field they were passing had been sheared. Hoover looked and then said, "Well, on this side, anyway."

Irvin and Ruth Poley, FRIENDLY ANECDOTES 1950

Dirk Bogarde's father, who was art editor of *The Times*, always treated his son's achievements as a film idol with horror. One day as he came off the train at Charing Cross he was greeted by yards of posters bearing his son's grinning face. He rang Bogarde to complain.

Did he realise how embarrassing it was to the family? Bogarde felt ill with guilt. It was not until years later that his father, on the off-chance, revealed that the reprimand had been ironic. Bogarde's years of anguish had been misplaced.

Nicholas Wapshott, The Times 18 *Mar* 1983

Carl Reiner took us to the Bistro restaurant which had originally been Mike Romanoff's famous meeting place for the Hollywood mighty. Clementina was all agog to see the stars in their natural setting. While Carl went off to get us a table she asked a small, slim, elderly bald-headed man sitting at the bar if he knew any of her screen idols.

"Well," he replied slowly, "a few of the faces do come in here from time to time. Stick around —"

Clementina then asked him why he was wearing an empty lipstick refill box on one of his fingers. He told her that he had hurt the finger in a car door and the little box protected it perfectly. By this time Carl had come back and as he ushered us to our table my beloved wife said, "Well, I don't see any stars yet, but that nice little man said they come in later."

"For your information, honey," drawled Carl, enjoying every word, "that nice little man is Frank Sinatra."

Michael Bentine, THE LONG BANANA SKIN 1975

See also **FAME**

CENSORSHIP

During the 1914–18 war a correspondent in France thought to brighten his copy with a quotation from Kipling's *Recessional* – "the captains and the Kings depart". Down came the censor's blue pencil with the official explanation that "no reference to the movement of war leaders is permissible".

Hamilton Fyffe , SIXTY YEARS IN FLEET STREET 1949

During the pantomime *Sinbad the Sailor*, at Manchester's Theatre Royal, there was a 30-second pause when George Robey was due to make his entrance. To an audience – waiting for the star of the show to appear – 30 seconds is a long time. Maggie Duggan was standing in the middle of the stage. The seconds ticked by. "What's happened?" whispered the audience, "Has something gone wrong?" Then Robey (as Mrs Sinbad) arrived in great agitation, and said to Maggie Duggan,

"I'm sorry I'm late, but I have been detained. In fact I have been blocked in the passage." Now, in those days there was only one slang meaning for "blocked" and that was sexual intercourse. George crowned the joke by putting the word into bogus French: "I have been blocked in the pass-sahge." The Manchester Watch Committee demanded changes in that scene. But they didn't intervene over Marie Lloyd's wink, which was *much* more suggestive.

Sir Neville Cardus, quoted Robin Daniels, Sunday Times 4 *Jul* 1976

When I was a foreign correspondent in Russia I wrote in a despatch that the prisons were so full that cells intended for twenty inmates held forty. The censor refused to pass it, but I insisted it was true. The censor said; "Just a minute. I will speak to Mr Rothstein." In a few minutes the censor came back smiling, and with my despatch in his hand. "You are both right and wrong, Mr Greenwall," he said. "Mr Rothstein tells me there are not forty but fifty prisoners to a cell." I duly made the correction in my despatch and the censor passed it.

Harry J. Greenwall, ROUND THE WORLD FOR NEWS 1935

John Gunther, the American writer and war correspondent told me that he had asked one of the censors for the text of our leaflet which we dropped over Germany. The request was refused. He asked why. The answer was, "We are not allowed to disclose information which might be of value to the enemy." When Gunther pointed out that two million of these leaflets had been dropped over Germany, the man blinked and said, "Yes, something must be wrong there."

Harold Nicolson, letter to Vita Sackville-West 14 *Sep* 1939

CEREMONY

Princess Alexandra was launching her first ship on a wind-buffetted platform on Clydeside. The bottle of champagne was handed to her and she said in a clear voice, "I name this ship *Jaguar*. God bless her and all who sail in her." The bottle shattered against the warship's prow. Crowds cheered. *But the ship stayed motionless on the slipway.* For a moment Alexandra was aghast. Then she put both her white gloved hands against the prow in a gesture of a mighty heave. And slowly *Jaguar* at last began her journey to the sea. It was Alexandra's first public triumph.

Vera Connaught, THE SECRET HEART OF PRINCESS ALEXANDRA 1962

Sir Robert Baden-Powell was the first man to enter Buckingham Palace in shorts. He wrote to the King for permission. It was granted – a revolution in court etiquette.

C. A. Lyon, Sunday Express 28 *Jan* 1934

I have just got back from my royal weekend with the Queen Mother. The Queen came over to lunch on Sunday looking a young girl. I told her how moved I had been by Prince Charles's Investiture and she gaily shattered my sentimental illusions by saying that they had both been struggling not to giggle because at the dress rehearsal the crown was too big and extinguished him like a candle-snuffer.

Noel Coward, DAIRY 27 *Jul* 1969

At the wedding of Princess Elizabeth, King George VI told King Peter of Yugoslavia to take his watch-chain off his uniform. "It looks damned silly and damned sloppy."

John W. Wheeler Bennett, KING GEORGE VI: HIS LIFE AND REIGN 1958

To Buckingham Palace for the Queen's reception. It was two and a half hours of tramping round the great rooms, eating bits of Lyons' pâté, drinking over-sweet warm white wine, everyone looking at everyone else, and that atmosphere of jocular ruthlessness which characterises the Establishment on its nights out. Wonderful paintings, and of course I was shown the bullet that killed Nelson.

As we were presented the Queen asked me when the National Theatre would open. I said I didn't know. The duke asked me when the National Theatre would open. I said I didn't know. The Queen Mother asked me when the National Theatre would open. I said I didn't know. The Prince of Wales asked me then the National Theatre would be open. I said I didn't know. At least they all knew I was running the National Theatre.

Peter Hall, DIARY 11 *Feb* 1975

For three years before the Great War I came over to compete for the Edward VII cup at Olympia. I won it outright, and when I returned to

Petrograd I was given a dinner by the Chevalier Guards. It was not a successful party because the Grand Duke Michael, who presided, had the King's Cup filled with champagne – over two bottles – and ordered me to stand up to drink it.

Having protested in vain, I lifted the great cup to my lips. Dimly aware of the laughter and cheers of other officers, I began to drink. "*Pey Dadna, Pey Dadna.*" The drinking song that lasts until all is consumed grew farther and farther away. Before the cup was half empty I fell unconscious owing to the fumes. My party ended sadly, before it had really begun.

Colonel Rodzianko, TATTERED BANNERS 1939

Sidney Webb, ennobled, refused to wear knee-breeches at Court, but was induced to scupper his principles when he heard what J. H. Thomas had told the King. "Poor Sidney can't put 'em on because his wife wears 'em."

Sir Robert Bruce-Lockhart, DIARIES 1915–1938 1972

CHARITY

Dropping a fifty-dollar bill into a tambourine held out to her by a Salvation Army player, Tallulah Bankhead waved aside the man's thanks. "Don't bother to thank me. I know what a ghastly season it has been for you Spanish dancers."

Dorothy Herrmann, WITH MALICE TOWARDS ALL 1980

Arthur Griffiths, Manchester newspaperman and born sentimentalist, with several of us was leaving the Manchester Press Club at 1 a.m. We were approached by a careworn and tattered old woman selling matches.

"Matches or bootlaces?" she croaked. Arthur burst in tears.

"My poor woman," he sobbed, "what are doing out at this time of night?" "Nowhere to go, gentlemen," she whined. "Nowhere to go?" gulped Arthur. "Where are you going to sleep?" "On the Infirmary Steps, sir."

At that moment a belated cab cruised up and Arthur, hailing the cabby, took a couple of half-crowns from his pocket and choking back his grief said: "Cabby, here are five shillings. Drive this poor woman to the Infirmary Steps."

James Dunn, PAPERCHASE 1938

See also **PHILANTHROPY**

CHILDHOOD

I threw my mother's spaniel out of the window because I had heard someone say that if you threw a dog into the water it would instinctively learn to swim. Reflection on this biological fact led me to wonder whether a dog thrown from a window would instinctively learn to fly.

Lord Berners, quoted Hugh Kingsmill, PARENTS AND CHILDREN

I took my youngest son Theodore to lunch with Henry Adams one day and as I was presenting him I said, "This is your uncle Henry (all my children called him that) and he knows everything." Teddy looked at him in round-eyed silence through part of the meal, watching his opportunity. During a pause in the conversation of the grown-ups the little boy leaned forward respectfully and said, "Uncle Henry, how do you feed a chameleon?"

Marjorie Terry Chanler, ROMAN SPRINGS: MEMOIRS 1934

I think even Scrooge would appreciate the true story of a nativity play in Yorkshire, where the form master believed in free expression and left a team of eight-year-olds to write their own script and produce it themselves.

The great day arrived, the hall was crammed with children, staff and doting parents. The curtains creaked back to reveal scene three, Mary in the stable. Enter Joseph with a briefcase.
Joseph: How's our Jesus then?
Mary: (after a long pause) He's been a right little booger all morning.

Jilly Cooper, Sunday Times 19 *Dec* 1976

Michael had taken a strong dislike to kindergarten. All persuasion having failed, his mother, in desperation, told him he would *have* to go. "All right, mother," Michael retorted. "If you want me to grow up into a damned bead-stringer, I'll go."

Parents Magazine Jun 1942

As a boy of four Ronald Knox suffered quite seriously from insomnia. Asked by a friend of the family how he managed to occupy himself during his sleepless nights he answered, "I lie awake and think about the past."

Clifton Fadiman, LITTLE, BROWN BOOK OF ANECDOTES 1985

A small girl arrived at school and told her teacher that they had a new baby at home. "How nice," said the teacher. "I wish I had a baby."

"It's quite easy," the child explained to her. "All you do is have a bath, put on a clean nightie, get into bed and send for my grannie."

Wilfred Pickles, HAVE ANOTHER GO 1978

CHIVALRY

After a meeting in a mid-western city a woman saw Alexander Woollcott standing alone in the lobby. Impulsively she went up to him to tell him of the pleasure his lecture had given her. "And," said the lady, who had grown grandchildren and fully admitted to having passed seventy, "I was encouraged to speak to you because you said you loved old ladies."

"Yes," said Woollcott, "I do. But I also like them your age."

Fannie Campbell, Reader's Digest Feb 1945

CHRISTENING

I was told the story of a nervous woman who, when the vicar asked her to name the baby, said "Lucifer." The outraged cleric said, "I christen this child *John.*" At which the poor woman protested and whispering to the vicar, explained that her baby was a girl and added "I said Lucy, sir."

Lady Oxford, Daily Sketch 21 *Jun* 1939

Christenings can be howling bad affairs, but of one which went off in a seemly and quiet way the mother explained afterwards that it was because "my husband and I have been practising on him with a watering can for a whole week".

Gerald Findler, HUMOUR FROM THE PULPIT AND PEW 1934

A priest in the West Indies was carrying out a baptism, and when he asked the child's name was told it was "Pindonshe". He duly christened the girl to discover afterwards that her actual name was written on a note pinned on the back of her dress.

Peterborough, Daily Telegraph 22 *Nov* 1985

CHRISTMAS

On Christmas Eve 1928 Princess Elizabeth was allowed to stay up late to listen to the carol singers, and when she heard "Glad tidings of great joy I bring to you and all mankind," she called out excitedly, "I know who Old Man Kind is." It seemed to her only natural that so many people should sing so enthusiastically about her grandfather.

Robert Lacey, MAJESTY 1977

We had just crossed the Antarctic Circle. It was light all night and the look-out man struck eight bells and the watch changed. Christmas Day 1902 was ushered in by a handful of sturdy Yorkshire seamen who marched aft and were greeted by the captain and officers of the little whaler *Morning* that eventually found Scott and the *Discovery* in her ice-girt winter quarters.

As the echoing clang of eight bells died away the men sang "O come all ye faithful" and when the last note of the hymn ceased we shook hands all round, then we "spliced the mainbrace".

The sun was just above the horizon and I felt the wonderful call of the Polar regions for the first time. There were two great white icebergs in sight, sentinels to that cruel, silent land with which my life has been so closely associated.

Admiral Sir Edward Evans, Sunday Express 24 *Dec* 1939

One Christmas Eve during the Great War the other girl understudy and I were sitting dismally in a room at the top of the theatre knitting khaki mufflers and wishing with all our hearts that we were downstairs on the stage, when we heard a voice singing along the passage, and a tall, lank, loosely jointed boy of about seventeen danced amazingly into the room. He high-kicked, he pirouetted, he waltzed round us both; then he hugged us both, gave us each a Christmas gift of a fancy handkerchief, and danced out again. The little handkerchief has long since been lost, but the fragrance of the incident remains. And the boy who remembered the understudies was Noel Coward.

Elizabeth Fagan, T.P's & Cassell's Weekly 4 *Dec* 1926

At Christmas we performed, as did then most junior schools, a nativity play, and as year followed year one progressed upwards from humble shepherd to a starring role (Joseph). I was much amused to see recently that an ambitious performer, envious to shine, and cast in the somewhat dull role of the Innkeeper, with just one negative response to supply, replied cheerfully when asked whether accommodation was available, "Oh yes, certainly, please come in," thus bringing the play to a shorter end than usual.

Arthur Marshall, Sunday Telegraph 28 *Dec* 1986

In December 1948 a Washington radio station telephoned various ambassadors in the capital, asking them what they would like for Christmas. The unedited replies were recorded and broadcast in a special programme the following week. "Peace throughout the world," proclaimed the French ambassador. "Freedom for all the people enslaved in imperalism," demanded the Russian ambassador. "Well, it's very kind of you to ask," came the voice of Sir Oliver Franks, the British ambassador. "I'd quite like a box of crystallized fruits."

Geoffrey Moorhouse, THE DIPLOMATS 1977

CHURCH

At St Mary Magdalene, Oxford, a host of rich characters were among the faithful who filled the pews Sunday by Sunday. There was the old lady I christened "the prophetess Anna" as she departed not from the temple day or night, and was always to be found pottering about doing flowers. She had lived most of her life in the Far East and I got used to her saying she was returning to her bungalow for tiffin, but when she referred to the verger as "the church coolie" I felt that she was going too far.

Colin Stephenson, MERRILY ON HIGH 1965

Once at the Ruri-decanal Chapter we had someone to talk on "The Place of Women in Church" which Father Hack listened to with ill-disguised impatience. The Rural Dean was unwise enough to ask him what he thought on the subject, to which he replied; "As far as I know there is only one place for women in the church, and that is on their knees – praying or scrubbing, and there is plenty of use for both."

Ibid.

CINEMA

Julie Andrews, after her stage success in *My Fair Lady* was turned down for the film part by Warner Brothers, and instead went on to win an Oscar for *Mary Poppins*. In her acceptance speech she said, "I'd like to thank all those who made this possible – especially Jack Warner."

Leslie Halliwell, FILMGOER'S BOOK OF QUOTES 1973

Down on his luck, Michael Arlen went to New York in 1944. To drown his sorrows he paid a visit to the famous restaurant "21". In the lobby he ran into Sam Goldwyn, who offered the somewhat impractical advice that he should buy a racehorse. At the bar Arlen met Louis B. Mayer, an old acquaintance, who asked him what his plans were for the future. "I was just talking to Sam Goldwyn –" began Arlen. "How much did he offer you?" interrupted Mayer. Arlen hesitated, "Not enough," he answered evasively. "Would you take fifteen thousand for thirty weeks?" asked Mayer. No hesitation this time. "Yes," said Arlen.

Clifton Fadiman, LITTLE, BROWN BOOK OF ANECDOTES 1985

Film producers usually think they can improve on a book's title. *Vanity Fair* was changed to *Becky Sharp*. When I was making *Disraeli* there was some talk about changing it to something more striking. I suggested that they should call it *Wild Nights With Queen Victoria*, but withdrew my suggestion when I found to my alarm that there was some danger of it being adopted.

Ibid.

The Royal Philharmonic Orchestra was engaged to perform the music for a film. The director wanted to run through the credit titles so that Sir Thomas Beecham could work out the timing. But Sir Thomas thought all this rather a waste of time. He looked impatiently at the long list of actors and technicians, then exclaimed, "Who are all these nonentities?"

Harold Atkins and Archie Newman, BEECHAM STORIES 1978

In 1960 Dirk Bogarde made *Liszt* in Hollywood, which made him determined never to work there again. He quoted from the script: "'Hiya Chopin, this is my friend George Sand. She's a great friend of Beethoven's' – that's a true line. It was eight months of hell except that I met George Cukor."

Nicholas Wapshott, The Times 18 *Mar* 1983

The famous sequence in the *The African Queen* with Bogart and the leeches was filmed on the back lot at Worton Hall. John Huston tormented his star for weeks, saying that Bogart would have to put live leeches on his bare legs or he wouldn't shudder properly when Katherine Hepburn removed them with boric powder. More than that, Bogart would be in breach of contract if he did not perform with real leeches. Spiegel backed Huston in this assertion.

A professional breeder of leeches was brought in to provide the specimens. But at the last moment rubber leeches were attached to Bogart's skin for the powdering, while the breeder provided the human flesh for the live leech that was shot in close-up. Only legend made Bogart suffer the real thing.

Andrew Sinclair, SPIEGEL: THE MAN BEHIND THE PICTURES 1987

Sergio Corbacci, the Italian director, had some eye trouble and there is a story that on the first day of every film he gets an assistant to disarrange a small item of an actor's clothing. Then, from hundreds of yards away, Sergio "notices" it and calls to the assistant to correct it – so reassuring any nervous actor or producer who may have started to wonder if he is working with a sightless director, considered a disadvantage in movies.

Ned Sherrin, A SMALL THING LIKE AN EARTHQUAKE 1983

I was sent to Alaska to do some filming and when we arrived we found that the script called for polar bears. As there are no polar bears in Alaska we wired to the studio for instructions. They sent us some from a Los Angeles zoo. There were seven of them and they had never been further north than Universal Studio, having been born in the zoo. We filmed them and sent them back, less two of their number. These poor fellows caught cold and died of pneumonia.

John D. Craig, DANGER IS MY BUSINESS 1939

Peter Croft went to Hollywood when he was seventeen as "technical adviser" to RKO who were making *Gay Divorce.* As the action took place in England his job was to keep it free of un-English details. They were shooting a scene of a hallway in an English house. "I didn't think the cactus plant looked very convincing," he says, "so I told the director. But he seemed rather devoted to it. He scratched his head in a puzzled fashion and said rather lamely, 'Well, it might be taken for an artificial one.'"

Sam Heppner, Evening News 30 *Aug* 1939

When I first started in movies they said my ears stuck out too far. They said I looked like a taxi with both doors open. Know what they did? Before every scene they glued them to my head. Then I looked like a whippet.

Trouble was, when I got on the set the hot lights caused the glue to melt and I'd be halfway through a scene when my ears would spring back to their natural position. Then they'd take me back to make-up and more glue. That went on for some time. Then one day my ears popped in the middle of a scene and they wanted to send back for more glue, but I refused. I'd made a couple of pictures by that time which were fairly successful, so they didn't argue.

Bing Crosby, quoted Michael Parkinson, Observer 16 *Oct* 1977

Scott Fitzgerald had done most of the work on a certain film, admittedly, then handed on to other script writers who no doubt tinkered about with it to some extent. Fitzgerald received 5000 dollars, at that time about £1000. The script was then sold by the studio to another, larger, studio, *which had already sacked Fitzgerald,* for 100,000 dollars, say £20,000, enough to set an author up for life, of which Fitzgerald never saw a cent.

Aaron Latham, CRAZY SUNDAYS: F SCOTT FITZGERALD IN HOLLYWOOD 1972

Rocky Graziano, the American world heavyweight champion, was making the perilous leap from the sweat science of boxing to the precarious world of show-biz. Someone asked him if he planned some training at a place like the famous Actors' Studio. "Why should I go to a place like that?" asked Rocky. "All they do is learn guys like Brando and Newman to talk like me."

Richard L. Crouser, IT'S UNLUCKY TO BE BEHIND AT THE END OF THE GAME 1983

Katherine Hepburn jibbed at plunging into a river infested with large crocodiles, during the filming of *The African Queen*. John Huston offered to have a few rounds fired into the water to scare off the beasts. "What about the deaf ones?" asked Hepburn.

Andrew Sinclair, SPIEGEL: THE MAN BEHIND THE PICTURES 1987

I remember a phone call from the MGM Studio. Bernie Hyman, the studio head, wanted my help on a plot problem that had arisen in a two-million-dollar movie being prepared for shooting.

"I won't tell you the plot," he said, "I'll just give you what we're up against. The hero and heroine fall madly in love with each other – as soon as they meet. What we need is some gimmick that keeps them from going to bed with each other right away. Not a physical gimmick, like arrest or getting run over and having to go to hospital. But a purely psychological one. Now what reasons do you know that would keep a healthy pair of lovers from hitting the hay in Reel Two?"

I answered that frequently a girl has moral concepts that keep her virtuous until after a trip to the altar. And that there are also men who prefer to wait for coitus until they have married the girl they adore. "Wonderful," said the Metro head of production. "We'll try it."

Ben Hecht, A CHILD OF THE CENTURY 1954

At a French airport the customs officer looked suspiciously at Alfred Hitchcock's passport in which his occupation was simply listed as "Producer." "What do you produce?" he asked. "Gooseflesh," Hitchcock replied.

Clifton Fadiman, LITTLE, BROWN BOOK OF ANECDOTES 1985

When first asked how he would adjust to writing for the wide screen the script writer Nunnally Johnson replied, "Very simple. I'll just put the paper in sideways."

Ibid.

Otto Khan went with Cecil de Mille to see his picture *The King of Kings*. The *tour de force* of this picture was a representation of the Dance of the Golden Calf. He sat back in the darkness watching an indiscriminate whirl of limbs. De Mille said to him, "Do you know how many people there are in that scene?" "No, I haven't any idea." "Two thousand five hundred," and then, "What do you think of that?"

"Nothing," was Otto Khan's reply.

De Mille was not pleased. "You're highbrow," he said.

Khan turned to de Mille. "Have you ever seen Velasquez' picture of the Surrender of Breda?" "No."

"If you look at that picture," said Khan, "you will have an impression in the background of a forest of spears and lances. If you count them you will find that there are precisely eighteen." He smiled sweetly at de Mille through the darkness and then added, "Velasquez was an artist."

Beverley Nichols, THE STAR-SPANGLED MANNER 1928

Producer Joseph L. Mankiewicz, stubbornly convinced that the film *Three Comrades* would make more money if the leading female character did not die, asked Scott Fitzgerald to change the script. "*Camille* would have made twice as much if Garbo had lived," he argued.

"How about *Romeo and Juliet* – you wouldn't have wanted Juliet to live, would you?" asked Fitzgerald. Mankiewicz, whose cultural experience did not extend beyond the film world, cast his mind back to the unsuccessful 1936 film version of the play. "That's just it," he retorted triumphantly. "*Romeo and Juliet* didn't make a cent."

Aaron Latham, CRAZY SUNDAYS: F. SCOTT FITZGERALD IN HOLLYWOOD 1971

Sitting next to a drama critic in New York, Louis B. Mayer, head of MGM and America's biggest salary earner, asked about a man nearby. He was told it was Serge Koussevitsky, the conductor. Asked Mayer, "Is he a good conductor?" On being told he was, Mayer said, "On your say-so then, he has a job with my studio, starting tomorrow."

A few minutes later Mayer said to the critic, "That's what you expected a Hollywood producer to say, isn't it? Well, I was only teasing." He then proceeded to recite at length Koussevitsky's background and accomplishments.

News Review 11 *Nov* 1948

M.G.M. bought the radio show *Date With Judy*, and then purchased the story called *Pigtails*, to be the basis for the picture *Date With Judy*. Then they bought a book *The Birds and the Bees* because they liked it better than *Date With Judy* as a title for *Pigtails*.

Sidney Solsky, quoted Andrew B. Hecht, Reader's Digest Oct 1946

After the sale of the motion picture rights to *On Trial* the movie director, James Young, called me up. He wanted my opinion of the scenario he had written. Flattered to be consulted by this august personage, for I was still a little in awe of actors and producers, I went to see Young in his room at the Lambs Club. I listened to his reading in utter astonishment; he had made the crucial revelatory scene of the play into a prologue! When he asked me, with obvious self-satisfaction, what I thought of the scenario, I hardly knew how to answer. I asked if he had seen the play and was hardly surprised when he said no. Not wanting to come right out and say he had destroyed the suspense, I discoursed as tactfully as I could upon the importance of the play's structure. He followed my exposition in sheer amazement. At its conclusion he crossed the room, put his hand on my shoulder and said, "Say, kid, you had a great idea there." It was my first contact with the motion picture industry.

Elmer Rice, MINORITY REPORT 1953

All the stars of Hollywood including Charles Chaplin, Marlene Dietrich and Carol Lombard attended the world premiere of Disney's *Snow White and The Seven Dwarfs* at the Cathay Circle Cinema.

Shirley Temple arrived accompanied by seven real dwarfs.

Margaret Morley, LARGER THAN LIFE 1979

Irving Thalberg sent an emissary to discuss with Arnold Schoenberg the possibility of his composing for movies. The emissary found Schoenberg indifferent to the idea, and thereupon launched into a long recitation of the possibilities for music in the film *The Good Earth*, leading up to a dramatic exposition of its big scene. "Think of it," he enthused. "There's a terrific storm going on, the wheat field is swaying in the wind, and suddenly the earth begins to tremble. In the midst of the earthquake Oo-Lan gives birth to a baby." "With so much going on," said Schoenberg mildly, "what do you need music for?"

Oscar Levant, A SMATTERING OF IGNORANCE 1940

CIVIL SERVICE

In the late 1970s Harold Macmillan spoke to the Young Conservatives. He told them, "In the Public Record Office there is a memorandum addressed to Queen Elizabeth I, written, we believe, by the young Walter Raleigh. He says, 'Tarry not, I beg you Madam, for the wings of time are tipped with death'". Then Macmillan paused, and continued to pause. There was anxiety in the audience. Had the old man been so struck by the truth of Raleigh's statement that he had lost his thread? He continued, "Civil servants don't write memos like that any more."

Bruce Anderson, Sunday Telegraph 4 Jan 1987

The Ministry of Works was considering a new design of lavatory seat for installation in the lavatories of government departments. The official in charge thought it necessary to consult his superior and accordingly sent a memo which read: "I should like to see you on this." The reply was, "At your convenience."

Kenneth Edwards, I WISH I'D SAID THAT 1976

CLERGY

The Rev. Frederick William Densham was the incumbent at Warleggan, Cornwall, from 1931 to 1953. When no one came to church he would lock it up and go to the Methodist Chapel. After years of non-attendance at church by his parishioners – his entries in the Service Book would read, "no fog, no wind, no rain, no congregation" – he cut out figures in wood and cardboard and fixed them to the pews. These figures, which he named after all the rectors at Warleggan, were preached to, offered the sacraments, and given absolution.

June Lander, ECCENTRICS IN CORNWALL 1983

When Dame Edith Evans was introduced to Billy Graham he told her, "We in the ministry could learn a great deal from you about how to put our message across." "You in the ministry have an advantage over us," replied Edith Evans. "You have long-term contracts."

Bryan Forbes, NED'S GIRL 1977

At St Mary and John, Oxford, I was given a special responsibility for the Infant School. The headmistress liked me to give them a little talk after prayers and would turn to me with a sweet smile and say, "Will you say just a word, Father?" When I was priested she said to the children, "You can now call Father 'Father' and mean it, because he is really a Father now." They looked at me with innocent eyes, but some of them were more sophisticated than she thought, and one little cherub came up to me afterwards and asked, "Who had the baby?"

Colin Stephenson, MERRILY ON HIGH 1965

Visiting in his parish one day, a clergyman knocked at the door of one church member but got no reply. He was annoyed because he could hear footsteps and knew that the mother of the family was there. He left his visiting card, writing on it, "Revelation 3.20. Behold I stand at the door and knock; if anyone hears my voice, and opens the door, I will come to him." The next Sunday, as the parishioners filed out of church after the service, the woman who had refused to open the door handed the vicar *her*: card with "Genesis 3.10" written on it. Later, he looked up the passage: "I heard the sound of thee in the garden and was afraid, because I was naked, and I hid myself."

Rev. William Hinson, Reader's Digest Jul 1978

A clergyman's wife from St Albans recently had her application form for a Marks and Spencer credit card returned because it did not contain "sufficient information". In answer to the question, "Who is your husband's employer?" she had written simply, "God."

Daily Telegraph 22 *Jul* 1987

CLICHE

As a master of colourful prose Winston Churchill was continuously against the obfuscatory language of over-wordy Whitehall officials. Asked once to look over a draft of one of Anthony Eden's vague speeches on the post-war world, he sent it back to the Foreign Minister with this curt note: "I have read your speech and find that you have used every cliche known to the English language except 'Please adjust your dress before leaving'."

Allan A. Michie, Reader's Digest Aug 1943

Groucho Marx despised cliches, especially those found in the fraudulent friendliness of business correspondence. After opening a bank account he received from an executive a standard letter ending: "If I can be of any service to you, please do not hesitate to call on me." Marx did not hesitate. "Dear sir," he wrote, "the best thing you can do to be of service to me is to steal some money from the account of one of your other clients, and credit it to me."

Leo Rosten, I REMEMBER GROUCHO 1982

CLUB

On his first visit to the Athenaeum Sir James Barrie asked an octogenarian biologist the way to the dining room. The biologist burst into tears. He had been a member of the club for fifty years. No one had ever spoken to him before.

Passing Show 23 *Apr* 1932

The late Lord Birkenhead used to stop off at the Athenaeum to relieve himself on his daily walk from his home to the House of Lords. When challenged, after adopting this practice for some time, as to whether he was a member, he exclaimed, "Good God, is this place a club as well?"

Douglas Sutherland, THE ENGLISH GENTLEMAN 1978

There was a great brouhaha when the Athenaeum went so far as to install a lift to enable the elderly members to avail themselves of the facilities of the club above ground level. Unfortunately the proportions of the new lift were almost exactly as if it had been designed to accommodate a coffin standing on end, which enabled the younger members to remark that its real purpose was to facilitate the removal of such ancient members as had died in their bedrooms.

Ibid.

A lady called at Brooks and asked the hall porter if Mr. X was in the club. "I can't say, madam." "Please find out, and if he is, say his wife wants him." "Sorry, madam, but members of Brooks don't have wives."

Sir Laurence Guillemard, TRIVIAL FOND RECORDS 1937

When the late Sir Iain Moncreiffe was elected a member of the Carlton Club it was questioned whether anyone so young as 18 – as he then was – should become a member. The chairman responded, "Yes, and the next candidate is 82. That makes an average age of 50. Ideal age for this club. Both elected."

Daily Telegraph 1 *Mar* 1985

The Garrick Club will soon have nothing left to hide. In her god-forsaken book *Men* Anna Ford recalls overhearing a member being complimented by a woman on the ubiquitous faded pink and soft green Garrick tie. "My God, please don't call it pretty," he squirmed. "This tie, if you recognise it, is only like this because the committee were choosing a club tie over tea, and in desperation over the colour were suddenly inspired by the sandwiches they were eating. Cucumber and salmon."

The Times 25 *Mar* 1985

A secretary's notice appeared in the Travellers Club in Paris before a visit by King George VI and Queen Elizabeth: "Members should limit their invitations to their wives and daughters, and should not invite their mistresses, unless they are the wife or daughter of another member."

The Times, Diary 28 *May* 1985

Every club has a complaints book where gentlemen can air their grievances. Thus one gentleman may complain that another snores too loudly in the smoking room, or consistently fails to raise the lavatory seat. A gentleman of my acquaintance resigned in a huff when three of his fellow members complained that he was helping himself too liberally to the milk pudding.

Douglas Sutherland, THE ENGLISH GENTLEMAN 1978

Derek Taylor recalls going as a teenager for a job at a research establishment during the war and being asked by a peer of the realm if he belonged to any clubs. "Yes," he replied, "the Ovaltineys." He got the job.

Godfrey Smith, Sunday Times 7 *Jun* 1987

COINCIDENCE

Berthold Beitz is director-general of Krupps; his mother had been in domestic service before she married. During a committee dispute with an aristocratic Krupps director he suddenly remarked, "By the way, Herr Von B, I know a woman who has held both you and me lovingly in her arms." After a shocked silence he added, "Yes, your nursemaid is my mother."

Observer, The man behind Krupps 12 *Feb* 1961

When Vera Czermak learned that her husband had betrayed her she decided that she would end it all by jumping out of her third-storey window. Some time later she awoke in hospital to discover that she was still alive, having landed on her husband. Mr Czermak, however, was dead.

John Train, TRULY REMARKABLE OCCURRENCES 1978

Going along Oxford Street in a bus I heard the conductor telling a woman the names of shops that had formerly stood on the site of a large store. Realising that he must have been either the freeholder, the builder or a postman, and judging him unlikely to have been either the first or the second of these I said to him, "How long ago were you a postman?" "How did you know I was a postman?" He inquired. "Quite simple, my dear Watson," said I. The man, who had evidently not read his Sherlock Holmes, nearly fell off the bus, for his name *was* Watson.

Cyril P. Foley, AUTUMN FOLIAGE 1935

Oliver Knussen, who yesterday joined the artistic directors of the Aldeburgh Festival as their ninth colleague, has an ominous track record. His composition *Fire*, commissioned by Benjamin Britten when Knussen was 15, was completed for the 1969 festival. After the opening night the Snape Maltings concert hall burned down. The piece has subsequently been known as *Capriccio for String Trio*.

The Times, Diary 27 *Jan* 1987

When I was doing a sick parade near Salonika, a Private Latimer presented himself. Thus I quizzed him, "Hallo Latimer, how's Ridley?"

Latimer looked at me wonderingly. "Ridley's next one in, sir." And he was.

Capt Eric Caplans RAMC. letter to Sunday Times, quoted Denys Parsons FUNNY HA HA, FUNNY PECULIAR 1965

My stepson Bunny was driving home from London to his cottage by the sea at about 2 a.m. one morning when a man driving out of a side road ran straight into his car. It was on the outskirts of a village, and the village constable happened to be near on his night rounds. He took out his notebook and said to the driver of the other car, "Your name, please." The man said, "Ian Purvis." My stepson who likes to play things deadpan, said nothing. The policeman then turned to Bunny and said, "And your name, sir?" And Bunny said, "Ian Purvis." "Look here," said the bobby, "this is no time for silly jokes." But it was true. One Ian Purvis had run into another Ian Purvis.

Dr Alan McGlashan, Sunday Times 5 *May* 1974

Towards the end of a recital in Berlin, just as Andres Segovia was concluding with a pianissimo there was a loud cracking noise. Segovia rushed off the platform. I visited him backstage and found him muttering, "My guitar, my guitar," as if they were the only words he knew.

Sometime afterwards he told me that his friend who had made the guitar had died in Madrid at the same time as the instrument had split in Berlin.

Gregor Piatigorsky, CELLIST 1965

Researching an anthology of obituaries, Harriet Bridgeman and Elizabeth Drury came across the misreported death of John Stonehouse who went missing, was presumed dead, and then mysteriously reappeared. It was in the *Gentleman's Magazine* of July 1733.

The Times, Diary 12 *Jul* 1982

An ambulance taking an injured motorcyclist to hospital at Exeter was diverted to another accident – and found the second casualty to be the first victim's brother.

Both brothers, Wolfgang and Bodo Solf, crashed at the same time and had left home on their new motorcycles at the same time, but in opposite directions. Both had collided with a car, suffering multiple leg injuries. Later their mother said, "At the hospital we asked to see our son, and the nurse said, 'You can see both of them.' I just could not believe it. My husband had to sit down in a chair, he was so shocked."

Western Times 22 *Aug* 1975

COLLECTING

Caruso had a passion for picture postcards and when on tour would buy them in ten-shilling lots, have them addressed to himself and forwarded to his next stopping place.

John Fisher, Everybody's Weekly 3 *Sep* 1938

Baron Ferrari, the world-renowned stamp collector, received the news of his wife's death as he was on the point of fixing a rare Greek stamp in its appropriate place in his collection. This blow so affected him that, unconsciously, he completely destroyed the stamp which he had in his fingers.

In 1917 the baron became ill and entered a sanatorium in Switzerland. While he was there a new patient, a provincial professor, came in to be treated. He had a small collection of stamps which he invited the baron to inspect. Suddenly the baron saw another specimen of the stamp he had destroyed when his wife died; the famous five-drachma Greek with the head of Hermes.

"I'll buy that stamp from you," he said to the professor. "How much do you want for it?". "The Greek five-drachma? Shall we say five francs?"

The baron produced a five-franc piece from his pocket, took the stamp and retired to his room. Some minutes later in walked the nurse. Baron Ferrari lay dead on the floor.

Oscar Ray, MILLIONS AND MILLIONAIRES

COMEDY

Douglas Fairbanks built a ten-acre set for *Robin Hood*, a castle with enormous ramparts and a drawbridge, far bigger than any castle that ever existed. With great pride Douglas showed me the huge drawbridge. "Magnificent," I said, "what a wonderful opening for one of my comedies. The drawbridge comes down, and I put out the cat and bring in the milk."

Charles Chaplin, MY AUTOBIOGRAPHY 1964

Charles MacArthur, writing the script of a screenplay asked Charlie Chaplin, "How could I make a fat lady, walking down Fifth Avenue, slip on a banana skin and still get a laugh? Do I show first the banana skin, then the fat lady approaching, then she slips? Or do I show the fat lady first, then the banana skin, and then she slips?" "Neither," said Chaplin without a moment's hesitation. "You show the fat lady approaching, then you show the banana skin, then you show the banana skin and the fat lady together, then she steps over the banana skin and disappears down a manhole."

David Niven, BRING ON THE EMPTY HORSES 1975

COMMUNICATION

Parliament was discussing the system of cheap form telegrams for the armed forces, and Sir Ian Fraser suggested that the phrase "I am going to have a baby" be included in the list. "It should be included," he explained, "because there are so many happy young women who would want it." "For the same reason," said Captain Edward Charles Cobb, "will you also add the message, 'I am *not* going to have a baby'?"

B. Bowker, Reader's Digest May 1945

An admiral was approaching Malta on his flagship after a lengthy spell at sea with a lot of dirty washing on board. As was his custom he ordered the yeoman of signals to have the washerwoman picked up. The yeoman showed the admiral the signal he had sent. "On arrival please send admiral's woman aboard." Incensed by this idiotic mistake the admiral ordered the yeoman to send an immediate correction. It read "*Re* last signal, please insert washer between admiral and woman."

Godfrey Smith, Sunday Times 1 *Mar* 1987

COMMUNISM

In Communist Hungary an agricultural inspector from Budapest was questioning a local farmer about that year's potato crop.

"Comrade Inspector," declared the latter, "under the beneficent rule of Communism the potatoes produced by the collective farms are so numerous that, if they were piled together in a single heap, they would reach as far as the feet of God Almighty."

"Don't be absurd, comrade," snapped the inspector, "you know very well that God is imaginary."

"True, Comrade Inspector," was the reply, "but so are the potatoes."

Kenneth Edwards, I WISH I'D SAID THAT 1976

COMPASSION

I once remarked to Bernard Shaw that Sidney Webb seemed to me somewhat deficient in kindly feeling. "No," Shaw replied, "you are quite mistaken. Webb and I were once in a tramcar in Holland, eating biscuits out of a bag. A handcuffed criminal was brought into the tramcar by policemen. All the other passengers shrank away in horror, but Webb went up to the prisoner and offered him biscuits."

Bernard Russell, PORTRAITS FROM MEMORY 1956

COMPLIMENT

Once when Princess Anne was watching show-jumping at Hickstead a fellow spectator, unaware of her identity, remarked, "Has anyone ever told you that you look like Princess Anne?" The Princess grinned and said, "I think I'm better-looking than she is."

Paul Walker, Leicester Mercury

During World War I Nancy Astor set up a Red Cross hospital at Cliveden. A very young Canadian, badly wounded, awakened to consciousness to see the fine Gibson-girl face gazing down at him. He said weakly, "I think you're the kind of person I'd like to take back with me as my wife." Nancy smiled. "Give me time to think it over," she said softly.

When the soldier became stronger he realised to his embarrassment that he had proposed to none other than the formidable Nancy Astor herself. The next time he saw her he broke into confused apologies. Nancy laughed. "I haven't had such a compliment in years."

Geoffrey Bocca, Sunday Express 22 Jan 1956

A gushing schoolmistress rushed up to Robert Atkins and said, "Oh Mr Atkins, I did enjoy you in *Midsummer Night's Dream*. Your Bottom was simply enormous."

Michael Bentine, THE LONG BANANA SKIN 1975

Well do I remember, how as I was leaving HMS *Lion* following a meeting with Beatty after the action of the Dogger Bank, the usually imperturbable Admiral Pakenham caught me by the sleeve. "First Sea Lord, I wish to speak to you in private," and the intense conviction in his voice as he said, "Nelson has come again." Those words often recurred to my mind.

Winston Churchill, WORLD CRISIS 1929

On the writing table in Clemenceau's study stood a charming little nude torso of a Greek female figure. He told A. J. Balfour that a lady had recently been to call on him, and reproached him for not remembering her.

"How can I forget you," he replied, pointing to the statuette, "when I have this portrait always before me?"

Sir Ian Malcolm, LORD BALFOUR 1930

Gracie Fields went to Shirley Temple's eighth birthday party and enjoyed herself as much as if she had been Shirley's own age. Gracie cut the birthday cake, and the two got talking. Shirley showed her a set of pictures of the Royal Family, of which she was extremely proud.

"Would you", she asked Gracie, "like to be a Queen?" "No," said Gracie, "would you?" Shirley smiled and said, "No, but I'd like to be a princess." Gracie kissed her and said. "Th'art that already, lass."

Bert Aza, Sunday Chronicle 6 *Aug* 1939

COMPOSER

I was immensely fascinated watching Benjamin Britten compose a score. I had had no idea of the amount of physical work required. He used to say that a composer was a manual worker and reminded me that there were more notes in one of Wagner's operas than words in all of Shakespeare's plays. He sat for eight or ten hours a day at his chore, as he called it.

Ronald Duncan, HOW TO MAKE ENEMIES 1968

In 1936 the Hungarian composer Dohnanyi gave a recital which included his own Rhapsody in C Opus 11 No. 3, a work requiring immense technique. I had not heard him for some years, and I got the impression that the programme was almost too much for him. This was borne out by what he himself said later on. "I am always asked to play my own works, but I do not like to do so now. They are too difficult."

Stuart Hibberd, THIS IS LONDON 1950

We walked slowly to the hall, round Langham Place to kill time. As we neared the Artists' Entrance we passed an itinerant fiddler giving a fairly good rendition of *Salut d'Amour.* The delighted composer paused and from his pocket produced half a crown. Handing it to the bewildered musician Elgar said, "Do you know what you are playing?" "Yes," he replied, "It's *Salut d'Amour*, by Elgar." "Take this. It's more than Elgar made out of it," responded the donor.

Fred Gaisberg, MUSIC ON RECORD 1946

George Gershwin was on the train journey for the premiere of *Sweet Little Devil* when the concerto for the first time came into focus. The train whistles, the rattle of the wheels, the strange symphonic sounds which even the unmusical ear can hear in the confused roar of a train when it moves rapidly – all these things excited him until by the time he reached Boston the construction of the rhapsody was complete in his mind. The *Rhapsody in Blue* is many things, but it includes the description of a train journey as its central theme.

Robert Payne, GERSHWIN

Igor Stravinsky tells the story of an exchange between himself and George Gershwin. "How much will you charge to come over and give me lessons in orchestration?" said George. "How much do you make in a year?" "A hundred thousand dollars," said Gershwin. There was a moment's silence and then Stravinsky said, "How about you giving *me* lessons?"

Bennett Cerf, TRY AND STOP ME 1947

In 1930 there were rumours that Sibelius had started work on his Eighth Symphony. I was staying in Finland in the late summer of 1931 and asked him, "What about the Eighth Symphony? I don't believe it exists." His eyes twinkled. He took a cigarette packet, opened it up and drew two sets of five lines. On them he wrote a large chord and said,

"That is the opening of my Eighth Symphony." Who knows? Perhaps I possess the only manuscript.

Harriet Cohen, Daily Telegraph 23 *Sep* 1957

After his one-act opera *Von Heute auf Morgen* was performed for the first time in Frankfurt, Arnold Schoenberg said to the orchestra, "Gentlemen, the difference between what you have played tonight and what I wrote in my score would make another opera."

Norman Lebrecht, THE BOOK OF MUSICAL ANECDOTES 1985

The young Igor Stravinsky took a new composition to Rimsky-Korsakov. "This is disgusting, Sir," said his teacher. "It is not permissible to write such rubbish until one is sixty." Rimsky remained in a bad temper all day and at dinner complained to his wife, "What a bunch of nonentities my pupils are. Not one of them is capable of producing a piece of rubbish such as Igor brought me this morning."

Richard Buckle, DIAGHILEV 1969

COMPROMISE

At one stage President Lyndon Johnson looked for a way to get rid of the head of the FBI, J. Edgar Hoover, but the difficulties appeared insuperable. Philosophically accepting Hoover's continuance in office, he observed, "It's probably better to have him inside the tent, pissing out, than outside pissing in."

Clifton Fadiman, LITTLE, BROWN BOOK OF ANECDOTES 1985

COMPUTER

"Out of sight, out of mind" when translated by computer into Russian and back again becomes "invisible maniac".

Arthur Calder-Marshall, The Listener

The manager of our bank objected to investing in a data-computer, considering it a needless expense. The head office overruled him, however, and plans for installation began. When delivery day came it was discovered that the components were too large to fit into the lift.

"How am I going to get this thing up to the third floor?" the delivery man moaned.

The manager saw no problem. "Plug it in," he said, "and let it work it out for itself."

R. M. Cordell, Reader's Digest Nov 1965

A colleague received through the post a folder and a newsletter from the International Press Division of Hachette, breaking the news that they intend to put their business operations in the hands of a computer.

"It was only after careful analysis, rehearsal and constant checking and rechecking that it was decided that the actual computer operation would begin," promised the letter. "The point which cannot be overstressed is the amount of time spent in checking the service date for each account."

A bracing prospect, slightly dimmed by the fact that the letter was sent to the wrong address. By the computer.

Philip Oakes, Sunday Times 2 *Feb* 1969

An army officer on manoeuvres asked a computer, "Shall I advance or retire?" The machine answered, "Yes." "Yes what?" asked the officer, and the reply came, "Yes, sir."

Lord Pearse, TREASURER OF LINCOLNS INN 1966

A man had two watches. One gained a second every hour. The other wouldn't go at all. The question was put to a computer as to which he should keep. The computer replied, "Keep the one that does not go." Asked why, it responded, "The watch that does not go will show the exact time once in every twelve hours, the other will only give the right time once every five years."

Sir Edward Reid, Speech to Overseas Bankers' Club, Guildhall, London 1 *Feb* 1965

CONCEIT

At dinner Lady Astor remarked that she considered men to be more conceited than women. Noticing that the comment had been heard around the table, she continued in a loud voice, "It's a pity that the most intelligent and learned men attach little importance to the way they dress. At this table the most cultivated man is wearing the most clumsily knotted tie." The words had no sooner left her lips than every man in the room surreptitiously reached up to adjust his tie.

Clifton Fadiman, LITTLE, BROWN BOOK OF ANECDOTES 1985

Alfred Austin said to me in all seriousness one day, "My child, have you ever noticed how many great men are called *Alfred* – Alfred the Great, Alfred Tennyson?" Here was my cue. A slight pause after which I, as a dutiful niece, added, "And *you*, Uncle Alf."

No one could fathom why Alfred Austin was made Poet Laureate, since his only claim to fame was his exquisite prose. I therefore asked a niece of Lord Salisbury point blank, "Why on earth did your uncle give the laureateship to my Uncle Alfred?" She answered, "Because it was absolutely the only honour Mr Austin would accept from the Government for his long years of service to the Conservative cause."

Mrs Claude Beddington, ALL THAT I HAVE MET 1929

When the critic Bernard Fay was writing his *Panorama of Contemporary French Literature* Jean Cocteau paid him a visit, in the course of which he declared, "Bernard, say whatever you like about me in your book, it little matters. I insist on only one thing. The word GENIUS. That's all, you understand me?"

In the event Fay could not bring himself to use the desired term and Cocteau protested vigorously in writing at the ignominy of being put on the same level as Aragon and Giraudoux.

Frederick Brown, AN IMPERSONATION OF ANGELS: A BIOGRAPHY OF JEAN COCTEAU 1969

When Lady Carina, daughter of the Duke of Norfolk, told her favourite nun, Mother Wilson, that "I have met the man I wish to marry – David Frost." The saintly lady breathed deeply. "Is David – er – religious?" The wife-to-be replied, "Yes, he thinks he's God Almighty."

Stephen Pile, Sunday Times 28 *Jul* 1985

When Churchill offered Mountbatten the Asian Command he asked for 24 hours to ponder the offer. "Why?" snarled Churchill. "Don't you think you can do it?" "Sir," replied Mountbatten, "I suffer from the congenital weakness of believing that I can do anything."

Larry Collins and Dominique Lapierre, FREEDOM AT MIDNIGHT 1975

Early in his career Elvis Presley was asked which was his favourite among all the records he had made. He answered that it must be *Don't Be Cruel*. Why? "Because it has sold most copies."

Dominic Kennedy, Radio Times 19 *Aug* 1971

I heard a lady say, "That man Bernard Shaw ought to be well sat on by somebody! What do you think? I said to him, 'Oh Mr Shaw why do you not go to the States and do a lecture tour? You would make a fortune out of it. I know the Americans are simply *dying* to hear you,' and Mr Shaw replied, 'I am constantly being asked to lecture in America, but the reason I don't go there is that I am frightened that the Americans will insist as soon as I land there on making me President of the United States!' Just think, the conceit of the creature."

Mrs Claude Beddington, ALL THAT I HAVE MET 1929

Lipehitz asked Gertrude Stein to come to his studio and pose for him and she agreed. Lipehitz found her an interesting subject and her egotism memorable. He recalls Gertrude's telling him very solemnly, "Jacques, of course you don't know much about English literature, but besides Shakespeare and me, who do you think there is?"

James K. Mellow, CHARMED CIRCLE 1974

CONDUCTOR

One of the favourite stories at Glyndebourne dealt with Busch's first orchestral rehearsal, when he raised his baton, then dropped his arms and before anyone had played a note said to the men in mock reproach and heavily accented English, "Already is too loud."

Rudolf Bing, 5000 NIGHTS AT THE OPERA 1972

One of the players among the second violins at a rehearsal of Beethoven's Ninth Symphony at Turin played a false note. "I would kill a man for that," cried Arturo Toscanini, who was conducting, and beat the man over the head with his baton. Toscanini was summoned for assault. In court he pleaded, "sublime fury"; his fellow Italians acquitted him.

Lionel Hale, News Chronicle 24 *Feb* 1936

CONFESSION

Only occasionally did Horatio Bottomley descend to the open confession which is so good for the soul. One day during lunch at the Savoy he was introduced to Arnold Bennett.

"I believe we have met before," remarked Bottomley. "Do you remember when I was owner of *The Sun*? It was during the time that Dr Parker, of the city Temple, edited the paper for a week. I believe you were one of his contributors."

"That's so," said Bennett. "Dr Parker was a friend of mine, and a very great man."

"Yes," said Bottomley, "a man after my own heart. He was one of the greatest humbugs I have ever known."

Sunday Express 28 *May* 1933

My father's tutor, Monsignor Contini, was once hearing a confession. At the end the penitent who was kneeling before him said, "Oh father, I was forgetting to tell you that I have stolen a pair of silver buckles." "Well, my son," said Contini, "you must promise to give them back immediately, or I cannot give you absolution." "Oh father," replied the penitent, "won't you have them?" "Certainly not, I absolutely refuse." "But father, what if when I give them back to the owner he refuses to accept them?" "Then in that case you will be able to keep them," and he gave absolution to his penitent, who went away happily.

When some time later Contini left the confessional he found that his shoes were minus their silver buckles.

Marchesa Stella Vitelleschi, OUT OF MY COFFIN 1937

Alfred Lunt told a story about an American Roman Catholic couple who were discussing the Rotary Club dinner which the husband had attended the night before. He said that after dinner a prize had been offered for the best answer to the question, "What gives you the greatest pleasure in life?" The husband, having had a few drinks, wrote his answer on a piece of paper saying, "Going to bed with my wife Elaine" but he thought this might shock his wife who was attractive but prudish, so he told her a harmless fib, and said that his answer had been "Going to Mass" and that he had won the prize – 100 dollars. Elaine, who was nothing if not devout, was upset that Mass should be made the subject of an after-dinner joke. So next morning, as soon as her husband had left the house to go to the office, she drove down to the Rotary Club building returning the prize accompanied by a note saying, "It is not true what my husband was saying last night. He only did it twice before we were married, once on our wedding day, and very seldom since."

Peter Coats, OF KINGS AND CABBAGES 1984

CONSOLATION

Curzon had no chance of succeeding Bonar Law. He was not wanted by anyone. Balfour, on being asked by a friend, "Will dear George be chosen?" replied, "No, dear George will not." Curzon's second wife, Grace Duggan, was "seriously rich" in American parlance. Balfour's friend said, "He will be terribly disappointed." "Oh, I don't know. He may have lost the hope of glory, but he still retains the means of grace."

Robert Blake, Observer, reviewing Roy Jenkins, BALDWIN 1 *Mar* 1987

CONVERSATION

When my brother Alec was Foreign Secretary he left my brother William, the playwright, alone after dinner with Macmillan, then Prime Minister. When he returned William was in a frightful state of nerves, though his excuse – that he was at a loss how to react to Macmillan, who was explaining that Lloyd George should never have gone into politics but should have been a ballet dancer – seemed reasonable.

Henry Douglas-Home, quoted Mark Amory, Sunday Times Magazine 17 *Apr* 1977

To luncheon with the Huntingdons to meet James Joyce. Desmond MacCarthy weighs in with talk about Charles Peace and the Partridge murders. "Are you," I say to Joyce, hoping to draw him into conversation, "interested in murder?" "No," he answers with the gesture of a governess shutting a piano, "not in the very least." The failure of that opening leads to Desmond starting on the subject of Richard and Lady Burton. The fact that Burton was once consul at Trieste sends a pallid but very fleeting light across the pinched features of Joyce. It is quickly gone. "Are you interested," asks Desmond, "in Burton?" "Not," answers Joyce, "in the very least." He is not a rude man; he manages to hide his dislike of the English in general and of the literary English in particular. But he is a difficult man to talk to. "Joyce," as Desmond remarked afterwards, "is not a very *convenient* guest at luncheon."

Harold Nicolson, DIARY 30 *Jul* 1931

New York. Lunch with Elizabeth Marbury, literary agent, at 13 Sutton Place. Find Mrs Vanderbilt there, representing society. Henry Van Loon, the historian representing literature, Wylie representing journalism – he is the editor of the *New York Times.* Now here were three people corresponding roughly to James Garvin, Ethel Smythe and Maynard Keynes. And this, with infinite slowness, was one of the many stories that Wylie told. "That," he said, "reminds me of a story I heard the other day down town. A man is taken from speakeasy to speakeasy. He returns to his wife after having music of a negro orchestra drummed in his ears. 'How are you feeling?' she says. He says 'Rather syncopated.' She looks up 'syncopated' in the dictionary and finds that it means 'passing rapidly from bar to bar'".

We laugh politely. But it is incredible that such a story should be told by people and to people who are really educated. It is this that I find so trying. They are so slow in conversation that it is like being held up by a horse dray in a taxi. And they never listen to what one says oneself.

Harold Nicolson, DIARY 8 *Jan* 1933

Conversation turning for some reason on Byron, C.M. Bowra remarked that in his hearing at the Gilbert Murrays recently a visiting notability had asked, "Are you interested in incest, Professor Murray?" to which the Professor of Greek had rather brusquely replied, "Only in a very general sort of way."

Anthony Powell, The Times, The Bowra World 19 Oct 1974

COOKING

A bishop visiting a small country town was the guest of a lady who did her own household work. He was awakened in the morning by his hostess singing, "Nearer my God to thee." At breakfast the bishop expressed his pleasure, but was taken aback by the lady's reply. "Oh lor' – that's the hymn I boil the eggs by. Three verses for soft, five for hard."

Gerald Findler, HUMOUR FROM PULPIT AND PEW 1934

For a while we lived in Vancouver where the cook was Chinese. Lucy Sampson, my nanny, one day went into the kitchen while he was preparing for a dinner party and discovered him mixing soup in what used to be called a domestic article. The delicate situation was resolved by my mother, who had to explain a lot of things to the cook. He thought the pot was a very big cup. Soup came off the menu that night.

Joyce Grenfell, JOYCE GRENFELL REQUESTS THE PLEASURE 1976

CORONATION

Before her coronation, Queen Alexandra sent for Archbishop MacLaglan to explain her predicament. Like most women of her age and generation she augmented her own hair with a toupee. If she were to be properly anointed she felt that the holy oil must actually touch her own body: she therefore begged the Archbishop to be sure some of the oil ran down her forehead. This he did; on returning to Buckingham Palace she refused to wipe the oil off, wishing to bear the mark of her anointing as long as possible.

Georgina Bettiscombe, QUEEN ALEXANDRA 1969

Edward VII, asked by Sir Frederick Treves what had impressed him most at his coronation, confessed that it had been "an incident which was not intended to be impressive, and that was the simultaneous movement of the peeresses in putting on their coronets". King Edward explained that "their white arms arching over their heads" had suggested inevitably, "a scene from a beautiful ballet".

Sir Philip Magnus, KING EDWARD VII 1964

It was the eve of King Edward VII's coronation. Suddenly to the pupils of our school there came a bolt from the blue: the headmistress decided not to give us a holiday on the day of the Coronation, although the mistresses had made arrangements to view the procession. The pupils held a conclave and decided to communicate with the King himself, and that I should write it. This was it.

"Dear King, as we are sure it is your wish that all schools should have a holiday on your Coronation day we think you ought to know that Miss O — the head of our school, is not going to let us have one.

So I am writing secretly to ask if you can possibly help us get it. Your affectionate subject, Gladys Storey."

In a day or two came back an answer. "Madam, by the King's orders I am writing to Miss O — to ask her for a holiday for your school on 26 June. I am, Madam, your obedient servant, F. Knollys."

Gladys Storey, ALL SORTS OF PEOPLE 1929

Who could but admire, with an awed wonder, Lord Castlerosse whom I found sitting all alone in an otherwise empty Savoy Grill during the Coronation, from which he had walked out saying, "I got fed up with the bloody thing."

Hannen Swaffer, World's Press News 23 Sep 1943

One thing I noticed in the Abbey at the Coronation of George VI which I don't think that many people did. You know, of course, cameramen weren't allowed in except at specified positions, but we were allowed to have binoculars. There was a German correspondent with a pair of binoculars which he kept pressing with his fingers. The binoculars were actually a miniature camera. He took 36 pictures and then went outside for a minute and changed the film, came back and took some more.

Cornelius Vanderbilt, World's Press News 20 *May* 1937

The first of the heads of state to arrive at the Abbey [for the Coronation of Elizabeth II] was Queen Salote of Tonga, with a bright red feather rising high out of her hat. Opposite her in the carriage was a frail little man in white, the Sultan of Kelantan. "Who can *he* be?" asked one of the beautiful young men attendant on Noel Coward as he watched the procession go by. The Master scrutinised the little figure opposite the monumental Polynesian lady. "Her lunch," he said crisply.

Robert Lacey, MAJESTY 1977

CORRESPONDENCE

In 1919 the 17th Earl of Derby wrote a letter to the Foreign Secretary beginning, "My Dear Curzon, I have always known you to be a cad. I now know you to be a liar." The letter did not go off in the night's bag from the Paris Embassy. The next morning Derby looked at it again.

"Hmm. Perhaps it's a bit too strong. I think I'll have another go." This time the letter began, "My Dear George, you and I have known each other too long to quarrel over so small a matter."

Randolph S. Churchill, LORD DERBY 1960

Tom Driberg, as a Member of Parliament, developed an infuriating technique to deal with the shoals of abusive letters. His secretary was instructed to reply, "Tom Driberg asks me to thank you for your letter. He regrets he is unable to answer it individually as he has had a great deal of correspondence on this subject; he is, however, most grateful for your support."

Russell Miller, Sunday Times Magazine 26 *Aug* 1974

John Peart-Binns, biographer of John Habgood, Archbishop of York, has unearthed a letter written by him when he was eight.

"Dear God, if you feel lonely up in the sky would you like to come down and stay with us? You could sleep in the spare room, and you could bathe with us, and I think you would enjoy yourself. Love, John."

Addressed to "Our Father Which Art in Heaven" it was opened by the Post Office and marked "Return to sender", which, as Peart-Binns comments, has fewer theological implications than "Gone away" or "Unknown at this address".

Kenneth Rose, Sunday Telegraph 31 *May* 1987

COURAGE

Caruso, singing in Brooklyn in 1921, broke a blood-vessel in his throat in the middle of a song. For a moment his voice quavered and the audience half rose to its feet in astonishment – they did not know what had happened. With a supreme effort of will he regained control of himself and sang on for another twenty minutes, though his wife, frantic with anxiety, begged for the curtain to be lowered. Handkerchiefs were passed out to Caruso, and with these he tried to staunch the flow of blood. At last, choking and with tears in his eyes, he had to stop. But the audience applauded as never before.

John Fisher, Everybody's Weekly 3 *Sep* 1938

Paderewski's hands were strong and very white. Each nail was insured for £1000. The hands were covered with a policy of £100,000.

Once he split a nail and finished a concert bleeding. Only the trail of crimson on the keys let it be known he was hurt. His playing was as strong as ever.

Bruce Clavering, Sunday Referee 9 *Aug* 1936

COURTESY

Lady Astor's maiden speech was – naturally – about the temperance question. She attacked Sir John Rees for his tolerance of brewers. Sir John listened patiently then rose to his feet and in Biblical language said, "The Hon. lady has been unto me a rod of chastisement. I must kiss the rod." The members laughed and Nancy blushed.

John Beevers, Sunday Referee 10 *Feb* 1939

While Basil Boothroyd was writing his biography of Prince Philip he was given a room in the Palace to work, and leaving it one day he accosted Sir Michael Adeane, the principal private secretary, walking towards the front of the building. Adeane listened sympathetically to a problem troubling Boothroyd, and the writer got the impression, faint as an echo, that he would like to be moving on. It was another minute or so before he said, "I do hope you'll forgive me, but I've just heard my house is on fire. I wouldn't mind, but as it is part of St James Palace —"

Robert Lacey, MAJESTY 1977

A friend of my mother's once gave a party for Winston Churchill. The buffet was cold fried chicken, an American tradition that the ageing statesman found greatly to his liking. He came to her for seconds. "May I have breast?" he asked. "Mr Churchill," my mother's friend replied, "in this country we ask for white meat or dark meat." "I *am* sorry," Churchill replied.

The next day the host received an orchid. A card bore the handwriting of the great man himself. "I would be most obliged if you would pin this on your white meat."

James C. Humes, HOW TO GET INVITED TO THE WHITE HOUSE 1977

Sir Edward Clarke's courtesy to women was never-failing. A lady introduced to him at a first night said, "Oh, Sir Edward, people say I am so like Lady X [a noted beauty]. What do you think?" "Well," replied

Sir Edward, "I never saw the lady, but I hope for her sake you are."

Derek Walker-Smith and Edward Clarke, THE LIFE OF SIR EDWARD CLARKE 1939

Joseph Conrad imported to his rural ambience in Kent the gestures of Continental courtesy, even though a stupid cleric once told him we don't do that sort of thing here – stiff bow from the hips, and a kiss for the hand of a lady, especially if she was pretty. One day a candidate for a housemaid's post came to the door. Conrad, unwarned, saw merely a personable woman – "Belle visage, très chic" – and performed the regular ritual. She fled in terror.

John Conrad, JOSEPH CONRAD: TIMES REMEMBERED 1981

Henry Davray told me that at some English house a foreigner arrived wearing what looked like an overcoat. The hostess urged him to take it off; said it was the custom, etc. He took it off and appeared in his shirtsleeves. Consternation of the hostess, especially as other guests were expected. Presently Laurence Housman came in and was advised of the situation. Housman took off his own coat and sat down in his shirtsleeves; then complained of the cold and demanded his hostess's permission to resume his coat; the foreigner followed his example. After that I was surprised to learn that Housman spoke no French at all. It seemed to me, somehow, that a man capable of that ought to be a perfect French scholar.

Arnold Bennett, JOURNALS 1896–1910 1932

At a royal dinner party at the Quirinal my father, the Marchese Vitelleschi, dropped some spinach on his white shirt front and I tried to draw his attention to it by making signs. But, deeply immersed in conversation, instead of pausing to inspect the damage, he took his serviette and began to rub vigorously at his shirt front, leaving on it a stain two or three inches in diameter.

The Queen immediately noticed the injury and exclaimed, "Vitelleschi! Look!"

On the refectory table at which we were seated were bowls of choice red roses. Like a flash my father took one of the roses and placed it in his buttonhole. He said, "The Italian colours, Your Majesty" (Red, white and green).

Marchesa Stella Vitelleschi, OUT OF MY COFFIN 1937

The conductor Hans von Bulow had a reputation for courtesy. Once, hurrying up a narrow, ill-lit staircase, he collided violently with a man coming down. "Idiot!" thundered the stranger. Hans lifted his hat. "Von Bulow" he said.

Reader's Digest Oct 1978

The music blared at a recent soccer match in Athens between a Chinese and a Greek side, and the crowd rose and stood in respectful silence. They assumed it was the Chinese national anthem. The Chinese also stood at attention, thinking it was the Greek. Then a voice sang out; it was a toothpaste commercial.

Simon Barnes, The Times 14 *Nov* 1987

COURTSHIP

Robert Baden-Powell married at the age of 51. He had seen a girl walking down Knightsbridge two years before. He had marked her walk with his swiftly estimating eye; it showed, he thought "honesty of purpose, common sense and a spirit of adventure". He did not know her, did not see her again until he recognised that free-striding gait on the deck of a ship. With characteristic Baden-Powell unconventionality, combined with shipboard freedom, he got into conversation with her. "Did you, two years ago, walk down Knightsbridge with a brown spaniel?" he asked. Within a year Miss Soames, soon to be Chief Guide, and Robert Baden-Powell were married.

Guy Ramsay, News Chronicle 9 *Jan* 1941

Thomas Beecham's sister had a friend called Utica Wells. When they were out walking one day Beecham said, "I don't like your Christian name. I'd like to change it." "You can't," the girl said, "but you can change my surname." And so they were married.

Daphne Fielding, THOSE REMARKABLE CUNARDS, EMERALD AND NANCY 1976

Shortly before he became a Bristol MP Tony Benn proposed to his beloved while sitting on an Oxford park bench. She said yes. Benn was so carried away by that golden moment that he wrote to the City Council pleading with it to let him buy the bench. In its astonishment the council agreed and Benn had it placed in the garden of his London home as a permanent reminder of his love.

The Times, Diary 8 *Aug* 1985

At one time John Betjeman and I were in love with the same young woman. Every time I threw out my personality most powerfully and was beginning to make an impression on her, John would come along looking terribly shabby and unshaven and unhappy. Instantly she turned all her attention on him. He got one girl after another. They all wanted to look after him.

Unnamed author, quoted Susan Barnes, Observer Magazine

The Duke of York's courtship of the Lady Elizabeth Bowes-Lyon had its difficulties. Hopelessly tongue-tied, at the critical moment he sent a friend to propose for him. Lady Elizabeth replied, "No, not until he comes and asks himself."

The Duke set himself to it. Once more speech failed. Pulling a scrap of paper from his pocket, he proposed in writing.

A.J.P. Taylor, THE IMPROBABLE KING 1957

In October 1929 Randolph Churchill came to London on 24 hours leave. Entering the Ritz Hotel he saw an old friend, Lady Mary Dunn. "Can you have dinner?" he shouted. Mary replied that she had to dine elsewhere. "However, I know someone who might," she added, "and I can tell you where to ring her. She's a girl called Pamela Digby and has just arrived from Dorset."

Randolph rushed to the phone box. A fresh voice replied. "Who are you?" he enquired. "Pamela Digby," came the answer. "Mary Dunn said I could invite you to dinner. What do you look like?" asked the insufferable Randolph. "Red headed and rather fat, but mummy says that puppy-fat soon disappears."

Three days later their engagement was announced.

Anita Leslie, Sunday Telegraph 21 *Apr* 1985

One day a letter arrived at Faber and Faber, from a Valerie Fletcher in Yorkshire, saying she had admired T.S. Eliot since she was a schoolgirl, and could she become his secretary? This remarkable request was declined. Years later, Mr Eliot's secretary left, and the letter from Yorkshire was remembered. Valerie Fletcher, with other candidates, was interviewed by Mr Eliot who had been enjoined not to reveal any preference to the candidates. Valerie Fletcher had a bandaged finger. At the end of the interview, Eliot said he hoped the finger would be better by the time she came to work on Monday. Three years later they were married.

Michael Davie, Observer 15 *May* 1983

They met at a dinner party in Oslo, and before they had got past the first course Commander Edward Evans had asked the blonde girl beside him, "Do you like soup?" Receiving her answer he replied, "Neither do I – let's get married."

He had in fact proposed to and been accepted by his Viking bride Elsa within 20 minutes, and it was always a happy marriage.

Reginald Pound, EVANS OF THE BROKE 1967

George Gershwin reserved one unpublished little waltz for affairs of the heart. "You're the kind of girl who makes me feel like composing a song," he would tell the enraptured lady of the moment, and lead her off to his suite. We would follow on tip-toe to hear him compose the familiar tune for her. "It will be dedicated to you," he would tell her soulfully.

Bennett Cerf, TRY AND STOP ME 1947

Harry Hopkins, who is a shy sort of chap, proposed to Louise Macy in this manner, "I was just talking to the President and I asked him whether he thought you would say yes if I asked you to marry me – and the President said he thought you would." Her answer belongs to the history books. "As usual," she said, "the President was right."

Walter Winchell, quoted Reader's Digest Oct 1942

It was almost 60 years ago that Lady Longford first met her husband, then Frank Longford, at a party at Oxford. He was asleep on a sofa, and she could not resist the temptation to awaken him with a kiss. Frank opened his eyes and fell instantly in love, before drifting, almost as instantly, back to sleep again.

Clare Colvin, Daily Telegraph 25 *Aug* 1986

When I was a struggling young musical student, living in a small *pension* in Munich, I was sitting in the garden one day, learning the words of a new opera. As I sang the words, "Come to me, my love, on the wings of light," there was a flutter, a flash of white, and there sitting at my feet, was a beautiful little creature who had dropped right out of the blue. It was Maria Hacker, a diminutive Bavarian actress. Stunting for a movie thriller, she had jumped from an aeroplane and landed, parachute and all, practically in my arms.

And that was She. I thought that she came to me from heaven. I still think so.

Lauritz Melchior, quoted Peggy McEvoy, Reader's Digest Jan 1940

An ancient courtier, it may well have been Sir Harry Stonor, told me that some years before he had proposed marriage to a rich Coats aunt of mine, who had refused his offer with the words, "My dear, I love men but I hate husbands."

Peter Coats, OF KINGS AND CABBAGES 1984

There is a famous Washington story that Mrs Wilson, wife of President Woodrow Wilson, has declared, "When Woodrow proposed to me I was so surprised that I nearly fell out of bed."

Sir Henry Channon, DIARY 1 *Jul* 1943

It was reported of one old don at Trinity College, Cambridge, that for thirty years he had never ventured outside the college gates. Into his room one day, however, there burst a friend of his youth, a cheery colonel from India, who with much difficulty persuaded his old friend to go for a walk before dinner in Hall. As they were passing through a meadow the don stopped short, and pointed excitedly to a stile where sat a youth with his arm around a girl's waist.

"Just look at that!" he cried.

"Well, what about it?" asked the colonel.

"What about it?" echoed the don. "I haven't seen that since I was a boy in Lincolnshire, and I always thought it was a local custom."

Sir Laurence Guillemard, TRIVIAL FOND RECORDS 1937

In 1924, during a rehearsal at His Majesty's Theatre of *Die Meistersinger*, Sir Thomas Beecham asked the clumsy young singer playing Walther, "Do you consider yours a suitable way of making love to Eva?" "Well, there are different ways of making love," parried the young man. "Observing your grave, deliberate motions," returned Sir Thomas, "I was remined of that estimable quadruped, the hedgehog."

Charles Neilson Gatty, THE ELEPHANT THAT SWALLOWED A NIGHTINGALE 1981

CREMATION

I go down to Hertfordshire with Jim Lees-Milne and Jack Rathbone to see Bernard Shaw's house, which he left to the Trust. . . . The grass path and the bed around the statue of St Joan are still strewn with his ashes and those of Mrs Shaw. The trustees and the doctor got both urns and put them on the dining room table. They then emptied the one into the other and stirred them with a kitchen spoon. They went out into the garden and emptied spoonfuls of the mixture on to the flower beds and paths. All this some fifteen days ago, but the remains are still there. Just like the stuff Vita puts down for slugs.

Harold Nicolson, DIARY 11 *Dec* 1950

CRICKET

The drink question got Nancy Astor into trouble in 1931 when she said that England had lost the Test because the Australians did not drink. At once the MCC, then in Johannesburg, sent her a cable: "We thank Lady Astor for the great interest she obviously takes in Test Cricket. We beg to state that she is guilty of a terminological inexactitude. For further information we suggest she applies to Richardson, Kippax, Ponsford, Grimmett, Oldfield and Hornibrook."

John Beevers, Sunday Referee 19 *Feb* 1939

Augustine Birrell once hit so hard that he smashed the bat I had lent him. Instead of grieving he called out gloriously, "Fetch me some more bats."

J.M. Barrie, THE GREENWOOD HAT

Mike Bore had a positive genius for getting on the wrong side of Geoffrey Boycott. At Middlesbrough, in 1972, Yorkshire had to lend Gloucestershire a fielder, and Bore was sent out to do the job. Boycott, then captain, was batting; when he was on 68 he hooked Procter and was caught – by Bore at long leg. Instead of staying on the boundary and looking sheepish in marched Bore with a great grin on his face to join the celebrating Gloucestershire fielders. When he got back to the dressing room he found that his irate captain had picked up Bore's cricket bag and thrown it into the opposition room.

David Bairstow, A YORKSHIRE DIARY 1984

Until 1977 Michael Foot turned out regularly for *Tribune* in the annual cricket match against the *New Statesman*, a feat for a man in his sixties who, 15 years previously, had suffered a car accident that almost killed him. In one of their matches the *NS* fielded a young bowler, the son of one of their contributors, who was alarmingly fast.

"Take it easy, lad," the *NS* captain instructed. "Remember he is not only a distinguished but a very old man."

The bowler duly took it easy, and bowled a slow ball down the leg side. Foot promptly swept it for four. He swept the next ball for four. The *NS* captain said, "Right, if that's the way he wants to play it, you can let him have it."

The bowler accordingly let him have it. Foot hit another four. He was then run out. Good judges believe that, if he had applied himself and been properly taught, he would have made a nearly, but not quite, first-class batsman, despite his short sight, a disability, after all, shared by Geoffrey Boycott and Clive Lloyd.

Alan Watkins, Observer 16 *Nov* 1980

King George of Greece was once bowled first ball in a cricket match at his English private school. He never forgot the incident. It helped him, he said, to face the poverty-stricken years of his exile with more courage than he might otherwise have shown. It enabled him, he told friends, to treat the misfortune of his expulsion from Greece as a stepping stone to ultimate triumph.

Sunday Referee, quoted Frank Muir, FRANK MUIR GOES INTO – 1978

We chanced to sit next to E.R.T.Holmes and were soon pumping him for cricket gossip about when he first captained Surrey when the great Hobbs was still playing. Once Holmes asked him whether he ever paid any attention to the bowler's arm, wrist, etc. Hobbs said "Never", and I believe it's true. All the great players have always played each ball on its merits as it approaches them. It is only the second raters and below who can be deceived by the googly hand-action.

Rupert Hart-Davis, THE LYTTELTON HART-DAVIS LETTERS 1978

Stanley Holloway's earliest ambition for his son Julian was that he should play cricket for England, and he gave him three Christian names – Julian Robert Stanley – because he thought J.R.S. Holloway would look good in the score book.

Stewart Knowle, TV Times 27 *Jul* 1972

Harold Larwood generously agreed to take part in a charity match. It soon became clear that the umpire regarded Larwood and his bowling with some disfavour when a dead-straight ball was intercepted by the batsman's pad. "How's that," called Larwood, confident that he had dismissed the batsman leg-before-wicket. "Not out," said the umpire. Larwood bowled again, faster this time, and the batsman made a slash at the ball, snicked it, and sent it straight into the wicket-keeper's gloves. "How's that?" again called Larwood. "Not out," said the umpire. Larwood took his full run and sent down one of his deadly deliveries. The batsman's wicket was blasted from the ground, bails and stumps flying through the air. Larwood turned to the umpire. "I damned nearly got him that time."

Oxfam, PASS THE PORT 1976

I remember a very wet morning at Leeds; they didn't cover the wickets in those days. At one o'clock the sun came beating down and of course this meant the wicket would become difficult for the batsmen. An hour or so later Wilfred Rhodes and Emmott Robinson went out to inspect the wicket. And I went with them. Rhodes felt the turf and said, "Emmott, it'll be sticky at four o'clock." Then Emmott bent down, pressed his fingers into the soil like an expert cloth-tester and said, "No Wilfred. Half past."

Neville Cardus, quoted Robin Daniels, Sunday Times 4 *Jul* 1975

Eleven good men and true who swish the willow every weekend have suffered an almighty ducking. It happened yesterday in 30 minutes and fifty balls when Saltwood village from Hythe dismissed Martin Walters works eleven for 0. Last night the losing captain, John Bradford, said, "Our batsmen were coming out quicker than team-mates could pad up." Winning skipper of Saltwood, Ernest Mills, said, "We were pleased as it was a batsman's wicket."

Rodney Hallworth, Sunday Express 25 *May* 1964

On July 15 1939, after the final curtain fell at Glyndebourne on what was to be the last performance of opera in that theatre for 11 years, John Christie came before the curtain to utter an idiosyncratic valedictory. There was, he told the audience, "serious news". With rumours of wars in all the papers the audience stirred uneasily. But the news which Christie felt could not wait until Glyndebourne's patrons returned home was news from Lords, not from Downing Street. For the first time since 1908 the annual Eton-Harrow match had been won by Eton.

Rudolf Bing, 5000 NIGHTS AT THE OPERA 1972

The parson of a village where a friend of mine lives was perturbed at the persistent shortage of rain. Cattle and roots were suffering; the outlook was gloomy. He decided to pray for rain at the morning service on Sunday. Then a troublesome thought struck him. "No," he told my friend, "not next Sunday. I shall put it off until the Sunday after. *I am not going to do anything to spoil the Test Match.*"

Sunday Times, quoted FRANK MUIR GOES INTO SPORT

CRIME

Charles Palmer, when he was assistant editor, told me that one day Horatio Bottomley, returning from lunch, heard him discharging the office boy. "What are you sacking him for, Charlie?" asked HB. "He's, been stealing the postage stamps," said Palmer. "Why worry about that?" said Bottomley. "We all began in a small way." That was his philosophy!

Hannen Swaffer, World's Press News 1 *Jun* 1933

Thieves once stole a detached London house. They first robbed it of all its furniture and fittings while its owner was away on holiday and then, expert housebreakers in more ways than one, proceeded to demolish the walls. No one interfered; the police and neighbours assumed that they were acting under the owner's instructions. When he returned he found a waste piece of land where his house had been and thought the cabman had brought him to the wrong street.

J.C. Cannell, WHEN FLEET STREET CALLS 1932

Francis Searchlights, the Bolton firm that supplies high-powered lamps to the Navy, the Fire Brigade and many others, held a demonstration of new and existing models beside the Thames at Windsor on Tuesday night.

Fifty yards away on the opposite bank they had tethered an eight foot by eight foot "iceberg" made out of marine ply. "And now", said the announcer "our 50-million candela [candle-power] Xenon searchlight will show you an iceberg."

The guests watched as the beam stabbed through the darkness to reveal – nothing. The iceberg had apparently been stolen and Thames Valley Police coldly reported yesterday: "The suspect melted away into the night."

Daily Telegraph 28 *Oct* 1982

Police and county highway officials are baffled over a spate of road sign thefts in Staffordshire. Over the past few months thieves have stolen about £15,000 worth of aluminium highway signs from county depots including Doxey and Hilton Park. "We don't know in which direction to look," said a county council spokesman.

Staffordshire Newsletter, quoted Daily Telegraph 3 *Dec* 1985

After making an impassioned plea for more bobbies on the beat, Martin Thomas, SDP candidate for Wrexham, left the HTV studio to find that his car had been stolen, along with a batch of literature on crime prevention.

The Times 27 *May* 1987

On February 18, 1981, Mrs Dora Wilson looked out of her window in Harlow New Town and saw a group of men loading her neighbour's priceless Persian carpets into a pantechnicon. "What are you doing?" she called, knowing her neighbours were on holiday. "We're taking them to be cleaned, madam," the workmen replied. Quick as a flash Mrs Wilson decided to take advantage of the service they offered. "Will you please take mine, too?" she asked. The men obliged. They were burglars.

David Frost, THE WORLD'S WORST DECISIONS 1983

A 48-year-old Chinese man reported an attempted mugging to Hong Kong police and handed over a fingertip which he had bitten off when a hand was clamped over his mouth. A 20-year old man was later arrested when he sought hospital treatment for a shortened index finger.

Daily Telegraph 21 *Dec* 1985

A cautionary tale from old Merseyside concerns a ten-year-old girl who was accosted by a man in a local park. She dodged him and rushed home and her mother called the police. Later the girl's teacher took her aside to ask what had happened at the police station. "They showed me photos of men to see if I could find the one who had spoken to me in the park." "Did you?" asked the teacher. "No," replied the girl, "But I saw one of Uncle Fred."

Daily Telegraph 30 *Dec* 1982

The illegibility of doctors' handwriting has always been a stock joke but –. Two men were jailed recently for forging prescriptions for an addictive pain-killing drug. They were caught because the chemist was suspicious about the writing on the forms. The grounds for his suspicions? He found he could easily read the "doctor's" writing on the prescription.

Observer 20 *Oct* 1985

CRITICISM

Brendan Behan was asked what he thought of dramatic critics. "Critics are like eunuchs in a harem," he replied. "They're there every night, they see it done every night, they see how it should be done every night, but they can't do it themselves."

Gyles Brandreth, GREAT THEATRICAL DISASTERS 1982

Zolotow: "What do you think of critics?" Brooks: "They're very noisy at night. You can't sleep in the country because of them." Zolotow: "Isn't that crickets? I mean critics." Brooks: "Oh critics. What good are they? They can't make music with their hind legs."

Maurice Zolotow interviewing Mel Brooks, New York Times 30 *Mar* 1975

Joyce Carey accompanied Noel Coward to the first night of Leslie Howard's *Hamlet* in America. As Howard delicately spoke the first line Noel clutched Joyce's arm. "Beautiful, beautiful," he whispered, but from then on nothing grew, the whole performance remained muted and impassive. At the end they went to Howard's dressing room and

Joyce wondered what Coward could possibly say. Coward embraced Howard and said, "Oh, Leslie, you know how I hate over-acting – and I know you could never over-act – but please, please, try."

Donald Sinden, A TOUCH OF THE MEMOIRS 1982

Nellie Melba gave her first public recital at the age of six, singing "Comin' thro' the Rye" while standing on a chair. Her first critic was a neighbourhood girl who, when asked what she thought of the performance, shrilled, "*Nellie Mitchell, I saw your drawers.*"

Joseph Wechsberg, RED PLUSH AND BLACK VELVET 1962

I think that the best audience review I heard came at the end of a Peter O'Toole *Macbeth* at the Old Vic, which was not as bad as many of us said, but rather worse. By the doors on the way out a man turned to his wife and said, "Well, all I hope is that the dog has not been sick in the car."

Sheridan Morley, Radio Times 27 Jul 1985

I went to the theatre one night with Philip Page. We were not speaking to Hannen Swaffer at that time. I believe he was speaking to us, but we were not speaking to him. We sat through a dreadful farce until, when they brought a coffin on the stage, we heard Swaffer's voice behind us saying, "I wish to God I was in it." Then we spoke to him again.

James Agate, speech at a dinner celebrating Philip Page's silver jubilee as a dramatic critic, Oct 1938

Gertrude Stein had just been reading some poetry by Pablo Picasso. "I read his poems," she told us happily, "and then I seized him by the shoulders good and hard. 'Pablo,' I said, 'go home and paint.'"

Bennett Cerf, TRY AND STOP ME 1947

CYCLING

The retiring Professor of Modern History at Trinity College Dublin, Gordon Davies, a dogged chain-smoking Englishman, recently startled undergraduates by announcing he had just completed a round-Ireland bicycle tour. Students were surprised that he had broken the habit of a lifetime by stepping beyond the pale of Co. Dublin.

It then emerged that the Professor had completed the trip on a stationary exercise bike in his college room. He followed a route on Ordnance Survey maps, ordered the relevant provincial papers from his city-centre newsagent and even broke for lunch when a lay-by appeared on the map.

Daily Telegraph 25 *Jul* 1981

Princess Patricia of Connaught (afterwards Lady Patricia Ramsay) told me that when a Cyclist Corps was started at Aldershot the Duke of Connaught was made Commander-in-Chief. He therefore took lessons because he thought he ought to be able to ride a bicycle when he attended any parade of the new Corps. When he was asked to inspect them he was still very wobbly on his machine but he gallantly rode forth from Government House. On the road he met an orderly who was also a beginner. The orderly, in trying to salute, went end over end on the road, and the Duke, in attempting to return the salute, fell on top of him.

Sir Frederick Ponsonby, RECOLLECTIONS OF THREE REIGNS

DANCING

At the Bal Negre I [Margot Fonteyn] was entranced as I watched the black dancers. One of them invited me on to the floor. I thought it rude to refuse, and nervously stepped out trying to follow his rhythm and movement. He steered me once round the room, then returned me to my table saying, "You're an attractive girl. It's a shame you can't dance."

Margot Fonteyn, AUTOBIOGRAPHY 1974

One of our extra-curricular jobs, while touring with ENSA during World War II, was to go to dances. I have a fatal attraction for small men and in Dacca I had a tiny persistent partner with a grip of iron and a fine Palais de Danse style, who led me through some dashing routines involving spins and swoops and gave me a lot of enjoyable exercise. When the evening was over he took the black Tank Corps beret from under his shoulder strap, put it on the back of his head and saluted me. "Ta," he said, "I enjoyed it." Me too.

Joyce Grenfell, JOYCE GRENFELL REQUESTS THE PLEASURE 1976

See also **BALLET**

DEAFNESS

Queen Alexandra's deafness was a sad handicap. Often when she came into the room King Edward would pretend to be asleep rather than exhaust himself by trying to make her hear.

Georgina Bettiscombe, QUEEN ALEXANDRA 1969

Was Queen Alexandra's last splendid malapropism due to her deafness, or a deliberate leg-pull? "Did you know Ma'am, that His Majesty has a new car?" "A new cow?" "No Ma'am, a new *car.*" "Yes, yes, I heard you. I understand the old one has calved."

Ibid.

Prince Louis Esterhazy's castle was near a big ammunition factory which exploded during the Great War. All the windows in the castle were smashed. The detonations were terrific. The old gentleman, sitting in an armchair, became conscious of a noise and said, "Come in." He thought someone was knocking at the door, and was quite delighted that his hearing had improved.

Eugene de Horthy, THE SPORT OF A LIFETIME 1939

Grandfather bought a brand-new hearing-aid. "It's so small," he said, "nobody notices it." "That's great," I said, "how much did it cost?" "Half past four," he replied.

Frank Muir, FRANK MUIR GOES INTO – 1978

DEATH

I remember, in Middlesex Hospital, waiting guiltily for last words from Brendan Behan for a newspaper. "Brendan," I whispered, "do you ever think about death?" He sat up, like an enormous Pooh bear, in a sheet like a toga. "Think about death?" he shouted. "Bigod, I'd rather be dead than think about death."

Alan Brien, quoted E.H. Mikhail, BRENDAN BEHAN 1983

In 1915 a mosquito performed a tragic and historic act. Somewhere in the Middle East it alighted on the upper lip of a golden-haired naval sub-lieutenant, and bit it. The lip swelled. The temperature of the god-like young man rose to 106 degrees. As he died a shudder passed through the British at war.

"We shall not see his like again," cabled the First Lord of the Admiralty, Winston Churchill. "He was willing to die for the dear England whose beauty and majesty he knew," said *The Times*. "Oh God, Oh God!" cried D.H. Lawrence. Even at a time when young men were dying under German fire it was recognised that the mosquito's victim was someone very special indeed. He was Rupert Brooke, the poet.

Robert Pitman, Sunday Express 10 *May* 1964

A strange result of Caruso's death was that the following day another obituary notice appeared in the papers. Carl Numan of Copenhagen, it read, died an hour after he had eaten twenty-six hard-boiled eggs, a feat which he had undertaken to accomplish if the report of Caruso's death was confirmed.

John Fisher, Everybody's Weekly 3 *Sep* 1938

When I told Dorothy Parker – what she didn't know – that a former lover of hers had died, a young, good-looking and well-to-do fellow who had suffered from tuberculosis, she said crisply, "I don't see what else he could have done."

Edmund Wilson, THE TWENTIES 1975

DEBT

On her fifth birthday Princess Margaret captivated James Barrie, a guest at Glamis. "Is that your own?" he asked pointing to a present on her plate. She said, "It's yours and mine." Barrie was so pleased with this graceful response that he put it into his play *The Boy David,* promising her a penny for every performance of it. By the time it was staged two years later he had forgotten his debt, but the king had not, and sent a message that if Barrie did not at once pay his daughter her royalties, he would hear from the royal solicitors. A contrite Barrie drew up a mock solemn agreement engrossed on parchment; the last thing, as it happened, that he ever wrote. He died before the sack of pennies could be delivered, and his executors discharged the debt.

Kenneth Rose, KINGS, QUEENS AND COURTIERS 1985

When, early in his illness, Valentine Castlerosse was persuaded by his mother and sister to see a priest, he wrote out a telegram to the *Cork Examiner* saying, for print, that he had taken the Last Sacrament. To Lord Beaverbrook, who stopped the wire, he explained, "There were some big bills due on Monday. I wanted to stave off the creditors."

Hannen Swaffer, World's Press News 23 *Sep* 1943

DECEPTION

When Brendan Bracken became Minister of Information, a journalist told him, "I don't believe a word you say, Brendan. Everything about you is phoney. Even your hair, which looks like a wig, isn't."

Charles Edward Lysaght, BRENDAN BRACKEN 1979

We noticed that every time Richard Nixon received the customary ovation at some whistle stop he would turn and say something to the dignitary on his right which was always received with a look of fascinated incomprehension. By moving in very close with the microphone we discovered why that was; instead of saying, "Really this is too flattering, too kind–" Nixon was moving his lips and saying nothing at all. On film he looked modest and grateful, but in fact he was silent. It was very curious.

Gerald Priestland, SOMETHING UNDERSTOOD 1986

DENTIST

In British East Africa a bishop needed a set of false teeth. He consulted his dentist. "Are you sure," he asked, "that you can make some that won't hurt me?" "I'm positive," said the dentist. "Go ahead, make 'em."

A week later the bishop put the new teeth in his mouth and bellowed as loud as King Lear, "Christ!" he exclaimed. "Jesus!" The dentist's face grew red. "Why, Bishop," he said, "if they hurt as much as that, take them out and I'll fix them." The bishop looked at him in surprise. "The teeth are fine," he announced. "Frankly, this is the first time in years I've been able to say those beautiful words without whistling."

Donald MacGregor, Reader's Digest Nov 1940

DETERMINATION

Hammerstein was resolved to secure Melba for his new Manhattan Opera House. She refused the enormous fees he offered and on one occasion he scattered a bundle of thousand-franc notes all over the room. He pestered her for a month, even to the extent of battering on the door while she was bathing. He won after a good fight.

Percy Colson, MELBA 1932

DIARY

Princess Alexandra had been given a diary. When you are only five and you have a diary there is a great urge to write in it. There were no world-shattering events to record that day. So instead the little girl wrote down her judgment on the masculine section of the human race. She wrote, "*Boys are soppy.*"

Vera Connaught, THE SECRET HEART OF PRINCESS ALEXANDRA 1962

My last attempt to keep a diary – a failure – was when aged 11 I exchanged Charles Lett's School Boy's/Girl's diaries for Christmas with my cousin Angela. After I had completed the personal particulars – size of collar – size of boots – hobbies – I gave up. Angela persisted for one day. Her entry remains vividly in my memory. "Shopped in morning," it read. "Sick in afternoon."

Hugh Casson, DIARY 1 *Jan* 1980

Sam Goldwyn found on his office desk one morning a copy of *The Making of Yesterday. The Diaries of Raoul de Roussy de Sales 1938–1942* which someone had submitted as possible movie material. Goldwyn looked at the book in amazement. "How do you like that?" he said "Only four years old and the kid keeps a diary!"

Gerald F. Lieberman, THE GREATEST LAUGHS OF ALL TIME 1961

Elderly Mrs Janet Winn of Hallfield Estate, Paddington, opened her diary at lunch time and found an entry in an unknown hand. "House burgled at 5 a.m." A burglar had stolen £25 from her wallet while she slept.

The Times 30 *Jun* 1961

DICTATORSHIP

When my interview with Mussolini was over I sent it as usual to his office to be vetted. The only alteration he made to my manuscript was significant. Somewhere I had written, "The Duce's laughter encouraged me to ask another indiscreet question." The word "laughter" had been crossed out, and "cordiality" stood in its place. Apparently no dictator may laugh.

Vernon Bartlett, THIS IS MY LIFE 1937

DIET

Jean-Louis Barrault's principal companion in his early days was Etienne Decroux, the new apostle of the old art of mime, who taught him how to live creatively on a diet of one kipper, 125 grammes of raisins, one lettuce with lemon juice, and a cup of coffee. This cost them four or five francs a day except when, as a special treat, master and pupil would indulge in a plate of boiled semolina.

Observer, Profile 23 *Sep* 1951

General Wingate maintained that every man should be his own doctor. One of his theories about health in the tropics was that eating half a dozen raw onions a day was the best way to stay fit. Sometimes he ate nothing but onions and grapes for days at a time.

Catherine Caufield, THE EMPEROR OF AMERICA AND OTHER MAGNIFICENT ECCENTRICS 1981

See also **FOOD**

DIPLOMACY

In a debate on the Middle East question Warren Austin, US delegate to the United Nations, exhorted the warring Jews and Arabs to "sit down and settle their differences like Christians".

Clifton Fadiman, LITTLE, BROWN BOOK OF ANECDOTES 1985

A French diplomat about to take up a new ambassadorship visited President de Gaulle before leaving the country. "I am filled with joy at my appointment," he said enthusiastically. The President frowned. "You are a career diplomat," he said. "Joy is an inappropriate emotion in your profession."

Ibid.

During an interview with the Queen a British ambassador returning from the Middle East was struggling to explain the character of the head of government with whom he had to deal. He approached it from this angle and that angle, and roundabout, using increasingly long words with a psychological angle, until the sovereign extracted him from his misery. "Are you trying to tell me," asked Her Majesty, "that the man is just bonkers?"

Robert Lacey, MAJESTY 1977

When President Nixon suggested to Golda Meir that she might send some of her generals to Vietnam to help with the war she replied, "Certainly, if we can have a couple of yours in exchange." When asked which two she said, "General Motors and General Electric."

Meriel McCooly, Radio Times

"A little laughter," suggested an American reporter to a Russian delegate at the United Nations, "might clear the air a bit around here." "Clear air," replied the dour Russian, "would enable us only to see our troubles more clearly."

Bennett Cerf, SHAKE WELL BEFORE USING 1948

DISARMAMENT

In an Aberfoyle hotel, Tam Dalyell got into heated debate about disarmament with a Young Socialist. Several minutes after it had ended he suddenly lunged at the girl with a fork, stabbing her in the arm. She spun round, grabbed it, and hurled it across the room. "Aha," said the empiricist, "so you *do* believe in defence."

Observer, Profile 28 *Aug* 1984

DISCIPLINE

I had lunch with a young woman aged three. After a perfect dickens of a row she had been sent to bed supperless last night for obstreperous and obstinate naughtiness. This affair with its horrid sequel must have provided her with sensations quite novel in her experience of the world. Today she exhibited the manners of a Count D'Orsay, the sweetness of a Louise de la Vallière, and the reasonableness of a John Stuart Mill. And yet there are parents who maintain that the best way to teach righteousness to children is by example only, never by correction or deprivation.

Arnold Bennett, JOURNAL 1929

DIVORCE

Mr Bayford, one time leader of the Divorce Court, met a young man at dinner who said he wanted to divorce his recently married wife. Mr Bayford asked him for the whole story. "I'd rather not go into details. These things are very personal." "You'll have to face a court full of strangers and be cross-examined. Better tell it quietly to a friend who wants to help you."

"Well," said the young man in a burst of confidence, "the fact is my wife insists on going to bed in her gloves."

Mr Bayford said that no doubt it was very annoying, but the law stopped short at habit as grounds for divorce. Years later they met again and Mr Bayford learned that all was now well with the marriage. "Do you mind telling me how you arranged it?" Mr Bayford asked. "Not at all. I found out the answer after seeing you. That night I went to bed in my boots."

Major Hugh Hole, LOOKING LIFE OVER 1935

Dance band leader Harmon Nelson was today granted a divorce from blonde film star, Bette Davis. The suit was undefended. "She reads," Nelson told the court, "to an unnecessary degree. She refused to put down a book even when company was present. On innumerable occasions she absented herself from the room to pursue her everlasting reading."

News Chronicle 7 *Dec* 1938

DOCTOR

Noel Coward, on being asked for a urine sample by the doctor in attendance at the Savoy: "No, no, really out of the question. Quite impossible." Doctor: "Just a teaspoonful." Coward, as he shows his visitor to the door: "I'm sorry. I haven't a teaspoon."

Leonard Rossiter, THE LOWEST FORM OF WIT

Farve [Lord Redesdale] disliked doctors. When the infant Nancy [Mitford] developed a foot infection which required lancing he grudgingly agreed to call a doctor, but insisted on overseeing the operation. Nancy was allergic to the anaesthetic and at one point her breathing grew shallow and almost stopped. Years later, when someone asked Farve how he had reacted to this he said, "I seized the doctor by the neck and shook him like a rat."

Peter Bushell, GREAT ECCENTRICS 1984

Exhaustive tests on a man who had tried to push his wife out of a window showed what the wife had known all along. That he was a very nasty old man. She asked if I would kill him "because we'd all be better off without him, doctor". "I'm sorry," I said, "but this service is not available on the National Health." "Can't I go private then?" she asked.

Anthony Daniels, FOOL OR PHYSICIAN 1987

This lady in Los Angeles told her doctor that she was certain she had picked up a certain serious illness. He advised her not to be foolish, that she couldn't possibly know if she had it. The disease, said he, carried no discomfort with it. "But, doctor," she protested. "That's exactly how I feel."

Walter Davenport, Colliers Magazine 18 Jul 1953

A patient came to one of our field hospitals with the complaint that he was unable to sleep at night, and the doctor advised him to eat something before going to bed. "But, doctor," the patient reminded him, "two months ago you told me not to eat anything before going to bed." The doctor blinked and then with professional gravity replied, "My boy, that was two months ago. Science has made enormous strides since then."

Lt-General Vandergrift, Reader's Digest May 1945

DOG

Stanley Baldwin visited Stanstead and spoke at a great fête in our grounds in July 1935. When one of our dogs, whom he approached sympathetically, nipped his finger he said calmly: "I quite understand how you feel. I want to do that to every supplementary question in the House at this time of year." He then took an iodine pencil out of his pocket and painted the scratch.

Lord Butler, THE ART OF THE POSSIBLE 1971

The Hon. Mrs John Barran is one of the famous Ruthven twins and a daughter of Lord Ruthven. Her dachshund, Snoutie, follows the prevailing fashion of a single pearl earring and choker collar and manages to look most attractive in them.

The Sketch, quoted Michael Bateman, THIS ENGLAND

This evening I had agreed to take Anne to the Queen for a drink. In turn each of us was taken up to talk to the Queen. There were some half dozen Labour Cabinet Ministers, the Crossmans, the Gunters, the Greenwoods, the Cousinses and the Castles. In our ten minutes she talked, as I am told she always does, about her corgis. Two fat corgis, roughly the same colour as the carpet, were lying at her feet. She remarked how often people fell over the dogs. I asked what good they were and she said they were Welsh dogs used for rounding up cattle by biting their legs. So we talked about whether cattle stepped on them. I said Suki, our poodle, was much quicker at avoiding cows.

Richard Crossman, DIARY 11 *Nov* 1964

"It was a small dog." The speaker was a man whose job it was for 10 years to attend the Emperor Haile Selassie's receptions and when the dog (which was allowed to sleep on the Emperor's bed) peed on the shoes of visiting dignitaries, to go round wiping off the urine with a satin cloth.

Ryszard Kapuscinski, THE EMPEROR 1984

Dog lovers protested when President Lyndon Johnson appeared in a photograph lifting up his pet beagles by the ears. He claimed the dogs enjoyed it. "My mother used to pull my ears," he said, "and it never did get that much attention."

Daily Telegraph, Obituary 24 *Jan* 1973

The magician Lafayette bought a diamond collar for his dog Beauty. A special bathroom was built for the dog at this house in Torrington Square and at night time the animal was served with a regular *table d'hôte* meal, complete from soup to sweet. Beauty's portrait hung outside the house with the inscription beneath it, "The more I see of men, the more I love my dog."

Will Goldston, SENSATIONAL TALES OF MYSTERY MEN 1930

Working on the Londoner's Diary in the *Evening Standard*, Bruce Lockhart had a quick eye for pointers in the morning papers. As when he spotted in *The Times* Personal Column that a dog had been lost near Churt. Could it be Lloyd George's? A few telephone calls elicited that it was and Bruce, his eyes sparkling, led that day's Diary with the story of how this self-same terrier which had once disgraced itself by biting the Italian Prime Minister, Signor Orlando, during negotiations at Rapallo, was now at large in Surrey.

Malcolm Muggeridge, THE INFERNAL GROVE 1973

The poor dog had a distressing malady. Mrs Dorothy Parker issued bulletins about his health. Confidential bulletins, tinged with scepticism. "He *says* he got it from a lamp post."

Alexander Woollcott, WHILE ROME BURNS: OUR MRS PARKER 1935

How neurotic is your dog? Fritz, a German Schnauser puppy, got so neurotic he howled all night – until his West End owner hit on the idea of putting him to bed with an alarm clock. The reassuring tick tock, said to remind the puppy of his mother's heartbeat, now sends Fritz peacefully to sleep.

Peter Chambers, Daily Express 5 *Nov* 1963

A reader who took his dog to a training class in Marlow, Bucks, promises me that he heard the owner of a large Alsatian, who was fitting his beast with a muzzle, ask "And you wouldn't have to wear it, would you, if you hadn't bitten your teacher?"

Peterborough, Daily Telegraph 27 *July* 1985

A kindly lady entered a New York store and asked for instructions for making a dog's sweater. "How big is he?" the salesgirl asked. The woman started to make gestures. "Maybe you'd better bring him in," suggested the girl. "Oh no, I can't," the dog's mistress said. "It's to be a surprise."

New Yorker 1939

During the Thanksgiving cold spell in Bronxville a young couple taught their Scotch terrier to keep his balance and slide downhill on a metal tray. That's all there is to the story except that now, every time there is a fall of snow, the terrier gets out the tray and goes coasting by himself.

Ibid.

A distinguished Peeress of the Realm became infected with the dog-breeding fever and by dint of the expenditure of vast sums of money found herself leading the champion on to the platform to receive the highest accolades the doggy world had to offer. Unfortunately the beastly little animal snapped viciously at the judge as he bent over to bestow a congratulatory pat – so viciously in fact that the little brute's false teeth flew out, resulting in immediate disqualification.

Douglas Sutherland, THE ENGLISH GENTLEMAN'S WIFE 1979

DREAM

I was given an umbrella with a skeleton's head on it. This came back to me in dreams with terrific effect, and for several nights running I ran down from the top to the bottom of the house in terror. The umbrella was taken away.

Maurice Baring, THE PUPPET SHOW OF MEMORY 1922

R.D. Blumenfeld described to me a curious dream he had had. He found himself in a boat leaving Calais for Dover. As they got out of the harbour he looked over the side, and was shocked to see the coffin of Edward VII floating past. Odds and ends of ordinary debris followed. They sailed on and on, panic growing. Then a wireless message came through to say England had completely submerged.

Reginald Pound, THEIR MOODS AND MINE 1947

Old George Chitty [a master at Eton] once consulted C. Miller, the college doctor, about his "raves". CM told him to tell him a fortnight later about his dreams. GC told him he could remember but one, and he didn't think it would help. CM heard it and agreed. It was very short – merely that he dreamt that his cook had given birth to a zebra.

Rupert Hart-Davis, THE LYTTELTON HART-DAVIS LETTERS 1978

Salvadore Dali told us that the anarchists had burnt his house. His conversation had a disastrous effect on Diana Cooper's night. She dreamed of women with flies coming out of their nipples, and babies with piano instead of human legs.

Sir Henry Channon, DIARY 17 *Feb* 1938

I once took a trip to Spain with John Dos Passos. When we got to a town I'd go out to the square or somewhere to see if I could find a girl. Dos would never go with me – he'd say, "I'll just stay here in the hotel, I think." One day I said to him, "Dos, don't you ever think about women?" "No." "Don't you ever dream about sex?" "No." What I went through with that man! He'd wake me up in the night, groaning and throwing himself around in his sleep. I'd say, "What's the matter, Dos?" He'd say, "Why, I thought there were some beautiful wild swans flying overhead." One day I said, "You know sometimes sex appears in dreams in very much disguised forms. You may be dreaming about sex without knowing it. Tell me one of your dreams – what did you dream about last night, for example?" He said, "Why, I dreamed I had a bunch of asparagus, and I was trying to give it to you."

E.E. Cummings, quoted Edmund Wilson, THE TWENTIES 1975

I am one of those people given to dreaming about the Queen. In one, I remember, I was just getting on very well with the Queen, when Prince Charles came in, dressed in Boy Scout uniform.

Graham Greene in an interview with J.W. Lambert, Sunday Times 3 *Mar* 1978

The late Francis Hope's mother once had a dream about Richard Crossman. She was seated in a dentist's chair and he, attired in a white coat, was about to attend to her teeth.

"Don't be silly, Dick," she said. "You know you're not a dentist." "I know I'm not, you fool," Crossman replied, "but I can work it out quite easily from first principles."

Hugh Gaitskell, who was staying in the same house, and to whom this dream was related at breakfast, said it perfectly expressed the reason he would not give Crossman any post in a Government formed by him.

Alan Watkins, BRIEF LIVES 1982

I had a dream the other day about music critics. They were small and rodent-like, with padlocked ears, as if they had stepped out of a painting by Goya.

Igor Stravinsky, Evening Standard 29 *Oct* 1969

I would like to offer another remedy for "clogged feet" in dreams with me it always succeeds. Whenever I am overcome in this way I immediately unscrew my feet at the ankles, and hurry on without them. One must remember, however, that the left hand foot has a left hand thread.

H.R.F. Keating, letter to the Daily Telegraph, quoted Denys Parsons FUNNY HA HA, AND FUNNY PECULIAR 1965

DRESS

Queen Alexandra asked me why all the naval officers next to whom she sat on State occasions had such a peculiar smell. I explained it was due to their packing their full-dress uniforms with moth balls when not in use.

Admiral Sir Frederick William Fisher, NAVAL REMINISCENCES 1938

Anyone who did not take Hilaire Belloc for an undertaker would very naturally think of him as a priest. He turned up at his agent's dressed typically in a well-fitting black fustian suit, dripping with soup, dandruff, grease and fishbones, and bulging at the pockets with newspapers and a bottle of white port.

A.N. Wilson, HILAIRE BELLOC 1984

It has always been an endless worry to me whether I would ever have a whole garment and an unladdered pair of tights to wear. Poor old Ted pointed out to me at mid-week that his jacket was torn and that he had a missing button which he couldn't get sewn on. My riposte was to pull out my winter coat, whose lining is falling apart for want of a stitch, and tell him how embarrassed I was at functions when people insisted on helping me into it.

Barbara Castle, DIARIES 1974–76 1980

John Christie, founder of the Glyndebourne Festival Opera was something of a dandy, but certainly no slave of fashion. At one time he owned 180 handkerchiefs, 132 pairs of socks and 110 shirts; yet he often wore a pair of old tennis shoes with formal evening dress. For a time lederhosen were practically a uniform with him and in the summer of 1933 all visitors to Glyndebourne were expected to wear lederhosen or dirndls.

Catherine Caufield, THE EMPEROR OF THE UNITED STATES OF AMERICA AND OTHER MAGNIFICENT BRITISH ECCENTRICS 1981

Reporters would sometimes tease the energetic and hard-working American lawyer, Clarence Darrow, about his dishevelled appearance. Darrow retorted, "I go to a better tailor than any of you and pay more for my clothes. The only difference is you probably don't sleep in yours."

Edmund Fuller, ANECDOTES 1942

Both the Queen and Mrs Thatcher wore the same shade of blue at a banquet. Downing Street asked the Palace if it could be told in advance what the Queen intended to wear, thus avoiding the embarrassment of duplication. A brisk reply advised Mrs Thatcher not to concern herself as "the Queen does not notice what other people are wearing".

Leslie Cunliffe, GREAT ROYAL DISASTERS 1987

Ian Fleming had a dark blue suit which he would send back to his tailor so often that the man would talk about "fixing some new cloth to Mr Fleming's original buttons."

John Pearson, LIFE OF IAN FLEMING 1966

Gandhi was asked about the clothes he proposed to wear in London and he replied, "My loin-cloth is an organic evolution in my life. My duty, as I conceive it to be, is to add nothing to my loin-cloth that the climate peremptorily demands," and with a twinkle he pointed out, "In your country you wear plus fours. I prefer to wear minus fours."

Evening News 30 Jan 1948

I was to photograph Pope Benedict XV. The audience was for midday and when I turned up at eleven thirty I was told I must wear evening dress! I rushed out, burst into a cafe that I had passed on the way to the Vatican and, waving a hundred-lira banknote under the head waiter's nose, I induced him to allow me to undress the smallest waiter in the establishment. Within a few minutes I had changed into "formal" uniform though, unfortunately, even the smallest waiter at the cafe was several sizes bigger than myself. Then back to the Vatican as fast as my legs would carry me. I arrived at one minute to twelve.

Bert Garai, I GET MY PICTURE 1938

Mrs Horace Greeley, meeting Margaret Fuller in the street, noticed that she was wearing kid gloves. "Skin of a beast," she said, shuddering with distaste. "Why, what do you wear?" asked Margaret. "Silk," replied Mrs Greeley. Miss Fuller wrinkled her nose with equal distaste. "Entrails of a worm," she said.

Edmund Fuller, ANECDOTES 1942

James Mason cannot have much interest in clothes. A typical Mason ensemble is a brown suit, a white shirt with stiff cuffs that looks like a hangover from Gerry, Lord Manderstoke, a floppy collar, a blinding tie, socks that almost fall over cheap shoes, and cuff-links as large as half crowns, but more theatrical. "I looted them in Germany," he says.

Roland Wild, Illustrated 16 *Feb* 1946

See also **FASHION**

DRINK

When we left the Dublin hotel, the skies were overcast. Brendan Behan looked gloomy. He said "The bars here are shut from 2.30 to 3.30. We call it the Holy Hour. The politician that introduced it in the Dail was shot an hour afterwards."

Robert Pitman, Sunday Express 12 *Oct* 1958

Gordon Bennett, editor of the Paris edition of the *New York Herald*, had occasion to enter the room of his sports editor, Billy Bishop, when that worthy was surrounded by six empty glasses which had just been thrust through the partition. "Did you see that, Mitchell, what that man had drunk?" he said to his secretary afterwards. "And, Mitchell, did you notice he was still sober, could talk coherently, answer my questions quite rationally, indeed behave like a man who had had nothing to drink at all? A man like that is worth a lot of money to us. *Double his salary*."

Bernard Falk, HE LAUGHED IN FLEET STREET

I calculate that between Winston's 80th birthday on November 30th and the following April when he retired I had no less than eight gargantuan dinners with him alone; the dinners being followed by libations of brandy so ample that I felt it prudent on more than one occasion to tip the liquid into the side of my shoe.

Lord Butler, THE ART OF THE POSSIBLE 1971

"You'd like a little whisky?" R.A. Butler once remarked to a newspaper visitor. "My wife's not here and she says I mustn't make tea. I'm afraid I've never really got the hang of boiling a kettle."

Anthony Howard, RAB: THE LIFE OF R.A. BUTLER 1987

"I hate the taste of beer," Clemmie [Churchill] said. "So do most people, to begin with," Winston replied. "It is, however, a prejudice that many people have been able to overcome."

Lord Boothby, MY YESTERDAY, YOUR TOMORROW 1962

Anthony Eden told me about Tehran. Winston Churchill had had a late and rather boisterous night in Cairo, and when they arrived at the aerodrome early next morning he had lost his voice. "I feel very ill," he whispered to Anthony. They then got into the plane. Winston, not being able to talk, was absolutely miserable. Aching with self-pity, he drummed on the table. Then he called his servant. "I'm feeling very ill. I have lost my voice." "Would you like me to fetch you a cough lozenge, Prime Minister?" "No you bloody fool, a whisky and soda."

Harold Nicolson, DIARY 5 *Jul* 1944

A drunk shambled into a bar and bet the barman that he could tell the ingredients in any drink the barman cared to mix. The barman stooped behind the bar and emptied into one glass the remains of several drinks – a Martini, a Scotch and soda, brandy, a rum punch, and so on. The drunk sipped the drink and one after another correctly named the contents. He offered to do it again, and this time the barman filled the glass with water. The drunk tasted it, thought reflectively, tasted it again and then said, "I don't know what it is, but it won't sell."

Allan Michie, Reader's Digest Dec 1946

See also **INTOXICATION**

EARTHQUAKE

On the afternoon of 14 January 1907, in Kingston, Jamaica, an acquaintance had returned early from his office and was having a cup of coffee on his verandah at 2.30. Suddenly he saw the trees at the end of his garden rise up some eight feet. A quick brainwave suggested an earthquake, and half unconsciously he jumped from the verandah for all he was worth. As he alighted on the lawn his home crashed down behind him.

Lord Frederic Hamilton, HERE, THERE AND EVERYWHERE 1921

The 1907 earthquake in Kingston, Jamaica, was followed by further milder shocks. I was engaged in shaving early one morning in our little wooden house, when I felt myself pushed violently against the dressing table, almost removing my chin with the razor at the same time. I suspected my nephew of a practical joke and called out angrily to him. In an aggrieved voice he protested that he had not touched me but had himself been hurled by an unseen agency against the wardrobe. Then came a perfect cannonade of nuts from an overhanging tree on to the wooden roof of our temporary modest abode, and still we did not understand. I had at that time an English valet, the most stolid man I have ever come across. He entered the hut with a pair of brown shoes in one hand and a pair of white ones in the other. "There's been an earthquake so perhaps you would like to wear your brown shoes today instead of your white ones." By what process of reasoning he judged brown shoes more fitted to earthquake conditions than white ones, rather escaped me.

Ibid.

ECCENTRICITY

Not content with being called anaemic, Sarah Bernhardt painted her face chalk white. Not content with being told by doctors she had a very short time to live she made herself a coffin of rosewood with silver handles and had herself photographed in it with her eyes closed and with her hands crossed. It was her way of proving to Death that she could outstare him. She placed the coffin by the bed so that it would be the first thing to strike her eyes upon waking; and she had it carried along with her wherever she went. Often, she slept in it. When guests came, she served tea on it.

Henry and Dana Lee Thomas, LIVING BIOGRAPHIES OF FAMOUS WOMEN 1942

Ballet dancer Robert Helpmann had been invited to take tea with the eccentric Lord Berners and was shown into the drawing room of the peer's mansion near Oxford. Helpmann found him with a silver tea service and a horse. Lord Berners greeted Helpmann, asked him whether he took cream and sugar, and fed buttered scones to the horse. No explanation was offered, and after the animal had been told it had eaten enough it was led out through the French windows. Much later, Helpmann asked about the horse's presence. "I'm very nervous," Lord Berners explained. "When people see the horse they become as nervous as I am, so that after a while I get over it. Then we can have a normal conversation."

Elizabeth Salter, BIOGRAPHY OF SIR ROBERT HELPMANN 1978

Hurrying along a London street on his way to an important ceremony for which he was already late, G.K.Chesterton could not resist the temptation to stop for a glass of milk at a dairy he had often visited with his mother. From there he dived into a nearby gunsmith's, purchased a revolver and cartridges, then hastened on to the ceremony – his own wedding. Before he and his bride reached the Norfolk Broads later in the day to begin their honeymoon he had helped her to miss trains and lose luggage, and explained that the gun would be useful "to protect us from the pirates that doubtless infest the Broads".

News Review 5 *Nov* 1936

Childless, the G.K. Chestertons loved children. Hoping to have a baby of her own, Frances underwent an operation at a clinic. One day matron called a doctor to deal with Chesterton. "I found him sitting on the stairs," complained the doctor, "where he had been for two hours, greatly incommoding passers up and down and deaf to all requests to move on." The oblivious Chesterton was perfecting a sonnet to his wife.

Maisie Ward, G.K. CHESTERTON 1944

When John Christie had an attack of lumbago during the war he rode the train to London with a hot-water bottle tucked in against his side. As we left the train at Victoria he calmly reached into his clothes, removed the hot-water bottle, and before the startled gaze of our companions in the compartment, poured its contents on to the platform.

Rudolf Bing, 5000 NIGHTS AT THE OPERA 1972

One evening it was very hot in the theatre at Glyndebourne and John Christie, having walked over to the house during the first intermission, took scissors out of his pocket when he returned to his seat and to his wife's horror cut off at the elbows the sleeves of his full-dress jacket and shirt.

Ibid.

John Christie had injured an eye in a game when a boy, and as a man he had the eye removed surgically and a glass eye substituted. He told everyone about the glass eye, and indeed recommended the removal of an eye to one and all as a way to improve the health of the rest of the body. A mutual friend told me that when the Queen Mother came to visit Glyndebourne, Christie took his eye out to show it to her.

Ibid.

W.E. Hocking, professor of philosophy at Harvard from 1914 to 1943, took up painting, and his wife Agnes, ever the worshipper at his shrine, used to startle the students by creeping across the platform in front of the lectern where he stood speaking, doubled over in order not to interfere with his flow of words, with one of his paintings clasped to her bosom. Having reached the other side she would snatch up another painting in exchange, and noiselessly repeat the exhibition. No reference was made to this unusual phenomenon by Professor Hocking, who carried on the discussion of the evening as though it were the most natural happening in the world.

Marion Cannon, SCHLESINGER SNATCHED FROM OBLIVION 1979

Alfred Jarry, the French surrealist writer, demonstrated his eccentricity one day in a Paris restaurant. Wishing to communicate with a woman fellow diner who was engaged in staring contemplatively at her reflection in a mirror on the wall, Jarry drew out a pistol and shot at the mirror. In the stunned silence that followed Jarry repocketed the pistol and smiled engagingly. "Now that the mirror is gone," he said to the lady, "we can talk to each other."

Phyllis Meras, THE MERMAIDS OF CHENONCEAU 1983

Alfred Jarry once fired his pistol into a hedge. From behind it appeared a furious woman shouting, "My child is playing here. You might have killed him." "Madame, I would gladly have given you another," responded Jarry gallantly.

Ambroise Vollard, RECOLLECTIONS OF A PICTURE DEALER 1936

When one sat to Percy Wyndham Lewis in his enormous studio mice emerged from their holes and lolled against the furniture, staring in the most insolent way at the sitter. At last, when Tom Eliot was sitting to him, their behaviour became intolerable. They climbed on his knee and would sit staring up at his face. So Lewis bought a large gong which he placed near the mouse hole and when matters reached a certain limit he would strike this loudly and the mice would retreat.

Edith Sitwell, letter to Lady Snow (Pamela Hansford Johnson) 8 Jan 1959

When Amy Lowell's car broke down the garage mechanic refused to repair it until she had identified herself and could guarantee payment of the bill. Miss Lowell told the man that she was the sister of the President of Harvard, and suggested he call her brother. The mechanic duly telephoned Harvard. Abbott Lawrence Lowell asked, "What's she doing now?" "Sitting on a wall smoking a big cigar." "That's my sister all right."

Bennett Cerf, SHAKE WELL BEFORE USING 1948

My Uncle Albert [The Hon Albert Victor Lyttelton] was insatiably curious. When moving staircases came in he tried to stop one by holding on to one of the stationary knobs at the side. A moment later he picked himself up from the floor quite satisfied by the proof that he could *not* stop it. Then he tried (at about 60 odd) to go *up* the stairs that were coming *down* and after a minute or so on what must have been exactly like a treadmill, found out that that, too, wouldn't do.

George Lyttelton, THE LYTTELTON HART-DAVIS LETTERS 1978

I once had lunch with Groucho Marx, a big lunch with terrapin and pitchers of wine. When he got the bill he studied it like a bank examiner, added it up three or four times, then sprinkled it with sugar and ate it.

Gipsy Rose Lee, Reader's Digest May 1946

A story is told of Ralph Richardson approaching a man on a railway station and saying, "My dear Robertson! How you've changed! You look younger – your face is round, you've got good colour, you've shaved off your moustache – my, how you've changed." Bewildered, the man said, "But my name isn't Robertson." Ralph started back. "What? Changed your name, too?"

Donald Sinden, A TOUCH OF THE MEMOIRS 1982

Uncle William refused to change his watch from Calcutta time and lived for 30 years in a London hotel eating breakfast at dinner time.

Annabel Williams-Ellis, ALL STRACHEYS ARE COUSINS 1983

Two former members of the diplomatic service met in London. "What's Winthrop up to these days?" "Last thing I heard he had gone completely off his rocker and gone off into the jungle to live with a monkey." "Good Lord, fancy that. Was it a male monkey or a female monkey?" "Oh, female of course. There's nothing queer about Winthrop."

Frank Muir, FRANK MUIR GOES INTO – 1979

ECONOMICS

In his late twenties J.M. Keynes was travelling in Africa with a Cambridge friend, Walter John Sprott. At one point they had their shoes polished by native boys. The economist handed them a miserly tip. Sprott suggested a more generous handout, but Keynes firmly declined. "I will not be a party to debasing the currency."

Charles H. Hession, JOHN MAYNARD KEYNES 1944

There are plenty of people in Grantham who remember Alderman Roberts and his little daughter, Margaret Hilda, who used to help run his shop. One such person has just given me a reminiscence which explains a lot about the Prime Minister's economic policies. "We used to dread it when young Margaret was helping out and used to serve us. Whereas her father gave us five sweets for a penny, she would only sell us four."

Peter Hillmore, Observer 15 *Dec* 1985

EDUCATION

James Barrie came of a solemn community, in which scholarship was much more highly esteemed than original work. When he told a lady of his acquaintance that he meant to be an author she flung up her hands in horror and exclaimed, "And you an MA."

W.A. Darlington, Everybody's Weekly June 1943

Samuel Beckett once taught briefly at Cambell College in Belfast. When he was told he was teaching the cream of Ulster he replied, "Yes, rich and thick."

The Times, Diary 21 *Feb* 1948

Professor John Berdan read to an English composition class a particularly inept theme and, as usual, called for comments. The students panned it unmercifully. "Interesting," commented Berdan, "because I wrote it myself." As the critics began to blush he continued, "You are quite right. The theme is incredibly bad. I spent two hours of painstaking effort last night making sure I had not omitted a single feature of poor writing and I believe I succeeded." The professor paused for dramatic effect. "What astounds me," he resumed, "is how you fellows can dash these things off day after day in ten minutes."

B. Jay, Reader's Digest Jun 1942

Robert Birley, headmaster of Eton tells me that the council school boys sent to Eton get on perfectly. One of them, whose father is still a house painter, is Captain of his House. The difficulty, of course, is in the holidays.

Harold Nicolson, DIARY 20 *Oct* 1954

When you come to think of it, it really was extraordinary that during the Sicilian campaign I was doing the education bill. Churchill really looked rather surprised when I took education so willingly. "Would you not prefer something more *active*?" he said.

Lord Butler, quoted Ronald Butt, The Times 13 *Jul* 1971

Maurice Lane-Northcott says he was invited to a do-as-you-like school run by a well known experimentalist in education who told him he had written a list of "bad" words on the blackboard which the pupils, mixed, were warned not to use during holidays at home. The local parson called to complain of the children stealing the altar cloth to make a tent with. This was bad enough; when his eyes caught what was on the blackboard he flung up his hands in horror and fled.

Reginald Pound, POUND NOTES 1940

Interview in the afternoon at Hobart House. The colonel said, "We've got two jobs for you. I don't know which will appeal to you the more. You can be welfare officer in a camp in India." (I said that was not one I should choose). "Or, you can be assistant registrar at a hospital." I said if I had to have one or the other I would have the latter. Then he said, "By the way, are you educated? Were you at University?"

"Yes, Oxford."

"Well, they're very much in need of an educated officer at the War Office G3, Chemical Warfare."

"My education was classical and historical."

"Oh, that doesn't matter. All they want is *education.*"

Evelyn Waugh, DIARY 11 *May* 1944

In Salisbury, Wiltshire, about 60 years ago a child was sent home from school because of her "unwashed smell". Within minutes the unrepentant pupil was returned to the complaining teacher bearing a scrap of paper in her grubby hand which bore the words: "Learn her, don't smell her."

Peterborough, Daily Telegraph 4 *Mar* 1985

When Woodrow Wilson was president of Princeton University, his busy routine on opening day was suddenly disrupted by the appearance of an overdressed mother clutching her bewildered young freshman by the hand. Planting the boy firmly in one chair and herself in another the woman proceeded to cross-examine the president concerning the intellectual background, moral atmosphere and general standing of Princeton. She knew nothing of the place, she said, because her father and grandfather attended Harvard. Her husband, a Princeton alumnus, wanted their son to follow in his footsteps, but frankly she had her doubts.

"William being our only son, we want him to have the very best of everything," she continued. "We want him to be absolutely outstanding in all his endeavours. We want him to receive an education which will mould him for great things. Can you assure me that William will do well here?"

"Madam," Woodrow Wilson replied, "we guarantee satisfaction or we return the boy."

Calvin M. Floyd, Saturday Evening Post

See also **SCHOOL, SCHOOLMASTER**

EFFICIENCY

Lord Ashford, Chairman of the London Passenger Transport Board, noticed one morning that the lid of his desk inkstand rattled. It disturbed him. He told his secretary it had to stop. Early next morning before the trains were running on the Underground, a maintenance gang examined the rails running through St James's Park Station, over which his office stands. Finally they discovered a little bump on one of the rails. It was smoothed away, the inkstand stopped rattling, and the passengers had one less jolt that morning on their way to work.

Owen Blake, Sunday Referee 12 *Mar* 1939

Sam Goldwyn's secretary came to him and asked if she could destroy the files that were more than ten years old. "Yes," said Goldwyn, "but keep copies."

Howard Dietz, DANCING IN THE DARK 1974

When Sir Oswyn Murray became Secretary of the Admiralty he instituted a staff conference system that was intended to increase the efficiency of various branches. At first he had some difficullty in making his idea understood. At an early meeting the only idea forthcoming was that the Government should supply every clerk in that section with a fountain pen and "with an allowance for its upkeep".

Lady Murray, THE MAKING OF A CIVIL SERVANT 1940

ELECTION

Julian Amery who contested Preston North as a Tory at the last election knows the constituency backwards and accordingly visited the obscure Carmelite convent called Carmel in quiet Fulwood Row. Visitors are allowed only on special occasions but Amery was able to chat with the Mother Superior through a special grille. "I found her full of wisdom," he says.

This was one of the convent's few contacts with the outside world, as the nuns have no radio or television, and never see a newspaper. On the other hand they are allowed a postal vote, a right which they exercise.

Came polling night, and after recounts and trepidation Amery was re-elected by just 14 votes. Oddly enough there are just 14 nuns at Carmel and, to put it mildly, it seems likely that their 14 postal votes went to the only candidate that they knew existed.

Atticus, Sunday Times 1 *Mar* 1966

Lady Astor canvassing for her first parliamentary seat in Plymouth, because of her status, and because she was new to the town, was allotted a senior naval officer as a minder, and together they went round knocking on doors. "Is your mother at home?" asked Lady Astor imperiously when one door was opened by a small girl. "No," replied the child, "but she said if a lady comes with a sailor they're to use the upstairs room and leave ten bob."

Sue Arnold, Observer Magazine 16 *Jun* 1985

Hilaire Belloc's passionate convictions prompted him in 1906 to seek election as an MP although he knew that, as a Roman Catholic, he would have to struggle to overcome the voters' religious prejudices. At his first campaign speech in Salford he appeared on the platform with a rosary in his hand and made the following declaration: "I am a Catholic. As far as possible I go to Mass every day. As far as possible I kneel down and tell these beads every day. If you reject me on account of my religion I shall thank God for sparing me the indignity of being your representative." He was elected.

Robert Hendrickson, THE LITERARY LIFE 1981

At an election meeting when I was Liberal candidate for Leicester I was handed a slip of paper on which was written, "Is the candidate in favour of Dwarf Battleships?"

The rule is, when understanding nothing about something, to talk at length about something you do know something about. So I prepared to launch forth on a general exposition of naval policy. Luckily I caught the agonised eye of my faithful and extraordinarily efficient election agent, who had hastily scribbled something on a piece of paper. Contriving to get it into my hands while delivering a harmless exordium, I opened it and saw, "It's a kind of potato." I rapidly, and I trust dexterously, revised my already issuing remarks.

Eliot Crawshaw-Williams, SIMPLE STORY 1935

When Andrew Faulds fought his election battle at Smethwick he knew the National Front would start a heckling campaign, so he decided to hit out hard at their first appearance. When heckling began at a meeting he paused, and said to the audience gravely, "I'm afraid I may have to tell you something about these gentlemen's personal problems." Then, leaning towards a National Fronter he boomed at him, "I think your relations with your girl-friend are not all they might be."

Norman Moss, Observer Magazine 3 *Apr* 1977

When Adlai Stevenson was standing for the presidency against Eisenhower a woman supporter said, "Every thinking person will be voting for you." Stevenson replied, "Madam, that is not enough. I need a majority."

Philip Howard, The Times 9 *Mar* 1987

EMBARRASSMENT

I played at the Duke of Windsor's birthday party soon after he abdicated. I was so worried that playing for him there might upset the King and Queen that I threatened to fire any member of my band who didn't keep it secret. Then, a few nights later, the King and Queen were dancing when I was playing. As they passed me the King stopped and said, "Mr Ambrose, did you fly to France or go by train?"

I didn't know what to say.

Bert Ambrose, Sunday Express 28 *May* 1961

When my first film *In Which We Serve* was shown in Leicester, the cinema, as a tribute to a local lad, gave me star billing. "Is he a relative of yours?" a schoolmate asked my brother David. He was deeply embarrassed. "Only distant," said David.

Richard Attenborough, Sunday Telegraph 15 *Aug* 1965

Tallulah Bankhead was sure to be included in any list of party-goers, and was almost sure to have said the one quotable thing, as when she inquired of a peer staring blankly at her, "What's the matter, darling? Don't you recognise me with my clothes on?"

Brendan Gill, TALLULAH 1973

When Tony Benn first took a ride in his official car he sat on the floor; the point being not only that he didn't like the trappings of office, but that he didn't want to be seen enjoying them.

Ivan Yates, Observer 1969

When we were in St Louis they gave a splendid party for me and there were a lot of pretty women there, one in particular – dark if I remember right. I was engaged in bidding her a rather affectionate farewell in the ladies' cloakroom when her husband came in. You may imagine in what an awkward situation I found myself. I had to think, and I had to think quickly. I turned to him and said, "Sir, you have surely failed to observe that this is the ladies' cloakroom." He turned and went out.

Lord Birkenhead, quoted Randolph Churchill, TWENTY-ONE 1964

Every day Father Hack's portly figure could be seen walking down Oxford's Cornmarket with a pile of books under his arm. One day, on a bus, a woman dropped a handkerchief into his lap. She was too embarrassed to retrieve it, but Hack could see her looking at something; to her horror he firmly tucked it inside his trousers as he thought it was his shirt hanging out.

Colin Stephenson, MERRILY ON HIGH 1965

At the beginning of the war the monks of Nashdom were evacuated to the Girl's School at Laleham, and I went over to see my cousin there. The discomfort was more than their rule required, for the rooms had been built for very small girls and the beds were to scale. Here all the rooms had been named after flowers and at night there was some activity as members of the Community crept round transferring the card reading "Pansy" to someone else's door.

Colin Stephenson, MERRILY ON HIGH 1965

That worthy Labour Cabinet Minister, the late Jimmy Thomas, found himself seated at an official dinner next to the Chinese Ambassador, Mr Wellington Koo, surely one of the most charming emissaries at the Court of St James. When the nauseating traditional turtle soup was served Jimmy Thomas turned to Wellington Koo and enquired, "Likee soupee?" Having received a polite acknowledgement, he felt that he had discharged his conversational duties and relapsed into silence for the rest of the meal. Mr Koo who, if I remembered rightly had been educated at Eton and Balliol, was later called upon to make a speech and did so in the most impeccable unaccented voice. As he sat down to well-earned applause he turned and asked smilingly, "Likee speechee?"

Douglas Sutherland, THE ENGLISH GENTLEMAN'S CHILD 1979

EMOTION

The indignation of the Italians over the denial of their claims upon the Adriatic coast at the Paris Peace Conference in 1919 caused the temporary return of Signor Orlando to Rome. The departure was the occasion of a considerable display of the Latin temperament. On the evening that it was to take place Balfour rose from the dinner table in his own flat in the Rue Nitot saying, "I must go now and put on my wading boots." His companions looked at him, startled. Was the strain of the Allied disagreements proving too much for him also? His next words reassured them. "To say goodbye to Orlando," he explained. "He was in tears when I left him, and I have no reason to suppose that he has stopped crying since."

Blanche E.C. Dugdale, LIFE OF LORD BALFOUR 1936

Noel Coward and Ivor Novello were watching a newsreel together in the Tivoli cinema when Chamberlain came on the screen delivering his "Peace in our time" speech. Coward was incensed, but Novello burst into tears of relief, weeping uncontrollably. "Stop it!" yelled Coward "Stop that immediately," and hit him.

John Heilpern, Observer 14 *Dec* 1969

The night Alexander Woollcott saw Thornton Wilder's moving play *Our Town* the producers found him seated on a fire escape in the theatre alley, sobbing. "Pardon me, Mr Woollcott," one of them said, "will you endorse our play?" Woollcott rose to his feet. "Certainly not," he blubbered. "It doesn't need it. I'd as soon think of endorsing the Twenty-Third Psalm."

Samuel Hopkins Adams, THE WORLD OF A. WOOLLCOTT 1943

ENERGY

Lady Astor's energy was extraordinary. After a long day in London in the House she would return to Clivedon about seven, change into tennis clothes and play two, or even three, sets of singles with one of her nieces, then down to the river (before the war) in her cream-coloured car, driven at speed; she would swim across the Thames, talking all the time about God, or advising someone on the bank how to live his, or usually her, life, touch bottom on the far bank, tell the swans to go away, and swim back, still talking.

The Times, Obituary 4 May 1954

ENTERPRISE

Richard Attenborough's first venture into actor-management was at the age of 12 when he put on a show at St Barnabas Hall in Leicester. To raise ten shillings for the hire fee he bought dozens of little notepads for a penny each, the same number of pencils for even less, tied the two together with coloured string and sold the package to his school friends for threepence.

Peter Waymark, The Times 22 *Nov* 1982

In Jeffrey Archer's Oxford days his most publicised coup was getting the Beatles for an Oxfam concert and arranging their dinner with Macmillan. During the visit Jonathan Aitken found himself standing next to Ringo Starr. "That guy," said Starr, "he'd bottle your pee and sell it for £5."

Observer Profile 25 *Jul* 1987

Hilaire Belloc failed to turn up when his friend G.K. Chesterton was received into the Roman Catholic Church. He did, on the other hand, attend the requiem for Chesterton in Westminster Cathedral and in the course of the Mass he managed to sell his exclusive obituary of his friend to four different editors.

John Gross, Observer, reviewing A.N. Wilson HILAIRE BELLOC 22 *Apr* 1984

I set up my first stall at a one-day fair at Axbridge, Somerest. It was a hoop-la stall. I had built the stall myself and by fairground standards I hadn't been very clever at the job. My pegs were small and my rings were generously large. My stock of prizes went rapidly and the quicker they went the bigger grew the crowd round my stall. My fairground colleagues thought I was heading for ruin when they saw my stall cleared of prizes by nightfall.

But it didn't work out that way. I had spent £10 on prizes but I had taken £15. Some of the other stall holders had lost hardly any prizes but they had taken only £3. They had the job of packing up their prizes and carting them to the next fairground. There they would use paint and a lot of time making those battered prizes attractive again. But I would buy new stock and attract more customers. Three years later I had a dozen men working for me.

Billy Butlin, Sunday Chronicle 31 *Mar* 1946

While in exile King Carol of Rumania told Sir Robert Bruce-Lockhart that during his reign he had selected fourteen of the brightest Rumanians for special training in the government service. He sent seven to England and seven to the United States to study their political and economic systems. "The seven who went to England were very smart – they all achieved great success in the government in Bucharest," said Carol. "What about the seven you sent to the United States?" asked Lockhart. "They were even smarter," said the King. "They stayed there."

Jacob M. Braude, SPEAKER'S AND TOASTMASTER'S HANDBOOK 1971

Walt Disney made his first little nest-egg as an 18-year-old ambulance driver in France in 1919, shortly after the Armistice. Together with a Southern con-man he transformed brand new German military head-gear into "sniper's helmets", by adding fake bullet holes, mud, blood and hair, to be sold as souvenirs.

Leonard Mosley, THE REAL WALT DISNEY 1986

On the night of the Tunney-Heeney boxing match I saw, from my New York hotel, dashing up Fifth Avenue, a procession consisting of a squad of cops on their motorcycles, behind them two ambulances, then another squad of cops, and behind them two police cars. Next morning at the press agency I was told: "We hired those ambulances as travelling developing rooms, and the escort of police was all part of the show to get a clear way through the traffic. We had the whole outfit outside the fight enclosure, and as the pictures were taken they were rushed to the waiting cars. We had a bunch of fellows in their shirt-sleeves waiting in the ambulances and when the final pictures were got on board the whole fleet, speed-cops leading, stepped on the gas and beat it down-town like bats out of hell.

David Ellbey, SHOOTING THE BULL 1935

I went to America in 1914 and got myself a job with a small picture agency. At first my work consisted in translating the scanty information provided with their photographs by the French and German agencies, but I soon evolved a theory that the value of a thing depends on what you call it and I began to exercise my imagination. For instance, if a photograph representing a couple of British soldiers in a field bore the title, "British soldiers at the front", I changed it to "British soldiers preparing to go over the top" and if there happened to be a smudge in one corner I added something about a shell exploding in the distance. As a result of my activities in this direction our pictures began to fetch better prices.

Bert Garai, I GET MY PICTURES 1938

An American wrote to Rudyard Kipling, "I hear you are retailing literature for a dollar a word. I enclose a dollar for which please send me a sample." Keeping the dollar, Kipling wrote, 'Thanks.' Shortly afterwards he received another letter, "Sold the 'Thanks' anecdote for two dollars. Enclosed please find 45 cents in stamps, being half the profit on the transaction, less postage."

Edmund Fuller, ANECDOTES 1942

In April 1968, learning that London Bridge was to be demolished, Mr Robert McCulloch bought it, sight unseen, for a million dollars and had the dismantled structure shipped to Lake Havaso City, Arizona. Mr McCulloch expected the sight of the old-world landmark to become a tourist draw. Only when several thousand tons of stonework had arrived in Arizona and had been erected in the desert did Mr McCulloch realise that London Bridge was not Tower Bridge.

David Frost, THE WORLD'S WORST DISASTERS 1983

When Lytton Strachey was in Rome, Princess San Faustino entertained him to luncheon and treated him and other guests to a long explanation of a scheme she had recently thought of to aid the unemployed. It was all dependent on growing the soya bean. Factories and synthetic chocolates and motor-cars and building materials and bath salts, all were to be made out of this magic substance. She worked the whole idea up to an enthusiastic but boring climax, when she turned to the guest of honour and appealed to him. "Mr Strachey, what do you think of my scheme?" He replied in his highest and most discouraging key, "I'm afraid *I don't like beans*."

Osbert Sitwell, LAUGHTER IN THE NEXT ROOM 1949

Dennis van Thal wanted to work in the theatre and obtained an interview with André Charlot, the famous impresario whose productions inspired even C.B. Cochran. "Mr Charlot," said Dennis, "I want to conduct a revue." "Can you?" asked Charlot. "I can." "Prove it." So Dennis then assembled an amateur band of ten instruments – 2 violins, 1 cello, 1 double bass, 1 pianist, 2 saxophones (doubling clarinets), 1 trumpet, 1 trombone, 1 drummer. He rehearsed the band, hired a hall, and invited Charlot, who arrived on the dot. They played a bit from the overture to *The Barber of Seville*, two fox-trots and a thing called *Nola*. At four o'clock that afternoon Charlot gave Dennis a contract to conduct *Hi-Diddle-Diddle* on its provincial tour and then in London.

James Harding, AGATE: A BIOGRAPHY 1986

Millet's *Angelus* during its sojourn in America was reproduced in a cheap print which sold very slowly until an astute publisher hit upon the notion of changing the title to *Burying the Baby*.

Thomas Bodkin, THE APPROACH TO PAINTING 1927

Hong Kong's efforts to stem illegal immigration from China have revealed a curious new trade which has developed in the past six months: the sale of tiger's dung. This, it seems, has become a successful dog-repellent, the smell of which can be used to scare away bloodhounds used by the Chinese army units to track and pursue fugitives. Cantonese security authorities recently arrested some young men caught scraping the cages of tigers in Canton zoo. Inquiries then uncovered the business. Prices reputedly range from the equivalent of £4 to £8 a basket.

Richard Hughes, The Times 28 *Oct* 1980

A fine example of Japanese enterprise is quoted in the Anglo-Japanese Economic Institute's latest bulletin. A fish-bait firm is to rent a million worms to a pollution control company which will use them to eat sludge collected from Tokyo paper mills. The resulting worm casts will then be sold as fertilizer.

Peterborough, Daily Telegraph 15 *Oct* 1976

A man wrote to a toothpaste company saying he had an idea which would increase their sales by twenty per cent, and asking for £1000 for the idea. After a lot of haggling the company paid up. The idea was to increase the size of the hole at the end of the toothpaste tube by twenty per cent. It worked.

Richard Askwith, Sunday Telegraph Magazine 27 *Sep* 1987

EPITAPH

I was taking my daughter Jan, age six, through the local graveyard. At a tombstone which carried an epitaph ending with the words, "Well done", she asked, "Does that mean he was cremated?"

Michael Aspel, CHILD'S PLAY 1985

H.L. Mencken, the American editor, coined his own epitaph which was engraved on a plaque in the lobby of the *Baltimore Sun* building. "If after I depart this vale you ever remember me and have thought to please my ghost, forgive some sinner, and wink your eye at some comely girl."

Clifton Fadiman, LITTLE, BROWN BOOK OF ANECDOTES 1985

In the churchyard at Ayot St Lawrence there is a tomb bearing the inscription "Jane Evesley. Born 1815 – Died 1895. Her time was short." Bernard Shaw felt that a place where the inhabitants who died at eighty were considered short-lived was the climate for him.

Hesketh Pearson, BERNARD SHAW 1942

ESCAPE

In World War II Josephine Baker joined the French Resistance. Her marriage to a Jewish businessman, Jean Leon, brought her to the notice of Goering and the Gestapo who decided to murder her. Goering invited her to dinner, having arranged to poison her fish course. Forewarned, Josephine excused herself as the fish course arrived, planning to drop down the laundry chute in the bathroom to a rendezvous with Resistance workers below. Goering produced his gun and ordered her to eat the fish before allowing her to retire to the bathroom. She managed to reach the chute, slid down, and her colleagues rushed her to a doctor who pumped her stomach. After a month she recovered but lost all her hair, and always wore a wig thereafter.

Irving Wallace, INTIMATE SEX LIFE OF FAMOUS PEOPLE 1981

Oliver Gogarthy was captured by his enemies on 8 January 1923 and imprisoned in a deserted house on the edge of the Liffey with every prospect of death. Pleading a natural necessity he got into the garden, plunged under a shower of revolver bullets and, as he swam the ice-cold December stream, promised it, should it land him in safety, two swans. I was present when he fulfilled that vow.

W.B. Yeats, Introduction OXFORD BOOK OF MODERN VERSE 1936

In Sofia I was asked by the politician Dimitrov to go with him to his country home for some fishing. Almost persuaded by his insistence I put my foot on the running-board of his car. Then I drew back, prompted by some force that gave me the resolution to say firmly, "Thank you very much, your Excellency. I really must stay in Sofia."

Fifteen kilometres away from the town Dimitrov's car was ambushed, the three Ministers, the ADC and the driver were riddled with bullets."

George A. Hill, DREADED HOUR 1936

A Czechoslovak family made a spectacular escape across the Austrian border on Wednesday night in a homemade hot air balloon. Robert Hutrya, aged 38, engineer and spare-time racing cyclist, flew his wife and two children over the border in a balloon strung together from old raincoats and propelled by domestic propane gas. Czechoslovak border guards spotted the balloon and fired flare rockets to light up the sky but were unable to halt its 50-minutes flight.

The Times 9 *Sep* 1983

The most original escape attempt from prison camp PGZ at Cheiti was made by someone who managed to lower himself into the town sewers and paddle along them on an air bed. Unfortunately they were full of inflammable gas and he blew himself up while lighting his pipe and had to be given hospital treatment before serving a sentence in solitary confinement.

Eric Newby, A TRAVELLER'S LIFE 1982

I am lucky to be alive. Before I was a year old a telegram was sent to my father saying, "Dreadful news. Stella dead." I was placed in a coffin and the lid screwed down. As father was carrying it down to the hearse he dropped it on the landing. From the coffin came a muffled cry and the lid was torn off amid exclamations about catalepsy and God's mercy.

Marchesa Stella Vitelleschi, OUT OF MY COFFIN 1937

Attempting a daring escape from a gaol in Sydney, Australia, a prisoner climbed underneath the bonnet of a lorry. At the lorry's next stop he climbed out and found himself in the yard of another prison, five miles from the first.

Reader's Digest Jul 1980

Two Scots, taken prisoner when France fell, escaped and made their way towards the Spanish border. They were about to row across a river when two Germans stopped them. They thought their number was up, but stalled in broken French and finally found that the Germans only wanted to cross, too. "So we paddled them across", said one of the Scots later, "and charged them five francs each."

John T. Whitaker, WE CANNOT ESCAPE HISTORY 1943

ESPIONAGE

The story of Sir Robert Baden-Powell's exploits as a spy may never be fully told. He went on a sketching holiday in the Austrian alps as mountain warfare troops tested their equipment, and was given breakfast by unsuspecting Austrian staff officers. In the evening he taught them how to do the hula-hula.

Jack Cox, Radio Times 22 Feb 1957

Disguised as the nephew of the skipper, Sir Robert Baden-Powell went to the Dardanelles in a grain ship and arranged for the engines to break down near the vital defences. While they were being "repaired" he went "fishing" in a small boat and learned all he needed to know.

Ibid.

The greatest achievement of "Room 40" during World War I was to decode a message from an ordinary comb entwined with sewing cotton. A brainwave of Sir Alfred Ewing's suggested that each space between the teeth represented a letter, so by unwinding the thread and following its course tooth by tooth a message was deciphered which led to the discovery of a nest of naval spies.

James Fairlie, Sunday Express 6 Jan 1935

My tour of instruction ended in a short course on invisible inks and their use. When all else failed, what my instructor referred to primly as BS, meaning bird shit, could be used and worked well, but procuring a supply was not so easy as might be supposed. For instance, my instructor once had to fall back on it when he was stationed at The Hague, and had imagined that crumbs spread out on a little balcony would bring a goodly number of sparrows along that might be relied on to leave behind a supply of BS. Not so; the birds duly arrived and ate the crumbs, but whether they were constipated, or out of delicacy, they left no droppings. In the end, he explained to me, he had to take a walk in a public park – which, fortunately, was spacious – and when he saw traces of BS he dropped his handkerchief as though by chance, and scraped the BS up. His dolefulness become almost unbearable as I pictured him walking mournfully about questing for BS and I tried to cheer him up by expressing unbounded admiration for the brilliant stratagem he had devised.

Malcom Muggeridge, THE INFERNAL GROVE 1973

The Germans, in their literal way, took P.G. Wodehouse's works as a guide to English manners and actually dropped an agent in the Fen country wearing spats. This unaccustomed article of attire led to his speedy apprehension. Had he not been caught he would, presumably, have gone to London in search of the Drones Club, and have thought to escape notice in restaurants by throwing bread about, like Bertie.

Malcolm Muggeridge, TREAD SOFTLY FOR YOU TREAD ON MY JOKES 1968

ETIQUETTE

While travelling in India in 1921 Georges Clemenceau was to meet a ruling prince, and the prince was quite perplexed over the etiquette of meeting. Who was to be the first caller? He had his dignity to think of, but then Clemenceau was a very great man. Well, neither should call on the other: both should come from the place where they were staying to a certain house. But then, in what part of the house should they meet? When these questions were propounded to the Tiger he growled, "Let him come how and where he likes. He can walk on the ceiling like a fly if he wants. I don't care a button. It is ridiculous to bother about such things."

Children's Newspaper 14 *Feb* 1929

Tony Snowdon was having a mild argument with his wife, Princess Margaret, and, having lit a cigarette, flicked the match towards an ash-tray and it fell into Princess Margaret's brocaded lap. HRH brushed it off quickly and, rather annoyed, said, "Really, Tony, you might have burned my dress," to which came the reply, "I don't care. I never did like that material." The princess drew herself up and said very grandly, "Material is a word we do not use."

I admit to having told this story several times, and it always arouses a storm-in-a-cocktail-glass of discussion. What other word? Stuff, perhaps?

Peter Coats, OF KINGS AND CABBAGES 1984

A lady received a card of invitation to a dance at Buckingham Palace and duly attended without having answered the invitation in writing. Happening to find herself next to the equerry who had issued the invitation she said, "I must apologise for not writing to accept your invitation. It was very remiss of me." "It's quite all right," replied the equerry. "There is no need to apologise. It's entirely our fault for having invited you."

Kenneth Edwards, I WISH I'D SAID THAT 1976

For one guest inside the Castle at the investiture tomorrow, a problem of dress has arisen. Most people will be wearing morning dress but he still has an arm in a sling after breaking it six weeks ago. He asked a functionary of a famous firm of outfitters what sort of sling he should wear. The answer came unhesitatingly. "Black silk, sir."

Peterborough, Daily Telegraph 30 *Jun* 1969

When a girl lit up a cigarette after the soup her hostess said icily, "We seem to have finished," and led the entire party from the room. That was the end of the dinner.

Katherine Whitehorn, Observer 27 *Aug* 1980

EUPHEMISM

A South African lady, an ATS officer, visiting Petworth House, expressed her simple needs to me by asking, "Where does one go to speak to the fairies?" I not unnaturally suggested, "The bottom of the garden," but the lady was affronted.

Lord Egremont, WYNDHAM AND CHILDREN FIRST 1968

EXAMINATION

Running short of time towards the end of an examination my sister came to the question, "Should there be limits to curiosity?" She thought for a moment then wrote, "Why ask?" She passed.

Andrew Briggs, Reader's Digest Feb 1978

When I was examining for Allahabad University I noticed that a European candidate frequently took what appeared to be notes from his pocket and, after a hurried glance, proceeded to write furiously. I had him brought up to my desk and told him that he had been seen to take notes from his pocket and each time he commenced to write rapidly. He then produced, not notes, but a photograph of his best girl.

E.J. O'Meara, I'D LIVE IT AGAIN 1935

At Radcliffe Gertrude Stein was a favourite pupil of Henry James. Confronted with an exam paper the day after a session of opera-going and parties, she wrote on her paper, "Dear Professor James, I am sorry but I do not feel like writing an examination paper on philosophy today." James wrote back, "Dear Miss Stein, I understand perfectly. I often feel like that myself."

L. Lucaire, CELEBRITY TRIVIA

EXCUSE

After Kingsley Amis sold his house in Hampstead for £250,000, the story goes, one of the walls fell down. "It was being shored up by all my books," Amis explained to the displeased purchaser.

Observer, Profile 26 *Oct* 1986

In 1904 I became my father's housekeeper. An Armenian named Ohannes was our cook, a very tiresome person. My father frequently gave him notice but he refused to go. I once found a crowd looking into our area where Ohannes was chasing the butler with a large saucepan, filled with hot potatoes. Finally my father said, "We must shut up the house in order to get rid of Ohannes. We will go to China."

We dismissed the household and installed a policeman and his wife as caretakers.

On the day of departure I waited for my father in a four-wheel cab piled with luggage. He walked slowly to the cab, put his head through the window and said, "It is raining my dear. We won't go."

And we never did.

Mrs J.D. Bailey, The Times 26 *Jul* 1963

When I was at boarding school I desperately needed a day off to finish an essay. So I wrote a note to my "house mother" that I was suffering from a severe attack of ergasiophobia. It usually passed with a day of rest, my note said, so I'd confine myself to my room and would she please inform my teachers that I was indisposed. She did so and no one broke into my room to drag me off to classes. It was late afternoon and my essay was finished by the time she submitted my note to the school doctor who must have smiled when he told her that ergasiophobia meant "a morbid aversion to any work".

James C. Humes, HOW TO GET INVITED TO THE WHITE HOUSE 1977

Ring Lardner was asked to speak at a banquet. He sent the chairman a telegram which was read out at the dinner. "Regret extremely my inability to attend your banquet. It is the baby's night out, and I must stay at home with the nurse."

Frank Crowninshield, Vogue 15 *Mar* 1942

On the training ship *Medusa*, in order to emphasise the difference between *meum* and *tuum*, orders were given that whenever a boy found anything lying about he was to take it immediately to the master-at-arms. One day I caught one of the boys with a lighted cigarette in his hand. I asked him why he was disobeying the regulations, which forbade the boys to smoke. He replied, "Please sir, I found this lighted cigarette lying about, and I'm taking it to the master-at-arms."

I was so touched by his ingenuity that I took no further action in the matter.

Vice-Admiral Humphrey Hugh Smith, AN ADMIRAL NEVER FORGETS 1938

Caspar Weinberger, the American defence secretary, had a ready answer to a question at yesterday's briefing on the NATO nuclear planning group meeting in Luxembourg. Asked why the Americans had asked the Australians and not New Zealand to participate in the research programme for a strategic defence system Weinberger said: "We didn't have the address."

Daily Telegraph 28 *Mar* 1985

When police came across unemployed Thomas O'Grady in a Cliftonville bank late one October night they asked him what he was doing and he replied, "I've come about my overdraft."

East Kent News, quoted Punch 8 *Jan* 1978

Billy Wilder, visiting Paris just after World War II was asked by his wife to send her a bidet. Unsuccessful, he sent her a telegram. "Unable obtain bidet. Suggest headstand in shower."

Leslie Halliwell, THE FILMGOER'S BOOK OF QUOTES 1973

A matronly chairperson announced – with no apparent irony – to a women's club in Exeter the other evening, "The report of our Committee on Solving World Problems will have to be delayed because three of our four members have not been able to get baby-sitters."

The Times Diary 5 *Jan* 1987

EXECUTION

When I was writing *In Cold Blood* I was present at the trial, I talked to the prisoners, they wrote to me from their death cells (there were four people in those death cells and between them they had killed fourteen people) and I was present when they were hanged – together. Just before the ropes were put round their necks one of them asked if he could speak to me privately. They said yes, and he just came across and kissed me and said, "Adios, amigo" and walked back.

Truman Capote, quoted J.W. Lambert, Sunday Times 8 *Aug* 1965

Through the half-open door in one room of the huts I saw Pastor Bonhoeffer kneeling on the floor, praying fervently to his God. I was most deeply moved by the way this lovable man prayed, so devout and so certain that God heard his prayer. At the place of execution he again said a short prayer, and then climbed the steps to the gallows, brave and composed. In the almost fifty years I have worked as a doctor I have hardly ever seen a man die so submissive to the will of God.

The doctor at Flessenburg Prison Camp

EXERCISE

A beautiful singer was asked to give the secret of her slim figure. "Confetti," she replied. Asked to explain, she said, "Every morning for 20 years when I have got up I have thrown a bag of confetti all over my bedroom carpet. Then I lean down and pick up each piece separately."

Brooklyn Daily Eagle 1936

Sir Winston Churchill once telephoned and caught Sir Alexander Korda ill in bed. "The trouble with you, Alex," he said, "is that you never take any exercise – use your hands. Look at me. I used to lay bricks. I still paint. What do you do with *your* hands?" "I talk with them," said Alex.

Paul Tabori, ALEXANDER KORDA 1955

EXPERIENCE

When Mrs Pat Campbell went to Hollywood in the early thirties to be considered for film roles she was handed the customary publicity questionnaire. She gave details of her name, the colour of her hair, her eyes, height, hobbies and so forth. When she came to the part headed "Experience" she wrote, "Edward VII."

Garson Kanin, HOLLYWOOD 1974

When a "Mulberry" harbour exhibition was opened in Liverpool Mr R.P. Biddle, newly appointed north-west region port director, stated that the first trials of the model section of the harbour took place in the Prime Minister's bathroom in a liner, when he was going to a conference in Canada.

The Times 8 *May* 1945

Professor J.B.S. Haldane, addressing a public meeting at Auchterarder, explained that many of the gases used in the Great War had been manufactured to very simple formulae because their main purpose was not to kill, but to incapacitate. To prove this he vaporised a spoonful of pepper over a spirit lamp. The hall was quickly filled with pungent smoke. People began running for the doors, dabbing at their eyes and clutching their throats. Looking after them Haldane said, "If that upsets you how would you like a deluge of poison gas from an air fleet in a real war?"

Peter Bushell, GREAT ECCENTRICS 1984

Nairobi. A Kenyan man has answered a call by Yorkshire Television to film water flowing out of a bath at the equator. The company wanted to test the theory that, because of the earth's rotation, water flows clockwise out of plugholes in the Southern hemisphere, anti-clockwise in the Northern hemisphere, and straight down at the Equator. "The water went straight down," reported the cameraman.

The Times 13 *Jul* 1974

To help find the way in which Smith, the 'Brides in the Bath' murderer, drowned his victims we carried out tests with a bath of water and a lady swimmer – with almost fatal results. It was decided to test sudden immersion so, from the ankle I lifted her legs very suddenly. She slipped under easily, but to me, closely watching, she seemed to make no movement. I gripped her arm, it was limp. With a shout I raised her head above the water. It fell to one side. She was unconscious. For nearly half an hour my detectives and I worked at artifical respiration. She explained afterwards that immediately she fell back with her legs in the air the water rushed into her mouth and up her nostrils, making her unconscious.

A.F. Neil, FORTY YEARS OF MAN-HUNTING 1932

EXPLORATION

When Admiral Byrd led his second expedition to Little America, in Antarctica, in 1934 he found everything as he had left it when he had evacuated it in 1930. On the previous expedition there had been an old Norwegian named Ronnie with the party. He was now dead, but his son had begged to come and now he strode over to the bunk where his father had so often slept. He touched the blankets with his fingers. Byrd saw him bend forward and scan the woodwork at the side of the bunk. Some letters were scrawled there, carved deeply in the wood. A name. But not the name of the old man who had lived there. They spelt the name of the son who was now looking at them.

It was a voice from the dead. But it was also the voice of encouragement. The young Norwegian turned to Byrd and cried with emotion, "The old man must have known I'd come."

G.M. McCarthy, Sunday Referee 8 *Mar* 1956

EXPLOSION

The most phlegmatic barrister I ever worked for was Mr Kenworthy Brown, the authority on Indian law. On the night of the Silvertown Explosion during the war, I was working in chambers in Temple Gardens which overlooked the Embankment, and the window in the clerk's office was fitted with wooden shutters secured by a heavy iron bar. There was a dull roar. The building rocked. The shutters burst open with a bang and I was pitched clean out of my revolving chair. Suddenly Mr Kenworthy Brown's bell rang. I took off the receiver and a quiet voice murmured, "Please do not bang the cupboard door."

Francis Pearson, MEMOIRS OF A K.C.'S CLERK 1935

EXTRAVAGANCE

One of Major Iain Grahame's first tasks with his newly commissioned lieutenant, Idi Amin, was to take him to the bank in Jinja so that he could open a bank account. The bank manager went to some trouble to explain to Idi what a bank account was and made him laboriously practise his signature so that he could sign cheques.

If Idi found signing his name difficult he found the principle of a bank account totally incomprehensible. After depositing his first week's pay to open the account – about £13 – he left Grahame outside the bank and went off on a shopping spree.

"I think he must have called at every shop on the way back to the barracks," Grahame recalled. "He ordered a car here, a sewing machine there, a new suit, crates of drink and Lord knows what else. By the time he got back he had run up an overdraft of about £2000. From then on no cheque of his was valid unless I countersigned it. It took a long time to sort out. I had a special file in my office, dealing with his bank transactions and it was my responsibility to make sure that he didn't go off the rails again. He wasn't being dishonest. He just couldn't grasp the significance of a cheque book."

Alexander Mitchell and Russell Miller, Sunday Times Magazine, Amin: the untold story 29 *Oct* 1972

A friend accompanying Maurice Baring on a train journey through Germany was astonished to see him, having failed to fit a new overcoat into his holdall, throw it out of the window without pausing in his conversation.

Catherine Caufield, THE EMPEROR OF THE UNITED STATES OF AMERICA AND OTHER MAGNIFICENT ECCENTRICS 1981

While walking in Piccadilly in a fur-lined coat and finding the day sultry, Sir Thomas Beecham hailed a taxi, threw his coat into the back and told the driver, "Follow me about. It might turn cool again."

Observer, Profile 7 *Jan* 1951

Commodore Gordon Bennett, who edited the Paris edition of the *New York Herald* was a man of strange habits. On one occasion he spent hours with his secretary going through the petty cash accounts and saved 7½d. "You see, my dear Mitchell," he remarked, "how necessary it is for me to keep my hand on things." Then, elated with his morning's work, he crossed the road and carelessly flung his favourite barber a thousand-franc tip.

Bernard Falk, HE LAUGHED IN FLEET STREET

Andrew Carnegie spared no money in beautifying his Scottish home. Marble was brought from Italy to form a staircase carved by a sculptor also brought from Italy. On one occasion his small daughter fell down the marble staircase. Carnegie immediately had it removed. It was buried in the estate grounds at a spot known only to those who placed it there.

Sunday Referee 21 *Nov* 1935

Night after night James Gordon Bennett, the American newspaper owner, would return to the same restaurant in Monte Carlo because of the perfect way it prepared a mutton chop. One evening someone else was occupying his favourite table. He ordered the owner to sell him the restaurant and purchased it for 40,000 dollars. Bennett then asked the diners at his table to leave, even though they were only half way through their meal. When Bennett had finished his mutton chop he left a large tip. He gave the restaurant back to its owner.

David Frost and Michael Deakin, BOOK OF MILLIONAIRES, MULTIMILLIONAIRES AND VERY RICH PEOPLE 1984

James Gordon Bennett's primary goal was to spend all his money. On one occasion he gave a 14,000 dollar tip to the guard on the Train Bleu, between Paris and Monte Carlo. The guard stepped off the train, resigned his job, and opened a restaurant.

Ibid.

While at Baden-Baden, Lord Castlerosse went into a flower shop to buy orchids for the great lady he was to dine with that night. Luxuries were scarce in Germany and they could only produce one spray. "Get some more," shouted Castlerosse, "more, more, more." "But how can we get them?" said the shop. "Wire for them – send planes for them," shouted Castlerosse in his most magnificent manner. The shop, overwhelmed by this terrific Irishman, said, "Yes, milord, it shall be done." So the telegraph wires hummed, airliners converged on Baden from the luxury towns of Europe, all carrying orchids for Lord Castlerosse. The fortunate lady on whom he was lavishing all this generosity found next morning she had enough orchids to fill a room. Then came the bill. It made even Castlerosse blanch. And it certainly put him off women for a while.

Max Aitken, Sunday Express 3 *Mar* 1939

When I first went down to Kent to see Joseph Conrad he had written to me that I should be met by a pony and trap which would bring me to the farmhouse where he was living. When I arrived at Ashford, however I found that the rustic equippage referred to had given place to a small open two-seater car, inexpressibly shabby and apparently in the last stages of dilapidation. It was certainly the saddest looking crock I had ever seen. In the midst of our talk that afternoon Conrad suddenly turned to me with the look of a naughty child and said in a hushed voice, "Please don't mention in your article that I have a car. You see, I am in receipt of a Civil List pension and if it were known that I have a car my pension might be withdrawn – for extravagance."

William Maas, John o'London's Weekly 15 *Sep* 1939

In 1944, just days after the liberation of Paris, Marlene Dietrich, still wearing her American GI uniform strode into the House of Hermes on the rue de Faubourg Saint Honoré and ordered a blue leather dress to be made especially by the couturier department. A few weeks later when she returned to pick it up she was presented with the bill by the firm's owner, Emile-Maurice Hermes. Dietrich took one look at the bill and paled. "Madame," suggested M. Hermes. "You will be able to wear it more than once."

Lynne Thornton, Connoisseur Mar 1982

Pierpont Morgan one day entered Agnew's the art dealers and spent a great deal of time examining a roomful of mezzotints. As he was seen to be marking several items in his catalogue the salesman said to himself, "The old blighter at any rate is going to buy three or four." The inspection finished, Morgan turned to the expectant salesman and said, "I will take them all – except the ones I have marked."

Bernard Falk, FIVE YEARS DEAD 1937

For a time I was court physician to an Indian rajah. One day he bought a fire engine, not to put out fires – his palace had no adequate water supply – but to amuse the ladies of his harem. With four horses harnessed to it, it dashed madly round the grounds. I am confident that no one who witnessed this display, except the rajah, had the slightest conception of the purpose for which this modern bit of machinery was built. They looked upon it as a great mechanical wonder – a sort of enormous toy made for their amusement. It finally blew up one day as it raced around the grounds, killing the engineer, the fireman, the driver, one of the horses, and wounding several onlookers.

Dr William E. Aughinbaugh, I SWEAR BY APOLLO 1939

I once knew a man with an income of £1000 a year who regularly lived for one month at the rate of £10,000 a year, and for the rest like a poor man on a shilling or two a day. Regularly he moved into a suite in an expensive West End hotel. Then when the amount allotted for the period of extravagance had been spent, resumed his place among the denizens of Rowton House, content to wait until funds accumulated to allow him once more to live like a lord.

Bernard Falk, HE LAUGHED IN FLEET STREET

I was visiting my brigade one day when there was an air raid alert. Seven Mirage Jets and Skyhawks came over the crest of the hill. Two turned off to attack a gun position but the others came at us. No one was hurt in the attack but a bomb exploded close to my helicopter, shattering the glass "bubble". I was just thinking "that's not done my helicopter much good" as I went to look at the wreck, when somebody shouted that the planes were coming back. I dropped in to the nearest hole, which happened to be the crater made by the bomb. As I was climbing out a marine shouted, "Do you know what you were sharing that hole with? The other two that didn't go off." And I looked round and saw two unexploded bombs behind me."

Major-General Sir Jeremy Moore, quoted Linda Hawkins, TV Times

FAME

Joss Ackland can remember being recognised only once, and that was after he had been seen week after week as Kipling in a TV serial. A man came up to him in a pub and exclaimed; "I know you!" Joss preened himself. Here was a recognition at last. So he was somewhat taken aback when the man said, "You played the dirty photographer in Z Cars." "And that," comments Joss, "was ten years earlier."

TV Weekly 9 Sep 1968

William Anders received his fair share of publicity after the Apollo 8 moon trip. Tired of being accosted by pressmen, photographers and the admiring public he escaped with his wife for a brief vacation in Acapulco. A few days after their arrival, however, as they relaxed on the patio of their holiday villa, a young man called and asked if he could take some photos. Groaning, Anders replied, "Okay, come on in." "Thanks," said the young man enthusiastically as he marched across the patio. "You've got the best view of the bay in the whole place."

Clifton Fadiman, LITTLE, BROWN BOOK OF ANECDOTES 1985

As a young, little-known writer W.H. Auden was asked what effect fame might have upon him. "I believe," he said after a moment's thought, "that I would always wear my carpet slippers." When fame did eventually come Auden was always to be seen in carpet slippers, even when wearing evening dress.

Book of the Month Club News

My advice to a young writer – who is merely thinking of fame – is to concentrate on one subject. Let him, when he is twenty, write about the earthworm. Let him continue for forty years to write about nothing but the earthworm. When he is sixty, pilgrims will make a hollow path with their feet to the door of the world's greatest authority on the earthworm. They will knock on his door and humbly beg to be allowed to see the Master of the Earthworm.

Hilaire Belloc, quoted Sisley Huddleston, PARIS, SALONS, CAFES, STUDIES 1928

Stanley Baldwin admitted the truth of the story that he was asked by an Old Harrovian in a railway carriage who saw him sporting the old school tie, "Were you not at Harrow in my time? What have you been doing since?"

Thomas Jones, letter to Lady Greig 1 *Jun* 1935

The PM [Stanley Baldwin] and Tom [Dugdale, Baldwin's PPS] drove to Buck's Club where they dined a little after 7 p.m. There was nobody there and they sat together eating oysters. After dinner the PM took out his pipe and began to light it. Simultaneously several shocked waiters rushed up. "No pipes here, Sir." Nobody recognised him, or his far-famed trademark.

Nancy Dugdale, DIARY 2 *Dec* 1936

"It's all very well drawing funny pictures," Sir Osbert Lancaster the cartoonist and satirist was told by his uncle, "but it won't get you anywhere. Why, I remember an awfully clever chap in my form at Charterhouse who did wonderful caricatures of all the masters. We all thought he had a great future, but I've never heard of him since." The awfully clever chap was Max Beerbohm, for whom Lancaster had a disciple's admiration.

The Times, Obituary 29 *Jul* 1986

A man on a bus once said to Sir Adrian Boult, "I know you quite well don't I? I see you often at Lords." Although Sir Adrian replied that well, he didn't have much time for that, the man went on, "Oh yes, I know. You're the policeman there."

Paul Jennings, Radio Times 7 *Apr* 1979

Lunch with Sybil Colefax. A good party, Lady Castlerosse, Diana Cooper, Charlie Chaplin, H.G.Wells, Tom Mosley. We discuss fame. We all agreed we should like fame, but should not like to be recognised. Charlie Chaplin told us how he never realised at first he was a famous man. He worked on quietly in Los Angeles, staying at the Athletic Club. Then suddenly he went on holiday to New York. He then saw "Charlie Chaplin" everywhere – in chocolate, in soap, on the hoardings, "and elderly bankers imitated me to amuse their children". Yet he himself did not know a soul in New York. He walked through the streets where he was famous yet unknown. He at once went to a photographer and had himself photographed as he really is.

Harold Nicolson, DIARY 26 *Sep* 1931

Every day Salvador Dali receives masses of press cuttings from all over the world. Russell Harty asked him if he read them. "Dali never reads," the maestro assured him in his usual adoring third person. "Dali weighs them. If they heavy, Dali happy."

Colin Bell, TV Times 1973

In London D'Annunzio asked a policeman the way to his destination and remarked, "I am D'Annunzio." The bobby did not understand, Whereupon the genius burst forth into oaths and commanded his secretary to present the ignorant lout with copies of all his work.

Edmund Fuller, ANECDOTES 1942

"How does it feel to be a celebrity?" Walt Disney was once asked. "It feels fine," he replied, "when it helps to get a good seat for a football game. But it never helped me to make a good film, or a good shot in a polo game, or command the obedience of my daughter. It doesn't even seem to keep fleas off our dogs – and if being a celebrity won't give one an advantage over a couple of fleas then I guess there can't be much advantage in being a celebrity."

Christopher Finch, THE ART OF WALT DISNEY 1973

Einstein has been bothered a good deal when he comes to New York by people who stop him in the street and say, "Aren't you Professor Einstein?" The Professor finally figured out a dodge. He says with great humility, in broken English, "Pardon me, so sorry. Always I am mistaken for Professor Einstein." People turn away, instead of asking him just what that theory is all about, as they used to.

New Yorker 1939

As a member of the Rank organisation I began receiving invitations to film premieres. Diana and I had been seeing a lot of Ava Gardner and one day I told her that we were attending the premiere of the latest comedy from Ealing Studios, *The Titchfield Thunderbolt*. "I love those Ealing films. Do you think I could come?" I telephoned the office and asked if I could have an extra ticket. "Not a hope." "Not even one?" "No. It is also the night of the British Film Academy Awards. All the seats were allocated weeks ago." "Oh dear, do you think there will be any returns?" "I doubt it. Why do you want another ticket?" "Ava Gardner wants to come." After a stunned silence – "I'll call you back, Donald." A little later, "You've got your extra ticket – we've moved J. Arthur Rank."

Donald Sinden, A TOUCH OF THE MEMOIRS 1982

In Havana a Cuban miss failed to keep a luncheon date with George

Gershwin. Later that afternoon he spied her on the Yacht Club terrace and exclaimed, "Hey, do you know that you stood me up?" "Oh, I meant to phone and tell you I couldn't meet you," said the contrite maiden, "But do you know something? I couldn't remember your name." George didn't recover for days.

Bennett Cerf, TRY AND STOP ME 1947

My father, Sir Cedric Hardwicke was going to direct *Caesar and Cleopatra* on Broadway and he took me to meet Bernard Shaw. When we left Shaw turned to me and said, "Young man, you will be able to tell your grandchildren that you met Bernard Shaw and they will say, 'Who the hell was he?'."

Edward Hardwicke, Radio Times 30 *Aug* 1986

Two very attractive girls who were obviously studying *Cider With Rosie* spotted me in the street the other day. I was looking forward to a little chat until one of them came up and said, "Excuse me, sir. Can you tell me where Laurie Lee is buried?"

Laurie Lee, Radio Times 3 *Nov* 1984

Willy Maugham and Lily Langtry were crossing to America together and one night on deck she mentioned a man called Eckmuhl, or something like that. Willy said he had never heard of Eckmuhl. "But," said Mrs Langtry, "he was famous on two continents." "And why was he famous?" asked Willy. "I loved him," she replied quite simply.

Harold Nicolson, DIARY 10 *Feb* 1934

When Claude Monet lived nearer to Paris men and women whom he did not know would boldly set up their easels beside his. "They would follow me about for days together," he said. "I could not get rid of them. Where I went, they went. What I painted, they would paint also. They made me look at their work and then, when not to be impolite, I had said two or three words, they would go away and tell the world they were pupils of Monet."

Frank Rutter, SINCE I WAS TWENTY-FIVE 1928

Robert Morley always enjoyed watching famous people. At the famous night-club 21 a rumour swept through that Joan Crawford was dining. Robert jumped to his feet and gazed round the room. Then he sat down with a stricken look on his face. "I forgot," he explained. "I've met her."

Margaret Morley, LARGER THAN LIFE 1979

Donald Peers, music hall and radio singer, went last week to the Passport Office in Dartmouth Street to collect his passport. A girl clerk noted his profession and said, "Do you really sing on radio?" and being assured that he did, replied, "Well I'm sorry, but I've never heard of you." Peers asked her name and replied sweetly, "Well, I'm sorry, but I've never heard of you, either."

News Review 2 Dec 1948

As I edged my way to my seat in the crowded cinema I had to clamber over two teddy boys. One of them looked up and a flicker of recognition crossed his face – I had been on the news earlier that night. He nudged his companion. "Look who that is." "Who is it?" "Ned Sherrin. He's on television. He's famous – like Lassie."

Ned Sherrin, A SMALL THING LIKE AN EARTHQUAKE 1983

Eugene O'Neill went to a night-club only once in his life. During a lull in the entertainment, the owner of the club made an announcement to the effect that America's greatest playwright was among those present. The spotlight soon found O'Neill and he was forced to stand and take a bow. Later, when ready to leave, he was presented with a bill for sixty dollars. He looked at it for a moment, took out a pencil, and wrote across it, "One bow – sixty dollars." He walked out.

Sidney Solsky, quoted Crosswell Bowen, THE CURSE OF THE MISBEGOTTEN: A TALE OF THE HOUSE OF O'NEILL 1959

The transient nature of television fame was well illustrated when I was buying a ticket for the Motor Show. The ticket-seller looked at me closely and said, "Aren't you what's-his-name?" "Yes," I said. "I thought you were," she said.

Michael Pertwee, NAME DROPPING

The spur of fame can start very young. One of my grandsons aged five had the duty of handing a bouquet to Mrs Thatcher at the end of a meeting. Having performed his mission, quite uninvited he climbed on to her knee. It made a pretty picture and the press cameras started operating. He was happily aware of this, for when his mother came to remove him he demurred, commenting, "People like to see my picture in the papers."

John Boyd-Carpenter, WAY OF LIFE 1980

I am neither disturbed – nor surprised – at the limitations of my "fame". In November 1964 I went to hear a lecture given by the Oxford Professor of Poetry, Robert Graves. He introduced me to a pleasant young woman who had attended it; well but quietly dressed, easy and agreeable, and we got on well. Graves laughed and said, "It is obvious neither of you has heard of the other before." Quite true. And I had not supposed the lady would have heard of me. Her name was Ava Gardner, but it still meant nothing, till people informed me that she was a film star of some magnitude, and that the press of pressmen and storm of flashbulbs on the steps of the Schools were not directed at Graves, but at her.

J.R.R. Tolkien, letter to his son Michael, LETTERS OF J.R.R. TOLKIEN, *ed. Humphrey Carpenter*

FAMILY

Last year, when I had the honour to be made an honorary Freeman of the Borough of Hammersmith, I said, "Mr Mayor, my wife and I have lived in this Borough for nearly fifty-four years. It must be a healthy neighbourhood. For we have four fine children, fourteen grandchildren, and five great-grandchildren. How all this happened without the slightest assistance or instruction from the BBC I am unable to explain."

A.P. Herbert, APH: HIS LIFE AND TIMES 1970

Sex education has been introduced at our son's school. He came home one day and announced that he had worked it out that he was related to his mother by birth, but to his father only by marriage.

Anon, Reader's Digest Sep 1978

FARMING

Victor Borge, the Danish entertainer, had just completed the purchase of a chicken farm. "Do you know anything about breeding chickens?" he was asked by a friend astonished to learn of the new acquisition. "No," replied Borge, "but the chickens do."

Clifton Fadiman, LITTLE, BROWN BOOK OF ANECDOTES 1985

In the Second World War Diana Cooper ran a smallholding at her cottage near Bognor, bustling about cheerfully among the muck-heaps and butter churns. When some ARP workers who were sleeping in one of the outbuildings protested at the smell of the goat, she replied with typical aplomb that the goat had, only that morning, made the same complaint about the ARP workers.

Philip Ziegler, DIANA COOPER 1981

The upstate New York mink farmers had a contract with the chicken farmers to supply them with chicken offal for their minks.

The chicken farmers had started to caponise their fowls by giving them large doses of Ostrodiol, the female sex hormone. This had produced a breed of chickens with very large breasts, cocks as well as hens. The hormones had settled in the chickens' guts which were sold to the mink farmers and this had affected the minks as well. The male minks had turned "queer" and refused to mate with the female minks, preferring their own sex.

This had resulted in a nil breeding return and a New York court was at that moment solemnly listening to this dramatic case. The headline was: "Upstate Mink Farmers Sue Chicken Moguls For Sex Failure."

Michael Bentine, THE LONG BANANA SKIN 1984

A farmer was asked what sort of year he had had. "Medium" came the reply. "What do you mean by 'medium'?" "Worse than last year but better than next year."

Peter Walker, Speech, Royal Horticultural Society 21 *March* 1979

Every year this farmer complained about the weather and the crops. It was too wet, or too dry, or too many weeds, or too many insects, or there was no market, or something.

Then came a year when crops were good. Prices soared. Bank accounts bulged.

"Pretty good year, you have to admit," a neighbour said.

"Middling," the farmer allowed. "But it's been terribly hard on the soil."

Reader's Digest 1978

FASHION

A young photographer had come the week before, wearing an earring in one ear. Sir Harold Acton had been intrigued by this one earring and, being far too polite to make personal remarks, wondered if it would be for reasons of health. Piercing the ears was said to be good for the eyesight. "Or do you think," he said, "that he might have belonged to some secret society?"

Maureen Cleave, Observer 21 *Feb* 1982

Marlon Brando dressed himself up so nattily for his first audition that none of the people there took him for an actor. "From that time on I determined to be the messiest dresser of them all," he says. Thus was the torn T-shirt launched.

Roderick Mann, Sunday Express 12 *Jul* 1961

In 1924 a hairpin fell in the soup, and so women bobbed their hair. The hairpin had been in the head of Irene Castle, and it was during a whirling dance performed with her husband, Vernon Castle, that the hairpin fell into one of the cash customers' plates of soup. Rather than repeat such an incident, Irene snipped off her hair.

Molly Castle, Daily Mirror 16 *Nov* 1938

When the mini-skirt came into fashion in the mid-60s Coco Chanel was asked whether she approved of girls exposing their knees and thighs in this way. "Thighs – of course," she replied. "But knees – never."

Clifton Fadiman, LITTLE, BROWN BOOK OF ANECDOTES 1985

Quite early in the war Norman Hartnell was summoned to discuss the Queen's costume for hostilities. It was comparatively easy to stick to the government rules for "austerity" dressing: a limited number of seams per dress, narrow collars and belts, a minimum of frills. Embroidery was forbidden, so Hartnell hand-painted garlands of lilac on one satin gown which, with jewels, became the Queen's standard uniform at diplomatic soirées.

Robert Lacey, GOD BLESS HER. QUEEN ELIZABETH THE QUEEN MOTHER 1987

A bishop of Texas visited London and was taken to a fashionable soirée at which the ladies' dresses were cut very low. His hostess asked condescendingly if he had ever seen such a sight. "Not since I was weaned," said the bishop.

Bennett Cerf, TRY AND STOP ME 1947

FATHER

My father was a great admirer of Churchill. I remember vividly that he took me to hear Churchill speak at some country meeting when I was 10 years old. It was a crowded meeting in a marquee and we were sitting quite far back; heavy rain started leaking through and people put their umbrellas up, and to my horror my father shouted out at the top of his voice, "Put those umbrellas down. I can't see Mr Churchill." There was a shocked silence; Mr Churchill looked up from his text with a grin. "Does anybody mind the rain dropping on them, because I don't mind it a bit?" Then everyone put their umbrellas down and I thought my father was a great figure for heckling like that and not being arrested or taken off to prison.

Robin Day, Observer 18 *Nov* 1984

When Daniel Parson was at prep school his housemaster benevolently invited him, with a privileged group of fellow pupils, to stay up and listen to the high-minded political BBC programme starring his famous father, Negley Parson, the ace American foreign correspondent.

The chairman's modulated, discreet preamble was interrupted by a loud ripping noise. It sounded as if scripts were being torn up. Then, over the murmur of studio perturbation and the master's fit of urgent coughing and fumbling with the wireless set, came a swelling phlegmy roar like a bull rhino lumbering in to charge.

Before the knob could be turned the faintly shrill protestations in that Portland Place *conversazione* were drowned by a rasping roar. "Mussolini, God dammit, now you listen to me . . . ." It seemed probable that Negley had been heavy-handed at the sauce, was smashed, whisky-inflamed and belligerently drunk.

Was the young Dan frozen with shame and embarrassment? Not at all. "I was thrilled to hear his voice. I felt terrific self-importance at having such a splendidly different father. He had great glamour. From the year dot I knew he wasn't as other fathers. There was no one with his charm, his charisma. I thought he was infallible."

Kenneth Allsop, The Sunday Times 5 *Nov* 1972

My father, Isaac Foot, took a tremendous interest and an unreasonable pride in the activities of his offspring, and we in our turn would go to him for guidance and encouragement. When I finally returned from Cyprus I was offered a commercial job at any salary I liked to state. I was not attracted by the prospect but I went to him and told him of the offer. He told me he would think about it, and next day at breakfast he said, "If you accept it your enemies would know what to say, but your friends wouldn't."

Sir Hugh Foot, A START IN FREEDOM 1964

FATHER-IN-LAW

In 1933, at the age of 27, John Betjeman married the daughter of Field Marshal Lord Chetwynd who said to him, "Well, Betjeman, if you're going to marry my daughter you needn't go on calling me 'sir'. Call me 'Field Marshal'."

Observer, Profile 8 *Feb* 1959

Winston Churchill was once entertaining a large and distinguished party at which Vic Oliver, his son-in-law, who married Sarah Churchill, was present. The men had divided into two groups. One clustered round the great man, and the others, clustered round Vic, did as best they could at the other end of the table. Conversation in the PM's group was animated; at the other end less stimulating. At last Vic Oliver could stand it no longer and called out, "Say, Pop (which Churchill must have disliked being called), do tell us what you are talking about." Churchill glowered and crossly replied, "We are discussing who is a really great man." "Gee, that would be interesting to know. Who did you decide, Pop?" "Mussolini." "Why Mussolini, Pop?" "Because he was one of the few men in history who had the courage to have his son shot."

Peter Coats, OF KINGS AND CABBAGES 1984

FEMINISM

When a man said to Beatrice Webb, "Much of this talk about

feminism is nonsense; any woman would rather be beautiful than clever," she replied, "Quite true. But that is because so many men are stupid and so few are blind."

John Mather, Daily Express 14 *Oct* 1947

A judge in the New York State Supreme Court has, after three years of litigation, allowed the former Mrs Ellen Cooperman to call herself Cooperperson. His ruling reversed that of a lower court last year when a judge called the new name inane and nonsensical. Mrs Cooperperson said her 10-year-old son Brian would keep the name Cooperman, because he was male and therefore not uncomfortable with it.

The Times 17 *Dec* 1977

See also **SUFFRAGETTE**

FINANCE

In 1938 Jack Frye, president of Trans-World Airlines telephoned Howard Hughes to say he needed 15 million dollars for re-equipment and couldn't get it. "Good God, Jack," said Hughes. "Don't you realise that's a small fortune?" Glad to have found someone who considered 15 million dollars "small" Frye persuaded Hughes to buy out the principal stockholders and acquire control of the airline.

Raymond Palmer, Observer 17 *Mar* 1968

Like many wealthy people Hetty Green, the American multimillionairess recluse, was wary of giving financial tips. When asked to suggest a good investment she replied, "The other world."

Ishbel Ross, CHARMERS AND CRANKS 1965

Herman Landau, who came from Poland and made a fortune in London, had had a bad day on the Stock Exchange. He remained in his city office after four o'clock, walking up and down with his hands behind his back, gazing at the floor, thinking things out. One of the cleaners seeing him said, "Have you lost anything, sir? Can I help you?" "I'm afraid you can't help me," he said. "But actually I've lost £32,000."

Herbert Buckmaster, BUCK'S BOOK 1932

I once did a deal with Tiny Rowlands about selling wattle in East

Africa and when we shook hands Rowland said, "By the way, what is wattle?" To which I replied, "Where is East Africa?"

Jim Slater, RETURN TO GO 1977

FIRE

When a vast fire broke out at his home, Crewe Hall, my uncle, Lord Crewe, asked for a writing table and chair to be brought on to the lawn. By the light of the flames he calmly penned a letter to an architect, "Crewe is now burning. Come and build it up again."

Lady Cynthia Colville, A CROWDED LIFE 1963

When one of those hellish Southern Californian brush fires destroyed the home where Aldous Huxley was living with his wife Laura they escaped with their lives, but Aldous's manuscripts, his precious collection of letters from great people of his day, and a library that had taken years to assemble were all reduced to ashes.

I was in New York when I heard of the disaster, and hurried to phone Aldous my sympathy. "It was a hideous experience," he exclaimed. I could visualise his quizzical smile when he added, "But it did make me feel extraordinarily clean."

Anita Loos, KISS HOLLYWOOD GOODBYE 1974

The magician Lafayette always insisted that the "pass door" – the small door which leads from the stalls into the wings – should be kept locked during his performance. This he did in order that no intruders should discover the secrets of his illusions. It was a foolish stipulation which cost him his life. When fire broke out on the stage of the Empire Theatre, Edinburgh, on 9th May 1911 he rushed to the pass door to make good his escape. For the moment he had forgotten it was locked, by his own orders. Before he could make his way to the other exit the stage was a raging mass of flames and smoke, and overcome by fumes he fell unconscious to the boards. When his body was recovered it was charred beyond recognition.

Will Goldston, SENSATIONAL TALES OF MYSTERY MEN 1930

FLATTERY

When my wife Peggy became chairman of the Political Committee of the Ladies Carlton Club and had frequently to introduce distinguished speakers, she asked Sylvia Kilmuir for advice on the technique. "Oh, it's easy," she said. "Just say 'beautiful, wonderful man'."

John Boyd-Carpenter, WAY OF LIFE 1980

FLYING

Just before taking off on an aeroplane flight the stewardess reminded Mohammed Ali, the boastful heavyweight boxing champion, to fasten his seat belt. "Superman don't need no seat belt," said Ali. "Superman don't need no aeroplane, either," retorted the stewardess.

Richard Crouser, IT'S UNLUCKY TO BE BEHIND AT THE END OF THE GAME 1983

When Lady Bailey, at the age of 37, made her 18,000 mile solo flight to South Africa in 1928 she had been on her way for a month when she made a crash landing at Tabora, Tanganyika, without being hurt. Another Moth was flown to her and she arrived in Cape Town some days later. As her husband came forward to greet her she said, "Hello, Abe. I'm sorry I'm late."

Daily Telegraph, Obituary 3 *Aug* 1960

It is a strange position to be alone, unguided, without a compass, in the middle of the Channel. I let the aeroplane take its own course. And then 20 minutes after I have left the French coast, I see the cliffs of Dover. The wind has taken me off course. I am going in the direction of the Goodwin Sands. It is time to attend to the steering. My beautiful aeroplane responds. I drop upon the land.

Louis Blériot, DIARY 25 *Jul* 1909

In the midst of the throng on the cliffs at Calais on the morning of July 25, 1909, I saw what appeared to be a cripple directing the mechanics as they tuned up the engine of the little monoplane. He pointed here and there with his crutch. The "cripple" was Louis Blériot. Some days previously he had badly burned his foot when the engine of his aircraft caught fire. He turned to me and said, "I cannot walk – but I can fly!"

George Mumford, Evening News, I saw the dawn of our age 25 *Jul* 1949

I was looking at my wrist-watch. Dawn was at hand. I was

Northcliffe's official timekeeper. The sky was grey, but officially the sun was rising. The moment had come. "Now," I said, "Off you go. Good luck and au revoir."

It was then that Louis Blériot put that astonishing question to Leblanc, "Where is Dover?" Leblanc waved his hand seaward. "It is over there," he said. Blériot nodded, then gave his head mechanic the sign to turn the propeller.

Hamilton Fyffe, News Chronicle 20 *Jul* 1934

I always make a point, on aeroplanes, to travel in the smoking compartment, because there won't be any kiddies there.

John Betjeman, Radio Times 28 *Aug* 1976

I took Elizabeth Bowen, the novelist, to tea with a somewhat menacing dowager, Mrs Bruquiere, who wore wire spectacles through which her lance-like gaze alternated benevolence with disapproval. There were only the three of us and we were set up round an assertive silver kettle. A note of formality had been struck, and formality at tea does not permit silences. Silences, however, there were, and one of them was broken by my hostess saying how fond she was of my sister-in-law, at that time living in Washington. "I must visit Helene," she concluded. "I shall fly down for luncheon. After all, it only takes an hour." The silence resumed until I broke it feebly by saying that it had seemed to take more than an hour when Elizabeth flew up a few days previously.

Mrs Bruquiere adjusted her spectacles and her tone. "Perhaps," she snapped, "you travel on public planes."

Alan Pryce-Jones, THE BONUS OF LAUGHTER 1987

Strolling towards Bond Street I saw in a shop window a little blue and silver aeroplane. Something influenced me to step inside and ask the price of the machine.

"Five hundred and fifty pounds," replied the salesman. I was just about to leave the shop when he added, "– and chromium plating is only five pounds extra."

That settled it. It was just like buying a motor-car. "Chromium plating five pounds extra!" I had always imagined that aeroplanes were extraordinary things, and yet this machine seemed very ordinary.

"Could one fly round the world in this?" I asked.

"Of course – easily," was the reply.

That settled it. In a week or two I was painting the name *Bluebird* on its nose, and was ready to be off.

Mrs Victor Bruce, THE BLUEBIRD'S FLIGHT 1931

In July 1954 Churchill appointed me Minister of Transport and Civil Aviation. He was always much concerned by the smallness of his majority in the House of Commons and when he saw me to offer this appointment he followed it up with an intimation that I should see to it that not more than five Conservative Members of Parliament ever flew together in the same aircraft. What in fact I was to do if a dozen of my colleagues booked tickets on the Friday evening plane to Paris, or indeed a foreign aircraft, was no more clear to me then than it is now. So I said hesitantly, "I see, Prime Minister, your idea is that you don't want too many eggs in one basket?" "No," he said, "I don't want too many baskets in one egg." So I left it there. I think he knew there was nothing he or I could do.

John Boyd-Carpenter, WAY OF LIFE 1980

Georges Clemenceau loathed flying and always avoided it whenever possible. Before one flight he was heard to admonish the pilot, "Fly very cautiously, very slow, very low."

Ian Hamilton, KOESTLER: A BIOGRAPHY 1982

I had difficulty in communicating my enthusiasm for flying to my children. I first took my elder sons flying when they were five and three. One merely wanted to know which way his spit would blow, and the other, mad about trains, wished to follow the railway lines.

Sir Geoffrey de Havilland, SKY FEVER 1961

As a novice flyer Amelia Earhart participated eagerly in the life around airports. Of her first flying coat she recalled, "It was 1922. Somehow I saved 20 dollars. With it I bought an elegant leather coat. *Patent* leather, shiny and lovely. But suddenly I saw that it looked *too* new. How were people to know that I was a flyer if I wore a coat that was too new? Wrinkles! That was it. There just had to be wrinkles. So – I slept in it for three nights."

George Palmer Putnam, SOARING WINGS

E.M. Forster made his first flight in a glider on his 90th birthday. His comment on the experience afterwards, "There is absolutely nothing in it. You go up. You come down."

Raymond Mortimer, TRY ANYTHING ONCE

When Caspar John was in his 20s he became a passionate aviator. Augustus (his father) lent him money towards the cost of a two-seater Avro Avian. On a visit to Wiltshire Caspar offered Lytton Strachey and Carrington a trip. Carrington adored it, but Strachey refused, complaining that his beard might foul the controls.

Rebecca John, CASPAR JOHN 1987

One of Freddie Laker's early enterprises was the air-car ferry from Southend. On one stormy day Freddie was at the airport comforting passengers after their short but rough flight across the Channel. As one group of people stepped from the aircraft Freddie spotted a man clutching an air-sickness bag. Rushing over, Freddie exclaimed, "You don't have to do that, give it to me. I'll dispose of it." The man glared at Freddie and in a booming but gummy Northern accent replied, "Nay tha doan't, lad, maa teeth's in theer."

Douglas Whybrow, The Times 22 Aug 1985

Following a dispute with his pilot Mr Levine, the American financier, on impulse flew his own plane from Paris to Croydon, where I saw him endeavouring to land. He was unable to do so, after several dangerous attempts which sent the aerodrome ambulance and fire engine scampering after him, until a Croydon pilot went up and showed him what to do. When the machine at last came safely to rest instead of to grief, as everyone expected, Levine stepped out with a grin. What seemed to tickle him most of all was that he could see the ambulance and fire engine below chasing him from place to place. He was still laughing at the joke when I took him back to London in my car.

J.C. Cannell, WHEN FLEET STREET CALLS 1932

When Charles Lindbergh, after his solo flight across the Atlantic, was presented to George V, the King asked the usual questions, including one which must have put the young aviator immediately at ease. "Now tell me, there's one thing I long to know. How did you *manage*?"

Kenneth Rose, KING GEORGE V 1984

I was supposed to go flying with Wilbur Wright. Unfortunately when he came to collect me he landed rather strangely and it took him the whole afternoon to tie the plane together again so by then it was dark and we never did get into the air.

Sir Harry Brittain, The Times 24 *Dec* 1973

During the very early days of El Al, Israel Airlines operations, their station manager at Heathrow airport occasionally found time to perform extra duties, such as taking any dog for a short walk on the runway while the plane was refuelling.

One day, while checking the cargo of a plane that arrived ahead of schedule, the manager noticed a large dog resembling a rather shaggy Alsatian. The dog looked at him with pleading eyes, so the kindly station manager tied a short rope to the dog's neck and led him out on to the runway. The dog happily made exploratory runs, bounding and sniffing about in sheer glee, with the station manager hard put to keep up with the unusually frisky animal.

After some farewell pats the dog was put in his cage, and the manager went back to his office to check his mail. There on his desk was an urgent telegram. It read, "Please be advised that a wolf bound for London Zoo is on board the plane. *Handle with extreme caution.*"

Walt and Ann Bohrer, THIS IS YOUR CAPTAIN SPEAKING

Passengers on a flight from Bangladesh to London waited for take-off after all the doors had been closed when a terrible banging on the passenger door could be heard. The crew refused to let the person on as he was too late for the flight. Only after they reluctantly opened it did they discover that it was the pilot.

Executive Travel Magazine, quoted Daily Telegraph 25 *Sep* 1985

Flying prospects on my birthday 6th December 1919 were not good, according to *The Times*. It is now difficult to imagine that a pilot, or even a passenger, would actually buy a newspaper in order to find out whether it was safe to "go up" but it must have been so, otherwise there would have been no point in publishing the information at all. "Unsuitable for aviation or fit only for short distance flying by the heaviest sort of machine," was what the communiqué said.

Eric Newby, A TRAVELLER'S LIFE 1982

"Breakfast in London, Lunch in New York", was the slogan on a British Airways poster, beneath which was a traveller's addition, "Luggage in Bermuda".

Nigel Rees, GRAFFITI RULES OK

An actress was in Theo Cowan's (J. Arthur Rank's publicity agent) office having hysterics at the prospect of travelling in an aeroplane. Theo tried to console her. "But there's nothing safer than flying – it's the crashing that's dangerous."

Donald Sinden, A TOUCH OF THE MEMOIRS 1982

My friend Jeff is an avid glider enthusiast. While gliding one day he watched the seagulls and noticed that they picked out the best thermals. Wanting to get the longest ride possible, he followed the seagulls. As they circled, so did he, it seemed the best possible idea for a long leisurely flight. "There was only one problem," he said afterwards. "I eventually ended up circling the rubbish tip."

Carol Webb, Reader's Digest Oct 1982

During World War I an observer was standing in the cockpit of his machine, aiming at a German plane with a camera-gun, when his pilot suddenly swerved and dived. An instant later, the plane seeming to respond madly to the controls, the pilot glanced back and was horrified to see the observer perched on the tail. When the plane had dived the observer and his camera-gun were left sitting in the air – and came down *on the plane* again, a foot from the rudder. There he was, clinging desperately. They made a slow pancake landing. The observer was unhurt, but the pilot never flew again. He had lost his nerve.

Basil Woon, EYES WEST 1940

The reputation of Concorde is clearly on the up and up. A woman telephoned a London travel agent the other day to ask how long Concorde took to get from England to America. "Just a minute, madam," said the travel agent. Satisfied, the woman hung up.

Daily Telegraph 10 *Oct* 1986

FOOD

At Faringdon, Lord Berners' home near Oxford, meals were served in which all the food was of one colour pedigree. I.e, if Lord Berners' mood was pink, luncheon might consist of beet soup, lobster, tomatoes, strawberries. And outside a flock of pink pigeons might fly overhead, for Lord Berners' pigeons were sprayed with harmless cosmetic dyes.

Norman Lebrecht, Sunday Times Magazine 18 *Sep* 1983

One morning at Glyndebourne some guests and a number of county people, one of them a general, were sitting about at breakfast when Childs, the butler, came in and said, "I am sorry to disturb you, sir, but cook is dead." There was a moment's uncomfortable silence, broken by the general who said, "Under the circumstances do you think I could have another sausage?"

Rudolf Bing, 5000 NIGHTS AT THE OPERA 1972

During the famous Sidney Street Siege, when two anarchists held police and Guardsmen at bay for several hours, Mr Winston Churchill and other officials who were present began to feel hungry. Suddenly a brave philanthropist appeared, bearing a tray of sandwiches, which were instantly seized and devoured by the officials, Cabinet Minister, police and reporters.

Later in the proceedings someone wondered about the identity of the philanthropist – who had charged highly for his services – and inquiries were made. It was the local cat's meat man in his wife's apron.

J.B. Booth, LIFE, LAUGHTER AND BRASS HATS 1939

Once at dinner, when the menu announced Roast Duck and the scouts at Merton brought Roast Lamb, Hugh Dyson remarked, "La Mallard Imaginaire".

Humphrey Carpenter, THE INKLINGS 1980

The chef of the Savoy Hotel in London, the renowned Escoffier, was desolate at being unable to get tickets for Dame Nellie Melba's sold-out gala performance. Melba somehow obtained him two seats. Next day, at lunch, an extraordinary dessert made its debut at her table, accompanied by a note from the chef, saying he had named it after her, Pêche Melba.

Josef Sxigeti, WITH STRINGS ATTACHED 1967

T.S. Eliot did nothing to discourage the idea that he was a connoisseur of English cheeses. "Let's lunch at the Athenaeum," he would say in the manner of a *bon viveur* of dairy products. "They keep a good piece of cheese there." Or, "Ah, Wensleydale, the Mozart of cheeses!" But at home for years Eliot never complained at the regular bit of old Cheddar which his housekeeper used to produce.

Roy Perrott, Observer 10 *Jan* 1963

"One of the things that still makes me laugh when I read Ian Fleming's books," says Noel Coward, "is the contrast between the standard of living of dear old Bond, and the sort of thing Ian used to put up with at Goldeneye. When Bond drinks his wine it has to be properly *chambré*; the tournedos slightly underdone, and so forth. But whenever I ate with Ian at Goldeneye the food was so abominable that I used to cross myself before I took a mouthful. Stewed guavas and coconut cream – salt fish and ackee fruit. I used to say, 'Ian, it tastes like armpits.' And all the time there was old Ian smacking his lips for more while his guests remembered all those delicious meals he had put in his books."

John Pearson, LIFE OF IAN FLEMING 1966

Reg Gutteridge, in Kinshasha, Zaire, to report on the Muhamad Ali –George Forman scrap went to his restaurant for dinner, discovered there was only one course – it appeared to be locally prepared chicken – and wolfed it down. The next night the same dish was served, and when the same meal came up on the third night Reg rebelled and politely asked the waiter if there was anything other than chicken available. "Chicken?" said the waiter. "We only have chicken on the President's birthday." "Then what have I been eating on the last couple of nights?" asked Reg. "Roast monkey," was the reply.

TV Times 7 *Oct* 1976

One of Howard Hughes' short-lived attachments was to Baskin and Robbins banana-and-nut flavoured ice cream. For some months he ate a scoopful with every meal. When it was noticed that stocks were running low a domestic was sent out for more. He returned empty-handed, reporting that the line had been discontinued. In a state of shock the staff contacted Baskin and Robbins and begged them to make up a special batch. Although the minimum order was three hundred and fifty gallons the purchase was authorised and the crisis averted. The very day the consignment arrived Hughes announced that he no longer liked banana-and-nut flavoured ice cream, and would try a scoop of French vanilla instead. His aides spent the next twelve months asking everyone they knew whether they liked banana-and-nut flavoured ice cream. Those who said they did were presented with a two-gallon drum.

Peter Bushell, GREAT ECCENTRICS 1984

Maria Huxley's attitude towards food made her a very peculiar housewife. Not that she didn't earnestly put her mind to the job. I recall a menu she worked out with the aid of a calorie counter to include all the nutrients for an evening meal. It consisted of a platter of string beans at room temperature surrounded by cold, sliced bananas. When Aldous diplomatically insisted on leading us to the Farmer's Market for a banquet Maria's wide blue eyes grew misty with chagrin.

Anita Loos, KISS HOLLYWOOD GOODBYE 1974

A secretary of mine died suddenly and, wanting to look up an old case, I went to search through his desk. There were nine drawers packed full – not of papers, but of cold buttered toast, mostly mouldy. The explanation is this; every day they sent him from the pantry a pot of tea and a plateful of hot buttered toast. Apparently he was never hungry then, but being unwilling, like every Irishman, to hurt even the parlourmaid's feelings, rather than send down the toast untasted he packed it away in those receptacles for learned records.

Dr Griffith MacDonald, REMINISCENCES OF A SPECIALIST 1932

"By the end of the war the food [in Japanese POW Camps] was pretty well dried up. The Japs could hardly feed *themselves*. We ate cracked wheat, warehouse sweepings, weevils. You'd shift the weevils to the side of your plate and eat them last. I often had three rings of them on the edge of the plate."

"What did they taste of?"

"They didn't taste of anything, funnily enough. We had to eat them for the protein."

J.G. Ballard in an interview with Martin Amis, Observer Magazine 2 *Sep* 1984

George Moore dismissed his sixth cook the day I left. Six in three weeks. One brought in a policeman, Moore made so much noise. Moore brought the policeman into the dining room and said, "Is there a law in the land to compel me to eat that abominable omelette?"

W.B. Yeats, letter to Lady Gregory, May 1901

H. G. Wells, seeing caviare for the first time, helped himself to a liberal quantity, thinking it some sort of vegetable. "You like caviare?" said his astonished neighbour. "Love it!" exclaimed Wells. It was a moment he never forgot.

John o' London's Weekly, 22 *Dec* 1950

The airport restaurant menu at Antalya in southern Turkey offers, with considerable prominence, an item it calls, "The Terminal Breakfast".

Peterborough, Daily Telegraph 15 *Jun* 1985

Sir, your recent articles on healthy eating remind me that when my eldest son was getting married two years ago, his fiancée's mother insisted that old-fashioned rice be thrown instead of confetti after the wedding. "Oh, all right," said the ecology-minded bride, "but it *must* be *brown* rice."

S.B. McClenahan, letter to The Times 3 *Jul* 1984

FOOTBALL

Sunderland footballers can expect some unusual tactical talks under their new manager, Lawrie McMenemy.

At his previous club, Southampton, he called a team meeting after signing Ivan Golac, a Yugoslav international, and began it by drawing a diagram of a ball and a goal on a blackboard. He spoke in English, but very, very slowly.

Alan Ball, the captain, said, "Don't be silly, boss. Ivan speaks perfect English." "I'm not doing this for him," replied McMenemy, "I'm doing it for the rest of you."

Daily Telegraph 28 *Jul* 1985

When Berwick Rovers had a purportive goal disallowed at Meadowbank, one of the half-dozen travelling fans lost control. Well, almost. "Referee," he yelled across the pitch, "you're a love-child."

Patrick Barclay, Independent 3 *Jan* 1987

At a political meeting at Wavertree, Randolph Churchill was haranguing his audience on the danger of Baldwin's India policy, which was likely to put the Lancashire cotton industry out of work. "And who is responsible for putting Lancashire where she is today?" he asked. The answer came from the back of the hall. "Blackburn Rovers."

Anita Leslie, Sunday Telegraph 21 *Apr* 1985

Brentford Football Club have paid transfer fees for their two new players to Her Majesty. They bought Steve Butler and George Torrence out of the Army.

The Times, Sports Diary 29 *Dec* 1984

In the mid-Fifties the Hungarian football team came over to England for that famous encounter labelled later "the match of the century". Arthur Koestler was a great football fan. "Which side are you going to support?" he asked me a few days before the match. I was taken aback. "I am a British subject now," I replied. "My loyalties belong to Britain. Naturally I shall support England." He shook his head. "Patriotism is one thing, football-patriotism quite another."

George Mikes, Observer 31 *Jul* 1983

The saddest entry in the House of Commons register of members' interest? Labour MP, Jee Ashton, lists his declarable shareholdings as "Two shares in Sheffield Wednesday Football Club. (No dividends paid since 1935)."

The Times, Diary 19 *Jan* 1987

It's a man's life in modern football. With hamstrings and ligaments and cartileges threatening you while the groin strains snap at your vitals, life is unquestionably tough. To make things worse, every week they invent a new problem. The latest tragic victim of a hitherto unknown footballing injury is Peter Whitehurst, who went down in agony when playing for Grantham of the Southern League in a pre-season friendly against Norwich City. The physio, Nigel Marshall, rushed on to the pitch, horrified at what he might find after Whitehurst had been involved in a clash of heads. He quickly discovered the truth; Whitehurst's earring had stapled his ear to the side of his head.

Simon Barnes, The Times 30 *Aug* 1986

FORGETFULNESS

James Agate published a collection of his early theatrical reviews, called *Buzz, Buzz* – a title taken from *Hamlet.* Thomas Beecham ran into him at St Pancras and told him, "I've just bought a book by you called *Buzz* – I can't remember the rest of the title."

James Harding, AGATE, A BIOGRAPHY 1986

John Drew had shaved off his moustache to play a part and his appearance was greatly changed. Shortly afterwards he met Max Beerbohm in the lobby of a London theatre, and could not remember who he was. Beerbohm's memory was better. "Oh, Mr Drew," he said, "I'm afraid you don't recognise me without your moustache."

Everybody's Magazine 1943

Not all interviews with Winston Churchill went smoothly. When Nigel Birch was summoned Churchill forgot what office he intended to offer him, so after a pleasant chat he dismissed him, none the wiser, and said he had much enjoyed talking to him. A frantic telephone call later in the day from a Private Secretary informed Birch of the office which had been intended for him.

John Boyd-Carpenter, WAY OF LIFE 1980

Christina Foyle showed me a hollow book which she found in a lot bought from a clergyman's widow in the Isle of Wight. It contained £350 in notes, the clergyman's savings of a lifetime. He had forgotten what he had done with the money. It was returned to the widow, who was practically penniless.

Louise Morgan, News Chronicle 27 Feb 1936

At a concert one evening members of the orchestra were concerned to see a look of bewilderment come over Josef Hofmann's face as he settled himself at the piano. Leaning towards a lady in the front row of the audience he whispered, "May I please see your programme, madam? I forget what comes first."

Henri Tomianka, FACING THE MUSIC 1973

Harold Macmillan's famous unflappable style was evident at a party at the Waldorf Hotel soon after he became chairman of the family publishing firm. The party was to launch a new series on European history, and Macmillan began on an encomium of the merits of the general editor, a Sussex don. Unfortunately he couldn't remember the name of the man. But he didn't pause for a second " – glad to have the services of that very able and learned man Doctor who I am glad to say is with us tonight". There wasn't the trace of space between "Doctor" and "who" in the sentence, and I doubt if many of the audience ever realised they had not been told who the learned doctor was.

Derwent May, Sunday Telegraph 4 Jan 1987

Once, when watching a play, the actor Walter Hudd found himself sitting next to a man whose face he thought he knew. All through the first act he cast sidelong glances; he could not concentrate on the play, he was certain they had met, but where? Who was he? In the interval he went to the bar and there next to him was the same man. There was nothing for it. He must face it out. "Forgive me, but don't I know you?" "Yes," said the man, "I'm your agent."

Donald Sinden, A TOUCH OF THE MEMOIRS 1982

Towards the end of his career A.E. Matthews was acting in a West End play with a scene involving a crucial telephone call which Matthews was to answer. The telephone rang on cue. He crossed the stage, picked up the receiver, and promptly dried. In desperation he turned to the only other actor on the stage and said, "It's for you."

Gyles Brandreth, GREAT THEATRICAL DISASTERS 1982

During the war I took Ellen Terry, whose memory was then beginning to fail, to a charity matinee of *Midsummer Night's Dream* at Drury Lane. The rain came down "like stair-rods" all day and, by the time I escorted her out of the theatre into my car there was in the street a very fair imitation of a waterspout overhead and a lake under feet. No sooner had I ensconced her in the car than she looked at me with that beaming smile (the sort "that 'ud wheedle a kettle off a hob") and said with a gurgling laugh, " *Isn't* it funny, dearest? I can't remember where I'm living." She could only offer two clues; (1) that she was not staying in her own flat, (2) that she must pass through something that looked like a churchyard with railings to reach the door. But between us the chauffeur and I took her to the right place.

Mrs Claude Beddington, ALL THAT I HAVE MET 1929

A yeomanry colonel introducing his officers to an inspecting general stopped before one of them and shaking his head and snapping his fingers, "This is Captain – Captain – memory like a sieve. I'll be forgetting the names of me hounds next."

Max Hastings, OXFORD BOOK OF MILITARY ANECDOTES 1985

See also **ABSENTMINDEDNESS**

FRAUD

Once after a performance in Boston an elderly lady met me at the stage door. She said I had reminded her of her only son she had lost in the war and she had spent her last few dollars to see me. A lump gathered in my throat and I pressed a ten-dollar note into her trembling hand. A few minutes later I met an actor appearing in the same show.

"A funny thing happened to me," he said. "A little old woman with tears in her eyes stopped me at the stage door and said she had spent her last dollar to see my show because I reminded her of her only son who was killed in the war, so I slipped her a ten-spot. It's very touching, isn't it."

I said, "It touched me, too."

Eddie Cantor, MY LIFE IN YOUR HANDS 1929

Recently a certain duke was persuaded by a bogus art dealer to hang a picture by "Hoppner" on the walls of his country mansion and announce that it was for sale. The duke thought it was a genuine picture although it was not a portrait of any member of his family. All he was interested in was that he would obtain a handsome commission if a sale was affected.

A rich American purchased the picture as coming from the duke's collection. In America they think a great deal of dukes. It was only afterwards that he discovered the picture to be a fake – a blend of portraits made by a skilled copyist.

The duke was indignant that he had been made a stalking horse for such a deception. The feelings of the American can well be imagined. He could not bring the case to open court because pride warned him that he would be the laughing stock of America. So he presented the "Hoppner" to a local picture gallery and claimed a lot of kudos by way of publicity.

Norman Hilton, PASSING SHOW 15 *Oct* 1932

FUNERAL

Lady Violet Bonham-Carter asked Margot Asquith if she planned to wear a certain hat, trimmed with ostrich feathers, at Lord Kitchener's memorial service. Margot answered, "How can you ask me? Dear Kitchener saw me in that hat twice."

Jane Abdy and Charlotte Greere, THE SOULS 1984

The actor Maurice Barrymore was the father of Ethel, John and Lionel. At his funeral the straps supporting the coffin became twisted. The coffin, already lowered into the grave, had to be raised again so than an adjustment could be made. As it reappeared Lionel impulsively nudged John and whispered, "How like Father – a curtain call."

Gene Fowler, GOOD NIGHT SWEET PRINCE 1944

Hugo Black, Justice of the US Supreme Court, was attending the funeral of a dignitary he heartily disliked, and whose funeral he would not have attended had it not been expected of him. Another judge, arriving late, tiptoed into his place next to Black and whispered, "How far have they got?" Black whispered back, "They've just opened for the defence."

Ralph Marquand, ANECDOTES FOR ALL OCCASIONS 1977

Harry Cohen, head of the Columbia film studios, was greatly disliked in Hollywood, but there was a large turnout at his funeral. An observer remarked, "It only proves what they always say – give the public something they want to see, and they'll turn up to see it."

Oscar Levant, THE UNIMPORTANCE OF BEING OSCAR 1968

When the Reverend Harold Davidson, the eccentric unfrocked rector of Stiffkey, had himself exhibited in a cage with a lion in a Skegness sideshow and was mauled to death on 30th July 1937, his widow caused a mild sensation at his funeral by arriving for the ceremony dressed all in white – white shoes, white stockings, white hat, white dress. When someone asked her why she had eschewed the traditional colour of mourning she smiled – and pointed to her black shoelaces.

Peter Bushell, GREAT ECCENTRICS 1984

Bernard Shaw told me that at the funeral of Thomas Hardy in Westminster Abbey, Barrie, walking as pall-bearer between Shaw and some other six-footer, deliberately made himself as small as possible so that people looking at the illustrated papers next day should ask who was the tiny figure.

Richard Prentis (James Agate), John o' London's Weekly 15 *Sep* 1939

It is not easy to make a funeral into a bright story, and I was once faced with the problem of entertaining millions of readers with the description of the last rites of a famous actress.

She had been born in a fishing village where she was to be buried and it occurred to me that some old fisherman might have taught her to row a boat when she was a girl.

A round of the pubs in the evening, buying drinks for ancient fishermen, seemed to prove that she hadn't, but I eventually found an acquiescent and intoxicated old man, and informed him quite bluntly that he had, in fact, taught the actress to row when she was a little girl, but that he had forgotten it.

I then went out and bought a bunch of flowers, wrote an inscription, "To and from, with love", and gave them to the astonished old man with a ten-shilling note, and told him to be at the graveside next day with the flowers and inscription.

He turned up rather late, still intoxicated, and the inscription, which was carefully copied out by the local correspondents, appeared in most of the papers – even *The Times*, I think.

Nathaniel Gubbins, World's Press News 6 *Apr* 1937

GADGETS

In the mid-1970s Stirling Moss, the former racing driver, owned a house in Mayfair almost entirely run by gadgets. The glass of the ground-floor windows was of the type which enables the occupant to look out whilst thwarting the attempts of the curious to look in. The toilet seat was kept permanently heated to body temperature and the bath could be run by remote control from either the study or the dining room. Beyond the study an interior courtyard contained a fountain, floodlit by a photo-electric cell which reacted to any marked diminution in natural light. At the press of a button a meal could be lowered on a small table from the kitchen in just eight seconds.

Peter Bushell, GREAT ECCENTRICS 1984

Christopher Serpell, when BBC correspondent in Washington, could never resist the gadgets with which Americans love to clutter their desks. Prominent among these was a small black box with a switch on the top boldly labelled "Do not throw this switch". When you inevitably did then the whole box heaved and groaned, the lid flew open, and a small green hand hand emerged and turned the switch off again. That is all it did.

Gerald Priestland, SOMETHING UNDERSTOOD 1986

GAMBLING

Abington Baird, usually known as the Squire, would bet on anything. During an argument with a friend he said, "I bet you a tenner you don't know the Lord's Prayer." "Done," said the crony and forthwith proceeded to say, "For what we are about to receive, may the Lord make us truly thankful." The Squire passed over a tenner saying, "My God, I never thought you'd know it."

Bertie Hollander, BEFORE I FORGET 1935

A friend saw Tristan Bernard, the French dramatist, on the promenade at Deauville, wearing a jaunty new yachting cap. When he remarked on it Bernard replied that he had just bought it with his winnings from the previous night's play at the casino. The friend congratulated him. "Ah," said Bernard, "but what I lost would have bought me a yacht."

Cornelia Otis Skinner, ELEGANT WITS AND GRAND HORIZONTALS 1982

During Horatio Bottomley's examination for bankruptcy J.M. Ashbury K.C. asked him, "Mr Bottomley why did you never tell me you kept racehorses?" Bottomley replied, "I gave you a correct answer. I never kept racehorses. They kept me."

Alan Hyman, THE RISE AND FALL OF HORATIO BOTTOMLEY

Mr Duff Cooper nearly remained in Oxford for ever. He gave a party to celebrate his success in his examinations. After the party there was poker. Mr Duff Cooper was fortunate.

There was a pistol on the table. An undergraduate who had been the heaviest loser picked up the pistol, removed the magazine, and, pointing the gun at the chief winner said jestingly, "Duff, you lucky devil, I'd like to shoot you." He pulled the trigger. There was a loud explosion and a bullet whistled past Mr Cooper's ear and buried itself in the wall. The undergraduate had neglected to remove the cartridge in the barrel.

R.H. Bruce-Lockhart, Evening Standard 4 *Aug* 1938

In spite of the large sums he earned on the stage Sir Charles Hawtrey never seemed to have any money. "When I was a schoolboy," I once heard him say, "I lost half-a-crown at a small race meeting. Ever since, I've been trying to get that half-crown back, and it must have cost me half a million."

J.B. Booth, LIFE, LAUGHTER AND BRASS HATS 1939

Lady Hildyard was a most charming hostess but an inveterate gambler, and South Africa with its fortunes won or lost overnight was a dangerous centre for the unstable. One day she came to me in great distress. She had gambled and lost an enormous sum, practically all Sir Henry's capital, and what should she do? I advised her to confess at once. All Sir Henry said was, "Never mind, my dear, I might have done much worse myself."

Adrian Carton de Wiart, HAPPY ODYSSEY 1950

A racing correspondent named Ted Humphreys won about £6000 at Goodwood. He decided to spend £3000 of it on a house in South London. But the estate agent he rang up was busy and could not show him the place until the following week. On Tuesday he went to the races. On Wednesday he went to the races. On Thursday he went to the races. On Friday there was about £900 left out of the £6000. Never mind. Ted still determined to buy a house, but a smaller one. On Saturday he went to Windsor races and lost the rest of the little fortune. I came back with him and he told me he hadn't a bean, "Not even enough to buy you a drink. You'll have to stand me one," was his cheerful exclamation.

Arthur J. Sarl, HORSES, JOCKEYS AND CROOKS 1935

During a holiday in Dieppe my father (Sir Nigel Playfair) often used to visit the casino. One night after he had been lucky he saw Richard Sickert sitting opposite him. He pushed all the money he had won over to Sickert. "Paint me a picture of the scene," he said. A year elapsed. Then the picture arrived.

Giles Playfair, MY FATHER'S SON 1937

Richard Strauss's passion was the German card game of *skat* , which he played at every opportunity. His first remark when working with a new orchestra was, "I need some players for *skat* . Who will join me?"

At the Bayreuth Festival, to keep him and the cast content, Winifred Wagner discreetly reimbursed the singers and musicians who nightly surrendered their earnings to the cardsharp conductor.

Norman Lebrecht, THE BOOK OF MUSICAL ANECDOTES 1985

As a plunger on horses – horses that ran oh so badly – Edgar Wallace became the favourite client of practically every large bookmaker in London. "Let us celebrate," he said on receiving £1000 for a serial – the first big money he had ever had from a publisher. The celebration carried him to Newmarket and when the last race was over he had twenty-three shillings out of his original £1000.

Leonard Russell, Daily Telegraph 23 Sep 1932

After an all-night session in a game of roulette a man had lost his entire fortune. The luck against him was uncanny, and not even a white chip was left. He sat by the table, staring disconsolately at the stack of chips of the happy men around him. Presently came the dawn, and a ray of sunshine. It found entrance into the room through a knot hole in the board wall. The playful ray fixed itself on the winning side of the table, right in front of the loser in a shape resembling a yellow chip. The sleepy croupier paid the bet on the sunny chip. The gambler bet again and again, now unshakably convinced that his ray of sunshine was the real thing. He broke the bank.

Ely Culbertson, THE STRANGE LIVES OF ONE MAN 1940

I knew a young army officer who bet £100 that he would eat a wine-glass, and the bet was accepted. He nibbled a tiny bit out of the glass every day for months – no time limit had been imposed – and eventually won the bet. And he was, apparently, none the worse.

Basil Toser, THE LIGHTER SIDE OF LIFE 1932

GARDEN

[On a visit to Max Beerbohm at the Villino Chiaro, Rapello] Miss Jungmann brought out strawberries gathered in the steep little garden outside. "From our garden," she remarked proudly. "I always say," said Max, with a quick, sly look, "that things from gardens just haven't got that special something which you find in things bought in shops, have they?"

S.N. Behrman, CONVERSATIONS WITH MAX 1960

A brother of mine laid out a new rock garden at his house in the country. The next year a neighbour wrote saying that he would be very grateful should my brother be able to supply him with any of his superfluous rock plants. My brother answered regretting his inability to accede to this request as, owing to the dry spring, his rock garden had failed absolutely, in fact the only growth visible in it consisted of several hundred specimens of "Leo Elegans". Much impressed with the sonorous appellation, his correspondent begged for a few roots of "Leo Elegans". My brother, in his reply, pointed out that the common dandelion was hardly a sufficient rarity to warrant it being transplanted.

Lord Frederick Hamilton, HERE, THERE AND EVERYWHERE 1921

When Edwin Lutyens was in India he received a letter from worried clients in England to say that the terrace garden he had conjured for them was collapsing. Lutyens, not unduly concerned, cabled, "Build buttresses. They are such jolly things."

Peter Coats, OF KINGS AND CABBAGES 1984

Marshal Lyautey asked his gardener to plant a tree in a particular part of his estate. The gardener objected that the tree the marshal had chosen was particularly slow-growing and would not reach maturity for at least a century. The marshal replied, "In that case there is no time to lose. Plant it this afternoon."

Leon Harris, THE FINE ART OF POLITICAL WIT 1966

Author Brendan Gill reports that the poet Robert Graves, a devoted gardener, has long been in the habit of naming compost heaps after friends. "During my visit," writes Gill, "he honoured me by naming his latest compost heap after me. A friend that Graves and I have in common – the banker-scholar Gordon Wasson – has recently been honoured in a similar fashion. I was understandably proud when, some months after my visit, I received a letter from Graves in which he mentioned that, "the Gordon Wasson is something of a disappointment, but the Brendan Gill is rotting nicely".

New Yorker 1978

Walled gardens were one of the joys of Teheran. One of the most spectacular belonged to the Iranian correspondent of the United Press agency, and as you were admitted through its gateway and progressed up a winding path towards the house you could not help being struck by a series of life-sized plaster casts of a naked woman posing among the flowers and bushes. It was something of an embarrassment when you got there to have the door opened by (very obviously) the model – his wife. And she knew you knew she knew.

Gerald Priestland, SOMETHING UNDERSTOOD 1986

GENERAL STRIKE

During the General Strike of 1926, the late Lord Jellicoe would have been addressed as P.C. Jellicoe. The Admiral called to see Sir Noel Curtis-Bennett, who was at the Civil Commissioner's Department and asked what he could do.

"We are still short of special policemen," replied Curtis-Bennett.

"Open air and a walk," said Lord Jellicoe. "Just what I want."

So for the remainder of the General Strike the Commander of the Grand Fleet took his spell of duty with an armlet and a truncheon, guarding a suburban gasworks.

Sir Harry Preston, LEAVES FROM MY UNWRITTEN DIARY 1936

In the General Strike of 1926 I became an engine driver on the London and North-Eastern Railway. I knew little about engine driving nor did my two firemen who, in ordinary life, were medical students. On our first trip we drew out of Kings Cross with a certain amount of difficulty, and proceeded slowly until we came to a long tunnel where, halfway through, the engine gave a last sorrowful puff – and stopped. Burning sulphur fumes filled our cabin, so dense that although a white hot furnace was only four feet away from where I stood, I could not see it. In the unprotected cabin the fumes were unbearable, and breathing in this difficult stuff we choked and coughed and spat. I snatched a sweat rag from my neck, dipped it in water and crammed it in my mouth.

Finally we were able to make the engine run backwards and emerged into daylight again. Had I been able to read the gradient chart I would have known the tunnel was uphill all the way. We managed to reach our destination eventually and were rewarded with tips amounting to three pounds and many packets of cigarettes from grateful passengers.

Rex Tremlett, EASY GOING 1940

GENEROSITY

When the Lady Astor was made a Freeman of Plymouth, the city which she represented in the House of Commons for so long, and to which she and her husband had made so many benefactions, she suddenly decided to give the marvellous diamond necklace which Waldorf had given her to the Lady Mayoress of Plymouth. Taking it off, she told the astonished Mayoress that she wanted it to be a present to the city so that it could be worn by the successive Lady Mayoresses of Plymouth.

Derek Patmore, Western Morning News 2 *May* 1968

There was a 16-year-old girl among my set of C.B. Cochran's "Young Ladies" who developed tuberculosis while in the show. Cochran immediately sent her to an expensive sanatorium in the country, where he would motor down to see her whenever he could, taking books and other presents to cheer her up. She remained there for many months, during which time Cochran had some severe reverses which brought him near to bankruptcy. One day, going down to see her, I met Cocky, his arms full of parcels. Just before he went in to see her he said, "Please don't tell her I had to come down by train. You see, I had to sell my car."

Elizabeth Frank, News Chronicle Feb 1957

Dorothy Day, founder of the Catholic Worker Movement in New York, was fined 250 dollars because her hostel for derelicts was not up to code. As she left for the court she walked past a gathering of bums looking for handouts. From their midst a man, who looked much like the rest, stepped out and pressed a piece of paper in her hand. "I just read about your trouble," he said. "I want to help out a little. Here's two-fifty." Miss Day elated over having, as she thought, 2 dollars 50, thanked her benefactor and hurried on. In the subway on her way to Manhattan Upper Court, she looked at the cheque. It was for the full amount of the fine, 250 dollars. And it was signed W.H. Auden. Miss Day was apologetic for not having recognised him. "Poets do look a bit unpressed, don't they?" she said.

New York Times, quoted Stephen Spender, W.H. AUDEN: A TRIBUTE 1975

One story about George Orwell says something about his real feelings towards the poor. A journalist who worked with him on *Tribune* described how he caught Orwell, with a guilty look on his face, stuffing something into a packet. It turned out that the packet was full of unusable verses which Orwell was returning to an unlucky contributor. He was looking guilty because he had added a bonus to the packet – a ten-shilling note.

Ian Cotton, TV Times 11 *Oct* 1973

GENTLEMAN

At dinner one evening in Belgium, Montgomery asked us for our definition of a gentleman. He clearly thought we weren't doing very well, and indeed we weren't, so he said; "Well, we'll ask Winston when he comes out next week."

On Winston's first night we had not been sitting down long before Monty duly said, "I have been asking these fellows for a definition of a gentleman – and they aren't very good at it. What's yours?" Winston thought for a moment and said, "I know one when I see one," and then added, "I supposed one might say – someone who is only rude intentionally."

J.R. Henderson, MONTGOMERY AT CLOSE QUARTERS 1985

GHOST

Andrew Gow once visited us during the grouse season at Douglas and, tired of walking, lay down where he could see over the valley of the Douglas Water. When we returned to him he asked if the local territorials were manoeuvering, and he described seeing men marching along the hillside and down the valley to the village. The Lanarkshire Yeomanry were not in the area that day, but he had described exactly the route taken by the Covenanting army, as they marched to fight and win over their oppressors, some hundreds of years before.

Lord Home, THE WAY THE WIND BLOWS 1976

GIFT

Sir Michael Adeane, the Queen's Private Secretary, would send out a six-thousand word document in advance to all hosts explaining the royal requirements. There were detailed instructions about gifts. Animals were not really welcome, explained Adeane's briefing, but his warning was not always heeded. Touring the Gambia in 1961, the Queen was offered a baby crocodile in a biscuit tin. It had to spend a night in the bath of Sir Martin Charteris.

Robert Lacey, MAJESTY 1977

GOLF

The Aga Khan once went to play golf with Lord Castlerosse, neither of whom could be described as lightweights. Lord Castlerosse spent some time in the professional's shop buying balls, and was interrupted by the entrance of his caddie with a serious face.

"I'm afraid you're going to lose today, my lord," he said. "His Highness is outside praying to his gods for victory."

"Indeed," said the Viscount and went outside to have a look.

The Aga Khan, to while away the time, was doing a little arms-above-the-head-stretch and toe-touching exercises. He won that game of golf.

Sir Harry Preston, LEAVES FROM MY UNPUBLISHED DIARY 1936

I associate AJB – as I always heard Arthur Balfour called – with Norfolk jackets and large canvas bags stuffed full with golf clubs. I used to be given sixpence to caddie for him on the Stanway garden links and I remember being puzzled and alarmed when my mother told me I must take great care never, never to get into the Tail of his Eye. For some time I supposed this mysterious prohibited area to be some extra feature peculiar to himself.

Cynthia Asquith, REMEMBER AND BE GLAD 1952

"May I half change?" This question to the house prefect in charge of games was how a junior boy would ask if he could change his school jacket for a blazer to be excused the compulsory games he hated and go to the Marlborough Down to play golf. John Betjeman was the only boy in the house who brought his golf clubs to school. Others had sets at home, but they either enjoyed games, tolerated them, or lacked the moral courage to do the same as John Betjeman. His request was seldom refused.

Arthur Byron, The Times 22 *May* 1984

"What is your handicap?" Lady Cunard asked Lord Castlerosse on the golf course. "Drink and debauchery," he answered, sadly but truthfully.

Philip Ziegler, DIANA COOPER 1981

Some months after the end of his term of office as president, Eisenhower was asked if leaving the White House had affected his golf game. "Yes," he replied, "a lot more people beat me now."

Richard Crouser, IT'S UNLUCKY TO BE BEHIND AT THE END OF THE GAME 1982

Roger Maxwell, an actor who always played generals, brigadiers, Conservative MP's, or alternatively butlers, was addicted to golf. He bought an old ambulance and fitted it out with an elegant bed, desk and dressing table, and in this he would drive off to wherever a tournament was to be held. Nobody thought of preventing an ambulance from driving straight to the eighteenth green where Roger would camp out for the duration with a grandstand view.

Donald Sinden, A TOUCH OF THE MEMOIRS 1982

When Ben Richter, one of the country's leading left-hand golfers, decided to turn professional he took advantage of his peculiarity. Hearing that the Triple-A Club of St Louis needed a pro he wrote to its president, Sidney Maestre, and applied for the job. "But a left-handed pro!" exclaimed Maestre. "I'll show you in two minutes why a left-handed instructor is better than a right-handed one," Richter said. "Face me and I'll show you something." Richter took his left-handed stance; Maestre, facing him, took his right-handed position. As Richter swung correctly, Maestre copied him easily. "It's like looking into a mirror," he admitted, and Richter was appointed club professional.

Colliers Magazine 1936

When John D. Rockefeller, the oil millionaire, drove into the rough and spent a long time poking in the grass for the missing ball his caddie mentioned to him that other members, when they drove into the rough, only looked for the ball for a minute or two, and if they did not find it, dropped a new one on the fairway and played on. "Ha!" said Rockefeller, "They must have barrels of money."

Sunday Referee 14 *Feb* 1957

There is a story of Owen Seaman, as a golfer, making an excuse for every bad shot until he got to the last green, when he threw down his putter and said, "That settles it. I'll never play in knickerbockers again."

R.G.G. Price, HISTORY OF PUNCH

Jim Thorpe, the American golfer and 1982 Canadian Open Champion, flew to Turnberry for the start tomorrow of the 115th British Open, took one look at the course and disconcerted the organisers by announcing, "Man, that rough is so rough it's not my ball I'm worried about losing. It's my caddie."

Daily Telegraph 16 *Jun* 1986

For two hours the committee of a golf club in South-East England debated whether women players might be allowed to wear trousers on the links. Their decision was: "Trousers may be worn by woman golfers on the course, but must be taken off on entering the club house."

Daily Mirror, quoted Michael Bateman, THIS ENGLAND

A golfing cleric who in the course of a game made several bad foozles remarked on each occasion in disgusted undertones, "Aswan." His opponent was intrigued. "Why do you say 'Aswan?'," he asked. "Because", replied the parson, "it is the biggest dam I know."

Gerald Findler, HUMOUR FROM PULPIT AND PEW 1934

After the Great War, when many Naval officers came under the "Geddes Axe" and had to retire, arbitrary methods had to be applied. Of two excellent officers one was axed because he was a good golfer, and would have something to occupy his life.

Lady Murray, THE MAKING OF A CIVIL SERVANT 1940

Not even my colleague, Captain Heath, with Professor Einstein and Dr Gallup to help him could work out the odds against that astonishing coincidence at Worthing golf course on Sunday morning when two brothers killed two seagulls with two balls during the same round.

News Chronicle, quoted Denys Parsons, FUNNY HA HA, FUNNY PECULIAR 1965

GOVERNMENT

The formal tones of Cabinet proceedings surprised me. It is really determined by a very simple thing. We don't call each other Dick and Harold and George as we do in the National Executive. We address each other as "Minister of Housing" or "First Secretary" or "Prime Minister" and this, corresponding to the House of Commons technique, does have a curious flattening effect and helps us to behave civilly to each other.

Richard Crossman, DIARY 22 *Oct* 1964

GRAFFITI

The actor Ernest Thesiger was in Moscow on a theatrical tour. He went into one of the public conveniences and, finding himself alone, wrote on the wall, "Burgess loves Maclean".

Michael Pertwee, NAME DROPPING

A friend of mine was being shown round a very distinguished school by the headmaster when he was taken short and asked if he could use the boys' lavatories. The headmaster, who prided himself on his liberal attitudes, gave him permission, but warned him not to be shocked by anything he might see written on the lavatory walls. Filled with curiosity my friend conducted a fruitless search in each of the compartments. He was just giving up when he discovered, etched with a nail file high up on one of the walls, the scandalous words, "Down with Harrow."

Douglas Sutherland, THE ENGLISH GENTLEMAN 1978

GREAT WAR *See* **WORLD WAR I**

GUEST

J.C. Ackerman, who was to become vice-chairman of the *News Chronicle* and Sir W.S. Crawford, the advertising expert, were invited by Northcliffe to spend the night at Elmwood, his country home. They met at Victoria Station, found on the bookstall there a book entitled *How to Behave at a Country House*, bought it for fun, and derived much amusement from its perusal in the train. On arrival at the other end Jack Ackerman as a joke, put the book into Crawford's bag. At Elmwood a footman, as usual, took the baggage. When Crawford went to his room to dress for dinner he found his clothes neatly laid out, and the little book propped up in a prominent place on the dressing table. It was, probably quite by accident, open at the chapter headed "Tipping".

Wareham Smith, SPILT INK 1932

Harold Baker, a dignified middle-aged barrister staying with the Asquiths at The Wharf, was once woken at one in the morning by a knock on his bedroom door. He opened it to find a footman who said,

"Lady Oxford says will you stop that hooting. She can't get to sleep." In fact the noise had been made by an owl. One wonders what wild train of mind had led Margot to think that a middle-aged barrister was spending the small hours of the night standing at his bedroom window imitating the cry of an owl.

Lord David Cecil, Observer, Staying With Margot 20 *Dec* 1981

The French playwright Tristan Bernard's frankness often went to extremes. One evening he had been invited to a dinner party at a house renowned for its excellent cuisine. An hour after the appointed time Bernard still had not arrived, and his hostess, anxious that the meal should not be ruined, telephoned to ask what had happened. "I'm so sorry," said Bernard, "but I'm not coming." "Not coming?" "No," said Bernard, "I'm not hungry."

Cornelia Otis Skinner, ELEGANT WITS AND GRAND HORIZONTALS 1982

Late in life I had a beautiful object lesson in behaviour to the unpunctual. The scene was a luncheon party at the Broughams', the appointed time 1.30. Till 1.45 we waited for Lady Cunard and at 2 o'clock she arrived, full of apologies – she had been buying a chandelier. Old Lord Brougham, a handsome patriarch with magnificent silver hair, looked straight in front of him and said in a pensive tone, "I once knew a man who bought a chandelier *after* luncheon."

Edward Marsh, A NUMBER OF PEOPLE 1939

After a dull weekend, Mrs Patrick Campbell took pen in hand and wrote in the hostess's elaborate visitor's book, "Quoth the raven."

Bennett Cerf, SHAKE WELL BEFORE USING 1948

We were aware of Hart Crane's midnight prowlings and also aware, to our dismay, of his nocturnal pick-ups. He said he'd go out for a nightcap, so it was with great relief that I heard him come in about 2 a.m. and softly close the stairway door. Then all was quiet. But in the morning, what a hideous awakening! Marcelle brought my morning coffee to me with hands that trembled with shock. "Oh, madame," she said, "*quel malheur, quel malheur*!" I jumped out of bed and followed her downstairs to see what was the matter. By that time it was ten o'clock and Hart had already departed, probably as silently as he had entered, but he had left behind him traces of great activity. On the wallpaper and across the pale pink spread, up and down the curtains and over the white chenille rug, were the blackest footprints and handprints I had ever seen, hundreds of them. No wonder, for I heard to my fury that he had brought a chimney-sweep home for the night.

Caresse Crosby, THE PASSIONATE YEARS 1979

I was due to leave for Windsor Castle, where Ted and I have been invited to stay the night. When he heard where I was going Harold [Wilson] said I would have a pleasant time. "But they unpack your bags for you there. Don't do what my sister did. When they opened her bag her corn plasters fell out."

Barbara Castle, DIARY 3 *Apr* 1968

I am one of the world's fainters, and have been in a situation where it was uniquely awkward to excuse myself from the table and find somewhere soft to faint. If you are at the top table, just two places from the Queen (at a banquet given by the Queen to Mr and Mrs Ford, at the British Embassy in Washington), it is not all that easy to make an inconspicuous exit.

Instead I used my smelling salts until the last moment and in the end only had time to reach the nearest door, through which I fainted dead away on to a pantry floor and broke my jaw. I suppose if you have to break your jaw there is something to be said for having both the Queen's doctor and the President's doctor in attendance.

And Henry Kissinger sent me books to read in hospital with a message saying, "Susan, you did not have to go to this length to avoid sitting next to me at dinner."

Susan Barnes (Mrs Anthony Crosland), Sunday Times 15 *Oct* 1978

Tam Dalyell's hilltop family seat, The Binns, stands in 260 acres overlooking his mining constituency. It is now owned by the National Trust for Scotland. The Dalyells live in a flat in the house. The Labour MP Eric Heffer was once woken up at 2 a.m. by blood-freezing screeches coming from the upper regions of the house. It sounded like the first Mrs Rochester having one of her turns. Heffer: "I think this house is haunted, Tam. I heard a ghost last night." Dalyell: "No. Those were our peacocks."

Observer, Profile 26 *Aug* 1984

There are regular house-parties at Chatsworth (seat of the Duke and Duchess of Devonshire) and Princess Margaret's name frequently figures on the guest list. Two days prior to one of her visits Sir Alec Douglas-Home slept in the room she was due to occupy. He told his hostess. "If I lie very still and don't turn over you won't have to change the sheets."

Peter Bushell, GREAT ECCENTRICS 1984

Einstein had perfected a beautiful technique for getting rid of unwanted guests. After he had been talking for half an hour a maid would come in with a bowl of soup. If he accepted it his guest would feel that he was interrupting a meal and feel obliged to leave. If, on the other hand, he was perfectly happy to go on talking, Einstein would wave the soup away, as if he couldn't imagine why it had arrived.

Nigel Hawkes, Observer 11 *Mar* 1979

At Welbeck Abbey, the Duke of Portland's house, Sir Alfred Fripp was a fellow guest of the Marquis de Villalobar, of the Spanish Embassy. This clever and amusing diplomat had the disadvantages of an artificial leg, an artificial hand, artificial hair and artificial teeth. One night he was late for dinner. The Duchess was getting worried, with Royal guests arriving, so she said to the Groom of the Chambers, "We will give him five minutes more, then we will have dinner." But before that five minutes was up the servant was back. "If you please, your Grace, the Marquis has come to pieces in the hall," he said. It had a marble floor!

Cecil Roberts, ALFRED FRIPP 1932

When Gandhi was Mrs Sarojini Naidu's guest and required supplies of goat's milk, fresh fruit, juice and other rarities she is reputed to have exclaimed, "You've no idea, Mahatma, how expensive it is to provide you with the wherewithal to fast."

Malcolm Muggeridge, Observer 19 *Oct* 1969

One of my father's friends, the Marchese Caprinica del Grillo, was invited to an evening reception by a prominent London hostess. He said that he would be reaching London very late, and was told to come along just as he was. But when he did arrive his lounge suit was frowned upon. He thereupon took his leave, and presently reappeared in full evening kit, covered with orders and decorations.

"We are here," he said as he caught sight of his hostess, advancing to kiss her hand. Then, to the surprise of everyone he took a cup of *consommé* in one hand, and an ice in the other, and poured them all over himself. His clothes were in an appalling state.

"It is you, dear clothes, who are invited," he said, "Not I. Therefore I am feeding you and not myself."

He bowed, turned, and walked quietly out of the room.

Marchesa Stella Vitelleschi, OUT OF MY COFFIN 1937

Having invited Charles Laughton and a number of other film stars to dinner one evening, pianist Arthur Rubinstein entertained his guests before dinner by showing them home movies of his children's amateur stage performances. The "audience" was visibly relieved when the last reel came to an end and dinner was served. "I've always regretted that I never had children," said Laughton to his host as they passed into the dining room, "and never more so than now. Because, Mr Rubinstein, if I had children I would make them play the piano to you."

Clifton Fadiman, LITTLE, BROWN BOOK OF ANECDOTES 1985

D.H. Lawrence came to luncheon at Montequforii and brought his wife. After lunch she jumped on all the beds to see if the mattresses were soft.

Edith Sitwell, TAKEN CARE OF 1965

As a guest in the Kaufmann household, Oscar Levant rather overdid his welcome. At the end of a prolonged visit Mrs Kaufmann hinted, "The servants always expect a little something and I knew you haven't any money, so I tipped them each three dollars and told them it was from you." Levant was outraged. "You should have given them five," he exclaimed. "Now they'll think I'm stingy."

Dorothy Herrman, WITH MALICE TOWARDS ALL 1982

For one year and one month Oscar Levant declared my house his house. For one year and one month he ate my food, played my piano, ran up my phone bills, burned cigarette holes in my landlady's furniture, monopolised my record player and my coffee pot, gave his guests the run of the joint, insulted my guests, and never stopped complaining. He was an egomaniac. He was a leech and a lunatic – but I loved the guy.

Harpo Marx, HARPO SPEAKS 1961

Bertrand Russell told us that Herbert Spencer suffered from a greatly over-active brain. He always went to dinner parties with two ear plugs in his pocket. If the conversation got too stimulating he put the plugs in his ears and remained silent for the rest of the evening.

Rupert Crawshaw-Williams, RUSSELL REMEMBERED 1970

Archbishop Trench and his wife were dining out. Forgetting he was not in his own house, he bent forward and remarked very distinctly indeed, "My dear, we must write down this cook as one of our failures."

Gerald Findler, HUMOUR FROM PULPIT AND PEW 1934

Denton Welch had visited Walter Sickert. As he left the house Sickert said, "Come again – when you have a little less time."

Edith Sitwell, TAKEN CARE OF 1965

To a rather impertinent Frenchman, who had asked to see her home, The Mount, in Massachusetts, and who said somewhat patronisingly as he departed that he approved of it all except the bas-relief in the entrance hall. Edith Wharton replied, "I assure you that you will never see it here again."

Percy Lubbock, PORTRAIT OF EDITH WHARTON 1947

A young unmarried clergyman had been given a living by a certain duke. He knew little about the usages of such exalted society, so when he was invited to visit his Grace for a few days he found himself in an astonishing state of nerves. He asked a more experienced friend for a few tips, for instance, as to what clothes he should take. The advice was minutely detailed; "Of course you'd take your swallow-tail and then, if you were a real toff, you'd take your servant with you." The young clergyman was careful upon every point, took his dress clothes *– and his parlourmaid.*

Dr Greville MacDonald, REMINISCENCES OF A SPECIALIST 1932

See also **HOSPITALITY**

HABIT

There is something very strange about Stanley Baldwin. At first sight he is a solid English gentleman but then one observes odd nervous tricks. He has an extraordinary unpleasant habit of smelling at his notes, and licking the edges slightly as if they were a flap of an envelope. He scratches himself continually.

Harold Nicolson, letter to Vita Sackville-West 4 *Dec* 1935

My efforts to keep up with Isaiah [Berlin, at New College, Oxford] were not helped by the distractions he introduced, presumably because trying to teach me occupied only one corner of his mind. In one of his rooms he kept a gramophone with an enormous papier-maché horn, on which he played classical music while I read my essay, or he would let loose clockwork penguins on the hearthrug.

Gerald Priestland, SOMETHING UNDERSTOOD 1986

The Marquis of Clanricarde owned large estates in Galway. On one stood the 200-roomed Portumac Castle. He was an absentee landlord, a hermit and a notorious miser who lived alone in dust-covered chambers in Albany, London. He belonged to famous social clubs, but was shunned by most of their members because of his habits.

He would, for example, stare at a fellow member, then, with deliberation, cock a snook at him, holding thumb and extended fingers to his nose like a street urchin. He would sit alone in a window alcove of one club overlooking the street, licking the tip of his long nose with his tongue.

John K. Garbutt, Sunday Express 31 *Jul* 1949

Every morning my grandmother as an old lady, went straight to the window to read what the thermometer on the wall outside had to say of the temperature. After that she looked through her letters before she picked up *The Times* to read the "Deaths", then on the front page. She was pleased when she found she had outlived another contemporary, and said so. *Then* she ate her egg.

Joyce Grenfell, JOYCE GRENFELL REQUESTS THE PLEASURE 1976

Author Sidney Sheldon and Groucho Marx were close friends and neighbours for many years. As Groucho got well into his eighties he started making a habit of visiting Sidney's house each afternoon for a snack of an apple and a piece of cheese. "It became such a ritual that my wife and I looked forward to it every day," Sheldon recalls. Groucho would eat his snack and walk back to his own house.

Then the Sheldons rented out the Hollywood house and moved to Rome where Sidney began work on a novel. One day he got a letter from his tenant who wrote, "We love the house, but there is one strange thing. Every afternoon there is a little old man, between 85 and 90, who knocks at our door and asks for some cheese and an apple. He's too well dressed for a tramp. Can you tell us who he is?"

James Bacon, MADE IN HOLLYWOOD

Once, as I sat talking to Gilbert Murray in his study while he walked up and down I suddenly asked, "Exactly what is the principle of that walk of yours? Are you trying to avoid the flowers on the rug? or are you trying to keep to the squares?" My own compulsion-neuroses made it easy for me to notice them in others. He wheeled round sharply. "You are the first person who has caught me out," he said. "No, it's not the flowers or the squares. It's a habit that I've got into of doing things in sevens. I take seven steps, then I change direction and go another seven steps, then I turn around. I consulted Browne, the Professor of Psychology, about it, but he assured me it isn't a dangerous fault. He said, 'When you find yourself getting into multiples of seven, come to me again.'"

Robert Graves, GOODBYE TO ALL THAT 1929

HANDWRITING

J.K. Galbraith won my heart the first time I wrote an essay for him to read. My handwriting has always been abominable, so when I went to his room the following week I diffidently enquired, whether he had found any difficulty in reading it. "None at all," he said to my relieved surprise, "but then, I am a palaeographer."

John Boyd-Carpenter, WAY OF LIFE 1980

A graphologist, shown a sample of the composer Arnold Schoenberg, concluded, "This man thinks he is at least the Emperor of China." Schoenberg, told of the man's comment said, "But did he believe I was justified?"

Norman Lebrecht, BOOK OF MUSICAL ANECDOTES 1985

HAT

A fellow journalist spotted G.K. Chesterton turning the corner of the street when a gust of wind blew his hat off. The journalist ran after it, followed by GKC. Eventually they retrieved it from the jaws of an oncoming bus. Mopping his brow, Chesterton panted his thanks. "But you shouldn't have taken the trouble," he said, "My wife has bought me a new hat, and she will be most disappointed – *most* disappointed – when she hears that the old one has only just been saved from well-merited destruction." "In that case why did you bother to run after it?" the indignant journalist queried. "It's an old friend," Chesterton replied, "and I wanted to be with it to the end."

Richard Ingrams, Telegraph Magazine 24 *Apr* 1974

As we were driving in the rain through Angoulême a lady in my party suddenly exclaimed, "Oh, there's a hat!" The car was violently stopped. She dashed into the shop and emerged with a 300-franc fashionable green hat, snatched from the provinciality of Angoulême. What an eye she had for a hat! We drove on.

Arnold Bennett, JOURNAL 1929

John Barrymore told me a story of the late Père Guitry who, accompanied by an outspoken friend, set forth to buy a hat, and after long consideration fixed his choice upon a wide-brimmed stetson. This he set upon his head and composing his features to suit its peculiarities asked, "How do I look?" "Like an old ponce," said his friend. With a pained expression Guitry returned the hat to the assistant saying, "Take it away. It ages me."

Roland Pertwee, MASTER OF NONE 1940

HEALTH

"The secret of health," Margot Asquith once told my uncle, Hugh Cecil, "is to have all your teeth out and drink a glass of brandy every day."

Lord David Cecil, Observer, Staying With Margot 20 Dec *1981*

Harry Preston kept insisting that people don't perspire enough, an old health theme of his. "It's the secret of my fairly long sojourn in this world. You ought to have a good sweat every day. Look at me, look at me," clicking his tongue and holding out his biceps not noticeably there. He then gave us a lecture on Fletcherism, and the importance of saliva in eating. Said he had prolonged the lives of Frank Curson, and J.J. Jarvis, the trainer, and that he would have been dead at forty if he hadn't taken himself in hand.

Reginald Pound, POUND NOTES 1940

Bernard Shaw was always on the look-out for a doctor who had meditated on headaches. One afternoon just after recovering from an attack he was introduced to Dr Nansen and asked the famous Arctic explorer whether he had ever discovered a headache cure. "No," said Nansen with a look of amazement. "Have you ever *tried* to discover a headache cure?" "No." "Well, that is a most astonishing thing," exclaimed Shaw. "You have spent your life trying to discover the North Pole, which nobody on earth cares tuppence about, and you have never attempted to discover a cure for headache, which everyone is crying out for."

Hesketh Pearson, BERNARD SHAW 1942

HOAX

My colleague A.J. McIlroy was the subject of a joke played on him aboard HMS *Invincible* on the way south to the Falklands War. The joker was Prince Andrew who challenged him to a game of snooker and arranged to meet him at the appointed time in the *Invincible*'s "snooker room". Mac declined to say how many circuits of the carrier he made in his search for the room, but he does confess that the entire crew seemed to be in on the joke and sent him on his way with new directions every time he stopped to ask the way.

Peterborough, Daily Telegraph 21 *Dec* 1985

Another of my stories was flashed on the city in a seven-column front page headline; "Earthquake Hits Chicago". A four-column cut of a fissure opened by the quake on the Lincoln Park beach accompanied the story. Gene Cour, the photographer, and I had spent two hours digging the fissure. There were other corroborations; housewives who reported dishes spilled from pantry shelves and broken, stenographers who reported the top of the Masonic Temple to have swayed dangerously, and several male citizens who had been thrown to the ground by the impact of the quake while at work in their shops. These were, of course, all my relatives with their true names attached. For several days, during which an angry rival press sought to belittle the *Journal's* great scoop of the earth's upheaval, my uncles, aunts and cousins stood firm in their memories of terror and shock.

Ben Hecht, A CHILD OF THE CENTURY 1954

Sir Edwin Lutyens was given to childish practical jokes. Once, staying with the Sitwells, he drew some strands of horsehair from a sofa, wrapped them in a piece of paper on which he had written a few words, and quietly deposited then in a desk drawer. Many years later Osbert Sitwell discovered the little package on which was written, "A lock of Marie Antoinette's hair cut from her head ten minutes after execution."

Clive Aslet, THE LAST COUNTRY HOUSES 1982

Oh, I had such fun just now. A woman telephoned and asked whether I was Fergus and Fergus, and would I have her fiancé's kilt ready by the first of March without fail? I said that we were an old Scottish firm, perhaps a wee bit old-fashioned, but I did not think a young woman should mention her fiancé's kilt. She gasped in astonishment. I said, "I am afraid I cannot answer so delicate a question and you must get your fiancé to write to us himself." "But he is in the Cameroons!" she wailed. "Oh," I answered, "I thought you said he was in the Black Watch." By then she was getting suspicious, so I replaced the receiver.

Harold Nicolson, letter to Vita Sackville-West 8 *Feb* 1956

Perhaps the most obvious April Fool's Day hoax was the *Sunday Times* story about a £50 million scheme using driverless buses in London. "Secret early morning tests have gone well," it said. If you believe that you believe anything. Not so the Department of Transport and the GLC. On the Monday morning London Transport received an irate call from the Transport under-secretary, demanding to know why he had not been told, and demanding further details. The LT board then passed a motion, censuring Dr David Quarmby, head of LT's buses, for not briefing his superiors on the scheme.

The Times, Diary 10 *Apr* 1984

See also **PRACTICAL JOKE**

HOME

Gilbert Chesterton and his wife were looking for a home in the country. Gilbert had no idea where to look, so they arrived at Paddington one morning and demanded tickets to the destination of the first train that left. The next train went to Slough. Gilbert and Frances got out and strolled through the lanes all day. At night they came to Beaconsfield, stayed at the White Hart, and bought a house there. That was Gilbert for you.

Dorothy Collins, G.K.Chesterton's secretary, Sunday Times 2 *Jun* 1974

Edith Evans was looking for a new house and I mentioned that I knew of a charming one in Herefordshire. "Oh no, dear," she said, "that's much too far out." "Do you mean somewhere like Chelsea or Hampstead?" "Oh, my dear, I've never lived further away than Hyde Park Corner."

Donald Sinden, A TOUCH OF THE MEMOIRS 1982

Dorothy Parker's apartment on West 57th Street was hardly pretentious. She said all she needed was space "to lay a hat and a few friends". The only things that belonged to her were a portable typewriter and a canary she called Onan, because he spilled his seed upon the ground.

John Keats, YOU MIGHT AS WELL LIVE: THE LIFE AND TIMES OF DOROTHY PARKER 1971

HOMOSEXUALITY

In the mid-1930s there was an influx of homosexuals to Fire Island, where the writer Gene Fowler had made his home. Asked how he felt about it he frowned. "I'm worried. I lie in bed at night and worry about them." "You think it is ruining the island?" "No, it's not that. The thing that worries me is, suppose it turns out that they are right?"

H. Allen Smith, LIFE AND LEGEND OF GENE FOWLER 1972

I shrieked with laughter when he (Lord Longford) was accused of being a homosexual. He replied, "I do have eight children." "Oh," said the other person, "that's just cover."

Elizabeth Longford, quoted Susan Crosland, Sunday Times Magazine 31 *Aug* 1986

The Wolfenden Report recognised the facts of homosexuality and tried to deal with them. Field Marshall Montgomery was utterly opposed to what he told me was the "Buggers' Charter". At the committee stage he tried to render the bill harmless by suggesting that the age of consent should be raised from the age of twenty-one to the age of eighty, adding with a disarming smile, that he himself would achieve four-score years at his next birthday.

Mervyn Stockwood, CHANCTONBURY RING 1982

Edna St Vincent Millay, on being shown the wonders of Villa Mauresque by her host, Somerset Maugham, and meeting her fellow guests, Cecil Beaton, Noel Coward and Gerald Haxton, exclaimed, "Oh, Mr Maugham, it's fairyland here."

S. N. Behrman, TRIBULATIONS AND LAUGHTER 1972

Lytton Strachey chose to appear before a military tribunal as a conscientious objector. To the the chairman's stock question, which had previously never failed to embarrass the claimant, "Tell me, Mr Strachey, what would you do if you saw a German trying to violate your sister?" he replied with an air of noble virtue, "I would try to get between them."

Robert Graves, GOODBYE TO ALL THAT 1929

At a party the conversation turned to the question of which great historical character the people there would most have liked to go to bed with. The men voted for Cleopatra, Kitty Fisher and so on, but when it came to Lytton Strachey's turn he declared shrilly, "Julius Caesar."

Michael Holroyd, LYTTON STRACHEY 1973

HONESTY

Lockett Agnew, a member of the firm of art dealers, was once asked £700 for a picture by a fellow art dealer. Agnew thought £600 adequate, but as the other would not budge he suggested over the telephone that they should toss up for the difference. "Very well," replied the other, "I'll call to you." "You blighter, you've won," shouted Agnew a second later. "It's seven hundred pounds, then." How many dealers would be so trusting?

Bernard Falk, FIVE YEARS DEAD 1937

I was on the whole a very good little boy, having been properly brought up by my poor but honest parents. When I first arrived at my prep school the headmaster, Mr Hornby, said that if anyone broke anything he must come and own up. A few days later I broke a small branch off a tree. I confessed the breakage to the headmaster. He reassured me, and told me that matters of such trivial nature were hardly worth reporting. I took comfort from this advice, and never reported any breakages again.

Randolph Churchill, TWENTY-ONE 1964

HONEYMOON

The honeymoon showed Aitken [Lord Beaverbrook] at his characteristic best and worst. He overwhelmed his bride with lavish gifts such as she had never known before. He gave her a brief taste of gay life in New York. Then carried her off to the West Indies and spent his time looking at business propositions. A letter of May 5 1906 to a friend gives some idea of this curious honeymoon: "While in Cuba I bought the Puerto Principe Electric Light Co for 300,000 dollars. I bought 200 acres of land in the city of Camaguey, and 217 acres to the north of Sir W. Van Horne's car works. I bought the old Mule Tram franchise, and I acquired the electric railway franchise in an almost completed condition. When the tramlines are completed they will pass through the lands I have purchased. On account of the congested condition of the population of the City I expect to make a very large profit out of selling business lots."

A.J.P. Taylor, BEAVERBROOK 1972

HONOURS

When the parsimonious French Government asked the Curies what official decorations they would like to have Madame Curie replied, "I pray to thank the Minister and to tell him that I do not in the least feel the need of a decoration, but I do feel the greatest need for a laboratory."

Practical Mechanics May 1940

While I was in America, in 1946, a cable reached me. "Clem says George wishes give you three-quarter length robe." I guessed that Clem must mean Mr Attlee, and probably George meant the King, but what on earth was the three-quarter length robe? I cabled back, "Mystified. Please elucidate," and by return came Reggie's reply. "Times crossword, silly." (Three quarters of the word robe is OBE). I was being honoured for my work in hospitals and camps and the decoration reached me by post in London a year later.

Joyce Grenfell, JOYCE GRENFELL REQUESTS THE PLEASURE 1976

I was on duty as gentleman usher at the first investiture of the Order of Merit, the founding of which was one of Edward VII's first actions on coming to the throne. Among the distinguished recipients of the Order was the great medical scientist, Lord Lister. The King took the ribbon with the jewelled Order hanging from it, and tried to pass it over Lord Lister's head. So wide, however, was the great man's head that the ribbon could not go over it, but remained halfway on, the jewel resting on Lord Lister's nose. The King tried to press it over, but in vain. The situation was embarrassing and becoming ridiculous. At last Lord Lister said, "I think, sir, I had better take it away in my hand," and lifting the ribbon and jewel off his head he retired in good order, leaving the King and ourselves to enjoy a gentle and discreet laugh at his expense.

Sir Lionel Cust, KING EDWARD VII AND HIS COURT 1930

Claude Monet had known poverty, indifference and contempt. Then one day Clemenceau, whom he knew well, said to him, "Monet, I am going to give you the Legion of Honour." Monet looked at him quietly and then said, "No, Clemenceau. I am sixty years old. You should have thought of it sooner." My father used to say that Monet died wearing the Grand Cross of Disdain of the Legion of Honour.

Sacha Guitry, IF I REMEMBER RIGHT 1935

HORSE

In New York, Bela Bartok longed for Hungary and its countryside. Walking in Manhattan one day he announced, "I smell horses." "In the middle of 66th Street?" exclaimed his wife. "Yes, horses," said Bartok, looking round and proceeding to cross the road. His wife and a friend watched him enter an unmarked building. They followed him inside and found it to be a riding academy. "What a peaceful, natural smell," said Bartok, inhaling deeply in the stable. "Sleeping horses."

Agatha Fassett, THE NAKED FACE OF GENIUS: BELA BARTOK'S AMERICAN YEARS 1958

Sir Alfred Munnings' deep regard for horses could not be denied. When one of his mares foaled he behaved as if it was a "blessed event". He toured the neighbourhood announcing it and his loud, graphic recital of the obstetric details in the Lamorna Inn had to be restrained, "on account of the ladies".

Frank Ruhrmund, Western Morning News 3 NOV 1965

HORSERACING

Elizabeth Arden insisted on treating her horses' bruises, not with the normal 25% petroleum jelly, but with her ten-dollar-a-jar Eight-Hour Cream. In place of the normal 2 dollar-a-gallon fly spray she used 20 dollar-a-gallon lotion, and had them rubbed down with Arden skin lotion. Outlandish though some of her ideas were, some of her innovations became standard practice. She insisted that her horses' legs be massaged for 20 minutes before and one hour after races. The Eight-Hour Cream proved as good for horses as it was for women, and began to appear in stables all over the world.

Constance Woodworth and Alfred Allan Lewis, MISS ELIZABETH ARDEN 1972

Elizabeth Arden's horse barn was painted in her racing colours, cherry pink, white and blue. Plants were hung over the stalls, soothing music was piped in and the animals were even sprayed with her Blue Grass perfume, which had been named in their honour and was the biggest seller ever made. "When I was a kid," one trainer commented, "my mother used to say only horses sweat, people perspire. That is not true in our stable, where it is the horses who perspire and the people who sweat."

Ibid.

When one of her horses became ill, Elizabeth Arden called the world-famous Mayo Clinic. The indignant specialist refused to diagnose for a horse. "What would you do if he were a baby?" Elizabeth enquired. "I wouldn't enter him in the Santa Anita handicap," the doctor tartly replied, and hung up.

Ibid.

David Niven, while making a film in Malaysia, stayed at the Kuala Lumpur Hilton Hotel, which overlooks the racecourse. From a balcony he watched the crowds and listened to the periodic cheering. But there were *no* horses. After each bout of cheering the crowd would work on their form sheets and place their bets. Niven asked the hotel management for an explanation. He was told the racing season was over. But Malaysians love the action so much that they come to the course with their transistors and listen to races broadcast from Singapore.

Hardy Kruger, Reader's Digest Jun 1978

A friend of mine, staying on the continent, was told by the hotel proprietor that he had bought it with his winnings on Hackler's Pride in the Cambridgeshire. "You must have had a good tip," said my friend. "No, I did not have a tip at all, it was like this: I used to be a waiter at the Café Royal. One of my regular customers often used to talk to me about horses. He came in about a fortnight before the Cambridgeshire, and he gave me a horse. I think he told me about nearly every other horse in the race on other occasions when he came in. Somebody said to me, 'That gentleman to whom you were talking last night is Mr Fallon, who trains Hackler's Pride. Did he tell you anything about it?' Now Hackler's Pride was the one horse he had never mentioned. I thought it funny. I determined to take the plunge. I drew out all my savings, and stuck the money on Hackler's Pride and – well, that's how I got my hotel."

Arthur J. Sarl, HORSES, JOCKEYS AND CROOKS 1935

An Irish trainer and his jockey were asked by the stewards to explain why their horse remained last every yard of the race. "Well sir, the fella's not very good at jumping, and the other horses knock the hurdles down for him."

The Times, Diary 1 Jan 1984

HORSERIDING

I recall Margot Asquith claiming to have invented the safety habit for women riding side-saddle, as they did in her youth. "Before I wore a safety habit," she exclaimed, "I had picked up every turnip in Leicestershire with my teeth." When this provoked a laugh she looked bewildered.

Lord David Cecil. Observer, Staying with Margot 20 *Dec* 1981

More than 40 years ago, after going through medical school, I eventually found myself alone, at midnight, in the large casualty department of a London hospital. A cavalry officer from a nearby training school appeared with his arm hanging limp. "Did you fall off your horse?" I asked. With dignity he replied, "Madam, I was thrown."

Sybil M. Hawkes, Western Morning News 29 *Oct* 1965

William Douglas-Home, the playwright, while an undergraduate, took part in a point-to-point on a horse named Nero. Though a fine shot and fisherman William could not ride and remembers Brian Johnston (later to become a famous broadcaster) as they approached the start, commenting "In a few minutes we shall hear the merry jangle of ambulance bells." At the second fence William cried, "Nero, my God, to thee," but could not persuade him over and retired gracefully.

Mark Amory, Sunday Times Magazine 17 *Apr* 1977

Diana Mitford attempted to teach her little sister Jessica to ride. Jessica had a tendency to keep falling off. This wildly annoyed Diana who said, "Do try to hang on this time, darling. You know how cross Muv will be if you break your arm again."

Peter Bushell, GREAT ECCENTRICS 1984

HOSPITAL

During World War I Nancy Astor created a four-ward hospital at Cliveden. Sometimes she visited the hospital before or after a ride, and on her rounds carried a whip. Entering the neurological ward she spotted a big Yorkshireman who appeared to be more the victim of melancholia than anything else. She abused him violently. "Get up," she commanded. "You haven't any guts." Taken by surprise the Yorkshireman climbed clumsily to his feet and Nancy began to use her riding crop. The soldier shielded himself as well as he could and started to giggle. From the other beds came welcome sounds of laughter, which swelled until the whole ward rocked. "There," said Nancy in triumph to the medical officers, who declared with gallant unanimity that she was the best doctor in the place.

Geoffrey Bocca, Sunday Express 22 Jan 1956

Waking up in his hospital bed after his car accident Michael Foot heard the melancholy strains of the English Methodist hymn, "I see the land across the sea, where mansions are prepared for me."

Foot thought he was in heaven, or in some spot conveniently adjacent. In fact the sounds emanated from a Salvation Army band performing in the street below.

Alan Watkins, Observer 16 *Nov* 1980

In hospital for a variety of ailments, Walter Mizner, the Broadway dramatist, submitted to a colonic irrigation with the worst possible grace. When it was finished he enquired of the nurse, "How about checking me for oil and water?"

Bennett Cerf, TRY AND STOP ME 1947

My wife was sharing a hospital room with a sophisticated grande dame. Her first evening there, a small bowl with a single rose floating on top was brought to the lady. My wife watched in wide-eyed astonishment as her room-mate plucked out the flower and began sipping the water.

'You shouldn't do *that*," she admonished, thinking the woman was a bit daft.

The woman chuckled gleefully and said, "How else could my husband send me my daily martini?"

Donald Marks, Reader's Digest Nov 1965

Robert Earl Hughes, who weighs 76 stone 3 lb and claims to be the world's biggest man, has created special problems for a hospital at Bremen, Indiana, which is treating him for measles, complicated by a heart condition. He has been classified as an out-patient simply because he is too large to pass through the hospital's entrance doors, and there is no bed there big enough for him. He was taken to hospital in his specially designed caravan-home and doctors decided the only way they could treat him was to leave him in the caravan. His condition today was described as serious.

Daily Telegraph, 7 *Jul* 1958

HOSPITALITY

Auden, sitting at the head of the table, would preface a meal by saying, "We've got a roast and two veg., salad and savoury, and there will be no political discussion." He had enough of the don about him to keep us all in order. Quite rightly, he would not tolerate argument or bickering during mealtimes.

Paul Bowles, of Auden in New York in 1940, quoted Charles Obsborne, LIFE OF W.H. AUDEN 1980

While serving a delicious soufflé at the end of a spectacular dinner, Cecil Beaton replied in answer to his guests' flattering comments on his hospitality, "It's just that I'm not grand enough to serve you Mr Kipling's treacle tart."

Nicholas Monson and Debra Scott, THE NOUVEAUX PAUVRES 1984

Hearing that Lloyd George was fond of hymns, Lord Beaverbrook invited him round to Stornoway House, his London home, one evening. Lloyd George, who was Prime Minister at the time, suspected some deep-laid political plot. When he arrived, however, it was to find the room full of Salvationists. Beaverbrook made him join in.

Edgar Middleton, BEAVERBROOK: THE STATESMAN AND THE MAN 1936

The dons once decided to hold a cocktail party for Max Beckmann. One of the prettiest of the young wives called to invite him. His wife, Quappi, answered the door. After being told of the invitation she disappeared to consult him and returned with the reply, "Mr Beckmann says no thank you. He has enough friends already."

Barbara Ellstop, Sunday Times 10 *Oct* 1965

One of my earliest memories of Princess Beatrice is of her coming to tea with my grandmother, and of my hauling her upstairs with the promise, "I've got something to show you which you will really like."

The something turned out to be a chair with a cane seat which could be lifted to reveal a chamberpot.

Alan Pryce-Jones, THE BONUS OF LAUGHTER 1987

Sir Herbert Beerbohm Tree often used to give parties in the dome of his theatre, but did not always enjoy them. At one rather dull party he heard that a member of the cast had drunk rather too much champagne and had been removed to his dressing room to recover. "Give him my sincere compliments," said Tree, "and tell him I am glad someone is enjoying this damnable evening."

J.B. Booth, LAUGHTER AND BRASS HATS 1939

At a party we went to in Sydney the hostess, along with a number of the distinguished guests, was smashed out of her head. As we left rather early in the proceedings the swaying party-giver said to Clementina, "Do come again dear. You were no bloody trouble at all."

Michael Bentine, THE LONG BANANA SKIN 1975

Andrew Carnegie was given scant warning that King Edward was on his way to pay him a surprise visit at Skibo Castle. The royal car was seen approaching but alas! Mr Carnegie's professional organist, who should have been at the wonderful organ to play the National Anthem as the King crossed the threshold, was disporting himself in the private swimming pool. Excitedly Mr Carnegie commanded him to come out of the water and to do his job at the organ, which stood in the entrance hall. A screen was rigged round the instrument to hide him from view, and so King Edward passed through the portals of Skibo Castle to the strains of *God Save the King* – which would have produced a most appropriate and even dramatic effect if only at the crucial moment of the King's entry, that screen had not fallen down to reveal the poor woebegone organist dripping wet in his bathing suit and shivering from cold and fright, as he sat at the keys.

P. Tennyson Cole, VANITY VARNISHED 1931

Sir Andrew Cohen had invited Ava [Gardner], Grace [Kelly], Clark [Gable], Frank [Sinatra], John Ford and me to stay for the weekend at Government House, Entebbe. Towards the end of the dinner I was intrigued to notice that the electric lights were dimmed as a result of an unseen signal, the governor rose and proposed the health of

Her Majesty the Queen. Lady Cohen took the ladies off and then Sir Andrew asked, "Would anyone like to look at Africa by night?"

All the men dutifully trooped out on to the lawn which stretched away to a balustrade. The sight was magical; a full moon hovered over the great lake and was perfectly reflected in the glass-like water. Cicadas creaked in the surrounding undergrowth and the scent from flowers and shrubs was powerful on the hot air. I stood there drinking it all in – suddenly I was aware of a splashing sound. I looked round and there was the entire hierarchy of Government House peeing on the lawn. "Would anyone care to look at Africa by night," has since become a euphemism in the Sinden household.

Donald Sinden, A TOUCH OF THE MEMOIRS 1982

Lady Diana Cooper took her own unconventionality wherever she went. When her husband Duff Cooper was British ambassador in Paris, a guest, an elderly Frenchman, arriving unexpectedly early, was surprised when Diana, unbuttoning her trousers to change into a skirt, asked him point blank, "And what can I do for you?"

Cecil Beaton, DIARY 29 *Oct* 1944

At Lake Tahoe in Nevada Sammy Davis Junior sang three songs to open a dinner show, then stopped and announced to the crowd of 850, "Folks, some nights I have it, and some nights I don't. Tonight I don't. Sorry to walk out on you – but the least I can do is have you all as my guests." He then paid the food and drinks bill for the entire audience, a gesture which cost him 17,000 dollars plus tips, and won him a million in goodwill.

Herb Caen, *San Francisco Chronicle*

After one of their brawls Scott Fitzgerald and his wife Zelda formed a set of house rules which were only partly facetious; "Visitors are requested not to break down doors in search of liquor, even when authorised to do so by the host and hostess. Weekend guests are respectfully notified that invitations to stay over Monday, issued by the host and hostess during the small hours of Sunday morning, must not be taken seriously."

Andrew Turnbull, F. SCOTT FITZGERALD, A BIOGRAPHY 1962

There were twelve, or possibly fourteen, guests. As we took our seats at the dinner table, John Galsworthy immediately began to discuss the deteriorating effect of educational uniformity on the incidence and development of genius. Apparently it is a time-honoured custom. The woman next to me told me that Galsworthy abominated desultory conversation. If the conversation lagged Galsworthy would rap on the table with the end of a knife and present a new aspect of the problem. "To what extent is genius influenced by the educational standard of the parents; with special reference to the cases of Thomas Chatterton and Shakespeare."

What a dinner! I was punch-drunk by the time we got to the sweet.

P.G. Wodehouse, BRING ON THE GIRLS 1954

Prince George, Duke of Gloucester, was a good-natured man. David Herbert, the brother of the Duke's equerry, has recalled an evening in Belgrave Square when a nervous guest laughed so loudly at his host's jokes that he shattered the back of his chair, one of a rare and beautiful set made by Chippendale. The culprit was too desolate, too embarrassed, even to apologise. But the Duke showed no chagrin. "How fortunate that it was *your* chair," he said, "you see there were only eleven of the original set so I had one copied to make up the dozen.It was yours."

Kenneth Rose, KINGS, QUEENS AND COURTIERS 1985

George Grossmith was engaged at a high fee by a society hostess to give his entertainment *My Piano and I* to her guests at a country house party. He found on arrival that he was expected to fraternise with the butler, and was quartered in the servant's hall. Equal to the occasion, Grossmith pretended to think that he had been hired to entertain the servants, and sitting down at a piano in the housekeeper's room, gave them his entertainment and then left the house.

P. Tennyson Cole, VANITY VARNISHED 1931

Charles Henry, 7th Duke of Richmond, was host to King George and Queen Mary each summer for Goodwood Races, in Sussex. The royal party were entertained to a succession of elaborate meals, the menus for which were submitted to Buckingham Palace for approval each April. Nearly 40 specially hired servants crowded into the house a mile from the racecourse as well as an orchestra. The Duke's grandson once attached a pedometer to the butler, Mr Marshall, for a single day in race week; it registered nineteen and a half miles. The Duke celebrated the departure of his royal guests by dining off plain beef and carrots.

Kenneth Rose, KINGS, QUEENS AND COURTIERS 1985

What was very embarrassing was, after a rather terrifying evening, Lord Home (the 13th Earl) would suddenly announce that he was going to bed. When one had been there once, one knew what that meant, but the innocent didn't know. And what it meant was that on the way to bed he turned an enormous switch which extinguished every light in the house immediately. People were caught in the bath a quarter of a mile away, in a house they had never been in before. You could hear them staggering about for hours.

Jo Grimond, quoted Mark Amory, Sunday Times Magazine 17 *Apr* 1977

Elsa Maxwell's most famous party was in New York's Waldorf-Astoria in 1937; chickens and scented goats were turned loose among the guests, and a champion hog-caller called up half a dozen pigs. One of her basic rules for a good party: ask the wrong people, then mix them up.

News Review 18 *Nov* 1948

Arthur Mayer, recently back from the Far East, swears to the truth of the following story: reaching Shanghai late one night, he was in his hotel room unpacking when the Chinese equivalent of a house detective knocked on the door. In his best pidgin English the dick asked, "Want gur?" "Want what?" asked Mayer. "Gur" answered the Chinese, and with appropriate gestures indicated what a "gur" was. The pantomime was so perfect that Mayer soon grasped the idea, but he was anxious only for a bath and a bed. He pointed to his grey hair and eyeglasses as an excuse for his strange lack of interest. As a pantomime artist, however, he was apparently not the equal of the Chinese. Half an hour later, when he emerged from his tub, there was again a knock on the door. The house detective had returned, this time accompanied by a charming if somewhat mature lady, her hair streaked with grey and a pince-nez on her nose.

Bennett Cerf, Saturday Review Of Literature 1946

Montgomery's allegedly austere habits gave rise to a number of anecdotes. His appalled reaction to the clouds of cigar smoke with which Churchill filled his tent in the desert was the subject of much amusement as was Churchill's reply to a question in the House of Commons to a complaint that Montgomery had invited Von Thoma to dinner in his desert caravan. "Poor Von Thoma," said Churchill, "I, too, have dined with Montgomery."

Lord Chalfont, MONTGOMERY OF ALAMEIN 1976

Jackie's [Kennedy] first cruise with Onassis was in October 1963. Just for Jackie the *Christina*'s crew of sixty had been augmented by two hairdressers, a masseuse, and an orchestra for dancing in the evening; just for her the *Christina* had been stocked with eight varieties of caviare, fresh fruits that had been flown in from Paris, rare vintage wines and buckets of mullet packed in ice.

Arianna Stassinopoulos, Sunday Times 12 *Oct* 1980

Eleanor Roosevelt collected people. We could accommodate 21 overnight visitors at a time, but Mrs Roosevelt often invited more. It was always musical chairs with the guest rooms at the President's House. "We've got them hanging from the hooks," Mr Crim told me one day as two new arrivals appeared, suitcases in hand, and we had to move one of the President's sons to his third bedroom that week, to make room.

J.B. West, UPSTAIRS AT THE WHITE HOUSE 1974

Bernard Hoffman, who was a photographer for *Life* magazine for some years, called on Carl Sandburg at his Michigan home in order to do a story. The weather was so cold that even the goats were virtually freezing outside. Whereupon Sandburg called them into the house and about fifteen of the shivering animals crowded into one of the rooms. Sandburg did not stop with this hospitality. He took up his guitar and played for the visiting goats. "They listened politely," said Hoffman.

North Callahan, CARL SANDBURG, LINCOLN OF OUR LITERATURE 1970

HOTEL

On a visit to King's Lynn we stayed one winter at the Globe Hotel overlooking the large cobbled market place. Early one morning shouts of "Fire" woke us. We ran out to ask where the fire was. My father, still shouting "Fire", said that was what *he* wanted to know, as he had asked for one in his sitting room at 6 a.m.

Mrs J.D. Bailey, The Times 26 *Jul* 1933

Just after the war, when I went to Paris for *Harper's Bazaar* I stayed at the Matignon. During the war it had been taken over by the Wehrmacht, and instead of loo paper there were, cut up into thrifty squares, inter-office memoranda which made interesting reading.

The hotel was also flea-ridden. After two sleepless nights I complained to the chambermaid. She affected not to believe me, but at the crucial moment of the argument a large flea scuttled on to the arm of a chair. "Voila!" I pointed. She bent over and examined it closely, then she straightened up.

"Ce ne peut pas être une puce Française," she declared. "Celle-ci doit être Anglaise," and she flounced out triumphantly.

Ernestine Carter, WITH TONGUE IN CHIC 1974

On arrival at a Chicago hotel Thomas Du Pont, the American senator, found that a lady who had previously occupied his room had left behind a frilly nightgown. He summoned the manager, handed him the garment and commanded, "Fill it and bring it back."

New Yorker 13 *Dec* 1952

The so-called proprieties bothered Alexander Woollcott not at all. The Gotham Hotel in New York, where he lived during the last four years, had a rule barring dogs. One day his friend Ina Claire came to call and the desk clerk announced her. "Send her up," said Woollcott. "I can't," said the unhappy clerk. "She has a dog." "Either Miss Claire's dog comes up," said Woollcott, "or I am coming down. And I am in my pyjamas." The dog came up.

Samuel Hopkins Adams, THE WORLD OF MR WOOLLCOTT 1943

I frequently stayed in a small-town hotel known for its appalling service. On my first visit I made the mistake of ordering early morning tea. Shortly before seven a girl threw open the door. "Sugar in your tea?" she shouted. "No thank you," I replied. As she banged the door shut she said, "Ah well, don't stir it then."

David Wright, Reader's Digest Jan 1978

HUMILITY

Ramsay MacDonald attended a big concert one Sunday afternoon at the Palladium. Gladys Faber and I went round to his box and she asked him if there were any of the artists on the bill he would care to meet. He said, "Your husband, and Mr Charles Coburn who sang 'The Man Who Broke the Bank at Monte Carlo' if it wouldn't inconvenience him at all." Gladys told him she was very proud, and all the artists were very proud to have him at the concert.

"Miss Faber, please, you mustn't say that," he said, "it makes me terribly humble, and – no one really likes to feel humble, whatever they may tell you."

Naomi Jacob, ME: A CHRONICLE ABOUT OTHER PEOPLE 1933

At lunch one of a party of French officers visiting Albert Schweitzer's hospital at Lamborene, perhaps an army chaplain, got up and made a solemn speech in which he beseeched the Lord to spare Dr Schweitzer in health and strength for many years. Schweitzer listened politely, and made a very short reply. "Let us hope the Lord is listening."

Frederick Frank, DAYS WITH ALBERT SCHWEITZER 1959

A small boy at my son's school was had up before the head for being a cocky little beast and urged to adopt humility. So he did, for a bit; then he lapsed into his old self.

"So how about the humility then?" demanded the head. "I *was* humble, for a fortnight," he said. "But nobody noticed."

Katherine Whitehorn, VIEW FROM A COLUMN 1981

HUMOUR

I played Vladimir Nabokov's hero, Hermann Hermann, in *Despair*, from a script by Tom Stoppard, for Rainer Werner Fassbinder. Rainer took me aside one day and asked me about the script. "What is this?" I told him it was a pun, a schoolboy joke. "Oh yes," he said. There is one thing about German humour which the English always forget. It is no laughing matter.

Dirk Bogarde, quoted Nicholas Wapshott, The Times 18 *Mar* 1983

R.A. Butler's most endearing aspect as a politician was his sense of humour, not the present prime minister's [Margaret Thatcher] most conspicuous quality. They encountered each other in a cattle market in Saffron Walden during a by-election in 1977. A week later they met in London "I bought that black bull we saw for you, Margaret," murmured Rab. Mollie Butler comments, "The look of stunned horror on her face was almost pathetic."

Robert Skidelskey, Sunday Times reviewing Mollie Butler, AUGUST AND RAB 6 *Sep* 1987

Ida Patlanski, a visiting British friend of ours, summed up New York's humour for me. Arriving for tea, still chuckling, she told us that she'd just bought a new hat at Sak's Fifth Avenue, and swept out of those imposing doors feeling like a dog's dinner. With a squeal of brakes a yellow cab pulled up opposite her, and the grinning driver leaned out.

"New hat?" he asked brightly. "Why yes," replied Ida, blushing with pleasure. "Don't do nuttin' for you," he said, and drove off.

Michael Bentine, THE LONG BANANA SKIN 1975

The only disadvantage I laboured under at St Paul's School, and being a Boy Scout made not the slightest difference, was that I had a curious sense of humour which meant that if anything came up in class that had a suggestion of *double entendre* it caused me to dissolve into hysterics for which I was punished, sometimes quite severely. In other words, I had a dirty mind.

For instance, on one occasion when we were reading Scott's *Marmion* aloud, it became obvious to myself and everyone else in the class that by the working of some hideously unfair natural process of selection it would fall to me to read a completely unreadable part of the romance in Canto Two, entitled "The Convent", which concerned the blind Bishop of Lindisfarne. And you could have heard a pin drop when I got to my feet.

"No hand was moved, no word was said
Till thus the Abbot's door was given
Raising his sightless balls to heaven – "

was all I could manage before going off into peals of mad laughter and to be beaten by John Bell, the High Master, who showed where his sympathies lay by beating me hard and then giving me a shilling. I have never forgiven Scott.

Eric Newby, A TRAVELLER'S LIFE 1982

HUNTING

Margot Asquith did not like the sportsman Lord Lonsdale, renowned for his fine horses and his courage in the hunting field. Someone in Lady Asquith's hearing once praised his prowess as a rider to hounds. "Jimmy?" she asked. "Anyone can jump. Look at fleas."

Cecil Maurice Bowra, MEMORIES 1966

When President Giscard d'Estaing went to Moscow in Khrushchev's day he insisted on going bear hunting. It was the wrong season, but Khrushchev, determined not to disappoint him, let him take off, having sent a bear on the aircraft ahead.

Nora Beloff, Observer Magazine 4 *Aug* 1974

Knowing Bernard Shaw hated blood sports and would agree with the sentiment, Lady Astor remarked, "I hate killing for pleasure." As he said nothing one of her children probed: "Do you hate killing for pleasure?" "It depends upon whom you kill," he answered.

Hesketh Pearson, LIVES OF THE WITS

A gentleman must realise that once he is in the saddle he must be as rude as possible to anyone who crosses his path. One quasi-gentleman, when he was asked by the Master what the devil he thought he was doing out hunting, was naive enough to reply that he only came out for the fresh air and exercise. "In that case you had better go home and bugger yourself with a pair of bellows," thundered the Master, riding off in pursuit of another victim of his scorn.

Douglas Sutherland, THE ENGLISH GENTLEMAN 1978

HYGIENE

Howard Hughes had a special fear of cross-contamination, and whenever he stayed at hotels he insisted that the trolley used to bring his meals to his room should remain outside the kitchen while food was being prepared, in case the wheels should accidentally pick up a cockroach.

Peter Bushell, GREAT ECCENTRICS 1984

I told Harold Macmillan about a dinner at the Algonquin when the editor of *Grove* found a cockroach in his salad. "Cockroaches," he mused. "It's strange. We don't seem to have them nowadays. I suppose it is because all our food is frozen or tinned. But when Dorothy and I were first married and living in London, the house was infested with them. We took advice and were told that the thing to do was to get a hedgehog. So we went to Harrods and bought one."

Richard Garnett, Independent 31 *Dec* 1986

Aboard SS *Moshulu*, East Side, York Dock, Belfast, 29 September 1938. Dear Mummy and Daddy, the first two mornings I cleaned the lavatories. They have no running water even if there ever was any, so you have to haul up water from the dock, and then use an iron rod to ram up and down them. The only way to use these lavs is to stand on the seats, which you are not supposed to do, but you have to. I had a fight because of this. "Take those bloody boots off," someone said when they found me standing on one of them. The doors have no locks on them, just like school. I wish Daddy had not insisted on my being so regular in my habits.

Eric Newby, A TRAVELLER'S LIFE 1982

Shaw's wife implored Nancy Astor to look after him (when they visited Russia) and make him wash his beard. These instructions Nancy carried out faithfully to the point of washing Shaw's beard personally, in the Metropolitan Hotel, Moscow, watched by the fascinated staff.

Geoffrey Bocca. Sunday Express, The Lady and the Commissar 5 *Feb* 1956

The Prince and Princess of Wales were walking among the crowds in South Australia. The princess made for a group of young children, the nearest of whom she patted affectionately on his tousled head. "Why aren't you at school today?" she asked. "I was sent home," the lad replied, "because I've got head lice."

The Times 13 *Apr* 1983

A new employee of a dairy dashed into a lavatory and was about to hurry out afterwards when the manager drew his attention to a notice, "Wash your hands before working." The youth replied, "It's all right. I'm going to lunch."

Frank Shires, President Food Manufacturer's Association, speech to Institute of Meat 28 *Apr* 1952

The medical authorities had great difficulty in persuading the Filipinos to safeguard their health by boiling their drinking water. I was making a tour of houses in one district and in each one I asked "Do you use boiled water?" and in each I received an affirmative reply. By the time I had reached the fifth house I decided I had better go into the question somewhat more thoroughly. "How do you use the boiled water?" I enquired. "We take a teaspoonful three times a day."

Dr Victor Heiser, A DOCTOR'S ODYSSEY 1936

HYPOCHONDRIA

Nov 21 1936. Driving back from lunch today, had an attack of nerves. At Oxford Circus was on my deathbed. Going up Great Portland Street was dead and buried. Along Albany Street calculated estate available after insurances raked in, horses sold and debts paid. Passing Stanhope Terrace made my will, ascended Primrose Hill and descended to the Everlasting Bonfire simultaneously and as we turned into England's Lane was critically considering Jock's [Alan Dent] first article as my successor in the *Sunday Times.*

All this turned out, of course, to be merely what Doctor Rutty, the Irish Quaker, called "an hypochondriac onubilation from wind and indigestion".

James Agate, DIARY 1976

If anyone in his household sneezed my father would cry for a servant to pack his bag. While this was being done he would pace about with lips tightly shut and a towel over his face to ward off germs. Mumbling to me to behave he would take his bag and move off to his mother's house until the sickness had departed from his own.

Vicki Baun, I KNOW WHAT I'M WORTH 1961

Caruso not only equipped himself with atomisers, and all sorts of gargling fluids, cold and cough cures, but obsession with his health extended to medicaments for headaches and migraines and to avoid catching any skin complaint he took everywhere with him his own linen. Before he occupied a hotel suite it had to be sprayed first with disinfectant, then with the perfume he brought with him for the purpose. He would take a bath and change his clothes after walking in the street or being in close contact with strangers in a public place – and before going to bed he saw that a mattress and piles of pillows were arranged around him on the floor lest he should fall in his sleep and hurt himself. Caruso was indeed the King of Operatic Hypochondriacs.

Charles Neilson Gatty, THE ELEPHANT THAT SWALLOWED A NIGHTINGALE 1981

Irving Thalberg asked Jean Harlow, "How did you make out with Howard Hughes?" "Well, one day he was eating a cookie and offered me a bite." When we all laughed Jean interrupted, "Don't underestimate that. The poor guy's so frightened of germs it could darned nearly have been a proposal."

Anita Loos, KISS HOLLYWOOD GOODBYE 1974

Igor Stravinsky was a notorious hypochondriac who went to see a doctor in every city he visited, but was constantly swallowing pills that he prescribed for himself. In 1934, soon after his son Theodore required emergency surgery for a ruptured appendix, Stravinsky had his own healthy appendix removed, "as a precaution". Then he ordered the same operation for his other three children.

Lawrence Elliott, Reader's Digest, Igor Stravinsky, Musical Revolutionary Jun 1982

ILLNESS

In 1906 Max Aitken (later Lord Beaverbrook) fell ill with an inflamed appendix. A year later he wrote to a friend who was also ill: "If anybody worries you, you will have to part with that person until the worry and annoyance passes away. My wife worried me, and the worry was entirely caused by her solicitude for my well-being, but this got on my nerves and my doctor was wise enough to send her away while I was left with nothing to grumble over, and I am satisfied that this hastened my recovery. Subsequently I was mighty glad to have her back again."

A.J.P. Taylor, BEAVERBROOK 1972

After a lunch at the British Embassy in Berlin, during Edward VII's visit in 1909, when smoking had begun, I was talking to Lord Hardinge when I saw the King collapse. The Queen rushed to him and tore open his collar. Edward VII remained for some time unconscious – Hardinge has told me since that he thought the King was dead. No one was allowed to enter the salon, and little by little the King recovered. He would not have it thought that he had been ill, and asked for another cigar. The room was re-opened and shortly afterwards everyone left. The incident was kept quiet; apart from the eye-witness I have mentioned no one knew anything about it.

Jules Cambon, quoted Genevieve Tabois, THE LIFE OF JULES CAMBON

I remember Mrs Haldane – the famous and distinguished mother of the present Lord Haldane – telling me of a professor of science and a near relation of hers who had received from an eminent Russian doctor a specimen of skin off a man who had died of a rare and virulent form of smallpox. He placed it in a cardboard box upon his mantelpiece. While he was out walking, his wife – looking for something she had left in the room – opened the box and caught smallpox.

Margot Asquith, LAY SERMONS 1927

When we passed through New York the temperature was below zero, and we both arrived here with bronchitis from the change of temperature. Ian [Fleming] had a high fever and was terribly cross. Happily Noel Coward came to call and proved himself a Florence Nightingale, changed Thunderbird's sopping pyjamas and turned his mattress and brought him iced drinks. Noel has always found Thunderbird fearfully attractive and jumped at the opportunity to handle him. While Noel fetched ice cubes from the frigidaire TB's language was something horrible. He blamed me for exposing him to homosexual approach.

Ann Fleming, letter to Evelyn Waugh from Goldeneye, Jamaica 4 Feb 1961

See also **DOCTOR, REMEDY**

IMAGINATION

Margot Asquith lived much of her time in a day-dream world founded on her experience of the real world so altered by her sense of the dramatic as to bear only an intermittent relation to it. She used to recount with zest and conviction how on the evening of 4th August 1914, when the Government met in 10 Downing Street to decide whether or not to go to war with Germany she lay overcome with agitation across the threshold of the door into the Cabinet Room, in which the Ministers were making their momentous decision. Even as a youth of 19 I found it hard to believe this piece of sensational biography. Surely some other observer would have noted that the Ministers could not have got in or out of the Cabinet Room without stepping over the prone figure of the Prime Minister's wife. But Margot believed it.

Lord David Cecil, Observer, Staying With Margot 20 *Dec* 1981

Most of my childhood games were played with an imaginary girl friend called Jeannie. What she looked like I can't remember but I recall that she was outrageously demanding. On her orders I stole tea, butter, cakes, jewellery and books, and hid them under a bush of catmint. The family found out about Jeannie on the day I stole the Sunday joint. Not without some sense of relief I allowed her to be banished from my life.

Richard Attenborough, Sunday Telegraph 15 *Aug* 1965

Louis Armstrong was once asked if he objected to the impressions of him given by other singers and comedians. "Not really," he shrugged. "A lotta cats copy the Mona Lisa, but people still line up to see the original."

Clifton Fadiman, LITTLE, BROWN BOOK OF ANECDOTES 1985

IMPRESARIO

I engaged Leonie Rysanek to make her debut at the Metropolitan in the *Macbeth*. It was an impossible assignment, even for a great artist. For the only time in my career I interfered with public behaviour at a performance. I hired a claqueur to station himself near the front of the house and at the moment of Miss Rysanek's entrance to call into the auditorium at an angle which would minimise the chance of her hearing it the words "Brava Callas". I counted on the American love for the under-dog to resent this intervention, and to balance the scales a little for Miss-Rysanek – who did indeed rise to the occasion with a splendid performance.

Rudolf Bing, The Times 14 *Oct* 1972

INCOME TAX

I had a letter brought to me in the trenches yesterday enclosing an Income Tax demand. It made me laugh as I extricated myself from a puddle of frozen mud to receive a request for £193 2s 6d, which is more than I have earned during the whole of my career in the Army.

Raymond Asquith, letter to his wife 20 *Nov* 1915

Sir Thomas Beecham said that after producing *The Faithful Shepherdess* by John Fletcher (1579–1625) he received a letter from the Inland Revenue asking for the address of Mr John Fletcher for the purpose of taxation, as they had been unable to discover his whereabouts. "I was able to reply that to the best of my knowledge his present residence was the South Aisle of Southwark Cathedral, and I went on to venture the opinion that he might find some difficulty in changing it."

Harold Atkins and Archie Newman, BEECHAM STORIES 1978

Joseph M. Schenck, the producer, tells the story of how Dad [Charles Chaplin] reacted to the discovery that he was far in arrears with his taxes. There was some close dickering back and forth between his lawyers and Uncle Sam. Mr Schenck remembers the outcome for he was with Dad in the hotel room in New York when his lawyers finally brought the news.

"We've agreed to pay the million," they said a little fearfully, expecting Dad to hit the ceiling. But my father only got up and walked to the piano as if he didn't have a care in the world.

"Well, I'm glad that's over," he said. "Let's have some fun." And he sat down and began playing.

Charles Chaplin Jnr, MY FATHER, CHARLIE CHAPLIN 1960

When the Inland Revenue demanded Property Tax on Uffa Fox's home – then a converted floating bridge – he sailed it up and down the river to a series of different addresses in different parishes until they gave up.

June Dixon, UFFA FOX 1975

I once saw John Galsworthy in a temper. He remembered, after paying his income tax, that he had left out a large sum he had received, and wrote to the authorities offering the extra amount due. They replied that the accounts were now closed, and nothing could be done about it. Galsworthy replied by sending a cheque for the amount. They returned it with a letter saying the Lords Commissioners had ordered that the correspondence must now cease. Galsworthy, enraged, went on worrying the authorities about it for a long time. How was it possible, he said, that the poorer classes should not be unduly burdened when the comparatively wealthy, like himself could escape so easily, if involuntarily.

Ford Madox Ford, IT WAS THE NIGHTINGALE 1934

One of the earliest remarks that I heard made by the first surveyor under whom I served when I joined the Inland Revenue Department was this: "There is not much we can do for you, madam, but I can let you have plenty of forms."

R.W. Harris, NOT SO HUMDRUM 1939

Inspectors of Taxes have acquired a reputation for wanting not only the greater part of one's income, but also the very clothes off one's back. I thought until today that this reputation was quite undeserved and indeed that it was probably the invention of some low music-hall comedian. I am now told by my accountant, who is professionally impeccable, that my own tax inspector now wishes to know whether I sell my old suits. I wonder if they ask deep-sea divers the same question?

Terry Thomas, letter to The Times 16 *Feb* 1957

INFIDELITY

One of the players in the Hallé Orchestra had an affair with a singer and after a time his wife heard of it. Intending to enlist Sir John Barbirolli's help she went to his room in Manchester's Free Trade Hall and sobbed out her story. Sir John listened sympathetically, and when she had finished tried to find some words of comfort. "You know, there's nothing to worry about. He's playing better than ever."

André Previn, ORCHESTRA 1979

I can remember dining in a well-known gentleman's club in Paris with two gentlemanly Frenchmen. As we supped a fine old Armagnac one turned to the other and remarked conventionally, "By the way, *mon brave*, since we are such old friends I feel I owe it to you to tell you that I am sleeping with your wife." I froze, my glass poised. Surely, I thought, this would be the classic case of pistols for two and breakfast for one. Not at all. "Indeed, *mon cher ami*," replied the other, looking at his friend in great interest. "Tell me, is she any good nowadays?"

Douglas Sutherland, THE ENGLISH GENTLEMAN'S MISTRESS 1980

James Thurber had an affair with a *New Yorker* secretary, but his blindness made for tactical problems. I worked as a boy in the Art Department. She was as ugly as sin, so it served him right. I would have to wait for him at the apartment until he was finished, and then I'd dress him. He could undress by himself, but he couldn't dress by himself, couldn't even cross the street by himself. Now since Helen Thurber would dress him in the morning she knew how he looked. Well, one time I put his socks on wrong side out, and when he got home I gather Helen asked him a lot of questions. The next day Thurber was furious with me – said I did it on purpose.

Truman Capote, quoted Burton Burnstein, THURBER 1975

INFLATION

When my elder son began his medical training seven years ago, he paid £28 for half a human skeleton. Three years later my younger son entered the medical school and the value of those bones had risen to £40. My daughter, who will soon begin training as a physiotherapist, is going to purchase half a skeleton. It will cost £70. What better investment is there than a skeleton in the cupboard?

Joan Tucker, letter to The Times 13 *Jun* 1974

I acquired a Fabergé cigarette case of which I was inordinately proud. I had bought it in a little semi-basement shop in Berkeley Street at the bottom of Hay Hill, kept by Prince Vladimir Galitzine. I paid for it with the first money I ever earned, and it cost £40. I thought myself very extravagant. I really had very little money in those days and was living in the very simplest of bed sitters. Twenty-five years later I sold it for £800. I do not know the moral of that story.

Peter Coats, OF KINGS AND CABBAGES 1984

A gushing woman once said to Paul Getty, "Mr Getty, I am told you are a billionaire." He looked at her mournfully with his curiously ravaged face and said, "That may be so, but you must remember a billion dollars is not what it used to be."

Ibid.

The latest drachma joke doing the rounds in Athens: Papandreou consults foreign financial experts on how to restore value to the currency.

"Drill a small hole in the one-drachma coin and fill it with gold," says the Swiss. No good; not enough gold in Greece. "Drill two holes and fill them with silver," says the German. No, not enough silver. "Drill three and fill with copper," says the French. Impossible – not enough copper. "Drill four holes," says the American financier in New York, "and sell them for shirt buttons at two drachmas each."

The Times, Diary 24 Jan 1983

INFLUENCE

King George V, approached by a friend who hoped that a word from His Majesty in the right quarter would solve a difficulty, said, "My dear fellow, I can't help you. You'd better write to *The Times*."

Helen Reid, letter to The Times 4 *Feb* 1979

INHERITANCE *See* WILL

INSULT

Elkan Allan sports a scrappy, dun-coloured pubic beard and was once massively put down by a mousy Rediffusion secretary who had listened patiently for several days while he speculated on what costume he should adopt for a fancy dress party. Finally she lost her patience and muttered, "Why don't you spray yourself with talcum powder and go as an armpit?"

Ned Sherrin, A SMALL THING LIKE AN EARTHQUAKE 1983

Rex Allen, a senior editor at Macmillan's, being told by an unreliable assistant, "I will make a mental note," replied, "On what?"

The Times, Diary 7 Jan 1982

Field Marshal Montgomery: Lady Astor, I must tell you that I do not approve of female politicians.

Lady Astor: That's all right. The only General I approve of is Evangeline Booth.

John Grigg, NANCY ASTOR, PORTRAIT OF A PIONEER 1980

During a rehearsal of a John Barrymore play the leading lady roused the star's ire, an incautious procedure, to say the least. Barrymore gave a pungent lecture on her paternity and her nocturnal pursuits. "Kindly remember," interrupted the actress, "that I am a lady." "Madam," snapped Barrymore, "I will respect your secret."

Bennett Cerf, TRY AND STOP ME 1947

In Beecham's early days there was an old cor anglais player well known for being late at rehearsals, and for his repartee. One rehearsal was in full swing when he arrived wearing a very striking suit. Beecham, without stopping, said, "Good morning. I presume you have been detained by a visit to your tailor?" "Not exactly, Sir Thomas," came the reply. "Your old suit turned very nicely."

Harold Atkins and Archie Newman, BEECHAM STORIES 1978

Asked by Sir Thomas Beecham to sing the soprano part in Handel's *Messiah*, a singer confessed that she did not know the oratorio, but accepted the offer. Meeting her some time later he asked how the task of learning the part was progressing.

"I've been working hard on it," she replied, "the score goes everywhere with me – to work, to meals, to bed at night."

"Then," he replied, "I trust we may look forward to an immaculate conception."

Ibid.

A Sibelius festival was supported by a large list of patrons and at rehearsal of one of the most delicate passages of *The Death of Melisande* one of them, a famous London hostess, burst into the hall with a clatter and a bang. Sir Thomas Beecham turned round and hissed savagely, "My dear lady, do you think this is Waterloo Station?"

Berta Geissmar, THE BATON AND THE JACKBOOT 1944

One of Lord Berners' acquaintances was in the impertinent habit of saying to him, "I've been sticking up for you." He repeated this once too often and Lord Berners replied, "Yes, and I have been sticking up for you. Someone said you aren't fit to live with pigs, and I said you were."

Edith Sitwell, TAKEN CARE OF 1965

A pompous woman, complaining to Lord Berners that the head waiter of a restaurant had not shown her and her husband immediately to a table, said, "We had to tell him who we were." Gerald, interested, enquired, "And who were you?"

Ibid.

Maria Callas's voice was slipping and her career was petering out. Her humiliation was complete. By the time Onassis married Jackie Kennedy in 1968 there was a grain of truth in one of his more cruel taunts. "What are you? Nothing. You just have a whistle in your throat that no longer works."

Arianna Stassinopoulos, Sunday Times 12 *Oct* 1980

Halfway up the long staircase, at the top of which Mrs Patrick Campbell's host and hostess were receiving the long chain of guests, there was a mirror. She paused in front of it, hitched up a shoulder-strap, patted her hair. Suddenly her eyes flashed. In the mirror she had seen an enemy advancing up the stairs behind her – and she had many enemies. Without turning her head, she caught my eye. The deep booming voice rang out. "It's tragic. I try to look like a lady, and all I look like is Lady P – "

The enemy in the mirror stiffened, stared, and swept up the staircase and Mrs Patrick Campbell turned towards me. "Oh dear," she said in an innocent voice, "do you think she heard?" "You know very well she heard, Stella. And you also know that you meant her to hear."

She shrugged her shoulders and we went on up the staircase.

Beverley Nichols, Daily Sketch 17 *Apr* 1940

Barbara Cartland came into remote contact with royal circles when her daughter Raine's stepdaughter became the Princess of Wales in 1981. When Miss Cartland was interviewed for the BBC radio programme *Today* the woman interviewer asked her whether she thought the class barriers had broken down in Britain. "Of course they have," replied Miss Cartland, "or I wouldn't be sitting here talking to someone like you."

Jilly Cooper, CLASS 1981

Milling about the ballroom with Wilson Mizner, I was stopped by Irene Castle, recently arrived from Paris. She tousled my tomboy bob. "I see you've taken my advice and kept away from hairdressers," she said.

Anita Loos, KISS HOLLYWOOD GOODBYE 1974

After my divorce from actor Louis Calhern he married Julia Hoyt. A month or so later I found in a trunk a box of beautiful calling cards engraved "Mrs Louis Calhern". It seemed a pity to waste them, so I mailed them to my successor. But, aware of Louis' mercurial marital habits I wrote on the top of one, "Dear Julia, I hope these reach you in time." I received no acknowledgement.

Ilka Chase, PAST IMPERFECT

The late Gilbert Harding fell asleep while attending one of Noel Coward's plays and snored loudly throughout the performance. Afterwards he apologised. Coward replied, "My dear fellow, don't apologise. After all I have never bored you half as much as you have bored me."

Kenneth Edwards, I WISH I'D SAID THAT 1976

Hannen Swaffer, a critic and theatre writer on the *Daily Express*, entered Noel Coward's dressing room unannounced, after the second night of S.N. Behrman's *The Second Man*, in which the critics had praised Coward's performance in extravagant terms. "Nowley," he sneered in his assumed cockney accent, "I've always said you could act better than you could write." "And I've always said the same about you," was Noel's instant reply.

Raymond Massey, A HUNDRED DIFFERENT LIVES 1979

Mrs Ronald Greville, one of the great London hostesses of the 1920s did not care for ladies whose jewels were more spectacular than hers. On one occasion after dinner a very rich and famous American lady suddenly discovered that the principal diamond had dropped from her necklace. Everyone got on their hands and knees, and then Mrs Greville's voice was heard, speaking to a footman. "Perhaps this might be of some assistance." She was handing him a magnifying glass.

Beverley Nichols, THE SWEET TWENTIES 1958

The Hon Mrs Ronald Greville did indeed have a sharp tongue. She annihilated one persistent enemy, Lady Cunard, with a single blow. "You must not think I dislike poor dear Emerald. I am always telling Queen Mary that she isn't half as bad as she is painted."

Kenneth Rose, KINGS, QUEENS AND COURTIERS 1985

At the Oxford Union in 1926 Winston Churchill tapped the rotund R.B. Haldane (later Lord Chancellor) and asked him what he proposed to call the baby. "If it's a boy I will call it George, after the King," said Haldane. "If it's a girl, Mary after the Queen. But if, as I strongly suspect, it is only wind I shall call it Winston."

John Parker, FATHER OF THE HOUSE 1982

When James Joyce met W.B.Yeats he tuned up his manner to a Wildean insolence and said, "We have met too late, Mr Yeats. You are too old to be influenced by me." To which Yeats retorted pontifically, "Never have I encountered so much pretension with so little to show for it."

Gerald Griffin, THE WILD GEESE 1938

The artist Frederick Leighton, who prided himself on his draughtsmanship, met Whistler one day in Piccadilly, and took it upon himself to remark on the other's techniques. "My dear Whistler, you leave your pictures in such a crude state. Why don't you ever finish them?" "My dear Leighton," was the response, "why do you ever begin yours?"

Clifton Fadiman, LITTLE, BROWN BOOK OF ANECDOTES 1985

I had a heated argument with some fellow examiners at Oxford last year. One I silenced, i.e. reduced to speechless fury, by telling him his attitude towards literature was that of a lavatory attendant.

G.W. Lyttelton, THE LYTTELTON HART–DAVIS LETTERS 1978

Beatrice Lillie was once accosted by a haughty dowager who scrutinised her through lorgnettes. Said the haughty Lady maliciously, "What lovely pearls, dear Beatrice. Are they real?" Lady Peel nodded her shapely little head. "Of course," purred the dowager, "you can always tell real pearls by biting them. May I try?" Bee flashed her most seductive smile. "Gladly, but remember, Duchess, you can't tell real pearls with false teeth."

Collie Knox, IT HAD TO BE ME

Told that Nancy Mitford was staying at a friend's house to finish a book, Dame Edith Evans remarked, "Oh, really? What exactly is she reading?"

Nigel Rees, QUOTE-UNQUOTE 1978

One day a tiresome stranger inflicted herself on our group, claiming some sort of distant relationship with the Mizner family. The lady kept addressing Ysobel as "Cousin Ysobel" until the latter politely remarked, "Pray cease calling me your cousin, madam; you see, I am illegitimate."

Anita Loos, KISS HOLLYWOOD GOODBYE 1974

When John Neville was playing Hamlet at the Old Vic during the fifties Robert Atkins was asked what he thought of him. "Well, with a little more sex and a little less sanctity he'd make a very possible Laertes."

Donald Sinden, A TOUCH OF THE MEMOIRS 1982

Some troublesome woman was being discussed and it was said, "Anyhow she is very nice to her inferiors." To which Dorothy Parker replied, "Where does she find them?"

Rupert Hart–Davis, THE LYTTELTON HART–DAVIS LETTERS 1978

A bore assured Dorothy Parker, "I simply cannot *bear* fools. "Apparently," said Miss Parker, "your mother didn't have the same difficulty."

Bennett Cerf, TRY AND STOP ME 1947

Lascelles Abercrombie had expressed an opinion with which the poet Ezra Pound violently disagreed. "Dear Mr Abercrombie," he wrote, "Stupidity beyond a certain point becomes a public menace. I hereby challenge you to a duel to be fought at the earliest possible moment that is suited to your convenience." Abercrombie was rather disturbed by the challenge, knowing Pound's skill at fencing, but then remembered with relief that the choice of weapons lay with the person challenged. "May I suggest," he replied, "that we bombard each other with unsold copies of our own books." Pound, having more "weapons" than his opponent immediately withdrew the challenge.

Noel Stock, LIFE OF EZRA POUND 1970

Burton Bascoe wrote that a certain actress's performance "sickened him". The next day she sent him a bottle of castor oil.

Bennett Cerf, TRY AND STOP ME 1947

At a luncheon party a certain actress, noted for her sarcasm, looked significantly at Rosalind Russell and said, "I dread to think of life at 45." "Why?" asked Miss Russell. "What happened?"

Reader's Digest Jun 1942

Dame Rebecca West, 84 this Christmas, was in coruscating form lunching at the Ritz last week. Summing up another great lady of her vintage (who had better remain nameless) she observed, "She looks at you as though you were a washing machine that had broken down."

Sunday Times 21 *Nov* 1976

A diva remarked, after a rival had just left a party, "What a woman. Nothing but I – I – I. Talk of a swollen head." Suddenly a car backfired out in the street. "There – it has exploded."

Charles Nielson Gatty, THE ELEPHANT THAT SWALLOWED A NIGHTINGALE 1981

In court during a recent libel action a lawyer listening to his opponent fumble through a difficult defence, scribbled a note to his colleague, "To call that man a silk is an insult to worms."

Observer 5 *Jan* 1986

A young lady was waiting at a bus stop. A young man driving slowly past in a flashy car was trying to catch her eye. He pulled up at the kerb.

"Hello, honey, lovely day for a drive."

The girl looked at him – and through him. He scowled and said with exaggerated politeness, "Pardon me. I thought you were my mother."

"I couldn't be," the young lady said coldly. "I'm married."

S. D. Schalk, Saturday Evening Post 6 *Nov* 1948

See also **REBUKE, RUDENESS, SARCASM, SNUB**

INSURANCE

Bud Abbott and Lou Costello once took out a 100,000 dollar insurance policy with Lloyds of London that stipulated payment if any of their audience should die of laughter.

J.D.Strauss and S.Worth, HOLLYWOOD TRIVIA 1981

When Peter Brough, the ventriloquist, asked his insurance company to increase the insurance on his dummy, Archie Andrews, from £5000 to £10,000 they replied that they would be glad to increase Mr Andrew's cover if he would present himself for a "medical".

Colin West, Illustrated London News 28 *Oct* 1950

All kinds of questions arose in the early days of the National Insurance Act as to the position under it of such part-time employments as those of puppy-walker and knocker-up, and whether footballers and leggers who propelled canal barges through tunnels by using their legs on the roof of the tunnel were employed by way of manual labour. I am not sure, but I believe it was decided that hands included feet.

R.W.Harris, NOT SO HUMDRUM 1939

A Glasgow pawnbroker was amazed recently when a young couple came into his shop, carrying between them what appeared to be everything electrical they owned, and pledged them for cash. The couple looked reasonably well-to-do. Had they suddenly hit hard times? Not a bit of it. When they came back a fortnight later to redeem their goods the couple explained that they had been to the continent on holiday and with a spate of break-ins in their area they hadn't wanted to leave their valuables at home, even though they were insured. So they put them in the safe keeping of the pawnshop.

The total value of their goods came to £300. At normal pawnbroker's annual rate of 20% they had to pay £2.30 to get their possessions back. Well worth it, they reckoned for the peace of mind it gave them.

Sunday Post 1980

INTOXICATION

Humphrey Bogart was a brilliant actor, much under-rated at the time. He and I had only one confrontation, and that was over his drinking. His taste for Scotch was famous; one day when we'd just started on *To Have And To Have Not*, he got back from lunch unsteady on his feet. I said to him, "Bogie, you're not that good an actor that you can cope when you've got a few drinks in you." "Too bad," he said, "I like my drink." "Right," I said, "then either I need a new actor or you need a new director." He never drank at lunch again.

Howard Hawkes, Radio Times 23 May 1974

W.C. Fields was suffering from one of his daily hangovers. "May I fix you a Bromo–Seltzer?" suggested the waiter. "Ye gods no," moaned Fields. "I couldn't stand the noise."

Edmund Fuller, ANECDOTES 1942

Scott Fitzgerald and his wife, arriving an hour late when the others had finished, sitting at table fell asleep over the soup that was brought in, for they had spent the two previous nights at parties, so Scott Fitzgerald said as he awoke for a moment, while someone gathered Zelda up, with her bright cropped hair and diaphanous gown, and dropped her on a bed in a room nearby. There she lay curled up and asleep like a kitten. Scott slumbered in the living room, waking up suddenly again to telephone for two cases of champagne, together with a fleet of taxis to take us to a nightclub.

Andrew Turnbull, S. FITZGERALD, A BIOGRAPHY 1962

Ring Lardner and Arthur Jacks made a trip to South Bend. At their hotel they had a stock of liquor which included some good Canadian whiskey and some Midwestern corn moonshine of very recent date. After a heavy night Jacks woke first in need of a drink. He tried some of the Canadian whiskey but it promptly came up. Undaunted, he tried again, with the same result. After he had made three or four unsuccessful attempts Ring opened one eye and said, "Arthur, if you're just practising, would you mind using the corn?"

Donald Elder, RING LARDNER 1956

A tame jackdaw was a familiar sight at my Brighton hotel. Its favourite remark was "Come on." One morning a visitor, who had had a hectic night, and was still in a hung-over condition, sat in the writing room penning a letter home. Suddenly a raucous voice croaked in his ear, "Come on." Clapping a hand to the region of his heart, he started round with a gasp. A strange black hood had perched on his shoulder. He thought the Old Gentleman had come for him at last. But it was only the jackdaw which had hopped in from the balcony. We had to give the unfortunate man brandy to pull him round.

Sir Harry Preston, LEAVES FROM MY UNPUBLISHED DIARY 1936

At Malta some of my shipmates had been enjoying themselves vastly with gin and ginger beer. When they were leaving in a native boat – a dghaiso – to return to their ship, they noticed that one of their number was missing. They had just ordered the dghaiso-man to go back to the steps when the voice of their shipmate, whose consumption of gin had exceeded his consumption of ginger-beer, was heard hailing, "Never mind boys. I've got lots of faith; I can easily run after you and catch you up." He proceeded to put his theory into practice, and was with difficulty rescued from a gin *cum* ginger beer *cum* watery grave.

Vice-Admiral Humphrey Hugh Smith, AN ADMIRAL NEVER FORGETS 1938

I was chief officer of the *Newark Castle* when she struck a submerged rock off Natal in 1908. The ship was abandoned, but later the Third Officer, finding her still afloat, boarded her again. He was amazed to find the lonely, pyjama-clad figure of a man crawling along the deserted decks.

"What's the meaning of thish, officer?" he hiccuped indignantly. "Wheresh all the blankey-blank stewardsh?"

It appears he had had one over the eight when he boarded the boat at Durban and had immediately turned in. Despite the noise, commotion and list of the ship he had blissfully slept through it all, and it was only with the greatest difficulty that the Third Officer persuaded him to leave the vessel.

Captain J.G. Whitfield, FIFTY THRILLING YEARS AT SEA 1934

An agency which is forever making mischief with speakers is alcohol. A friend of mine, an eminent poet, once managed to deliver himself of a 25-minutes lecture while far gone in wine. As soon as he had accomplished that amazing feat the chairlady thanked him profusely and joined in the continuing applause. The bewildered poet, hearing his name spoken and seeing all the handclapping, stumbled to his feet, stepped to his desk, and began the same lecture all over again.

Frank Crowninshield, Vogue 15 *Mar* 1942

Police in Corpus Christi, Texas, answered an emergency call from an angry housewife, and found they were expected to arrest her husband who was indoors, drunk.

When they pointed out he had a perfect right to be drunk in his own home, the wife dragged her husband out into the street. The police then arrested him.

Reveille, quoted Denys Parsons, FUNNY AMUSING, FUNNY AMAZING 1969

INVALID

During World War I, Queen Alexandra gave unstinted time and energy to hospital visiting and was completely uninhibited in her approach. She noticed a man looking particularly downcast, and was told that he had just realised that his knee would be permanently stiff and useless. Immediately the Queen was at his bedside. "My dear man, I hear you have a stiff leg. So have I. Now watch what I can do with it," and lifting up her skirt she swept the lame leg over his beside table.

Georgina Bettiscombe, QUEEN ALEXANDRA 1969

I went down to Chartwell in 1953, when Churchill was still convalescing from his stroke and his nurse wheeled him to look at his beloved goldfish pond. On one side of it were some stepping stones leading to the other end. Without saying anything he started to try to negotiate these. I plunged into the water on one side and held him up while the nurse came along behind. We got him safely over and then wheeled him back to the summer-house where we sat, myself drenched, discussing English history, as depicted in the Weald of Kent laid out before us.

Lord Butler, THE ART OF THE POSSIBLE 1971

INVENTION

On January 21, 1915, Queen Alexandra wrote Fisher a letter which must have astonished even that believer in unorthodox methods of warfare. Zeppelin raiders had recently appeared over Sandringham and dropped bombs in the neighbourhood. "Please let me have a lot of rockets, with spikes or hoops on, to defend our Norfolk coast," she demanded. "I am sure you could invent something of the sort which would bring down a few of these rascals."

Georgina Bettiscombe, QUEEN ALEXANDRA 1969

James Logie Baird, inventor of television, dabbled in many things. He had studied engineering and matters electrical at university, but among the things that in turn claimed his attention were the selling of a patent medical sock he had invented, and a shoe-cleaner, again his own invention.

William Stapley, Sunday Referee 3 *Feb* 1935

Diana Cooper's capacity for abstract thought seems to have been roughly that of a strawberry mousse and since, like most girls of her class and period, she had received little formal education, her practical ideas were unlikely to be helpful either. When the blitz began she contacted the War Office suggesting that large magnets should be placed in the London parks to attract the bombs.

John Carey, Observer, reviewing Philip Ziegler, DIANA COOPER 20 *Sep* 1981

Jacques–Ives Cousteau, the underwater explorer and inventor of the aqua-lung, was inventive even as a boy. At the age of 11 he got hold of the blue-prints of a 200-ton marine crane and built a 4-foot model. His father, a lawyer, showed Jacques's handiwork to an engineering friend, who examined it closely and asked, "Did you help him with this?" "No," replied *père* Cousteau, "Why?" "The boy has added a movement to this crane which is not on the blueprints, and it is patentable."

James Stuart Gordon, Saturday Evening Post, Cousteau, Master of the Deeps 1973

Thomas Edison had a summer residence of which he was very proud. He enjoyed showing visitors round his property, pointing out the various labour-saving devices. At one point it was necessary to pass through a turnstile in order to take the main path back to the house. Considerable effort was needed to move the turnstile. A guest asked Edison why it was that with all the other clever gadgets around, he had such a heavy turnstile. Edison replied, "Well, you see, everyone who pushes that turnstile around pumps eight gallons of water into a tank in my roof."

Edmund Fuller, ANECDOTES 1942

The Sitwell Egg, invented by Sir George Sitwell, had a yolk of smoked meat, a white of compressed rice, and a shell of synthetic lime. This was intended to be a convenient and nourishing meal for travellers. Sir George decided to put the marketing of his egg into the experienced hands of Sir Gordon Selfridge, founder of the famous Oxford Street shop. Wearing a silk hat and a frock coat, he appeared in Selfridge's office one morning without an appointment and announced, "I am Sir George Sitwell and I have brought my egg with me." He told no one what Mr Selfridge said, but soon after this encounter the egg project was quietly dropped.

Catherine Caufield, THE EMPEROR OF THE UNITED STATES OF AMERICA AND OTHER MAGNIFICENT BRITISH ECCENTRICS 1981

At Elm he [Sir George Sitwell] invented a musical toothbrush which played *Annie Laurie* while you were brushing your teeth, and a small revolver for killing wasps.

Sir Osbert Sitwell, THE SCARLET TREE 1945

Mr Standing started as a floor-sweeper and is now a research chemist. He is the inventor of the firm's caramel pudding, and in his spare time he makes electric organs.

Brighton Evening Argus, quoted Punch 2 *May* 1973

INVITATION

There was a famous funfair at Margate to which we often used to go in the evenings, and I shall never forget the excitement in my office in the City when one day a telegram arrived: "Meet me in Dreamland tonight at ten o'clock. Noel Coward."

Lord Boothby, RECOLLECTIONS OF A REBEL 1978

When Margot Oxford asked Lytton Strachey if he slept with his beard inside or outside the blanket he answered, "Come and see."

A.L. Rowse, MEMORIES OF MEN AND WOMEN 1980

Something awfully funny happened to me. A young American soldier was looking at the outside of the Houses of Parliament. I said to him. "Would you like to go in?" He told me, "You are the sort of woman my mother told me to avoid."

Lady Astor, quoted Christopher Sykes, NANCY: THE LIFE OF LADY ASTOR 1972

Presenting the graduation prizes at a girl's school, Sir Cyril Dyson found it difficult to think of something different to say to each girl. As an attractive seventeen-year-old approached him across the platform he could come up with nothing more original than, "And what are you going to do after you leave school?" With a coy flutter of the eyelids the girl replied, "Well, I *had* thought of going straight home."

Oxfam, PASS THE PORT 1976

On a visit to Russia Nancy Astor denounced in round terms to Stalin the nurseries she had seen. "Send a good sensible woman to me in London," she said, "and I will take care of her and show her how children of five should be handled." A gleam came into Stalin's eye. He pushed forward an envelope and asked for her address. Some weeks later a group of buxom Russian nurses presented themselves before Nancy in London, sent by Stalin. Nancy saw them and screamed, but duly arranged for them to be given courses at various London nurseries.

Christopher Sykes, NANCY: THE LIFE OF LADY ASTOR 1972

JARGON

Cordell Hull, Roosevelt's Secretary of State has developed to a fine point the art of saying nothing elaborately. To one ticklish question he replied, "That situation is complicated by the interplay of many phases which are receiving our most careful analysis. However, each phase is made up of many individual circumstances. These we are attempting to investigate so that we will have a true comprehension of the entire development." Then to the confusion he had created the Secretary added, "We always want to be helpful to you gentlemen."

Benjamin Stolberg, American Mercury, Cordell Hull, the Vanishing American Apr 1940

My mind buzzed with the talk of two businessmen with whom I shared a restaurant-car table. Eavesdropping was inevitable. The pair talked entirely in abbreviations. One would say, in effect, "Is that GMJ under the RPD?" and the other would respond, with every appearance of delight, "Only the SLV." I was still wondering, with Malvolio, what this alphabetical position might portend, when we steamed grumpily into Birmingham.

J.C. Trewin, John O'London's Weekly 30 *Mar* 1951

My son had a note in his report that he was very adept in the use of visual aids for learning. I telephoned his teacher and asked, "What does that mean – 'the creative use of visual aids for learning'?" She replied, "He copies from the child in the next seat."

Orben's Current Comedy, quoted Reader's Digest Jun 1982

JEALOUSY

Joan Collins had been very friendly with the director George England. When his wife revealed symptoms of pregnancy, Miss Collins understandably lost her temper. "That's my baby she's having." she screamed at England.

New York Times 6 *May* 1984

W.H. Davies developed an *idée fixe* that Walter De La Mare was a deadly rival whose widely publicised fame threatened to eclipse his own. Davies, angered by what he considered over-praise of De La Mare in the press, bought a target pistol of some kind, and practised shooting at a portrait of De La Mare which he tacked up on the landing of his boarding house.

Richard Stonesifer, W.H. DAVIES 1963

D'Annunzio kept telling Eleanora Duse how pretty a certain Madame le Bargy was. They were staying in the same place and, one lunch time, Duse appeared at the table, picked up Madam le Bargy, carried her off down the corridor, opened the door of her room and hurled her on to the bed, shouting to D'Annunzio, "There you are. You love her, so there she is." Then she double-locked the door and left the pair. D'Annunzio commented, "Our friend is mad."

The other members of the lunch party had to release the couple with a ladder.

James Fenton, Observer, reviewing William Weaver, DUSE 20 *Sep* 1984

Pavlova, was jealous of Nijinsky. One evening when they appeared together the audience shouted his name louder than hers and she fainted behind the curtain in an uncontrollable fit of jealousy and resentment.

Romola Nijinsky, NIJINSKY 1934

JEW

Obliged to find an apartment of their own, my parents searched the neighbourhood and chose one within walking distance of the park. Showing them out after they had viewed it the landlady said, "And you'll be glad to know I don't take Jews." Her mistake made clear to her, the anti-semitic landlady was renounced, and another apartment found. But her blunder left its mark. Back on the street my mother made a vow. Her unborn baby would have a label proclaiming his race to the world. He would be called "The Jew".

Yehudi Menuhin, UNFINISHED JOURNEY 1977

JOURNALISM

The Mexican earthquake proved to be a "journalist's torment" – the words of my colleague Tony Allen-Mills who arrived in the shattered capital from New York to find there were no telephone or telex machines in operation. But Allen-Mills hit on his own desperate remedy. He jumped on a plane to San Antonio, Texas – a 90-minute flight which resulted in the following exchange at US immigration. "What is the purpose of your visit, sir?" To which our man replied, "To make a telephone call."

Peterborough, Daily Telegraph 8 *Oct* 1985

Sir James Barrie once told me that he had been happy writing for the *Nottingham Journal* at a salary of three guineas a week and added, "One great innovation of mine has gone unapplauded. You see now how every newspaper at the beginning of the year presents its readers with a vast survey of the past twelve months, and a blithe prophecy of the future? Well, I was the first to do that. How I laboured at it! I wrote the whole thing. Did the world gasp? No. Not even the proprietor made any comment."

Cecil Roberts, HALF WAY 1931

During World War I, whenever news was lacking, James Gordon Bennett, owner of the *New York Herald* filled the empty spaces with "Deleted by the French censor".

Brian N. Morton, AMERICAN IN PARIS 1984

S.N. Behrman worked for a time on the *New York Times Book Review,* but was dismissed after it was discovered that while running a queries and answers column he had sent inquisitive letters to himself to relieve the boredom.

The Times, Obituary 11 *Sep* 1973

A woman wrote to Arnold Bennett begging him to help her become a journalist. "But what can I write about here," she asked, "buried in the country twelve miles from a shop?" "The fool," said he. "What better subject could she have than Twelve Miles From a Shop?"

Mrs C.S. Peel, LIFE'S ENCHANTED CUP

I used to sit at the kitchen table, watching TV, listening to women like Ann Morrow Lindbergh and Golda Meir talking about their own careers. I decided it wasn't fulfilling to clean chrome taps with a toothbrush, so I set out to write a column for housewives. It was the only subject in life I could discuss for more than five minutes. Fifteen years later I am still writing for housewives, but they've changed. I'm writing for a different woman now. She is no longer standing behind a curtain looking out. She has taken a bus and gone to town.

Erma Bombeck, IF LIFE IS A BOWL OF CHERRIES, WHAT AM I DOING IN THE PITS? 1979

General William Booth was in full spate. Suddenly he stopped and stabbing a finger at a young man busily writing at a table in front of him called out, "Young man, are you saved?" To which the astonished individual replied, "Me, sir? No. I'm a reporter."

Colin R. Coote, EDITORIAL: THE MEMOIRS OF COLIN COOTE

Arnold Bennett, after writing a strong personal letter to the *Daily Mail* in reply to an attack on him by Lord Birkenhead, learned at the last moment that the *Mail* had telephoned asking for an article. "So," he wrote in his journal, "I crossed out the 'Sir' and 'Yours truly' and called it an article and charged them £40 for it."

Wilfred Whitten, John o' London's Weekly 20 *May* 1933

W.R. Hearst offered columnist Arthur Brisbane a six-month vacation on full pay as a reward for his dedicated and successful work. When Brisbane refused Hearst asked him why. The journalist advanced two reasons. "The first is that if I quit writing for six months it might damage the circulation of your newspapers," he paused for a moment and then, "the second is that it might not."

Ralph Marquand, JOKES AND ANECDOTES FOR ALL OCCASIONS 1972

In a Lancashire and Yorkshire match in 1919, the year in which I began writing about cricket, one of the great characters of that period took eight or nine wickets for next to nothing and won the match for Lancashire. I was so impressed by this terrific display of bowling that I went back to the office and wrote about 1500 words. The chief sub-editor said, "Good God, we don't have room for all that copy," and so my report was submitted to C.P. Scott who didn't know a thing about cricket. As soon as he had read the piece he said, "This must go in, without cuts." Not long afterwards I became the cricket correspondent of the *Manchester Guardian.*

Sir Neville Cardus, quoted Robin Daniels, Sunday Times 4 *Jul* 1976

One Friday Haslam Mills [of the *Manchester Guardian*] told me he was going to send me, on the following Monday afternoon, to the Manchester Hippodrome where a great comedian, Little Tich, was appearing.

"Cardus, this being your weekend off, and in view of the fact that on Monday you will be writing about Little Tich, I don't want you to have any social engagements on Saturday or Sunday." He was talking to me as though I were a member of society. My social engagements in those days involved a poached egg on toast and a cup of coffee in a Lyons Corner House. "No sir," I assured him. "I won't have any social engagements." He said, "I want you to be alone. Tomorrow, if it is a fine day, go for a walk. Go alone, Cardus, and meditate on Little Tich."

We used to take those music hall notices very seriously and we would write them with an almost self-conscious sense of style. Arnold Bennett once said that he read the *Manchester Guardian* primarily for its music hall notices.

Ibid.

Lord Beaverbrook and Lord Castlerosse went everywhere together. Once, when they were in Monte Carlo, Beaverbrook wanted to send an article on it to the *Sunday Express*. He turned to Valentine, "You go in one room and write an article, and I'll go into another and do the same. And the better one goes to London."

When the articles were finished Max compared them. "Yours goes," he said to Valentine, and that's how Valentine Castlerosse became a journalist.

Sir Bruce Lockhart, Sunday Express 27 *Oct* 1957

I have a notion that the real advice I could give to a young journalist is to write an article for the *Sporting Times* and another for the *Church Times* and to put them in the wrong envelopes. It is the only theory upon which I can explain my own undeserved success.

G.K. Chesterton, quoted Times Literary Supplement 17 *Apr* 1974

"Mr Coward, have you anything to say to the *Sun*?" an interviewer once asked him. "Shine," said Noel pleasantly.

William Marchant, THE PLEASURE OF HIS COMPANY 1980

If a reporter came to Joseph Conrad for an interview and apologised for not knowing his work he would say, "Sir, you are a hypocrite. I don't blame you for not reading my books, but don't come here pretending you are terribly sorry, because you do not give a damn whether you have read them or not."

John Conrad, JOSEPH CONRAD: TIMES REMEMBERED 1981

One of Hugh Cudlipp's first jobs as a reporter on the *Penarth News* was to cover a performance of Handel's *Messiah* by the local choir. Though he knew nothing about the *Messiah* he just managed to scrape together 2000 learned words by diligent research in Grove's *Dictionary of Music.* But his editor had asked for no fewer than 3000 words. Cudlipp had an inspiration. Opening a new paragraph he wrote "The names of the choir were –" His editor was delighted. "How much are we paying you?" he enquired kindly. "Two and six, sir," replied Cudlipp hopefully. "I'm glad," mused the editor. "I'm glad." And that is all he was paid.

Geoffrey Smith, Sunday Times 8 *Oct* 1972

It was told of René Cutforth, the BBC reporter, that he once emerged from Broadcasting House to find the police holding back the crowd from a man who had been knocked down by a car. "Let me through, officer," pleaded René, "it is my duty as an ordained minister of the church." Whereupon he knelt beside the victim with hands clasped, extracted the information that he was a diplomat from one of the nearby embassies, and earned a few guineas telephoning it to the news agencies.

Gerald Priestland, SOMETHING UNDERSTOOD 1986

A woman horsewhipped her husband's mistress and then refused to talk to reporters. Phyllis Davies of the *Daily Mail* was on the job, but like the others she could not see the woman. She disappeared from the group of reporters near the house. A little later a big car drove up and a woman with a big bouquet got out, walked up to the door and knocked. The door was opened by the enraged wife. Before she could speak Phyllis said, "Accept these on behalf of the women of England." Taken aback, the woman invited her in and Phyllis got her story.

V. Brodsky, World's Press News 16 *Mar* 1939

On Saturday I saw signs of a wedding at the Savoy Chapel near the Strand. I was the only onlooker holding a camera. "They might be an important couple," I thought hopefully. "I'll stay around a bit." I waited just long enough to hear a commotion at the church door, to see the verger dash out of the vestry and make a bee-line back to the church door, a glass of water in his hand. The bride, I discovered, was being carried through the porch and lowered to a grass strip outside.

"Pity," I thought, feeling sorry for the frightened bridesmaids and the guests, looking as if praying someone would tell them what to do. "Tough on the bride, too," my mind wandered on, and then I suddenly realised what was happening. What a picture!

I soon had my camera in use, and with particulars collected from a distressed verger I hurried to Fleet Street. At London News Agency I was half way up the stairs. MacArthur, the agency manager appeared at the top.

"Well old man," he drawled, "what have you got this time?"

"A wedding," I gasped. "Savoy Chapel." "There's not much in that, is there?" he asked gently. Still fighting for breath I stammered, "The bride fainted."

MacArthur pushed me up the stairs. My plates vanished into the dark-room and I was giving details of the wedding fiasco to a caption writer. Every detail of the unhappy scene had been captured, with a pretty bridesmaid having a quiet weep, in a corner. When the evening papers came out I saw my pictures in the *Star*, the *Evening Standard* and the *Evening News*.

Edward J. Dean, LUCKY DEAN: REMINISCENCES OF A PRESS PHOTOGRAPHER 1944

The "Anglo-Saxons" (as Le Général used to call us) have always had some difficulty in appreciating the grandeur that was de Gaulle. The first question that the United States press corps asked the head of the Free French in 1940 was "What colour pyjamas do you wear?"

Richard Holmes, The Times 2 *Dec* 1982

After climbing the long flight of stairs to the Vatican audience chamber and then walking down again I found a reporter waiting to interview me on my impressions. "Now, Miss Dressler," he began with the brisk competence that seems to inflict all young reporters, "what in that noble old pile impressed you most?" "The absence of an elevator," I gasped. "I do wish they'd get a lift for old women like me."

Of course I did not expect the young man to take me literally. Imagine my chagrin, therefore, when I picked up the morning paper to discover on the front page, "American Actress Annoyed Because she has to Climb Vatican Stairs." After this I was always careful to label my attempts at humour as such.

Marie Dressler, MY OWN STORY 1935

A pressman named Field was once rushed off to Walsall to cover a big fire. At the station he told a cab driver to take him to the scene but neither he, nor anyone else, knew anything about it. Something was obviously wrong. Field phoned his office. "This is Field. There isn't any –" A voice cut him off. "All right. We know all about it. Come on back. The fire's in Warsaw."

William R. Turner, EYES OF THE PRESS 1935

In 1962, when working for Reuters, Frederick Forsyth was posted to East Berlin where he nearly started the Third World War. Returning home late one night he found his path impeded by Soviet armoured divisions; tanks, rocket-launchers, motorised infantry, rumbling along the Karl Marx Allee in the deep dead of night. As soon as he reached his telex he filed a story that a Russian assault on West Berlin was imminent. Sir Alec Douglas-Home, the British prime minister of the time, and the US president Lyndon Johnson had to be woken up, and NATO was put on red alert. Then a wise old hand at Reuters in London suggested he check if it was a rehearsal for the May Day parade. It was.

Observer, Profile 22 *Mar* 1987

Horace Greeley, publisher of the *New York Tribune* had one linguistic quirk. He insisted that the word "news" was plural. Accordingly he sent a cable to a member of his staff that read, "Are there any news?" Back came the reply. "Not a new."

Ralph A. Marquand, JOKES AND ANECDOTES FOR ALL OCCASIONS 1977

Interviewing President Coolidge was the journalist's idea of a nightmare. A secretary introduced us and left us together. We sat down and looked at each other. Nervousness had seized me. I felt idiotic. I made a remark about the beauties of Washington in autumn. President Coolidge looked at me. I looked at President Coolidge. That grim thin pink line that formed the President's lips opened a fraction. "How long are you staying?" he drawled. I told him. We looked at each other; the silence continued.

"Waal, goodbye," and my interview with President Coolidge was over.

Harry J. Greenwall, ROUND THE WORLD FOR NEWS 1935

One of Frank Magee's first jobs was at the command of Hannen Swaffer, then with the *Daily Mirror*. "Go and be the first to climb Mont Blanc this season," said Swaffer.

Magee set out with only £20 in his pocket to cover expenses. Arriving at Chamonix he realised that he was tackling a job that would cost far more than £20. He wired Swaffer for more money. Swaffer wired back, "The greater the task, the greater the glory," but sent no money. In reply Magee wired, "God Alps those who Alp themselves. Send £100."

The money duly arrived but the top was never reached, Magee being defeated by avalanches. When he got back Swaffer asked him what his thoughts were at the moment when the avalanche came sweeping down. Said Magee, "I offered up a prayer that I might return safely to give you a kick in the pants for sending me on such an awful journey."

Michael Popham, World's Press News 11 *Aug* 1938

Even at the *Manchester Guardian*, that shrine of meticulousness, George Mair's fastidious temperament evoked admiration. "Man," whispered a Scottish reporter, "he once telephoned a semi-colon from Moscow."

James Harding, AGATE, A BIOGRAPHY 1986

During the early 60s, when Kingsley Martin was editor of the *New Statesman* he had occasion to stop at the desk of a young sub-editor he had recently hired. He complimented him on his work. Pleased by the praise the young editor hesitated a moment and then said, "Thank you, Mr Martin – but may I say that I've recently married and we do find it hard to get by on twenty guineas a week." Martin (a Socialist, one should add) looked at him in astonishment, then said, "Good God! You mean you haven't got a private income?"

Mordecai Richler, quoted Clifton Fadiman, LITTLE, BROWN BOOK OF ANECDOTES 1985

I was being tried out as a reporter on the ill-fated *Evening Times*. The editor sent me a telegram "A ship is on fire in the Thames, somewhere near Tilbury. Telephone a good story."

Trembling with excitement and eager to make a good impression I raced for Tilbury. No one had heard of the boat. Then came a clue that sent me off to Purfleet. There they told me that the ship was "only a mile or two away". In the pouring rain I trudged across immeasurable stretches of marshland, located the burning liner, trudged back to a telephone box and dictated the most vivid and picturesque description of a burning liner ever written.

Soaked to the skin and completely exhausted I returned to London to see my story in print. I bought a copy of the paper. In the stop press column were the words, "At five o'clock the liner was still ablaze."

Sydney Moseley, THE TRUTH ABOUT A JOURNALIST

Northcliffe took the closest interest in the Leader Page articles. He was keen on names being original and unusual. Walter Callichan contributed freely; sometimes half a dozen articles a week. One day he sent for Walter. "We must have a good alternative name for your woman-interest articles. What do you suggest? What about Mortimer? We haven't a Mortimer. When is your birthday? Very well, call yourself in future January Mortimer." It became the most familiar and popular name on the page.

Reginald Pound, POUND NOTES 1940

At one time Northcliffe ran a campaign for the adoption of a *Daily Mail* hat to replace the ubiquitous bowler. I was loyal enough to wear one of the monstrosities myself, but at the end of a fortnight my friends refused to be seen with me in the street. One night, therefore, I put the hat in the dustbin. The next evening, on returning home, I said, "Thank God that damned hat has gone." "No it hasn't," my household informed me. "After the dustman had been we happened to go out, and there was that hat beside the dustbin." I went out to the dustbin and jumped on the hat.

Wareham Smith, SPILT INK 1932

I was writing copy for the "stop press" when Northcliffe came into the room and casually picked up some proofs from the basket. One was about an accident in which two people had been badly injured, a lamp-post uprooted and paving stones torn up.

The Great Man caught my eye and said quietly, "Do you mind about the lamp-post?" Wondering what was coming I replied that I didn't. "Do you mind about the displaced paving-stones?" Again I had to admit that I had no interest in them whatever.

"Then why pad the story with minor details? All the public care about is that two people were damn nearly killed." And he slowly walked into the machine room.

Arthur J. Sarle, HORSES, JOCKEYS AND CROOKS 1936

In the early 1890s Lord Riddell acquired the *News of the World*. Meeting Frederick Greenwood, the editor of the *Pall Mall Gazette* at his club one day he mentioned that he owned a newspaper, told Greenwood its name and offered to send him a copy. The next time they met Riddell asked Greenwood what he thought of the *News of the World*. "I looked at it and then I put it in the wastepaper basket," said Greenwood, "But then I thought, 'If I leave it there my cook might read it.' So I burned it."

J.W. Robertson-Scott, THE STORY OF THE PALL MALL GAZETTE

Forbes Ross, the original "Harley Street Specialist" was always good for a yarn, so when I wanted a day off I would tell Charles Watney, News Editor of the *Daily Mail*, "Ross has a good story," and then get it.

"I want a really good column today," I said to Ross once.

"I've got one," he said, "Let's take oatmeal." Then he went on to explain how – and proved it from facts and figures taken from blue books – while oatmeal was all very well for Scots ghillies who could digest anything, it lay like a plaster on the stomachs of sedentary workers and shortened their lives by years. "Oatmeal is Poison", said the *Daily Mail* poster next morning. I was terribly proud of this until I was sent for by Alfred Harmsworth. "You've got to deny this story!" he shouted. "I'll give you two hours. All the patent-food people are cancelling their advertisements."

I went the round of food specialists, but found no one who would knock the story down. Triumphantly I returned. Harmsworth was waiting. "It's true," I said. "Get out!" he yelled. "I'll give you another hour or you're sacked."

So I went – back to Gower Street and Forbes Ross. "You've got me into a deuce of a row," I explained. "That's easy," he replied, and producing the same blue books, from them disproved the entire story.

Hannen Swaffer, World's Press News 17 *Jul* 1937

Things did not "commence" in the *Manchester Guardian* they "began". Neville Cardus once used the phrase "from thence" and received a courteous rebuke from C.P. Scott. He dared to argue that Fielding had used it in *Tom Jones*, and so had Smollett. "Did they?" replied Scott. "Neither Mr Fielding or Mr Smollett would have used it twice in my newspaper."

John Harding, JAMES AGATE, A BIOGRAPHY 1986

After much argument by his advertising manager, C.P. Scott was persuaded to have the name of the *Manchester Guardian* displayed outside the office in neon lights. "Very well," he agreed, "but only on condition it does not twinkle."

Ibid.

During a period of twenty-one years Raymond Gram Swing spent in Europe as a foreign correspondent he refused to cable stories on divorce or murder. Once, just after he had sent over a long and careful treatise on the gold standard, his paper demanded a story on a murder. He complained by cable that forcing him to write such a story would be like compelling "a highly trained surgeon to clean up the operating room after a delicate operation".

Richard O. Boyer, New Yorker, Profile 1942

When I was working for the *Daily Mail* I was sent to Russia but, finding revolution-racked Petrograd little to my liking, I decided to return home. *The Mail* sent cables urging me to stay. Finally I decided to send a cable, "Will stay another month if salary doubled." I took it to the Post Office. The counter clerk was busy. I had to wait. Again I reflected, "Why not ask impossible terms which will assure my return?" And I added the word "retrospectively". When I had written the word it looked so impudent that I was about to scratch it out, but at that moment the clerk took the form out of my hand and the die was cast. Next day came the answer "Terms accepted". I cabled to my wife to buy a ring and stayed.

Alex M. Thompson, HERE I LIE 1937

Two aspiring journalists were passing the new insurance building now in process of construction when one of them remarked on the chamois-like antics of a craneman who was running along a narrow plank. "One false step and that fellow is a news item," said his companion.

James Dunn, World's Press News 30 *Jan* 1936

When Pope Benedict XV was dangerously ill a premature report of his death was flashed to a New York newspaper. A special edition bore the headline across its seven columns on the front page: POPE BENEDICT XV IS DEAD. And the triple-column lead, set out in bold, heavily leaded type read: "Pope Benedict XV is no more. Death took the leader of the Catholic world at an early hour this morning. His passing was easy and beautiful, and slowly, as he sank into his last sleep, the watchers at his bedside caught the murmur 'Peace. Peace.' as the Pontiff breathed his last."

Then the report was denied, so another edition appeared with equally large headlines reading: POPE HAS REMARKABLE RECOVERY.

David Ellby, SHOOTING THE BULL 1935

The well-intentioned *Daily Mirror* campaign against the Colorado Beetle, for each genuine specimen of which, delivered to the Ministry of Agriculture, they offered a £10 prize, was withdrawn at the urgent request of the Ministry. The Ministry had had an immediate response, people arriving with various types of beetles and claiming the £10, although the *Mirror* had emphasised that claims should go to them and beetles to the Ministry. The main fear however was that the offer might lead to a black market in the beetle and attempts to import specimens. There was, in fact, one case of a man arriving at Customs with a Colorado beetle in a matchbox.

World's Press News 3 *Jul* 1947

JURY

Lord Justice Bowen was not able to depress his faculties to the level of the ordinary witness or juror. Once, a man was tried before him for burglary. It was proved that the prisoner broke and entered a dwelling house at night, and that he was arrested on the roof, with his boots slung round his neck. The defence was that the prisoner, when passing the house, saw the door open and went on to the roof without any felonious intent. Bowen, in his charge to the jury, said that if they thought the prisoner's presence on the roof was due to his love of fresh air, and that if the locality of his boots showed that he had taken them off so as not to disturb the people sleeping in the house, they would acquit him.

They did!

Ernest Bowes-Rowlands, IN THE LIGHT OF THE LAW 1931

When President Roosevelt was a young lawyer just getting started in New York he was retained to handle a difficult civil case. The opposing lawyer was a very effective jury pleader and completely outshone his youthful rival in the argument to the jury. However, he made one fatal mistake: he orated for several hours. As he thundered on Roosevelt noticed that the jury wasn't paying much attention. So, playing a hunch when his turn came, he rose and said, "Gentlemen, you have heard the evidence. You also have listened to my distinguished colleague, a brilliant orator. If you believe him and disbelieve the evidence you will have to decide in his favour. That is all I have to say."

The jury was out only five minutes, and brought in a verdict for Roosevelt's client.

Drew Pearson and Robert S. Allen, WASHINGTON MERRY-GO-ROUND 1940

A client of ours was summoned for jury service at Inner London Crown Court one Monday last month, the same day as he was due to stand trial at the Old Bailey for conspiracy to rob and firearms offences. He was worried because he realised that he could not fulfil both commitments and he did not know which court he should go to.

T.M.S. Tosswill, letter to The Times 23 Nov 1982

JUSTICE

An Arab youth in the Batinah province of Muscat murdered his maternal uncle and went to his chief and confessed. This was the chief's ruling: "In the bottom of yonder dry well will be planted some spears with their spikes pointing upwards. My judgement is that thou start from there" – and he indicated with his cane a spot some fifteen paces from the well-mouth – "then shalt thou turn thy back upon the well and walk backwards until thou fallest into it. Thus will the stain be removed from thy name. Whether thou diest or livest the crime thou has committed will be expiated."

A wave of horror spread through the circle of tribesmen. The youth moved calmly backwards towards his doom, and reaching the brink, leapt as he was bidden. But at that instant ten stalwart Badus, who ostensibly were watching the ceremony, threw their arms about him as he was about to fall, having been ordered to do so.

"Go back to thy tribe," the youth was told, "thy coat is black no longer."

Bertram Thomas, ALARMS AND EXCURSIONS IN ARABIA 1931

KOREAN WAR

During the retreat from the Yalu, cold was a far worse enemy than the Chinese army. If you took your shoes and socks off you could get frostbite so badly that you had to be flown home. It was a recognised method of escaping from the front – so long as you didn't develop gangrene and die in the process.

René Cutforth, Radio Times 22 Apr 1971

Lieutenant-Colonel "Jumbo" Phillips of the 8th Hussars preserved every cliché of the British cavalry going to war. While his unit prepared their Centurion tanks for embarkation Phillips issued his own hints to officers about their preparation. He suggested taking fishing gear, four rolls of lavatory paper, and a shot gun – "though not your best gun" – and ammunition "because Eley cartridges may be difficult to obtain".

Max Hastings, THE KOREAN WAR 1987

On 23 April 1951, second day of the battle of the Imjin River, I was in a truck bringing up mortar ammunition. About four miles short of Gloucester Hill we were ambushed and captured. I escaped during an American air strike but did not known what had happened to the battalion. I walked around for some 30 hours in no-man's-land until I heard some Gloucester voices. I walked out and went up to them only to find they were prisoners. We were taken to the Yalu River and stayed there the next 2½ years.

Tony Preston, Radio Times 22 Apr 1971

LADY

I recall an acquaintance telling me that his wife, having advertised for domestic help, answered her doorbell and was greeted with the words, "Are you the woman that wants a lady to work for her?"

D.A. Nicholson, letter to Daily Telegraph 28 Feb 1979

In South London, at any rate, a distinction is made between women and ladies. A notice which appears outside a certain place of worship says, "Women's Fellowship. Wednesdays 3 p.m. All ladies welcome."

Martin Hawkins, letter to Daily Telegraph 1 *March* 1979

LANGUAGE

J.M. Barrie and I always took our hasty meals in a public house opposite the Duke of York's Theatre while the rehearsals for *Peter Pan* were being held there. I noticed that he always ordered Brussels sprouts and never ate them. One day I asked him why. JMB replied, "I cannot resist ordering them. The words are so lovely to say." Try them yourself with a slightly Scottish accent.

William Nicholson, Sunday Referee 5 *Dec* 1931

During the Anglo-American occupation after World War II the German economic director incautiously complained that the grain supplied by the Americans was "chicken-feed". It was indeed largely maize and the director had described it with literal accuracy, being no doubt unaware that the words he chose had, in the United States, another idiomatic and derogatory meaning. "Three hundred million bucks," exclaimed General Clay, American Military Governor, "and the bastard calls it chicken-feed."

Observer 12 *Jan* 1964

Occasionally the calm of the Elysée Palace is shattered as when an exasperated de Gaulle bellowed at one of his staff, "Monsieur, you are a *godelureau*!" This was one of the less easily cowed characters around the palace, and he said blandly, "A godelureau, mon général, what is that? I must look it up in the dictionary." It struck de Gaulle that it couldn't be what he thought it was – a simpleton. But he could never admit to using a word he wasn't sure of so he waved the man out and looked it up himself and found that a *godelureau* was "A gallant, a lady's man". So he called the man back to his office and said, "Monsieur, you are not a *godelureau*."

Pierre Galante, THE GENERAL 1968

Lunching with English friends at the time of her husband's retirement, Madame de Gaulle was asked what she was looking forward to in the years ahead. "A penis," she replied without hesitation. The embarrassed silence that followed was broken by the former president. "My dear, I don't think the English pronounce the word like that. It is ''appiness'."

Robert Morley, BOOK OF BRICKS 1978

To greet the new French cabinet, Asquith, Lloyd George and I went to Paris. The discussion was naturally all in French. Such part as was taken by us was left to, or it would be more correct to say thrust upon, myself. Asquith could not, Lloyd George would not, and I *had* to speak French. In French I knew my vocabulary to be limited, my grammar to be imperfect, and my genders to be at the mercy of chance; further, I am told that my accent is atrocious. But with my back really against the wall, something relevant could always be made forthcoming. When the Council was over and we three British ministers were safely outside, Lloyd George said to me, "You know, your French was the only French that I could understand."

Lord Grey of Fallodon, TWENTY-FIVE YEARS 1929

We returned from Panama after dark. As the night air from the swamps has the reputation of being deadly, every window in the car was shut. I noticed a Peruvian in some difficulties with the conductor owing to his lack of knowledge of English. He had opened a window and sat in the full draught of the night air. A pleasant young Irishman named Martin noticed this. "By Gad! That fellow will get fever if he sits in the draught from the swamps. I'll go and warn him." I told Martin that the South American spoke no English. "That's all right," said Martin, "I speak a little Spanish myself." Taking a seat by the Peruvian, Martin tapped him on the shoulder, pointed a warning finger at the window and said slowly and impressively, but in a strong Galway accent, "Swamp-o; musn't-sit-in-the-draught-o, get chill-o; get chill-o catch fever-o; catch fever-o, damned ill-o; damned ill-o, die-o." He repeated this twice, and upon the Peruvian turning a blank look of incomprehension on him returned to his place saying, "I don't believe that fellow understands a single word of Spanish."

Lord Frederic Hamilton, HERE, THERE AND EVERYWHERE 1921

Arabic is one of the most difficult languages for an Englishman to learn. A slight change in accent may change the entire meaning of a word. I was telling a large gathering of sheikhs about a forthcoming Agricultural Exhibition. Unfortunately I gave the Arabic word for exhibition *marad* a short first "a" instead of a long one, and my audience was horrified to learn that a virulent epidemic was about to take place.

"Is this true?" one old sheikh asked in a trembling voice.

"Yes, it is perfectly true," I replied, "and I want this epidemic to be the biggest one there has ever been in Egypt, and I expect you to help me with it, and see that all your people are in it."

This sounded so bloodthirsty and alarming that the sheikhs began to mutter to each other and then one of them turned to me and asked "Why is this to happen?" "Because the Government desires it," I replied.

Fortunately someone explained the mistake and the meeting dispersed with relieved laughter.

Major C.S. Jarvis, THREE DESERTS 1936

Russian foreign minister Molotov coined a word during a session with British and American representatives. Observing the way they indicated approval by nodding and saying "Okay", Molotov to indicate disapproval shook his head from side to side and declared "Nokay."

Leonard Lyons, Reader's Digest Mar 1946

I once knew a rather charming Oxford professor who went all through America under the impression that his fanny was his suitcase. I understand there was quite an outbreak of virtuous indignation among the coloured porters of Omaha when he rushed round the station asking them if anyone had been tampering with his fanny.

Beverly Nichols, THE STAR-SPANGLED MANNER 1928

Richter, the conductor, never learned to speak much English. At a rehearsal at the Queen's Hall he was disturbed by the women caretakers who were noisily dusting the seats, and after a time, in desperation, he turned round and waved his arms at them, shouting in imploring tones, "You wifes, you wifes down there – don't care please – don't care just now." They did not understand his words, but they guessed his meaning.

Mathilde Verne, CHORDS OF REMEMBRANCE 1936

Sir George Sitwell knew nothing of modern slang. Shocked by the bad behaviour of an acquaintance who had offered him a piece of jewellery and failed to deliver it he complained to Osbert about modern manners. "Such a pity to promise people things and then forget about them. It is not inconsiderate – really inexcusable." The cause of this lament was a passing remark, "I'll give you a ring, Sir George, on Thursday."

Catherine Caufield, THE EMPEROR OF THE UNITED STATES OF AMERICA AND OTHER MAGNIFICENT BRITISH ECCENTRICS 1981

Elaine Stritch began to sing, "When the tower of Babel fell," and pronounced it to rhyme with "scrabble". Noel Coward stopped her and said, "It's 'baybel' Stritch." "I've always said 'babble'. Everyone says 'babble'. It means mixed-up language, doesn't it? Gibberish. That's where we get 'babble' from."
"That's a fabble," said Noel.

William Marchant, THE PRIVILEGE OF HIS COMPANY 1975

While eating at a small French restaurant a tourist was quick to notice a fly in the soup. Summoning the waiter he stabbed an accusing finger at the soup bowl and cried, "*Le mouche.*" "No monsieur, *La mouche,*" the waiter corrected. "Good grief," said the man, "You've got good eye sight!"

Mayfair 1981

LAW

When practising at the bar the tables were once turned on Mr Justice Avory. "Let me see," he remarked to a witness, "you've been convicted, haven't you?" "Yes," came the reply, "but that was through the incapacity of my counsel." "It always is," said Avory, "and you have my sincere sympathy." "I deserve it," was the unexpected answer, "seeing you were my counsel."

Daily Telegraph, Obituary 14 *Jun* 1935

During a case in which the learned counsel opposed to him quoted something from the Book of Job Sir Horace Avory said, "I object. That evidence is quite inadmissible, seeing you are unable to put Job in the witness box to prove it."

Gordon Lang, MR JUSTICE AVORY 1935

F.E. Smith once appeared for an omnibus company which was being sued for damages by the parents of a boy whose right arm was said to have been crippled in a collision. It was alleged that he could no longer work, and could not raise his arm above the level of his shoulder. Smith was very sympathetic and pleasant and took great pains to put the boy at his ease.
"Will you please show us how high you can raise your arm now?" he said.

With face contorted the boy slowly raised his arm to the level of his shoulder.

"Thank you," said Smith, "and will you now please show us how high you could raise it before the accident."

In a second the arm was thrust high in the air and the case was lost.

Second Earl of Birkenhead, LIFE OF LORD BIRKENHEAD 1939

Some years ago I was defending a Chinese in the Old Street magistrate's court. When asked to take the oath the defendant asked for a saucer, declaring it to be essential. A saucer from the police canteen was produced. Holding the saucer aloft my client said, "May my soul be broken as this saucer is broken if I do not tell the truth." Then he hurled the saucer to the ground. It bounced with a ringing tone and hurtled across the courtroom quite undamaged.

H.M. Croome, letter to The Times 28 *Oct* 1987

At times Sir Henry Curtis-Bennett liked to shock the court, so that when the jury considered their verdict they would still be reeling under the surprise of his pleading. Imagine, for instance, the feeling of a jury, asked to decide whether a defendant was a knave or a fool, when Curtis stood up and said, "You may think my client a fool. I tell you myself–he *is* a fool. But you can't convict on that or the courts would be full."

Roland Wild and Derek Curtis-Bennett, CURTIS 1937

In one of his cases things were going badly for Sir Henry Curtis-Bennett, and even he had difficulty in keeping a confident expression while the most damning admissions were extracted from his own witnesses. However, a solicitor happened to pass his seat, and Curtis-Bennett whispered in his ear. The solicitor replied, and Curtis-Bennett burst into a paroxysm of silent laughter that no one in the court failed to observe. It was as if he had just heard news that completely expelled his anxiety and revealed, once and for all, the folly of the opposition case. Judge, jury, his own client, and even his learned friend could not help but think that Curtis had just heard something that would shake the case to pieces. And his confidence was immediately transferred to the case for the defence.

"What did you say to Curtis that pleased him so much?" the solicitor was asked. "Nothing," was the reply. "I only told him it was raining outside."

Ibid.

A motor horse-box carrying a live horse can travel at 30 m.p.h. If the horse dies in transit the vehicle immediately becomes a carrier of horseflesh and by law must reduce speed to 20 m.p.h.

Daily Mail, quoted Denys Parsons, FUNNY HA HA, FUNNY PECULIAR 1965

A smart trick used by prosecuting attorneys is to have a criminal's confession txped with many naIes aNd places misspelled. When reading it, the criminal invariably scratches out the errors and puts corrections in the margin. His handwriting is therefore on many of the pages, which prevents him and his lawyer from making the claim, in court, that the accused has signed, but not read, the confession.

Freeling Foster, Colliers Magazine 28 *Jun* 1949

H.M. Customs is forbidden to burn any more obscene books, because they were breaking the rules of a smokeless zone by making black smoke.

The Guardian, quoted New Statesman

A lawyer who was appearing in the Indian Supreme Court cited an English authority to support his case. "How can you refer to an English case in an Indian court?" one of the judges asked. "The difference between English law and Indian law is as great as the difference between trousers and *dhotis*." "But your lordship will appreciate," retorted the lawyer, "that the underlying principle of both is the same."

C. Rashmikant, Reader's Digest Apr 1978

LAWN TENNIS

Baseball player Ralph Kiner was telling Lindsey Nelson about his wife, the former tennis star, Nancy Chaffee. "When I married Nancy I vowed I'd beat her at tennis some day. After six months she beat me 6–2. After a year she beat me 6–4. After we'd been married a year and a half I pushed her to 7–5. Then it happened. She had a bad day and I had a good one and I beat her 17–15. "Good for you, Ralph," exclaimed Lindsey. "Was she sick?" "Of course not," Kiner shapped indignantly. "Well, she was eight months pregnant."

James C. Humes SPEAKER'S TREASURY OF ANECDOTES 1978

Suzanne Lenglen, the French tennis champion began her meteoric career by winning the world's hard court championship at St Cloud at the age of fourteen. A few weeks later her home in the Oise country was shell-ridden. As the guns of the German legions were rumbling in the ears of Compiègne Suzanne left her home and went out curiously into the street. Her father, stout-hearted in the hour of peril, had declined to flee. Presently a German officer, advancing faster than his fellows, appeared on the scene. He stopped, saluted the small citoyenne. "You are the little Suzanne, unless I am much mistaken," he said in excellent French. "I beg you to quit immediately while there is still time." The warning was conveyed to the Lenglen household and acted upon, but not before the championship cup, which the daughter of the house had first won on her fourteenth birthday, had been carefully buried – to remain in its hiding place for five years.

A. Wallis Myers, MEMORY'S PARADE 1932

I first played tennis for the sake of my health. I was a pale, thin little person and father and mother were afraid I should always be an invalid, so they encouraged me to keep in the open air. Tennis transformed me into a nut-brown maid, sparkling with health, who preferred to play with boys because they could run faster and hit harder.

Suzanne Lenglen, Quoted A. Wallis Myers, MEMORY'S PARADE 1932

LEADERSHIP

When given his first command, as captain of the destroyer *Daring* in 1934, Mountbatten asked his first lieutenant to prepare for him a card index giving particulars of the 159 members of the ship's company. While shaving every morning he studied these cards and after inspection on Sundays he arranged to have 40 men meet him on the quarterdeck. As the men came forward individually to salute him he would greet each one with some such remark as, "Oh yes, James, isn't it? You're in the engine room. I understand you've been having a little trouble at home recently. I know it's not easy having a mother-in-law to support as well as a wife and two children." The effect was magical. According to one friend, "After that, the ship never looked back."

Ray Murphy, THE LAST VICTORY

All morning an instructor on my staff had been explaining leadership to a class of police recruits. Calling a man to the front of the class he handed him a piece of paper on which was written, "You are in charge. Get everyone out of here without causing panic." The recruit was at a loss for words and returned to his seat. The second man tried, "The chief drill instructor wants us outside. Go!" no one moved. A third man glanced at the paper, smiled and said, "All right, men. Break for lunch." The room emptied in seconds.

Howard Dean, Reader'Digest Sep 1981

LIBEL

We had a very disturbed Easter. Boofy Gore (Earl of Arran) has identified himself with a gangster called "Boofy Kidd" in Ian's new horror-comic (*Diamonds Are For Ever*). The passage runs thus: "Kidd's a pretty boy. His friends call him Boofy. Probably he shacks up with Wint. Some of these homes make the worst killers. Kidd's got white hair though he's only 30. That's why he works in a hood." Lord Lambton telephoned Boofy, read the paragraph to him and advised him to see his lawyers. Boofy became demented, pompous, hysterical, telephoned to me, said his life was ruined, said Ian was Eton's most popular author and his son would read it, said his oldest friend had done him a grave injury; I pointed out that though married, Ian and I were separate entities, that I had neither written nor read the book. But that only increased his misery and rage.

Ann Fleming, letter to Evelyn Waugh 4 *Apr* 1956

LONGEVITY

"How is it," a reported asked George Moore on his eightieth birthday "that you enjoy such good health in your eightieth year?" Moore answered, "It's because I never smoked, or drank, or touched a girl – until I was eleven years old."

Bennett Cerf, THE LIFE AND SOUL OF THE PARTY 1956

All my family live to a good age. When my grandmother was 101 I heard her shouting to my uncle that he should not go out cycling without his overshoes. He was 81 and thought he was too old to be told what to do.

Victor Borge, The Times 2 *Jan* 1984

LUCK

Jean Cocteau was once asked if he believed in luck. "Of course," he replied. "How else do you explain the success of those you don't like?"

Jacob Braude, SPEAKER'S AND TOASTMASTER'S HANDBOOK 1971

On January 24 1971, Major General Idi Amin Dada, Commander of Uganda's armed forces, was out duck shooting. When he returned about seven in the evening a tank stood outside his house. From it emerged Sergeant-Major Mussa, a fellow Kakwa tribesman, to tell him he had intercepted President Obote's instructions that the general's supporters should be arrested and killed.

That afternoon the telephone had rung in Jinja barracks. The operator had left the room for a moment and Sergeant-Major Mussa happened to be passing. So he took the call. It was President Obote calling from Singapore, wishing to speak to Lieutenant-Colonel David Oyile-Ojok, one of his most devoted supporters Mussa put through the call but listened and heard Obote tell Oyilr-Ojok to arrest Amin and his supporters and then finish them off. Mussa ran for his life, collected his West Nile friends together, then seized the armoury just as Obote's Lango tribesmen and their Acholi kinsmen were arriving. There was a fight, with some bloodshed, and the Amin faction remained in full control. Amin was in luck again.

Judith Listowel, AMIN 1973

It happened on board the *Queen Mary*, outward bound for America. Harry Parr Davies, Gracie Fields personal accompanist and musical director was leaning over the ship's rail when his spectacles fell off his nose and dropped overboard.

They were the only pair he had. He could't see his music properly without them, which was going to make rehearsing on board ship pretty difficult. In despair, he told Gracie. Gracie went to the purser's office to see if she could buy another pair from any of the shops on the *Queen Mary*. As she did so a steward was pinning a notice on the door. It read, "Found; a pair of spectacles. Apply purser"

Gracie said, "If nobody claims these can Harry try then on and see if they suit him?" The purser agreed, Harry tried them on and found they were his own glasses. The man who had found them occupied a cabin on a lower deck. "Most extraordinary thing," he confessed. "I opened my porthole and put my hand out to see if it was raining. And into my hand fell a pair of glasses."

Bert Aza, Sunday Chronicle 30 *Jul* 1939

I went out on an Irish Sweepstake story one year. When the name of a South London woman sputtered out of the ticker-tape I went in search of her. She answered my knock and looked at me through a haze of steam from a saucepan she was holding in her hand. When I broke the news that she had drawn a horse in the Sweepstake she went deadly white. The saucepan slipped from her hand. Hot potatoes rolled in all directions and the lady collapsed.

I put down my camera and lifted the lady into a sitting position. The door was pushed open and a man stood staring down at us. "What the –?" he began. His appearance was as much a surprise to me as mine was to him. The woman stirred as he took a step towards me and regained consciousness in time to save the situation.

The woman's horse won her £25,000 and shortly afterwards I attended a party at their new home in Forest Hill, waited upon by three servants and driven home in a new car.

Edward J. Dean, LUCKY DEAN; THE REMINISCENCES OF A PRESS PHOTOGRAPHER 1944

"I have a new Ford car," William Dean Howells said. "In going over some boxes of old papers I came upon two bankbooks, each of which indicated an unused balance. I verified these records and drew the money which in a most miraculous manner exactly equalled the cost of a car."

Hamlin Garland, MY FRIENDLY CONTEMPORARIES 1932

MARRIAGE

Before Margot Tennant's marriage to Asquith it was rumoured that she was going to marry Arthur Balfour, who merely said that, on the contrary, he had rather thought of having a career of his own.

Daphne Bennett, MARGOT; A LIFE OF THE COUNTESS OF OXFORD AND ASQUITH 1984

In 1925 Allin Mackay's father, appalled at the possibility of family entanglements with a song writer, said to Irving Berlin, "What will you do if I cut my daughter off without a cent?" Said Berlin, "In that case I'll have to settle a million on her myself."

News Chronicle 25 *Jul* 1936

Clementine Churchill was sitting next to General de Gaulle at a luncheon and thinking to herself, during one of the many silences, how difficult Mme de Gaulle's life must be. Her reverie was interrupted by the general's remark to her, "Vous savez, madame, it must be very difficult being the wife of Mr Churchill."

Cecil Beaton, SELF-PORTRAIT WITH FRIENDS 1979

It was terribly hard work being married to a Huxley. "If I were not a man," said Julian frenetically, "I should like to be a tugboat."

Juliette Huxley, LEAVES OF A TULIP TREE 1986

Christopher Isherwood, temporarily living in Amsterdam, had not Erika Mann, daughter of Thomas Mann. Branded as a public enemy of the Third Reich, she was threatened with the loss of her German citizenship and hoped to find an Englishman she could marry so that she could become a British subject. She asked Isherwood if he would be willing to marry her but he refused, and instead suggested that she should write to his friend Wystan Auden, explaining the situation. She did so. Auden wired back: "Delighted."

Charles Osborne, W.H.AUDEN; THE LIFE OF A POET 1979

Someone once asked the millionaire, Harold Lever, "What kind of a socialist are you? You married your wife because she has four million. Harold's reply was, "I married my wife because she had four million? I would have married my wife even if she had only two million."

Charles Forte, AUTOBIOGRAPHY 1986

Walter Sickert, the artist, married three times. His first wife, who brought him some money to spend, was a daughter of Cobden. One of his favourite openings was, "I was standing under the statue of my first father-in-law, in Camden town –"

George Malcolm Thomson, Evening Standard 2 *Jul* 1947

Adlai Stevenson told Joan Fontaine that he greatly regretted that, as he entertained political ambitions, it would not be possible for him to marry an actress. "It is just as well," replied a dignified Joan, "my family would hardly approve of my marrying a politician."

Paul Levy, Observer 14 *Jan* 1979

When Gloria Swanson's mum heard that she had married a titled gent in Paris she hastily phoned her lawyer. "What's a markee?" she asked. "It's one of those things," he explained, "that you hang in front of the theatre to keep the rain off the customers." "My God," exclaimed the good lady, "Gloria married one this morning."

Bennett Cerf, TRY AND STOP ME 1977

MATHEMATICS

Edison employed in his office a graduate named Upton of Princeton University who had studied also in Germany under the great Helmholtz. One day the inventor wanted to know the eubical content of the pear-shaped bulb that he made for electric light. Armed with sheets of foolscap and rows of figures, the mathematician tackled the problem. After waiting a few days Edison asked him for the result.

"I haven't finished yet," Upton replied, displaying his charts.

"Let me show you how to do it," said Edison. He poured water into a bulb. "Now measure the water and you'll have the answer," he directed.

W A Simonds, EDISON; HIS LIFE, WORK AND GENIUS 1935

Godfrey Harold Hardy had a brilliant collaborator in Ramanujau, the self-taught Indian mathematician whom he had helped to bring to England in 1914. Ramanujau became fatally ill with tubercolosis soon after being made a Fellow of the Royal Society in 1918. Hardy often visited him in hospital. One day, depressed at his friend's condition and at a loss for conversation he nervously stammered out, "The number of my taxi was 1729. It seemed to me rather a dull number." Ramanujau, much distressed by his off-hand remark replied, "No Hardy! No Hardy! It is a very interesting number. It is the smallest number expressible by the sum of two cubes in two different ways."

Catherine Caufield, THE EMPEROR OF THE UNITED STATES OF AMERICA AND OTHER MAGNIFICENT BRITISH ECCENTRICS 1981

Einstein, a keen amateur violinist, was practising sonatas at home with his pianist friend, Arthur Rubinstein. Someone walked past the door of their room and overheard Rubinstein as he pointed out a false entry on Einstein's part. "Oh, Albert," he was saying, "can't you count?"

Steve Race. BBC. Radio 4, My Music 5 *Mar* 1979

MEANNESS

When I was painting the Duke of Albercorn, as a Governor of De Beers I could have thrown away – because they were so shabby – the dress clothes he used to leave behind him after each sitting. Yet, always, he wrapped them up carefully, and gave me instructions just where to keep them, and when he untied the parcel on his return he used to quiz the garments so suspiciously that I could see that he feared that I might have been wearing them.

F. Tennyson Cole, VANITY VARNISHED 1931

Though amply provided for, Diana Cooper retained a talent for scavenging that would have done credit to a coyote. Once, after staying with Lord Rosebery, she begged for a loan of his Rolls-Royce to take her to the station and, on the way down to the car, stole the breakfast kipper from the tray outside his bedroom door, to eat on the train.

Philip Ziegler, DIANA COOPER 1981

Often when the Marquis of Clanricard dined at his club he would eat sandwiches from a paper bag, and follow with a banana dipped in coffee. Once he ordered cutlets. When they were served the marquis carefully rolled them in a napkin and put them in his pocket.

He even foraged in street dustbins in West End news for kitchen refuse. Wives of taxi-drivers, thinking him poor, gave him food. Sometimes he would take strips of fat he collected from dustbins and ask the chef at one of his clubs to cook them for him. The request was, not unnaturally, refused.

Yet at this time the marquis owned 56,000 acres, and his income was probably £80,000 a year.

John L. Garbutt, Sunday Express 31 *Jul* 1949

Cocteau told the story that when one of his boyfriends decamped with a valuable Dali the master said, "Never mind, we will give you another," and Salvador Dali's wife Gala added, "Yes, we will give you another for only the price we would charge a dealer."

Meryle Secrest, SALVADOR DALI, THE SURREALIST JESTER 1986

At 16 Paul Hawlyn applied to the bookseller Anton Zwemmer for a job. The interview was brisk. "Who wrote *Ulysses*?" "James Joyce, sir." "Excellent. The job's yours." "But, er, Mr Zwimmer, how much will you pay me?" "I hate to talk money, dear boy. Don't you know it's an honour to work at Zwemmers?" (They settled for 25s – 6d a week.)

Observer, Profile 30 *Nov* 1986

Sir Squire Bancroft was notoriously tight-fisted, his style of management being in complete contrast to that of Sir Herbert Beerbohm Tree, who took Bancroft to view His Majesty's Theatre, which Tree had recently built and lavishly equipped. Gazing at the building from the opposite side of the street Bancroft remarked, "There'll be an awful let of windows to clean."

S.N.Behrman, PORTRAIT OF MAX 1960

MEMORY

Sir Thomas Beechan once arrived late for a performance and as the curtain was about to rise he leaned over to the leader. "We are performing *Figaro* tonight, are we not?" "Oh no, Sir Thomas," said the leader, "It is *Seraglio.*" The conductor smiled. "My dear fellow, you amaze me," he replied – and as the curtain went up launched into the opera, completely from memory.

TV Times 20 *Apr* 1979

Professor Francis Edgeworth, a Fellow of All Souls Cambridge, had a distinguished intellect and a fabulous memory. On his one journey to America, laid up in his cabin by sea-sickness, he managed to reconstruct about half of the *Iliad* in Greek.

A.L.Rowse, GLIMPSES OF THE GREAT 1985

MISPRINT

Punch discovered a misprint in one of my peace poems in the *Irish Times*. My verses had depicted a family dreaming of the homecoming of their soldier from the wars while. "All night lies beneath the stars, And dreams no more out there."

The *Irish Times* printed it as "All night he lies beneath the stairs" and made matters worse by adding: "Only a true artist could achieve this effect of quietly hopeless tragedy." *Punch* seized upon this and said that if I could express a wish for the New Year, it would probably be to meet the editor of the *Irish Times*. Oddly enough, a week or two later I found myself sitting next to him at a public dinner and, as an opening gambit to our conversation, remarked that we had recently been in *Punch*. To my surprise he blushed violently, and said something about having dismissed two printers, for it was the fourth time in the last month or two he had found himself in *Punch*.

Alfred Noyes, TWO WORLDS FOR MEMORY 1953

MISUNDERSTANDING

James Agate's memorial service was arranged by two old friends: when one of them telephoned to the theatre where the other was working to tell him that the plans had been made the call was taken by a stage door keeper who was nearly 90 and renowned for the surrealist quality of the messages he transmitted. On this occasion the note read, "Mr A.Gate will be at Sir Martin Fields at 11.30 and would like you to join him."

James Harding, AGATE, A BIOGRAPHY 1986

When John Gielgud told the actors in a play that all the men must wear jockstraps under their leotards a voice asked, "Please, Sir John, does that apply to those of us who only have small parts?"

Kenneth Edwards, MORE THINGS I WISH I'D SAID 1978

A man came to Gielgud's dressing room to offer his congratulations. "How pleased I am to meet you," said Sir John, recognising the man's face. "I used to know your son. We were at school together." "I don't have a son," answered the man coldly. "*I* was at school with you."

Robert Morley, BOOK OF BRICKS 1978

The journalist Frank Giles married Lady Katherine Sackville, who as the daughter of an earl retained her title after her marriage. On a journey abroad they received an invitation from the British embassy addressed to Mr and Mrs Giles. Concerned at the breach of protocol, Giles rang the embassy and started to explain, "She isn't exactly Mrs Giles." "That's all right," said the voice at the other end cheerily. "Bring her along anyway. We're not at all stuffy here."

Los Angeles Times 15 *Dec* 1981

On his way to Stockholm for the Nobel-prize-giving ceremony T.S. Eliot was interviewed by a reporter who asked him for which of his works the prize had been awarded. Eliot replied that he believed it was for the entire corpus. "And when did you publish that?" asked the reporter. Eliot observed afterwards that *The Entire Corpus* might make rather a good title for a mystery story.

David Wallechinsky and Irving Wallace, THE PEOPLE'S ALMANAC 1975

The official transcript of a recent American presidential exchange with reporters had Jimmy Carter referring to "a GNC". Everybody was baffled, running round trying to find out what this new agency was all about. Twenty-four hours later the White House Press Office issued a correction. It wasn't "a GNC" but Aegean Sea.

Washington Post 1976

Dr Michael MacDonald, director of the Scottish Tartans Museum, was in America. A silver-haired lady fixed her gaze on his 17th-century sporran and asked, "What, exactly, do you keep in your scrotum?"

The Times, Diary 18 *May* 1983

Godfrey Tearle told me that in *Anthony and Cleopatra* in 1946 at the Piccadilly Theatre the young actor playing his servant Eros was suddenly taken ill and an unprepared replacement was pushed on at the last moment to assist in removing Anthony's armour. Godfrey spoke: "Unarm, Eros; the long day's task is done. Off! Pluck off!" The young replacement looked aghast. "I'm so sorry," he said, and retired from the scene.

Donald Sinden, A TOUCH OF THE MEMOIRS 1982

Looking one day at the enormous nude statue of Achilles at Hyde Park Corner I heard a Londoner say to a visitor, "No, no, dear – Big Ben is a clock."

Donald Sinden, A TOUCH OF THE MEMOIRS 1982

MODESTY

I was dining at White's Club. General Alexander, fresh from his triumphs in Italy, came into the club in a flannel suit, and was greeted by a contemporary who lived in Ireland, and did not follow the war very closely. "Hello, Alex. I haven't seen or heard of you since the war started. What have you been doing with yourself?" To which Alexander replied, "I'm still soldiering."

Lord Ismay, MEMOIRS 1960

Those who know Field Marshal Auchinleck insist on his modesty. They relate that when he became known as "The Auk" his officers came to him with the suggestion that their corps should henceforth bear the insignia of that ancient, ungainly bird. Ridiculing the idea of a personal build-up, he chose the elephant instead.

Alan Moorhead, Daily Express 1942

Photographer Yousef Karsh and his wife were having lunch with Neil Armstrong after a photographic session. Armstrong politely questioned them about the many countries they had visited. "But Mr Armstrong," protested Mrs Karsh, "you've walked on the moon. We want to hear about your travels." "But that's the only place I've ever been," replied Armstrong apologetically.

Clifton Fadiman, LITTLE, BROWN BOOK OF ANECDOTES 1985

My brother Sacheverell, my sister-in-law and I were lunching with Lord Berners (Gerald to his friends) when his stately, gloomy, immense butler Marshall entered the room, bearing an immense placard. "The gentleman outside says would you be good enough to sign this, my Lord." Gerald inspected the placard and wriggled nervously. "It wouldn't be any use, Marshall," he exclaimed. "He won't know who I am – probably never heard of me." It transpired that the placard was "An appeal to God, that we may have Peace in Our Time."

Edith Sitwell, TAKEN CARE OF 1965

When Benjamin Britten was staying with me in Devon I asked him to witness my signature on some conveyance. He wrote his name and address and then paused. "What shall I put down where it says 'profession'?" "Composer," I said. "Or should I put musician?" "Composer," I repeated firmly. He wrote the word quickly, almost guiltily, as though forging a cheque.

Ronald Duncan, HOW TO MAKE ENEMIES 1968

The outstanding lesson of Cézanne's life was his modesty. In his hours of depression he went to the Louvre in quest of renewed energy and came out refreshed saying, "I think I shall do some good work tomorrow."

Ambroise Vollard, CONFESSIONS OF A PICTURE DEALER 1956

Marie Curie did not know how to be famous. An irresistible timidity congealed her as soon as curious glances were fastened upon her. The Curies were dining at the Elysée Palace with President and Mme Loubet, who asked, "Would you like me to present you to the King of Greece?" Marie innocently and politely replied, "I don't see the utility of it," then, perceiving the lady's stupefaction she blushed and said hurriedly, "But naturally I shall do whatever you please. Just as you please."

Eve Curie, MADAME CURIE 1937

I most admired Clark Gable for his lack of vanity. He was equipped with a premature set of false teeth for which he felt no embarrassment. One day I happened on him at an outdoor faucet where he had stopped to wash off his denture. Clark grinned, pointed to his caved-in mouth and said with an exaggerated lisp, "Look, America'th Thweetheart."

Anita Loos, KISS HOLLYWOOD GOODBYE 1974

Photographer Yousef Karsh had been commissioned to take an official portrait of Pope John XXIII. He was accompanied to the Vatican by Bishop Fulton Sheen. Pope John watched uneasily as Karsh set up his equipment. Turning to Sheen he remarked with a sigh, "God knew seventy-five years ago that one day I would be pope. Why couldn't he have made me more photogenic?"

Clifton Fadiman, LITTLE, BROWN BOOK OF ANECDOTES 1985

When Harold Macmillan became Prime Minister in 1957 his appointment took second place on the front page of his local newspaper in Sussex to a report of a Brighton and Hove Albion football match. He used to keep the cutting on his desk at No. 10 in order, as he said, to prevent himself indulging in the impulse towards self-importance.

The Times, Diary 31 *Dec* 1986

Thomas Mann, the German novelist, was introduced to an American writer of some note who abased himself before the famous novelist, saying that he scarcely considered himself to be a writer in comparison with Mann. Mann answered him civilly, but afterwards he remarked, "He has no right to make himself so small. He's not that big."

Edmund Fuller, ANECDOTES 1942

An American girl visited Beethoven's home, saw the piano at which Beethoven wrote the Ninth Symphony, flung herself at it and banged out a few notes. "I suppose you get a lot of famous people here," she said to the guide. "Ja, Fraulein. Paderewski was here a few days ago." "Say, did he play, too?" "Nein, Fraulein. He thought he was not worthy."

Bruce Clavering, Sunday Referee 1936

The ceremonial effusions expected of a Laureate proved an embarrassment to John Masefield, whose dutiful compositions were submitted to *The Times* with a stamped enveloped for their return if they were unsuitable.

Alan Bell, The Times 20 *Sep* 1982

An orchestra once applauded Arturo Toscanini during rehearsal after he made them play a difficult passage in a way they themselves had never known. He looked up, distressed and bewildered. "But for God's sake, that's not me. That's Beethoven."

Observer, Profile 30 *Jun* 1946

MONARCHY

A pompous young minister once used the royal pronoun "we", referring only to himself, in the presence of Edward VII. The King picked him up at once. "Only two people are permitted to refer to themselves as 'we' – a monarch and a man with a tapeworm inside him."

Patrick Mahony, BARBED WIT AND MALICIOUS HUMOUR 1956

For a year or two after the death of Edward VII, Lord Esher attempted to guide King George V through such intricate issues as the Parliamentary Bill and Home Rule for Ireland. But his insinuating ways did not commend themselves to that quarterdeck monarchy. When Esher reminded him that it was the duty of the Sovereign to accept the advice of his Ministers, even if they required him to sign his own death warrant, the King floored him with the sensible reply, "I would shoot through the head any Minister who brought it to me to sign."

Kenneth Rose, Sunday Telegraph reviewing James Lees-Milne, THE ENIGMATIC EDWARDIAN 12 Oct 1986

When the census forms came round George V signed the Buckingham Palace census paper himself, filling in his occupation as "King of Great Britain and Northern Ireland. Emperor of India", and Queen Mary's as "home duties".

Peter Ross, Sunday Referee 25 *Dec* 1938

During the opening of the new King's College hospital by King George V and Queen Mary in 1913 a little girl who was to have presented a purse to the Queen was overcome by shyness. She was about to flee when the Queen noticed her. "Why, you surely aren't afraid of me?" she asked in a low voice.

"Oh no, please your Grace," she whispered back. "I was only afraid of the King."

Everyone smiled, including His Majesty.

"Why," exclaimed the little girl confidently to the Queen, "he's ever so different when he smiles. I'm not afraid *now*."

And so the procession of the purse-bearers continued smoothly after all.

Herbert Fitch, MEMOIRS OF A ROYAL DETECTIVE 1936

Go to the Chelsea Flower Show. Ten minutes before King George V arrived an agitated equerry telephoned from the Palace to warn them that HM was in a furious temper. This did not diminish the anxiety of Christabel McLaren, wife of the president this year, at the prospect of taking a walk round the garden with him for over an hour. When he arrived, however, he appeared to have quieted down and to have quite enjoyed himself. His remarks on being confronted with various plants are characteristic of the royal mind. He was shown one hybrid of extreme delicacy and importance, and after gazing at it for a minute in heavy-eyed silence remarked, "What a large quantity of moss they have put round the roots. I wonder how they manage to get so much moss." At another point he was shown some very rare plants for which explorers have risked their lives. "Yes," he said, "people risk their lives for many curious objects. What, for example, would happen if this tent came down on our heads?" Christabel, unaware whether this was Royal humour or merely Royal sense of association, hedged by replying, "That, sir, would indeed be terrible." "It would indeed," the King answered.

Harold Nicolson, DIARY 19 *May* 1931

The butler, Mr Osborne, sent me down to the swimming pool with two drinks. When I got there what did I see but His Majesty painting Mrs Simpson's toenails. My Sovereign painting a woman's toenails. It was a bit too much. I gave notice at once.

An unnamed Palace footman, quoted Michael Thornton, ROYAL FEUD 1985

It is a useful tip never to accept the rather sticky meringues that are frequently served at Royal Garden Parties. The day after a garden party the gardeners frequently find meringues with false teeth stuck in them where they have been hurriedly disposed of behind a rose bush on the approach of Her Majesty.

Douglas Sutherland, THE ENGLISH GENTLEMAN 1978

Of the Queen's relationship with Harold Wilson a member of the outer Royal circle remarked, "Funny, really; the Royals will often get on famously with a bit of a rum cove. Attraction of opposites, I suppose."

Alan Hamilton

See also **ROYALTY**

MONEY

An American reporter asked Maria Callas, "Madame Callas, you were born in the United States, raised in Greece, and live in Italy. Which language do you think in?" Callas replied, "I count in English."

Rudolf Bing, 5000 NIGHTS AT THE OPERA 1972

A female client whose legal problems Clarence Darrow had solved burbled, "How can I ever show my appreciation, Mr Darrow?" "Ever since the Phoenicians invented money," replied Darrow, "there has been only one answer to that question."

Edmund Fuller, ANECDOTES 1942

The Western Union Company offered Edison a hundred thousand

dollars for one of his inventions. Such a sum was beyond his comprehension. "The money is safer with you," he said. "Give me six thousand dollars a year for seventeen years."

Jacob M. Braude, SPEAKER'S AND TOASTMASTER'S HANDBOOK 1971

MOTHER

"You can't really understand Tam Dalyell unless you meet his mother," says one of his friends. "She used to stride around West Lothian in yellow stockings, referring to Cromwell as *that man*!"

Observer, Profile 28 *Aug* 1984

Lady Louise Moncrieff was a remarkable woman. She kept her high spirits and sense of humour in spite of being the mother of sixteen children. When her last child was born, her sister, Lady Elizabeth Arthur, was present and called out, "It's all right, Louise, you have got another little boy." And the reply of the poor tired lady was, "My dear, I really don't care if it's a parrot."

Lord Ormathwaite, WHEN I WAS AT COURT 1937

MOTHER-IN-LAW

When Paul Latham bought Hurstmonceaux Castle his future mother-in-law eyed a nearby residence, a mock Tudor half-timbered cottage with interest and remarked that it would do very well for her as it was so near. Paul immediately had it demolished.

Peter Coats, OF KINGS AND CABBAGES 1884

In India, while I was on tour with Ensa during the war a cockney lad called out to me from his hospital bed at the end of the ward, "Sing us 'Deep Purple'." I wished I could. I knew the tune but not the words. I asked him if he wanted it for some special purpose. "Yes – my mother-in-law's varicose veins."

Joyce Grenfell, JOYCE GRENFELL REQUESTS THE PLEASURE 1976

MOTORING

Out driving, and late as usual, James Agate urged his chauffeur to go faster and faster and to ignore the restrictions of a built-up area. A police motorcyclist gave chase and stopped them. The policeman dismounted, took off his gauntlets, and bent down grimly at the open window. On seeing the driver his face relaxed. "Hello" he said, and planted a smacking kiss on the driver's lips. "On your way, and don't get caught again."

The car drove off.

"Do you know him?" asked Agate in astonishment.

"I can't remember his name, sir," replied the chauffeur, "but we were in the Guards together."

James Harding, AGATE, A BIOGRAPHY 1986

Peter Arno, the New Yorker cartoonist, imported a racing car from Europe for his own personal use. Among its unique features were bumpers made of platinum. Once the car was safely through customs at New York he had the bumpers taken off and replaced with steel ones, selling off the platinum at a large profit.

Brendan Gill, HERE AT THE NEW YORKER 1975

When Margot Asquith had a fancy for learning to drive a car – luckily for the safety of herself and others the fancy did not last long – she appeared dressed in riding breeches and a flying helmet. She was close on 70.

Lord David Cecil, Observer, Staying With Margot 21 *Dec* 1981

One of my earliest motoring memories is of going for a drive in Paris with Arnold Bennett. Motoring was an adventure in those pre-war days. The machine drove up with incredible noise, dust and smell. It was shaped like a governess cart – which comforted Nanny a little. Mr Bennett sat next to the chauffeur on a very high seat like a carriage box. We clambered into our seats through a little door at the back of the car and sat there very high in considerable trepidation. After a great many terrifying explosions, accompanied by Nanny's outcries of alarm, the motor-car gathered speed and rushed at fifteen miles an hour along the avenues through the forest.

Eva Le Gallienne, AT 33 1935

I really felt sorry for the Queen when she said she had received a large number of critical letters because of something I had said in

Parliament about mothers not taking children on their knees in the front of cars.

Apparently she had been in the estate car in Windsor Park with Andrew in the back and had taken Edward on her knee in the front seat. Some photographer had snapped her and she had been flooded with hostile mail saying Barbara Castle said she oughtn't to do that.

Barbara Castle, DIARY 3 *Apr* 1968

The money I earned was legendary – a symbol in figures for I had never actually seen it. I therefore had to do something to prove I had it. So I procured a secretary, a valet, a car and a chauffeur. Walking by a showroom I noticed a seven-passenger Locomobile which, in those days, was considered the best car in America. The thing looked too magnificently elegant to be for sale. However I walked in and asked, "How much?"

"Four thousand nine hundred dollars."

"Wrap it up," I said.

The man was astonished, and tried to put up a resistance to such an immediate sale. "Wouldn't you like to see the engine?" he said.

"Wouldn't make any difference – I know nothing about them," I answered. However, I pressed the tyre with my thumb to show a professional touch.

Charles Chaplin, MY AUTOBIOGRAPHY 1964

Shortly after the last war my great-uncle discovered a way of overcoming the discomfort which tall men suffer in certain cars. He bought a hearse, not because he had any intention of dying, but because it was the only vehicle capable of accommodating a favourite armchair, which he duly had fixed to the floor.

He entered his hearse by the spacious door at the back; his chauffeur was obliged to use the tradesman's entrance at the front. The expanse of window afforded my uncle an excellent view of the passing scene which former occupants had never enjoyed.

Incidentally my uncle received many courteous salutes from the police and was much gratified when members of the public doffed their hats.

Hugh Leggatt, letter to The Times 7 *May* 1987

Harpo Marx once arrived at Alexander Woollcott's house driving a broken-down model-T Ford. "What on earth do you call that?" scoffed Woollcott. "This is my town car," said Harpo grandly. "The town must be Pompeii," observed Woollcott.

Howard Teichmann, SMART ALEC: THE WIT, WORLD AND LIFE OF ALEXANDER WOOLLCOTT 1976

In 1912 Mr R.N. Matthewson, of Swan Park, Alipore, Calcutta, collected his new car from the makers in Lowestoft, Suffolk. The car was shaped like a swan and had a Gabriel horn with eight organ pipes and a keyboard which worked off the exhaust system. The swan's beak opened by a lever. A second lever sent half a pint of hot water from the radiator into the swan's nostrils. This was forced out by compressed air, making an authentic swan-like hissing sound.

Mr Matthewson, well pleased with his swan car, took it back with him to India, where it was as great a success as it had been on the roads of England. Unfortunately it caused such crowds to gather that the police were forced eventually to ban the swan car from the streets of Calcutta.

Catherine Caufield, THE EMPEROR OF THE UNITED STATES OF AMERICA, AND OTHER MAGNIFICENT BRITISH ECCENTRICS 1981

The driver of an electric brougham sat outside, perched high up on a box, fully exposed to the elements – which would have been necessary if he had been driving a horse – while the passengers were accommodated in its leather upholstered and buttoned interior in considerable comfort.

I first travelled in an electric brougham, aged five, on a night of thick pea-soup fog and torrential rain in December 1924, from my grandparents' home in Winchester Street, Pimlico, back to Hammersmith Bridge with my mother and father and an uncle and an aunt, all warm and dry and full of food inside, while the driver was drenched with rain and half asphyxiated by the fog on the outside.

I laughed till I cried all the way shrieking, "He hasn't got a lid on."

Eric Newby, A TRAVELLER'S LIFE 1982

I was given a parking ticket. I said to a policeman, "What do I do with this?" "Keep it," he said. "If you manage to collect three of them you get a bicycle."

Denis Norden, quoted Police Review

One day one of Howard Hughes's starlets announced that she was abandoning her career to marry one of his chauffeurs. In order to prevent such a thing happening again Hughes instructed his staff to dismiss all the heterosexual chauffeurs and engage homosexual ones. This simply generated a further set of problems. Two of the new employees were arrested for kerb-crawling and propositioning young men. Hughes sacked them, not for immorality but for "expressly disregarding my instructions about always driving in the middle of the road in order to avoid picking up leaf mould and other detritus on the tyres".

Peter Bushell, GREAT ECCENTRICS 1984

Mr Sims, an eccentric millionaire who took me on a trip to Europe, on arriving in Paris hired three cars – one upholstered in grey, to go with a grey suit, a second in blue, to go with a blue suit, and a third in brown, for a brown suit. The driver of each car was to be appropriately clad. Each morning the three cars would come to the hotel to await his pleasure. Sims would make his choice according to which suit his whim had indicated for that day. If he changed at noon we would shift cars.

Dr William E. Aughinbaugh, I SWEAR BY APOLLO 1939

Gertrude Stein ordered a new Ford, a two-seater which arrived in December 1920, stripped of all the amenities. Riding in the car for the first time Alice B. Toklas remarked that it was nude. "There is nothing on her dashboard, neither clock, nor ashbox, nor cigarette lighter." Gertrude answered "Godiva" and that became the name of the car. It was in Godiva, parked at the kerbside, that Gertrude often scribbled her poems on odd scraps of paper. She had discovered, while waiting for Alice to attend to errands, that her lofty position in the driving seat was an inspiring spot in which to write.

James K. Mellow, CHARMED CIRCLE 1974

Sir Herbert Beerbohm Tree was fundamentally a Victorian and found certain aspects of Edwardian life very frightening. He had a morbid dread of motor cars and continued to use horse-drawn transport almost to the end of his days. When he did at last consent to ride in a car it proved a terrifying experience. He slid almost at once to the floor and remained there for the duration of the journey, viewing the passing scenery from between his fingers.

Peter Bushell, GREAT ECCENTRICS 1984

Billings, Montana. A man driving on an interstate highway was attacked by a mouse that had apparently been sleeping in the heater vent of his car and got too hot. Walter Miller's car ended up in a ditch and the mouse ended up dead.

The Independent 13 *Nov* 1986

A middle-aged lady, who had recently learned to drive, conscientiously followed what she had been taught: that, in starting her car from cold, she should pull out the choke. This she conscientiously did, and then would hang her handbag on it and motor around all day with a cloud of blue smoke pouring from the exhaust. This is why second-hand cars advertised as "carefully driven by one lady owner" should be regarded with some suspicion.

Douglas Sutherland, THE ENGLISH GENTLEMAN'S WIFE 1979

MUNICH CRISIS

Neville Chamberlain was not pedantically exact in his treatment of the King. A constitutional rule lays down that the Prime Minister must have the King's permission to leave the country. Chamberlain announced his flight to Munich in the House of Commons without consulting his colleagues or warning the King.

Another rule provides that an international agreement must have royal approval before it is concluded. While at Munich Chamberlain signed with Hitler the declaration for "Peace in our time", without this authority. The King was persistently ignored.

A.J.P. Taylor, THE IMPROBABLE KING 1957

MUSIC

Sir Thomas Beecham was staying at a house near Glyndebourne and was disturbed one morning by a cacophony of bugles, other brass instruments and drums emanating from the nearby village green. It was the band of the local Boys' Brigade.

Sir Thomas suggested that it should play a little further off.

"You know what's the trouble with you, sir," said the youthful leader. "You just don't appreciate good music."

Harold Atkins and Archie Newman, BEECHAM STORIES 1978

The first time I had the opportunity of meeting Sir Thomas Beecham – an awe-inspiring occasion – I asked him whether, in view of his usual habit of conducting both operas and symphonies without a score, it would be an embarrassment to him to be compelled to use one. His head moved slowly from side to side, his eyes veered powerfully towards me like searchlights, and stopped. Rolling his tongue gently from one side of his mouth to the other, and pulling gently at his beard, he said, after what seemed a long time, "My dear fellow – I find all music an embarrassment."

Leisurely he rose from his chair, moved it back a couple of inches, walked unhurriedly across the room, mixed a whisky and soda, and was immediately engaged by another member of the party. I hoped that that one didn't ask him about scores.

C.B. Rees, Radio Times 12 *Jul* 1946

If ever a man could be said to be born to perform a certain task, Sir Thomas Beecham was born to perform Delius. When Sir Malcolm Sargent was rehearsing his orchestra in a piece by Delius some years after Beecham's death, a sudden storm blew up. There was a flash of lightning, followed immediately by a crash of thunder which blew the fuses and plunged the hall into darkness. In the momentary silence that followed Sir Malcolm was heard to say lugubriously, "He doesn't like it."

Henry Adaskin, A FIDDLER'S WORLD

At a wartime concert the piano stool was too high for the soloist so Sir Adrian Boult called for a saw and "adjusted" the legs. He claimed to be the only conductor who had saved a concert with a saw and enjoyed the subsequent heated correspondence with the owners of the stool.

Michael Kennedy, ADRIAN BOULT 1987

My father, the pianist and composer Leslie Bridgewater never forgot the discipline of his early years on the concert platform. When he was nearly 70 he wrote, for his own use, a fiendishly difficult piano study which he named *The Egg Timer.*

Asked the reason for this odd title he would explain, "Every morning I put my egg on to boil and I play this study before removing it from the pan. If it is soft-boiled I know I am in good form. If it is slightly over-cooked I must find time for at least two hours practice. And if it is hard boiled there is nothing for it but a week's hard work at the piano."

Hazel Whiteley, Reader's Digest Aug 1978

President Carter was very interested in the arts, and I suspect that to some extent his eagerness to immerse himself in culture reflected his small-town origins. On one occasion after Horowitz had given a recital at the White House, Carter told me that during the entire concert Horowitz had missed only one note.

Zbigniew Brzezinski, POWER AND PRINCIPLE: MEMOIRS OF A NATIONAL SECURITY ADVISER 1977–1981 1983

At the Star and Garter hospital for paralysed soldiers at Richmond one day in 1917, after that fine violinist Jelly D'Aranyi (niece of the great Joachim) had played, as only she can play, some intoxicating Hungarian dances, a nurse came up to us in a great state of excitement and said, "Isn't it wonderful? That boy over there – he has never moved since he was hit through the spine – until just now. He began to jerk his arms when Miss D'Aranyi was playing. I could hardly believe my eyes!" I don't know about believing my eyes, but I could scarcely see out of them for a few seconds, and the same hope shot through all three of us. "Perhaps there's a chance for him now?" Dear Jelly was an envied woman that day.

Mrs Claude Beddington, ALL THAT I HAVE MET 1929

The newly exiled Ernst Krenek was applauded politely when he played the piano in the US premiere of his aggressive and atonal *Second Piano Concerto* in Boston in November 1938. Afterwards his publisher heard a patrician lady comment on it to another. "Conditions in Europe must be dreadful."

Hans Heinsheimer, MENAGERIE IN F SHARP 1947

Pachmann turned everything to music, even his wine. He held a glass of champagne to the light, pointing at it and saying – "Bubbles! Golden, sparkling bubbles! I show you." And before one could rise to stop him he had rushed into the darkness of the next room, seated himself at the piano and played, with magical perfection, a shimmering treble passage from Chopin's Third Scherzo. After which the champagne tasted quite flat.

Beverley Nichols, TWENTY-FIVE 1926

At a musical party at which Paderewski was present, Richard Harding Davis, the American journalist, was asked to play a little piece he had composed. He advanced confidently to the piano, but once seated he stared at the keys in a puzzled fashion. Finally he turned to the great Polish pianist and declared, "I can't find the starting note. I composed my tune on a Steinway and this is a Weber. Where would the note that is under the 'w' on a Steinway be on a Weber?"

Fairfax Downey, RICHARD HARDING DAVIS: HIS DAY 1933

Paderewski was introduced to a polo player with the phrase – the stupid phrase of a society hostess – "You are both leaders in your spheres, though the spheres are very different." "No so very different," smiled Paderewski. "You are a dear soul who plays polo. I am a poor Pole who plays solo."

Bruce Clavering, Sunday Referee 9 *Aug* 1936

Dine with Sibyl Colefax. After keeping us waiting half an hour the King (Edward VIII) arrives and we go in to dinner almost at once.

After dinner Arthur Rubinstein plays some Chopin. After he has played three times the King crosses the room and says, "We enjoyed that very much, Mr Rubinstein." I am delighted at this, since I was afraid Rubinstein was about to play a fourth time. It is by now 12.30 and the King starts saying goodbye. This takes so long that at our end of the room we imagine he has departed, and get Noel Coward to sing one of his latest songs. The King immediately returns on hearing this and remains for another hour, which is not very flattering to Rubinstein.

Harold Nicolson, DIARY 10 *Jun* 1936

Erik Satie thought it might be amusing to compose music *not* to be listened to, "musique d'ameublement" or wallpaper music. Milhaud had some of it played in the interval of a concert of works by "Les Six" and Stravinsky. No sooner had Satie's music started than people began returning to their seats. Satie pleaded with them. "Carry on talking! Walk about! Don't listen!" But no one paid him any attention.

Norman Lebrecht, BOOK OF MUSICAL ANECDOTES 1985

Arthur Schnabel, rehearsing a Beethoven Concerto with Otto Klemperer in Los Angeles, began to signal his own preferred *tempi* to the orchestra from the piano stool. As soon as the conductor noticed what he was doing he stopped the rehearsal. "Schnabel!" rasped Klemperer, "*here* is the conductor!" "I know that," replied Schnabel, "and *here* is the pianist. But *where* is Beethoven?"

Peter Diamond, quoted Norman Lebrecht, BOOK OF MUSICAL ANECDOTES 1985

Dr Albert Schweitzer had come home to the Alsatian village of Gunsbach from his jungle hospital in Africa and had promised to play the organ. I travelled with him on the last stage of his journey across France. He had not had time to practise, so he practised in the train by tapping out rhythms with his feet as if he were dancing. A peasant and his children in the same compartment watched fascinated as Dr Schweitzer stamped out the bass notes of a Bach Fugue on his imaginary pedal board.

Roland Pullen, Sunday Express 30 *Aug* 1959

The hostess at a musical party asked Bernard Shaw, "What do you think of the violinist?" To which Shaw replied, "He reminds me of Paderewski." The bewildered lady said, "But Paderewski is not a violinist." "Neither is this gentleman," said Shaw.

Mrs Claude Beddington, ALL I HAVE MET 1929

The music of Shostakovitch was the first to be performed extra-terrestially. On 12 April 1961 Yuri Gagarin, the first cosmonaut, sang for the benefit of an audience at Mission Control the Shostakovitch song, "My homeland hears, my homeland knows where in the skies her son soars on."

Nicolas Slommsky, quoted Norman Lebrecht, BOOK OF MUSICAL ANECDOTES 1985

At the dinner given for Richard Strauss by the Lotos Club at its old home in Fifth Avenue near Forty-Second Street I sat next to him while he wrote some bars of one of his most difficult compositions for me in spite of the hum of talk and blare of quasi-popular music about us. During a discussion about making musical sounds mean anything he said, "I can translate anything into sound. I can make you understand by music that I pick up my fork and spoon from this side of my plate and lay them down on the other side."

David Bispham, A QUAKER SINGER'S RECOLLECTIONS 1920

I knew a Russian peasant who could make his horse micturate by whistling softly. That same whistling sound I have heard in several pieces of electronic music, and it makes me suffer the same desire as the horse. But some electronic sounds have the effect of colonic irrigation also, on me at least.

Igor Stravinsky, DIALOGUE AND DIARY 1968

Benson, when Archbishop of Canterbury, once complained that in my Mass "God was not *implored*, but was *commanded* to have mercy." It was explained that what was intended was an expression of intense terror. "Indeed," said the Archbishop. "I can only repeat that to me it sounded like orders issued in an extremely peremptory manner."

Dame Ethel Smyth, AS TIME WENT ON 1936

When I was a soloist at a concert conducted by Arturo Toscanini the maestro paced the dressing room in which I practised repeating, "You are no good; I am no good." "Please maestro," I pleaded, "I will be a complete wreck." Then, as we walked on stage he said, "We are no good but the others are worse. Come on, *caro,* let's go."

Gregor Piatigorsky, CELLIST

At the midday rehearsal of a concert at the Queen's Hall, Exeter, there was a smell of fish which became increasingly objectionable. Sir Henry Wood was told that it was fish for a sea-lion. A menagerie was appearing at the theatre. On account of the concert everything had been removed except the sea-lion which was in a tank under the stage. "Unless he was being continually fed he would bark and spoil the music," the manager explained.

Western Morning News 3 *Mar* 1969

The Scherzo of Vaughan Williams' 'London' Symphony has a perky subject for flutes and piccolo with accordion-like harmonics below it. Somebody told Vaughan Williams that this conjured up a vision of the Ratcliffe Highway on a Saturday night with lamp-light shining on to damp pavements. "Surprising," he commented, "what people can read into a tune."

Observer, Profile 4 *Apr* 1948

NAME

As a nice Jewish boy in Baltimore, Larry Adler heard that the family was of Russian extraction and named Zelakovitch, but that his grandfather, tired of being at the end of the queue, leapt over the alphabet and became a German eagle.

Anthony Burgess, Observer 11 *Nov* 1984

When Dave Burnaby chose the stage as a profession, his father thought that perhaps it was better for him not to use the family name. He consented and under another name joined Lilly Langtry's company. While they were rehearsing *The Crossways* for tour King Edward VII ordered a Command Performance. Davy wrote home and told them he was to make his first professional appearance at the Imperial before the King. His father wrote back to congratulate him. "I think perhaps after all you might use the name of Burnaby."

Guy Fletcher, Radio Times 14 *Aug* 1936

At school it is always, "Take that for being a sonofabitch, and *that* for being Winston Churchill." In the States I'd give my name and some guy would say, "Is that so? Well, I'm Eisenhower." I flew into one African state without permission and told them who I was and they just said I must be drunk and put me inside.

Winston Churchill Jnr, Sunday Times 6 *Aug* 1967

Princess Elizabeth's response to the arrival of her sister and to the floral character of her double name has been relentlessly recorded in every version of either sister's life. "I've got a baby sister, Margaret Rose," Elizabeth told Lady Cynthia Asquith, "and I'm going to call her Bud." "Why Bud?" asked Lady Cynthia. "Well, she's not a real rose yet is she?" replied the four-and-half-year-old girl. "She's only a bud."

Robert Lacey, MAJESTY 1977

Gladys ffolliott, the actress, took a house which had a defective staircase down which she fell, broke her ankle and sued for damages from the landlord.

Gladys ffolliott stepped into the witness box to give evidence. A smart young barrister named Harris was appearing for the other side. "Miss Gladys ffolliott – spelt with two small fs I notice."

"It has been spelt in that manner since the days of Edward the Second of England," Gladys returned.

"Ah, a name redolent of romance."

"Exactly, as yours, Mr Harris, is redolent of sausages."

The judge laughed and she won the case.

Naomi Jacob, ME: A CHRONICLE ABOUT OTHER PEOPLE 1933

One morning I was writing in my office in St James's Palace when a footman came in and said a Mr Acorn wanted to see me. As I did not know Mr Acorn I sent the footman back to inquire what he wanted. The man returned and said, "The gentleman says he knows you very well and will tell you what he wants when he sees you." I answered, "Please say that I am very busy and will he write to me saying what he requires," and then I added, "Don't leave him alone in the hall."

At that there was a burst of laughter, the door opened – and in walked King Haakon of Norway.

Lord Ormathwaite, WHEN I WAS AT COURT 1937

When Leslie Henson finally left the Winter Garden Theatre, after playing there for twelve or more years, the stage doorman who daily had handled his letters and seen his name on posters and on the star dressing room door, said to him on the last night, as he said to him every other night, "Good evening, Mr Henderson."

Joyce Grenfell, JOYCE GRENFELL REQUESTS THE PLEASURE 1976

The Foreign Secretary, Sir Geoffrey Howe, was perturbed to hear that the President of the European Parliament pronounces his name as "Sir Geoffrey Who". I am told that Sir Geoffrey derives some solace from the fact that the President's surname is Pflimlin.

Peterborough, Daily Telegraph 28 May 1986

When, in 1914, King George V changed his family name to Windsor, the Kaiser is said to have commanded a performance of "The Merry Wives of Saxe-Coburg-Gotha".

Sir George Arthur, KING GEORGE V 1929

Though I have no objection to *Pêche* Melba, I have the strongest objection to my name being calmly taken for any object which the proprietor considers suitable, from scent to hairpins. America is particularly prone to this sort of piracy. I was wandering down a street in New York one day when I suddenly stopped short before an immense drug store, across the windows of which were splashed advertisements for Melba perfume. "Ah," I thought, "I think I deserve a bottle of this." So I went inside. I said, "May I smell the perfume Melba?" "Certainly," said the assistant, and sprayed some on my wrist. One sniff was enough. I hated the stuff. Then, I humbly asked who had given them the permission to call this "creation " Melba. "Oh, that's all right," drawled the assistant. "We found out her name is Mrs Armstrong and we've just as much right to call this stuff Melba as she has."

Dame Nellie Melba, MELODIES AND MEMORIES 1925

NAVY

An American admiral, spotting a blip on the radar screen, ordered his radio operator, "Tell that ship to alter course 15 degrees." The word came back "You change *your* course 15 degrees." When a more heavily phrased message met with the same response he snatched the microphone and bawled. "You change your course 15 degrees. I am an admiral in the United States Navy." A calm voice replied, "And I'm a lighthouse."

Profile magazine, quoted The Times, Diary 3 *Sep* 1986

An admiral in his flagship was standing off shore, watching a junior officer's attempt to take his craft alongside the harbour wall. Young and inexperienced, he made a thorough mess of the job and so was surprised to see the signal "Good" hoisted on the flagship. His elation with the thought that he had got away with it was, however, somewhat punctured when, after a considerable delay, the word "God" was added to the message.

Douglas Sutherland, THE ENGLISH GENTLEMAN 1978

NUDITY

At the superior nudist camps a nice distinction was made. The butlers and maids who brought along the refreshments were forced to admit their lower standing by wearing loincloths and aprons respectively.

Robert Graves and Alan Hodge, THE LONG WEEK-END 1940

When four girls were fined on charges of "over-exposure" in a show called *G-String Revue* at a Virginia carnival one of them challenged a woman police officer's evidence that the girl was nude. She had, she said, a G-string round her ankle.

Reveille, quoted Denys Parsons, FUNNY AMUSING, FUNNY AMAZING 1969

The first woman I saw stark naked was Tallulah Bankhead. Aged about nine, I was taken backstage to meet her. My father knocked on her door and a voice said, "Come in," and there was Miss Bankhead, smiling and nude. She was not put out, but we moved out fast.

Michael Pertwee, NAME DROPPING

NUN

Of the four convents in the Cowley St John district one was the Magdalen Road Mission House where our parish sisters lived. On his arrival Fr Painter had said that there must be younger sisters, as the youngest in the house was well over 70. Their Order hadn't any younger models available so they decided to withdraw. Their place was to be taken by Sisters from Laleham Abbey whose redoubtable Mother Sarah came to inspect the house. "Good heavens, what a state the ceilings are in," she said. The old Sister Superior thrust her hands deeper into her sleeves and replied, "We never raise our eyes."

Colin Stephenson, MERRILY ON HIGH 1965

The nun assigned to guard St Peter's Basilica from immodestly dressed tourists was withdrawn from duty today after suffering a nervous breakdown. She said she could no longer stand the taunts from the tourists, the shoving from the photographers and the jibes from the press. During the past few weeks Sister Fiorella has refused entry to thousands of women in mini-skirts, see-through blouses, low-cut sweaters and skirt and trousers combinations which left midriffs bare.

The Times 5 *Aug* 1971

OBESITY

Max Wilkinson, associate editor of *Good Housekeeping*, has been fretting at his expanding girth. The other day he got a terrific jolt when his overcoat wouldn't button in the middle. Later he discovered that two of his assistants had carefully moved all the buttons two inches to the right.

Bennett Cerf, Saturday Review Of Literature 1945

OBSCENITY

Being of an irritable disposition W.C. Fields would often give vent to unprintable curses, which led him to invent his own set of swear words which, when uttered through gritted teeth, sounded infinitely more abusive than the originals. His favourite curse, "Godfrey Daniel!" became a kind of catch phrase, and so realistically foul did it sound that audiences marvelled at the leniency of the censors in allowing such vulgarity.

Philip Jenkinson, Radio Times 28 *Oct* 1971

One of my grandmother's foibles was washing her feet in a handbasin at journey's end. On a visit to Scarborough she slipped on wet lino and her big toe became firmly stuck in an old brass tap. Rather bad-tempered, built like Bismarck, and said to be related to George III, it took the fire brigade several hours to free her, and her vituperations could be heard over Punch and Judy on the beach. "That woman's language made my pansies die," complained the rather nervous landlady as we left.

Paul Pickering, Sunday Times 9 *Aug* 1987

President Truman's salty language was a bone of contention. He was known to slip a "hell" or "damn" into his public utterances, causing quite a furore, unlike most presidents, who only curse privately. Mrs Truman was for ever saying, "You shouldn't have said that." A story that made the rounds had a famous woman Democrat rushing to the White House to plead with Mrs Truman to have Harry clean up his language. It seems he'd called someone's statements "a bunch of horse manure". Unruffled, Bessie Truman is said to have smilingly replied, "You don't know how many years it took to tone it down to that."

J.B. West, UPSTAIRS AT THE WHITE HOUSE 1974

At one time I had to inspect the prison at Portland every six months. On one occasion a convict escaped but after having been at large for several days he gave himself up. He explained that he had disguised himself as one of the bluejackets, but that the naval men he had to mix with had used such bad language that he preferred to return to prison.

Sir Frederic William Fisher, NAVAL REMINISCENCES 1936

A man was charged at Sheffield Police Court yesterday with using obscene language to a clockwork mouse which refused to perform on the pavement.

Manchester Guardian, quoted Michael Bateman, THIS ENGLAND

At the age of 18 James Agate had already been seized with irrational fits of panic, as when, taking his three-year-old sister for walks on the pier, he was terrified lest he should snatch her up and throw her into the sea. Having changed once for a tennis match he went back to tidy up his clothes on the bed. "If you do that, you will do it all your life," he remembers telling himself. He went back, and he did it all his life. The thought of sleep-walking oppressed him, and he never slept high up in a building or without a piece of furniture against an open window. Neither did he care to have razor or matches in the bedroom. He forced himself to keep awake in railway carriages, and was scared of travelling in an empty one. Railings and lamp-posts had to be regularly touched, and cracks in pavements to be sedulously avoided. The gas was turned off four, eight, sixteen or thirty-two times, always in multiples of four. In company, when fully dressed, he observed a ritual that compelled him to touch, in repeated sequence, his left breast, his right, his middle, his sides, as if looking for something that wasn't there, or as if to find continual reassurance that all was well.

James Harding, AGATE, A BIOGRAPHY 1986

Among my most eccentric patients was a man who owned three hundred pairs of shoes, each one unworn and each one kept in a canvas bag. He would not be parted from them and took them with him (in the charge of a special valet) whenever he went abroad. In Holland he got himself, his whole family and his entourage locked up for the night because he declined with an Englishman's obstinacy to have his shoe-cases opened at Customs. I treated him for indigestion, with some success. Happily I was not asked to treat him for his shoe madness.

Dr L.G. Briggs, THE SURGEON GOES TO SEA 1939

OLD AGE

In a BBC interview to mark his eighty-ninth birthday the French conductor Pierre Monteux was asked what were his remaining pleasures in life. "I still have two abiding passions," he replied. "One is my model railway, the other – women. But at the age of eighty-nine I find I am getting a little too old for model railways."

Oxfam, PASS THE PORT 1976

At the age of ninety-one Justice Holmes resigned from the Supreme Court and spent the following summer at his country home in Massachusetts. Old friends from Boston came to see him, bringing their grandchildren, whose company Holmes greatly enjoyed. Sitting on the porch with Betsy Warder, aged sixteen, and discussing life with her he said, "I won't refrain from talking about anything because you are too young, if you won't because I am too old."

Catherine Drinker Bowen, YANKEE FROM OLYMPUS 1948

An uncle of mine, a retired headmaster, said that the first time he felt old was when he was in a queue at his local post office to collect his old age pension and found himself behind a former pupil who was there for the same purpose.

Paul Kelvin-Smith, letter to The Times 24 *Jul* 1985

OPERA

So total was the absorption of Gobbi and Maria Callas in their roles that when, during a full dress rehearsal three days before opening night, Maria's wig brushed against a lighted candle and caught fire, she went on singing and continued to do so even as smoke poured from behind her head, and Tito Gobbi rushed across the stage to put the fire out.

Arianna Stassinopoulos, Sunday Times 12 *Oct* 1980

Sir Thomas Beecham used to tell this story of a meeting with King George V in the Royal Box at Covent Garden. Did the King enjoy the opera? asked Beecham. What was His Majesty's favourite? "*La Bohème*," barked the Sailor King. "Why, sir?" asked Tom, to be told, "Because it is the shortest I know."

TV Times 26 *Apr* 1979

Turandot received its first performance seventeen months after Puccini's death (in 1924). Although a final scene had been added by Franco Alfano, Toscanini chose to end the opera with Liu's death, on the last notes Puccini had inscribed. He laid down his baton and, pre-empting applause, turned round to make the only speech of his life to an audience. "Here Death triumphed over Art," he said, and left the pit. The lights went up, and the audience dispersed in silence.

Howard Taubman, TOSCANINI 1951

OPPORTUNITY

Joseph Beecham, at the time Mayor of St Helens, had engaged the Hallé Orchestra from Manchester to present a concert in the town. On the day fixed for the performance the Hallé conductor was taken ill. It looked as though the concert would be cancelled. But one of the Hallé players said to Joseph Beecham, "Why not let your son conduct us? He knows the whole programme backwards." And he did. The young musician piloted the orchestra through his first major concert, including two symphonies, Beethoven's Fifth and Tchaikowski's "Pathètique". From that time on, Thomas Beecham was a committed musician.

TV Times 26 *Apr* 1979

I had written a play about my experiences looking for work, and so I took this dirty manuscript, typed with one finger, up to the BBC. I childishly thought that all I had to do was walk in there, but of course I was promptly turned away by the doorman. So I went into a public house nearby. I had a shilling in my hand. The most awful thing a man can contemplate is his last shilling. I had to decide whether I would have half a pint and walk part of the way, or a pint and walk all the way home. I had a pint, and got into conversation with a big fellow sitting there.

I told him what I had been doing, and he gave me three pounds to get home. Two days later I got a telegram asking me to see a BBC producer. The fellow I had talked to in the pub was Gilbert Harding.

Dominic Behan, Sunday Express 29 *Oct* 1972

Bob Hoskins became an actor by mistake. He was an accountant at the time. "I was sitting in the bar of the Unity Theatre at King's Cross in 1968. I was waiting for a mate and I was three parts pissed. And this bloke comes round and says, 'Right. You next. Have you seen the script?' So I went upstairs and they said 'Read it. Aloud.' And I got the leading part. It was a play called *The Feather Pluckers*."

The first night came. An agent spotted him, and from then on Hoskins the actor was in business.

Elizabeth Dunn, Observer Magazine 31 *Aug* 1986

Malcolm Sargent was given his first chance of conducting by Sir Henry Wood, who had commissioned him to compose a work for a Leicester music festival. He did so, calling his composition *Impressions of a Windy Day*. As he was late in delivering it an annoyed Sir Henry registered his displeasure by exclaiming, "Conduct it yourself." He did, and from that day he never looked back.

Western Morning News 4 *Oct* 1967

OPTIMISM

Horatio Bottomley remained optimistic all through his trial at the Old Bailey, charged with converting funds of the Victory Bonds Club for his own use.

Only the day before the verdict he said to his trainer, James Hare, who asked him what he thought of his chances, "Oh, it'll be all right, Jimmy. The telephone will ring at about two o'clock to tell you I've been acquitted. As soon as you get the message you can open a magnum to celebrate." The telephone did ring, not at two o'clock, but at half past three, with the announcement that the squire of the village had been found guilty and sent to penal servitude for seven years. Poor Hare had to go out to the lawn at the back of the house to break the news to Mrs Bottomley and her daughter.

Sunday Express 28 *May* 1933

OSTENTATION

At dinner I warmed to Lady Grey, who regaled us with nonsense. She told us about a woman who wanted to have diamonds put in her teeth so that she could even say "Good morning" brilliantly.

Cecil Beaton, DIARY 15 *Feb* 1927

I took Leslie Hore-Belisha to lunch at the Savoy. He wouldn't pass a flower shop without dragging me in to buy a gardenia for a button-hole. I said I wouldn't dream of wearing a conspicuous button-hole if a button-hole at all. He said, "You're wrong. I believe in these distinctive touches. They embellish your personality and help to fix you in people's minds." He then handed me the gardenia as if there could be no further argument. Perhaps there couldn't. But I didn't wear the gardenia.

Reginald Pound, THEIR MOODS AND MINE 1937

When Idi Amin invited his commanding officer's three sons to Sunday lunch he insisted on collecting them by car, despite the fact that he lived only 20 yards away. After lunch he solemnly drove them back again.

Alexander Mitchell and Russell Miller, Sunday Times Magazine, Amin: The Untold Story 29 Oct 1972

PAINTING

In 1931 I came to London for the premiere of *City Lights* and Winston Churchill invited me to Chartwell for the weekend. In the dining room I noticed a still-life painting over the fireplace. Winston saw me showing a keen interest in it.

"I did that."

"But how remarkable," I said enthusiastically.

"Nothing to it. I saw a man painting a landscape in the South of France and said, 'I can do that.'"

Charles Chaplin, MY AUTOBIOGRAPHY 1964

I was conducting a stranger round the Bencher's rooms at the Middle Temple Hall. We went up to a portrait of Lord Halsbury. I explained what a Lord Chancellor was. He said, "I think the colours are not standing." I ignored his comment but was glad he was interested and took him off to the Inner Temple Bencher's rooms. "This," said I "is the famous hanging judge, Henry Hawkins, Lord Brampton." The modest man said he was sorry, but the colour had certainly not stood. I asked, with freezing *hauteur* whether he was familiar with the picture. He said, diffidently, "Well, yes. You see, I painted it." He was the Hon. John Collier, MA.

Major Hugh Hole, LOOKING LIFE OVER 1934

At Cope's School of Art in South Kensington I really worked for the first time in my life. Arthur Stockdale Cope was a man who inspired labour. He had an unfailing gift for discerning when a student was painting "prettily" with the obvious intent of putting a frame round his study. For such a one he had no mercy, and exploded paint or graphite over the prettiest part of the canvas. I have seen him strike a wax vesta across the face of a study which offended his sense of the proprieties. "Every brush work a pain to you," was his slogan. He was a first-rate master and got his pupils on like a house on fire.

Roland Pertwee, MASTER OF NONE 1940

Roger Fry was taking Lady Violet Bonham-Carter round the Post Impressionist Exhibition at the Grafton Gallery. He led her up to Matisse's *La Ronde*. "What do you think of *that*?" Lady Violet, whose soul was already fatigued by its adventures among so many novel masterpieces, gazed up at it in stupefaction and at last brought out apologetically, "I don't think I quite like the shape of their legs." "Ah," said Roger in a tone of triumph, "but don't you like the shape *between* their legs?"

Edward Marsh, A NUMBER OF PEOPLE 1939

Roger Fry, the earnest-minded painter, would rush, slithering on his knees, holding a paint-brush in his hand, along a strip of wall-paper spread on the ground, pausing only to admire the results brought about by the brush, or a spilt cup of coffee, or the design made by his dog having sat down on the wet paint. "Really *rather* an interesting effect," he would say.

Edith Sitwell, TAKEN CARE OF 1965

Meissonnier's battle pieces, his *Retreat from Moscow*, his *Ney Defending the Rearguard* are familiar from ten thousand reproductions. In his studio a pupil is at work, preparing the stage for the day's work. He opens boxes and takes out toy guns and ammunition, weapons, trees, soldiers, houses, horses. He ranges them in battle array on a thick carpet of sparkling white powder that looks like boracic. Then he sprays the whole scene with gum arabic and dusts it over with more powder. The field is ready. Meissonnier comes in. "What a fine winter landscape," he observes.

He explained his methods.

"When I painted my *Retreat From Russia* instead of boracic acid I used castor sugar. What an effect of snow I obtained! But it attracted the bees from a neighbouring hive. So I replaced the sugar by flour. And then the mice came and ravaged my battlefield and I had to finish my picture from imagination."

Ambroise Vollard, RECOLLECTIONS OF A PICTURE DEALER 1936

Sir William Orpen was commissioned to paint the scene of the Versailles Treaty. He made the sketches. He worked for nine months, putting in the portraits of over forty statesmen and generals. Then he rubbed them all out. His soul revolted. He must tell the truth. And in his picture the body of the Unknown Soldier lies in the Salle des Miroirs, guarded by two gaunt wraiths from the trenches. He said, "The pleasure this completed picture gives me, however critics may rage, is worth the £2000 it cost me."

Sidney Dark and P.G. Konody, SIR WILLIAM ORPEN: ARTIST AND MAN 1932

When Monet, in 1923, was asked by the Minister of Fine Arts for a canvas to be hung in the Louvre he said, "I'll give you one, but I shall choose it myself." This was agreeable and Monet chose the celebrated *Déjeuner sur l'herbe.*

"May I enquire," the minister asked, "why you choose this canvas rather than another?"

"Mr Minister," Monet replied, "I chose it because it was rejected by the Salon of 1887."

Sacha Guitry, IF I REMEMBER RIGHT 1935

After producing masterpieces like the *Loge* Renoir came out of the Louvre one day exclaiming, "With all their blasted talk of modern painting I've been forty years discovering that the queen of all colours is black."

Ambroise Vollard, RECOLLECTIONS OF A PICTURE DEALER 1936

John Singer Sargent sighed gustily at my work. He had a habit of pulling his beard and making sad, puffing sounds in it. Now and then he said most illuminating things. He had looked long and miserably at a study I had done of an old model in modern clothes. At last he said, "I suppose it didn't occur to you that you are not painting a man with clothes on, but the play of light on different surfaces. This study of yours suggests to me that you have been out shopping; that you bought a coat, collar and tie, and dressed him up in them. It is a miserable result."

He drew a deep breath and went away.

Roland Pertwee, MASTER OF NONE 1940

Alexander Trauner, the Hungarian painter who worked in Paris, recently discussing forgeries with Picasso, asked, "How can you remember which are yours?"

Picasso replied, "If I like it I say it is mine. If not I say it is a fake."

Sunday Times 10 *Oct* 1965

PARLIAMENT

On the day she took her seat in the House of Commons Nancy Astor gave a dinner party for some of her friends. After dinner there was a division on the Scottish Land Settlement Bill, and Nancy duly recorded an obedient vote for the government. She then came back into the Chamber for a moment before going home. On her way out, before reaching the sacred Bar, she saw a friend, Sir John Rees, and she stopped for a short chat with him, to the latter's great confusion. Lowther's voice was heard calling, "Order! Order!"

Nancy looked round to see what the excitement was and, seeing nothing, she continued her chat. Again the Speaker called for order and Sir John hastily explained to her that to stop on the floor of the House and converse on the sanctified side of the Bar during a session was a grave offence. A report of the time describes Nancy "skipping" over the Bar, and then through the doors and out.

Christopher Sykes, NANCY: THE LIFE OF LADY ASTOR 1972

On the occasion of an important debate ambassadors packed the Distinguished Visitors Gallery. Nancy Astor arrived wearing a huge bunch of scarlet carnations. Will Thorne shouted across the floor of the House and asked for one. Under the chilly eye of the Speaker she strolled across and put one in his buttonhole. Then she handed one to Mr Attlee, and put one each in the coats of Mr Baldwin and Sir John Simon. The House rang with laughter, but she was quite unperturbed.

John Beevers, Sunday Referee 19 *Feb* 1939

My first weeks in the House of Commons were a sheer nightmare to me. It was just horrible – and I was scared to death. I never dared go anywhere about the House. I can recall as well as yesterday one occasion when I actually sat there for five hours after I wanted to get up and leave – all because I was afraid to walk out of the House through all those groups of unfriendly men.

Nancy Astor, Sunday Dispatch 26 *Nov* 1946

Attlee was at his most effective at Question Time, for this was a period when both ministers and back-benchers understood the merits of brevity. Once Henry Strauss, an amiable but pedantic Cambridge academic, asked by way of a supplementary question if the Prime Minister could explain "whether nationalisation and socialisation are the same thing?" "Very much the same," said Attlee, to the House's great pleasure. A

Prime Minister in the 1970s would have taken 50 words to reply.

Douglas Jay, CHANGE AND FORTUNE 1980

I once asked Lord Balfour how he liked speaking in the House of Lords. He laughed and said, "Fairly well. Happily my style of oratory does not require applause, otherwise I should have felt badly. They listen carefully but do not express their feelings. It is a cold House."

Lord Riddell, John o'London's Weekly 5 *Apr* 1930

I sat on the front bench for the Prices and Incomes Board debate for most of the day with my head and limbs aching. The mood of the House was very curious. When Roy Hattersley came to wind up, he flopped too. Working away vigorously in an effort to stir things up, he aroused more and more of our own left-wingers' hostility, while the Tories just chatted impertinently. He, too, sat down limp with incomprehension and disappointment. He said to me that speaking in the House in its mood that night was like trying to pedal a bicycle through a field of rice pudding. I knew exactly what he meant.

Barbara Castle, Diary 21 *May* 1968

In the House of Commons in 1967 the debate on David Steele's Abortion Bill was droning on when Norman St John Stevas, a dogged opponent of legalised abortion, launched into a speech moving an amendment. Andrew Faulds, who had been elected to the House only a year earlier, fidgety and fed up with this rearguard action, rose to intervene. He asked the Speaker, "Is it in order for an honourable member to delay this necessary Social measure when he has not the capacity to put a bun in anybody's oven?"

This produced as much of an uproar as the scattering of exhausted members could muster. R.G. Grant-Ferris complained that the words were "Offensive, gross and disgusting", and Mr Faulds withdrew on the Speaker's orders.

Norman Moss, Observer Magazine 2 *Apr* 1977

Michael Foot prepares his speeches in his head in his Hampstead Heath walks. When he was Employment Secretary and accordingly required to read chunks of Civil Service prose concerning complicated negotiations he would in effect say, "I hope the House will bear with me while I read this boring stuff before I get on with my speech."

Alan Watkins, Observer 16 *Nov* 1980

George, Viscount Gage, said to the Earl of Arran, "Did you get any reactions in the House of Lords to your Buggers' Bill – threats, or anything like that?" "Very little." "And what about your Bill for the protection of badgers?" "None at all." "Not many badgers in the House of Lords."

Peter Coats, OF KINGS AND CABBAGES 1984

Jack Jones, the Labour member for Silvertown always has something to say, and says it with punch, point and drive. Some old bore in the House was making a long dry-as-dust speech, and saying, "what would be necessary for the purpose of this experiment would be a moratorium and –" At that moment Jack Jones could stand it no longer. He shouted, "Moratorium! We don't want a moratorium. What we want is a crematorium, and you ought to be in it."

Naomi Jacobs, ME: A CHRONICLE ABOUT OTHER PEOPLE 1933

Lloyd George could never keep away from the House of Commons. I once met him behind the Speaker's Chair on a Friday afternoon, when it was empty. I asked him what on earth he was doing and he replied, "To anyone with politics in his blood this place is like a pub to a drunkard."

Lord Boothby, RECOLLECTIONS OF A REBEL 1978

James Stuart, the Secretary of State for Scotland, was a man of strong character and few words. Once when he was winding up a dull debate in the Commons someone shouted "Speak up!" He looked surprised and said, "Mr Speaker, I did not think anyone was listening."

John Boyd-Carpenter, WAY OF LIFE 1980

James William Lowther, first Viscount Ullswater, Speaker of the House of Commons 1905–1921, made a famous aside when a wearisome member said in the course of a speech, "I ask myself–". Lowther was heard to mutter, "And a damn silly answer you'll get."

The Times, Obituary 1949

On my first visit to the Members' Entrance of the House of Commons I was solemnly given a single coat hook, my name written beside it, and it was there I saw my first piece of parliamentary red tape, an actual piece of the stuff, hanging below the hook. The attendant explained that I should hang my sword from the tape, should I ever decide to attend the House of Commons wearing a sword. My disbelieving guffaw of laughter was met with doleful eyes; it was, sir, *tradition*.

Cyril Smith, BIG CYRIL 1978

Sir Waldron Smithers, who sat for Chislehurst, was an extreme Tory out of a vanished age. Deeply religious – he had an organ on which he played hymns in his house at Chislehurst and he preached whenever he could find the opportunity – he was also not insensitive to the consoling effect of alcohol. On one occasion Hugh Dalton, then Chancellor of the Exchequer, was winding up in a crowded House about the action he had taken to deal with one of the periodic economic crises of the time. In his booming voice, which was his greatest handicap, he quoted with self-satisfied emphasis, the particular date on which he had taken what he claimed was the necessary action. Sir Waldron, who was sitting on the back bench under the Gallery on the Opposition side, and did not appear to be very clearly following the argument, sprang to life at the mention of the date. "My birthday!" he exclaimed in a voice as loud as Dalton's. It was some minutes before the Chancellor could proceed, and his peroration was ruined.

John Boyd-Carpenter, WAY OF LIFE 1980

During a long and boring debate in the House of Commons a Press Gallery reporter threw down his pencil and groaned under his breath, "Oh, adjourn". The exclamation was louder than he meant it to be, Mr Speaker caught the word, put the motion to the House, and it was carried. This is probably the only occasion a reporter has adjourned the debate.

Alan Dick, INSIDE STORY 1943

PARTY

Fred, a Portsmouth party-goer, was left chained naked to some railings. When released he fled wearing a borrowed grass skirt and two coconuts. Said neighbour Mrs Margaret Gaiter, "I thought it was disgusting. You expect this kind of behaviour at the weekend, but not in the middle of the week."

Charles Nevin, Sunday Telegraph 26 *May* 1985

PASTIME

Franklin Pierce Adams belonged to a poker club that included among its members an actor called Herbert Ranson. Whenever Ranson had a good hand his facial expression was so transparent that Adams proposed a new rule for the club. "Anyone who looks at Ranson's face is cheating."

Robert Dennan, THE ALGONQUIN WITS 1968

Asquith entered into card games with extraordinary zest, but without pretension. His bridge was a shameless, if heroic, gamble with destiny. No one who has witnessed it will forget the relentless incaution of his bidding, which he would force up to any level which would ensure his playing the hand. If the result was favourable he would claim it as the reward for serpentine strategy. If, as often happened, it was adverse, his partner was left to draw what consolation he could from the standard formula, "We had to do it. They would have gone out." Margot, whose bridge was serious, found protest unavailing, and ultimately, to the great relief of both, he was exiled to a "bad" table, where he could indulge his adventurous bent without qualm or scruple.

J.A. Spender and Cyril Asquith, LIFE OF LORD OXFORD AND ASQUITH 1933

Lynn Fontanne told us how Chips Channon, who crossed and recrossed the Atlantic during the First World War, was once asked if he was ever afraid of being torpedoed, and had replied, "We did have a scare once, in a Portuguese liner, but I was playing bezique with Sarah Bernhardt and don't remember much about it."

Peter Coats, OF KINGS AND CABBAGES 1984

Nancy Astor gave Edward VII no encouragement; he was not welcome at Cliveden. He had a mania for cards; she wouldn't play and is said to have told the old roué that she couldn't tell the difference between a king and a knave.

A.L. Rowse, MEMORIES OF MEN AND WOMEN 1980

Sir Edward Elgar's diversions included throwing boomerangs and making "stinks" in his laboratory, an outhouse known as The Ark. It was furnished with shelves and a bench and innumerable bottles, retorts, Bunsen burners, test tubes and all the paraphernalia of an analytical chemist. There Elgar would retire and ease the burden of his destiny as a composer by pretending to be a chemist.

W.H. Reed, ELGAR AS I KNEW HIM 1937

W.H. Auden, finding T.S. Eliot engrossed in a game of patience, expressed surprise at his apparent enjoyment of this trivial occupation. "Well," said Eliot thoughtfully, "I suppose it's the nearest thing to being dead."

Peter Ackroyd, T.S. ELIOT 1984

King Farouk had an unbeatable way with cards and no one ever won against him because he would put his cards down and say, "I have won. I have better cards." He was once in a game of poker and an opponent had the effrontery to declare that he had three queens. Farouk retorted that he had three kings, and when someone turned up the cards to reveal only two kings Farouk snarled, "I am the third."

Omar Sharif, quoted Daily Telegraph 14 *Aug* 1986

To a partner during a game of bridge, who asked to be excused to visit the men's room, George S.Kaufmann said, "Gladly. For the first time today I'll know what you have in your hand."

Malcolm Goldstein, GEORGE S. KAUFMANN 1978

Debo Mitford (now the rather imposing Duchess of Devonshire) had some imposing pastimes during her childhood. When she was not checking through the still-births in *The Times* she could be found squatting in the chicken run in an effort to imitate the exact expression of pained concentration adopted by the egg-laying chickens.

Peter Bushell, GREAT ECCENTRICS 1984

PATRIOTISM

During the war, when I was director of Women's Services, and visiting munitions factories it took a long time to popularise trousers, which are necessary for safety in many kinds of work. One elderly woman flatly refused, and an exception was made in her favour. When, however, the King visited the town and there was a parade of munition workers she cast away her skirt and put on trousers. "Why," said my sister, "you've got your trousers on Mrs –" "Yes," said Mrs – "I'm a loyal woman, I am. I put 'em on to please the King, and I'll take 'em off again tomorrow."

Mrs C.S. Peel, LIFE'S ENCHANTED CUP 1933

PET

A taxicab driver once demurred at transporting Mrs Patrick Campbell and a disagreeable pooch named "Moonbeam". But she swept into the vehicle commanding, "The Empire Theatre, my man, and no nonsense." The dog, never housebroken, misbehaved en route, and the driver gave Mrs Campbell a furious I-told-you-so look as she descended. "Don't blame Moonbeam," she informed him loftily. "I did it."

Bennett Cerf, SHAKE WELL BEFORE USING 1948

Winston now stays in bed all morning. He has a tame budgerigar whom he calls "Toby". It keeps fluttering about his bedroom. Winston is convinced that it talks. Everyone else thinks it merely twitters, but he is positive that again and again it repeats the cheerful phrase, "Sir Winston will be pleased."

Harold Nicolson, DIARY 4 *Jul* 1956

Churchill's poodle, Rufus, ate in the dining room with the rest of the family. A cloth was laid for him on the Persian carpet beside the head of the household, and no one else ate until the butler had served Rufus's meal. One evening at Chequers the film was *Oliver Twist*. Rufus, as usual, had the best seat in the house, on his master's lap. At the point when Bill Sykes was about to drown his dog to put the police off his track, Churchill covered Rufus's eyes with his hand. He said, "Don't look now, dear. I'll tell you about it afterwards."

Stephen Shadegg, CLAIRE BOOTHE LUCE 1970

In Tokyo Jean Cocteau had bought a pet grasshopper which he kept in a little cage and often brought to my cabin. "He is very intelligent," he said, "and sings every time I talk to him." He built up such an interest in it that it became our topic of conversation. "How is Pilou this morning?" I would ask. "Not very well," he would say, "I have him on a diet."

When we arrived in San Francisco I insisted on him driving with me to Los Angeles as we had a limousine waiting. Pilou came along. During the journey he began to sing. "You see," said Cocteau, "he likes America." Suddenly he opened the car window, then opened the door of the cage and shook Pilou out of it.

I was shocked and asked, "Why did you do that?" "I give him his freedom." "But," I answered, "he's a stranger in a foreign country – he can't speak the language."

Cocteau shrugged. "He's smart, he'll soon pick it up."

Charles Chaplin, MY AUTOBIOGRAPHY 1964

George V hated to be parted from his pet parrot Charlotte. At Sandringham he would come to breakfast with the bird perched on his finger, then let her forage over the table. If Charlotte disgraced herself by making a mess the King would slide a mustard pot over it so that the Queen should not see it.

Kenneth Rose, KINGS, QUEENS AND COURTIERS 1985

The most faithful friend of Hetty Green, the eccentric American multi-millionairess, was a mongrel dog which had the unfortunate habit of biting her visitors. Most of the dog's victims, anxious not to offend, tolerated the animal, but one friend had had enough. "Hetty," she said reproachfully, "that dog just bit me again. You've got to get rid of him." Hetty refused. "He loves me," she explained, "he doesn't know how rich I am."

Parade Magazine 17 *Oct* 1982

PHILANTHROPY

Stanley Baldwin once left £100 at a home for retarded girls, and with it this note. "From one who once saw St Mary's Home and having been feeble-minded from the cradle regarded it with simpathy [sic] and understanding. Passing thro this vally of shadoes as a useless Fantum himself he desires to be the humble means of bringing a ray of light to kindrid unfortunates."

J.C.C. Davidson, MEMOIRS OF A CONSERVATIVE 1969

Beaverbrook was captivated by Dr Charles Wilson, later Lord Moran, who urged him to provide a new medical school for St Mary's Hospital. Beaverbrook decided to survey conditions for himself, He went along to the out-patients department and studied the crowded benches. There was a cafeteria serving tea and buns.

"I wondered whether it was a profit-making enterprise. I had just breakfasted on orange juice, toast, butter, honey and coffee. While I did not seek food it was my intention to gain information. So I asked the attendant at the counter, an old lady of benign countenance, 'How much for a bun and a cup of coffee?' The old lady answered, 'A penny for tea and a bun.' Certainly the cafeteria was not operating at a profit. I went back to my place on the bench. The old lady came over and whispered, 'If you haven't got a penny you have the tea and bun free.' I thanked her and replied with truth. 'I am not hungry.'"

When Wilson came in and greeted Beaverbrook the old lady was greatly distressed. She ran after Wilson whispering, "What shall I do? I've made a terrible mistake. Shall I apologise?" Wilson replied, "Do nothing. You've got us our money."

A.J.P.Taylor, BEAVERBROOK 1972

Andrew Carnegie gave away 8000 organs, costing £1,400,000, dotted all over America and Britain. Any denomination could have them – Catholic, Swedenborgian, Jewish. "You can't always trust what the pulpit says, but you can always depend on what the organ says," was Carnegie's comment.

Philip Morton, Sunday Express 2 *Oct* 1949

William Morris, later Lord Nuffield, wandered into the Office of the National Council for Social Services one day, wearing a creased old raincoat, and asked to see the secretary, an official who was not unfamiliar with cranks, but patient by nature. They got round to a project, at that time languishing for lack of means, to assist old people. The courteous official humoured what he thought was a mildly inquisitive engineer with time on his hands. Finally Morris said, "All right, I'll give you £50,000 for the pilot project," and went on his way.

Sir William Emrys Williams, Observer 25 *Aug* 1963

Dighton Probyn, Queen Alexandra's devoted Comptroller, did his best to keep some sort of control over her charitable giving, but she had ways and means of evading his vigilance. On one occasion she sent for Lord Knutsford, chairman of the London Hospital, and with great secrecy fished out from beneath her sofa cushions a crumpled envelope which contained a cheque for £1000 and another £1000 in notes, which she pressed in his hand as a gift for the hospital.

Georgina Bettiscombe, QUEEN ALEXANDRA 1969

PHOTOGRAPHY

When I was working in a leper colony in Venezuela I was photographed with twelve of my leper patients and the leper pharmacist. The photographs were intended for a weekly paper, but were never used as the editor thought them too grim. About six months later, however, I received a copy of the paper, on the front page of which was one of the photographs with the caption, "Venezuelans are lovers of large families and parents always try to keep their children with them when possible. This picture shows a wealthy coffee haciendo on the verandah of his coffee plantation, surrounded by his daughters and one son."

Dr William E. Aughinbough, I SWEAR BY APOLLO 1939

A portrait of Crippen was on demand for illustration of an article on crime. The reference library had only a poor one in stock, so I went along to the waxworks and photographed Crippen's effigy. With such a perfect likeness no one would be the wiser. And to this day the picture is still used – all unknowingly – as a genuine photograph, of the murderer.

William R. Turner, EYES OF THE PRESS 1935

I was wandering through St James's Park hoping to get a saleable picture of romping children or a new creation in hats. I stopped at Grosvenor Gate and prepared to snap the Life Guards coming from St James's. The policeman on point duty sidled up, looked in the opposite direction and whispered, "Want a good picture, chum? A really good one?"

He pointed to a perambulator that bowled along like a miniature automobile. "That's Princess Elizabeth," he murmured, "out in her pram for the first time."

Getting a picture of the sleeping princess was not easy. I walked with the nursemaid and told her I wanted a picture of a pretty baby. The nursemaid said nothing. She kept walking and I kept walking, determined to storm Buckingham Palace if necessary.

In the end I got my picture of the Royal baby, nodded gratefully to the intrepid policeman and started running for Fleet Street.

My boss, Mr MacArthur yelled, "A scoop! First pictures of the Royal baby. Wait till they see these!"

Princess Elizabeth at that time had not been photographed by court photographers, and no pressman had had anyone to point her out. The pictures appeared in every morning and evening paper. Provincial papers ordered it, and a firm of postcard printers bought it.

Edward J. Dean, LUCKY DEAN: REMINISCENCES OF A PRESS PHOTOGRAPHER 1944

There is a wonderful photograph of Albert Einstein by Ernst Haas which shows him rubbing his chin in a pensive mood, apparently contemplating the mystery of the universe. In fact the picture was taken immediately after Haas had asked Einstein where he had shelved a particular book.

John Naughton, Observer 21 *Nov* 1982

During King George V's Jubilee a photographer named Ferguson had permission to work from the Victoria Memorial in front of Buckingham Palace, but owing to the tremendous crowds, having permission was one thing, and getting to the scene of operations was another. He spoke to some first-aid men.

"I simply must get to the Memorial," he said. "Tell me, if I were suddenly taken ill, or something, could you fellows get me through the crowd?" A great idea! The base of the Memorial had been adopted by the ambulance men as a sort of headquarters and so, after a few "Mind your backs," Ferguson reached his goal.

William R. Turner, EYES OF THE PRESS 1935

In Berlin, soon after the war, I obtained the first photograph of the ex-Kaiser wearing his newly grown beard. I bought it from an old court photographer and expressed it to London – which was just as well for the old man changed his mind and pursued me to the railway station trying to return the cheque. "For God's sake, Herr Garai, let me have it back," he babbled, "I don't know what made me do it. I am a miserable wretch, a traitor –"

In vain I assured him that the picture was already on its way to London, and therefore beyond my reach. The poor old fellow was beside himself, and even threatened to throw himself in front of my train unless I returned the picture.

Fortunately he didn't carry out the threat, and later cashed the cheque.

Bert Garai, I GET MY PICTURE 1938

An Englishman was accused of murdering a friend in Rio de Janeiro harbour. One evening he returned in his yacht with the body of his friend who, he asserted, had been killed by falling from the masthead. An oar was missing, and doctors said that the wound might have been caused by such a weapon. And the friends had quarrelled two days before. But it fortunately happened that a passenger entering the harbour on a steamship had taken a snapshot which included the yacht. When developed, a black spot was visible against the sail. This, on enlargement of the photograph, appeared quite distinctly as a man falling from the masthead towards the deck. As a result of this extraordinary coincidence, and on the evidence of the photograph, the accused man was, of course, acquitted.

Henry T.F. Rhodes, CLUES AND CRIMES 1933

During the trial of Reuben Bigland before Mr Justice Darling I was in court with a small camera. In order to keep it firm for a time exposure I stuck it to a panel with some putty. Seeing two officials coming towards me I hastily took it down. To reach the door I would have to pass the two officials. I tried to look as innocent as I could, but they barred my progress. "You mustn't do that here you know," one of them whispered. "Do what?" I countered. "Take photos." "Oh really. Isn't it allowed then?" "No." "Then it's no use my staying then," I said and left the court taking my photograph with me.

William R. Turner, EYES OF THE PRESS 1935

PLAGIARISM

One day there came in to *London Opinion* an excellent story signed by one Barron Shore. I was on the point of dictating a letter of acceptance when the chords of memory began to vibrate. There were some droll references to whiskers. Who was always getting fun out of whiskers? Frank Richardson, of course. An examination of one of Richardson's volumes revealed the fact that Barron Shore had copied an incident of a thousand words and submitted it as his own.

This was a serious business. Had we failed to detect the trick we should have published the stolen story, and thereby have let ourselves in for a penalty for infringement of copyright.

I wrote to the person calling himself Barron Shore, asking if the story he had submitted was his own, and if he was requiring payment for it; and upon his assurance that this was so I instructed our solicitors to prosecute the man for attempting to obtain money by false pretences. They were of the opinion that he would be difficult to convict on a mere attempt to obtain money. So we sent him two guineas for Frank Richardson's story and had him brought up at Bow Street.

The magistrate was the aged Mr Mersham, who should have retired twenty years earlier. He fined the peccant *litterateur* ten shillings and two shillings costs. He had our two guineas in his purse, so that deducting the out-of-pocket expenses which his interview with the magistrate had cost him, he was left with thirty shillings profit.

Lincoln Springfield, SOME PIQUANT PEOPLE 1923

POETRY

When I was in Ireland I received a letter from Alfred Austin, the Poet Laureate, asking if I would let my flat for a few weeks. I agreed and terms were arranged. Shortly before his occupation I received a letter from him that he had a small request to make, namely, that I would not leave a dog in the flat. Never having, at that time, owned a dog I was able to reassure him, but told him that I equally had a small request to make to him, namely that when he vacated my flat he would leave no poems.

Sir Lionel Earle, TURN OVER THE PAGE 1934

When T.W.H. Crosland was editing a Sunday paper for Edward Hulton he was rash enough to print some lyrics by great poets. One by Shelley caught the eye of the magnate. "I don't want that sort of thing in my paper," he said. "I suppose he'll be a friend of yours. Tell him not to send any more." Of Keats he said, "That's not bad. Who is this chap Keats? Can we get him on the staff?"

Hamilton Fyffe, SIXTY YEARS IN FLEET STREET 1949

At a meeting of the Oxford Poetry Club T.S. Eliot was the guest of honour and agreed to answer questions about his work. An undergraduate asked him what he meant by the line from *Ash Wednesday* "Lady, three white leopards sat under a juniper tree." Eliot answered, "I mean 'Lady, three white leopards sat under a juniper tree.'"

Allen Tate, T.S. ELIOT: THE MAN AND HIS WORK 1966

The Duke of Devonshire came into the library at Chatsworth while I was arranging one of the cases that contained the rarer books, and asked me to show him some of the more precious among these. I took out the first edition of *Paradise Lost*, which he seemed not to know. The Duke sat down with the book and to my astonishment, began to read the poem aloud from the first line. He read on for quite some time, stopping once to say, "How fine this is! I had forgotten how fine it was!"; then the Duchess came in and, poking her parasol into the Duke whimsically remarked, "If he begins to read poetry he will never come out for his walk."

Bernard Holland, LIFE OF THE DUKE OF DEVONSHIRE 1911

I came to London, Tuesday. Lunched at the Webbs. Apropos of Squire's poem in the current issue of *Statesman* the Webbs were both funny. Mrs Webb particularly. She said, "Poetry means nothing to me. I always want to translate it back into prose."

Arnold Bennett, JOURNALS 1911–1921

Yeats would come to see me, five miles from Dublin, striding over the snow-bound roads, a gaunt young figure, mouthing poetry, swinging his arms and gesticulating as he went. Dublin policemen used to eye him in those days as if uncertain whether to run him in or not. But by and by they used to say, "Shure, 'tisn't mad he is, nor drink taken. 'Tis the poetry that's disturbin' his head," and leave him alone.

Katherine Tynan, TWENTY-FIVE YEARS 1913

At my prep-school one of the masters, Hope-Gill asked the class what it thought poetry was. I said it was something that had to be said, "but it would sound silly if you said it in prose". He gave a great cheer. "Lord let thy servant depart in peace – somebody understands."

Gerald Priestland, SOMETHING UNDERSTOOD 1986

POLICE

When Dashiell Hammett worked as a detective for the Pinkerton agency the chief of police of a southern city sent him a detailed description of a wanted criminal which included even the mole on the man's neck. The description omitted, however, the fact that the man had only one arm.

Diane Johnson, DASHIELL HAMMETT 1982

Peter Imbert, when Surrey's deputy chief constable, was on his way in his chauffeur-driven Jaguar when he picked up a police radio call for help. A villain was making a getaway and a young constable needed assistance. Immediately, Imbert diverted his car to the scene where he jumped out and cornered the thief in a back garden. When the regular uniformed officers caught up they witnessed Imbert, in his civilian clothes, lecturing the captured crook.

"Who are you then?" ventured the senior sergeant as Imbert handed over the offender.

"Just a passer-by," he replied.

Sunday Times, Profile 2 *Aug* 1987

According to this week's *Tribune* police in the East End of London found themselves the target in local schools of a rumour that people were dying by the dozen in nearby police stations. After some investigation they finally got to the root of the rumour from a pupil who had been on an open-day visit to a local police station. He told how he had seen on a blackboard behind the sergeant's desk, "13 charged – 3 dead". Pupils on other visits had seen the same message with varying numbers. Relieved police spokesmen were then able to announce that the figures referred to the rechargeable batteries for officers' radios.

Daily Telegraph 27 *Jul* 1985

POLITENESS

An American once complained to Marshal Foch about the insincere politeness of the French. "There is nothing in it but wind," he said. "There is nothing but wind in a tyre," said Foch, "but it makes riding in a car smooth and pleasant."

Edmund Fuller, ANECDOTES 1942

In Libya, in February 1986, the crowd was queueing to get into the Libyan equivalent of the Conservative Party Conference. They squeezed into the auditorium. Six television cameras were positioned through the hall. Five men in army uniforms sat on the podium and took turns to shout into the microphone. They were echoed by the audience who jumped up in their seats to wave their fists and scream with revolutionary zeal; "We will die for Qaddafi", "Death, death, death to the USA", "Shit, shit, shit on the US Sixth Fleet".

One young man who chanted and waved his fist in the front row, standing on his seat, accidentally bumped the head of an American reporter, a living example of the great Satan. "I am terrible sorry," he said. "It was an accident. I will stand a little higher up."

He resumed his chant. "Death, death, death to Reagan."

David Blundy and Andrew Lycett, QADDAFI AND THE LIBYAN REVOLUTION 1987

POLITICS

My Music host Steve Race met Jeffrey Archer at this week's The Man of the Year beano. Said Archer, "I do so love your programme." To which SDP member Race replied, "Thanks very much. I wish I could say the same about yours."

The Times, Diary 4 *Oct* 1985

We had a very rare experience at the Cabinet today. We had to settle the rate of pension for the widows of soldiers and sailors killed in the war. Finally the question emerged whether a childless widow should get 5/– per week, as now, or 7/6, or 6/6, proposed by Kitchener as a compromise. The argument for not more than 5/– is almost overwhelming, but as the childless widows are estimated to amount to no less than a third of the whole, and they would be left as they are, a 5/– rate would generally be condemned as mean and ungenerous. I said I would do what I had done only twice in 7 years, take a division in the Cabinet. The voting was very curious: for 7/6 – 1; for 5/– – 8; for 6/6 – 9. So 6/6 carried the day. Churchill was the one for 7/6.

H.H. Asquith, letter to Venetia Stanley 13 *Oct* 1914

Sir Austen Chamberlain visited his old nurse. He told her he was in politics. She said, "Why? There are enough of the family in politics already. I always hoped you'd do something useful."

Bruce Clavering, Sunday Referee 10 *May* 1936

Why, Hugh Cudlipp asked his old friend Sydney Jacobson, Editorial Director of IPC Newspapers, as they took their customary constitutional in Lincoln's Inn Fields, had they not become politicians. Because, Jacobson explained, politicians go out of office. "We are always in power."

Godfrey Smith, Sunday Times 8 *Oct* 1972

Ted Heath's first task after the 1966 election defeat was to form a shadow cabinet. My advice was asked on only one aspect. We still thought in terms of appointing a "statutory woman". "Who should it be?" asked Ted. "Margaret Thatcher," was my immediate reply. There was a long silence. "Yes," he said, "Willie Whitelaw agrees she's much the most able, but he says once she's there we'll never get rid of her, so we both think it's got to be Mervyn Pike."

Jim Prior, A BALANCE OF POWER 1986

When I was 11 I wanted to be a sailor. Then I met Lloyd George. "What do you want to be a sailor for?" he demanded. "There are greater storms in politics than you'll find at sea. Piracy, broadside, blood on the decks – you'll find them all in politics."

Julian Amery, Observer 2 *Jan* 1966

While addressing a political rally in his constituency Robert Menzies, the Australian prime minister, was interrupted by a woman heckler shouting, "I wouldn't vote for you if you were the Archangel Gabriel." Menzies riposted, "If I were the Archangel Gabriel, madam, you would scarcely be in my constituency."

Kenneth Edwards, I WISH I'D SAID THAT 1977

After a meeting last night a man entered into conversation with me. "By the way," he said, "do your family object to you standing for Labour?" "Well, my mother said I had betrayed my country." He was a Press Association man, and all the papers this morning have been ringing Mummy up. Oh my God!

Harold Nicolson, letter to his son Nigel, when standing unsuccessfully in the Croydon by-election 26 *Feb* 1948

When Enoch Powell was answering questions during the 1974 election one of the very few in the audience not mesmerised by him shouted "Judas!". Powell turned – and the expression on his face was one of indescribable and immeasurable anguish. "Judas," he said, "was paid. I am making a sacrifice." And he was.

Patrick Cosgrave, The Times 14 *June* 1982

Paderewski, the pianist, became Prime Minister of Poland, but I felt like Clemenceau who said to him at a conference at the ill-fated Versailles Treaty, "How is it that an artist like you can stoop so low as to become a politician?"

Charles Chaplin, MY AUTOBIOGRAPHY 1964

During an unsuccessful attempt to win a Sheffield seat, Tim Renton, currently Minister of State at the Foreign Office, looked through an open window at a burly steelworker soaking himself in the bath. Embarrassed, Renton turned to the garden and saw that it was full of primroses.

"Did you know that primroses were Disraeli's favourite flower?" he asked hopefully. "Is that so?" the steelworker replied from his bath. "In that case I'll dig the buggers up tomorrow."

Kenneth Rose, Sunday Telegraph 28 *Dec* 1986

PORTRAIT

I received a commission to paint a beautiful lady who counted millionaires among her admirers. "You know, Mr Cole," she said as she handed me the final payment, "this has been an excellent picture, really most valuable. I showed it to Mr A (mentioning the name of a millionaire) and of course he bought it for me. Then I showed it to Mr B (mentioning the name of a second millionaire) and he bought it for me as well. So you see, I give you your five hundred guineas, and I have got five hundred guineas as well."

P. Tennyson Cole, VANITY VARNISHED 1931

Queen Elizabeth II spends several sessions every month sitting to have her portrait painted by artists commissioned by high commissions, town halls and regimental messes. "Now then," she has been known to say as she enters the room, "with teeth or without?"

Robert Lacey, MAJESTY 1977

The Sun edition of James Joyce's *Tales Told of Shem and Shawn* was illustrated with a portrait of the author by the Rumanian sculptor Brancusi, a sketch of an abstract spiral intended to suggest the labyrinthine nature of Joyce's thought processes. When the portrait was shown to his father in Dublin he remarked, "The boy seems to have changed a good deal."

William Wiser, THE CRAZY YEARS: PARIS IN THE TWENTIES 1983

In 1906 Gertrude Stein posed eighty times for Picasso's portrait of her, after which he wiped the face off, saying he couldn't "see" her any more, and then finished the likeness in Spain, where he couldn't see her at all.

Edmund Fuller, ANECDOTES 1942

Stressemann's volubility made impossible a long, reasoned statement advocating the 1926 Locarno Pact. Lord d'Abernon therefore adopted the device of being present when Stressemann was having his portrait painted by Augustus John, who resolutely refused to allow his sitter to speak. Stressemann enjoyed the humour of the situation, but I am told he was not pleased with the portrait.

Lord Riddell, John o'London's Weekly 27 Sep 1930

Patrick Tuohy, when James Joyce was sitting for his portrait, began to philosophise about the importance to an artist of capturing his subject's soul. Joyce replied, "Never mind my soul. Just be sure you have my tie right."

Richard Ellmann, JAMES JOYCE 1959

POVERTY

I remember Attlee bringing to an end a certain discussion on fuel rationing with the remark, "The proposal is based on the supposition that everyone can store coal. They can't. In most of the East End they've only a cupboard under the stairs." And then, with a quick reminiscent smile "Why, when I lived there I used to keep it under the bed. And the first time I bought too much and had to sleep on a hump like a camel."

Francis Williams, Illustrated 24 Jul 1948

All Aneurin's stories of his schooldays centre round the combats between him and William Orchard, his headmaster. He was a bully and a snob. On one occasion Orchard picked on a little boy, asked him why he had not been to school the day before, and when the boy replied that it was his brother's turn to wear the shoes, mocked him and raised a titter from the class. Aneurin picked up an an inkwell and threw it at him.

Michael Foot, ANEURIN BEVAN 1962

Horatio Bottomley had been a Member of Parliament, a newspaper owner and editor, a journalist, an author, a theatrical impresario, a racehorse owner. He had been twice a millionaire, and yet, when his life was nearly over, he sought – and was refused – an old age pension.

Daily Express 27 *May* 1933

To the customs officer who asked if he had anything to declare Gandhi replied, "I am a poor mendicant. All my earthly possessions consist of six spinning wheels, a can of goat's milk, six homespun loincloths, one towel – and my reputation, which cannot be worn."

Evening News 30 *Jan* 1948

When Henri Gaudier and Sophie Brzeska were living together in England as brother and sister under the name of Gaudier-Brzeska, they were reduced to such poverty that while Gaudier was out Miss Brzeska made a doll, took a shawl which she wrapped round herself and her "baby" and went to the street corner to beg. She collected sixpence in pennies, and with it she bought some bread, margarine and tea, and because Henri was fond of cakes she bought one small cake. When Henri got home he found an excellent tea waiting for him. To Sophie's surprise he was very angry, saying she must never do such a thing again. Instead they visited public houses in the neighbourhood, and Henri did drawings of the customers at a penny each.

H.S. Ede, SAVAGE MESSIAH 1931

In order to feed his family, which he was unable to do by selling his stories, Ernest Hemingway resorted to catching pigeons in the Luxembourg Gardens when the gendarme on duty went into a cafe for a glass of wine. Having lured the pigeons with a handful of corn Hemingway dispatched the luckless creatures with a twist of the neck. He then concealed the bodies under the blanket on his son Bumby's baby carriage in order to take them home to be cooked and eaten.

Phyllis Meras, THE MERMAIDS OF CHENONCEAU 1983

PRACTICAL JOKE

Kingsley Amis has an awesome gift for mimicry. One day just after the war he and two friends were strolling along to the Lamb and Flag when a motor cyclist, clearly with the same destination, propped his machine against the kerb nearby. When he had got some distance across the pavement Kingsley made his motor-bike-failing-to-start noise. The man stopped dead in his tracks and stared at the machine narrowly. Then he walked back and knelt down beside it. Some minutes later he entered the pub with a subdued expression on his face.

Philip Larkin, quoted Observer, Profile, Kingsley Amis 26 *Oct* 1986

Dined at Barrie's. He told us he had had Asquith and Birrell to dinner the other night and had arranged with Asquith's daughter-in-law and another female friend that they should dress up as housemaids and serve the dinner. They did so. The daughter-in-law wore a black wig. Neither Birrell nor Asquith recognised the women. But after dinner, in the drawing room Asquith said, "One of those maids was extraordinarily like my daughter-in-law." Barrie told this practical joke with great restraint and humour.

Arnold Bennett, JOURNAL *Oct* 1918

In *Pelleas and Melisande,* when Sarah Bernhardt and Mrs Patrick Campbell changed parts on alternate nights, they tested one another's technique and composure with some practical jokes. Sarah had a horror of frogs, so Mrs Campbell put a clutch of them at the bottom of the well. Sarah Bernhardt, as Pelleas, peered into the well, caught her breath at the sight of the frogs, but avoided a recoil. The next night

Sarah put a large convex mirror at the bottom of the well so that when Mrs Campbell looked in she saw a gigantic, mongol-like face gazing back at her. She, too, did not miss a cue or falter over a line.

Lord Chandos, FROM PEACE TO WAR 1968

In Paris, James and Gloria Jones's friend Jean Castel owned a popular bar and restaurant down a side street in St Germain. For a long time this establishment and its owner had been terrorised by an old Romanian woman who stood outside in a dirty dress playing a squeaky mandolin and occasionally shouting obscenities through the doorway. Castel complained about her to anyone who would listen. She was ruining his business and her music was driving him insane. Castel announced to his friends that he was going to take a much-needed vacation in Tahiti.

About twenty-five of his friends, led by the Joneses, put up 100 dollars apiece and bought the Romanian woman a round ticket to Tahiti the day before Castel was due to leave Paris. He took his plane and many hours later he landed at the airport in Tahiti. He descended the ramp and almost collapsed at the sight which greeted him; the Romanian woman strumming her mandolin and saying, "Welcome to Tahiti, Monsieur Castel."

William Morris, JAMES JONES: A FRIENDSHIP 1978

A meeting of the Defence Committee included a number of senior Ministers and the Chiefs of Staff. But as can happen with such august gatherings it made very little progress. Churchill became bored with it. Any other Prime Minister would have suggested adjournment to an unspecified date. But Churchill preferred to break it up in his own way. He suddenly interrupted, pointing a finger at the window and said in a loud voice, "What was that bird?"

Ministers, generals and others started to give quick identification.

"I think it was a jay, Prime Minister."

"A big seagull," said another.

In the confusion he got up from his chair and began to leave the Cabinet Room. On his way he passed me, and somewhat daringly I said, "I didn't see a bird, Prime Minister."

"There wasn't one," he said with an immensely pleased grin, and stumped happily out of the room. He had evidently enjoyed seeing these eminent men make fools of themselves in attempting to please him.

John Boyd-Carpenter, WAY OF LIFE 1980

My brother William (Douglas-Home) found a stuffed crocodile and put it into a stream in the garden. Then he led Aunt Olive towards it planning to frighten her. When they were halfway across the bridge William put his hand down and Aunt Olive went on talking, and looked down, and you could see a look of baffled fury coming over William's face. Eventually they came back to the house and he said, " Most extraordinary woman. When I said, 'Look out, Aunt Olive, there's a crocodile,' she looked down and said, 'Oh, I didn't know they came this far North.' And then we had to drag the bloody great thing back to the basement."

Henry Douglas-Home, quoted Mark Amory, Sunday Times Magazine 17 *Apr* 1977

Among Sir Geoffrey's posthumous papers two letters were discovered. Evidently there had been an advertisement in *The Stage* magazine about a night club called Eliot's. The directors of Faber and Faber sent a spoof letter to T.S. Eliot formally expressing anxiety about the possibility that these extra-curricular activities might reflect badly on Faber and Faber.

Eliot wrote a very long and elaborate reply. He said he was writing at 1 a.m. He begins by expressing his anguish at the charges levelled against him. Then he more or less admits that he does, in fact, run the club after hours. Then with feigned mounting confidence, he begins to defend the club. The Faber directors, he writes, are worried about Faber and Faber's connection with the club. But has it not occurred to them that the club might be equally worried, and with much better cause, about its connection with a publisher? "If someone behaves badly at a night club, you chuck him out. At a publisher's, you take him out to lunch."

Michael Davie, Observer 15 *May* 1983

William Le Quex, the author of many popular mystery stories, was much addicted to practical joking. One of his efforts was to hoax the whole of the inhabitants of the Devonshire village in which he then lived. On several nights, when there was no moon, he donned a black suit with a skeleton painted on the front and back in luminous paint, and wandered in a cemetery. Within a few days the village was in a state of horror.

Eventually the bolder among the yokels armed themselves with pitchforks and scythes and bill-hooks and made a frontal attack *en masse* on the alleged ghost, and only just in time was Le Quex able to jump behind a gravestone and strip off his skeleton and disappear into the darkness. Next day Le Quex learned that next time the rustics meant to arm themself with shotguns. The ghost did not appear again.

Basil Tozer, THE LIGHTER SIDE OF LIFE 1932

Groucho Marx's first professional appearance was made at the age of 13, as a boy soprano in church. He was fired for puncturing the organ bellows with a hat-pin, and went into vaudeville as a female impersonator.

Alvin Johnson, Woman's Home Companion Sep 1936

Dame Nellie Melba habitually chewed gum, for preference a piece of Australian wattle gum, on opera or concert nights to keep her mouth and throat moist. Making an entrance at Covent Garden, she took her gum from her mouth and put it on a little glass shelf, provided for the purpose in the wings. When she came off the stage she went to the shelf, picked up the gum, as she thought, and put it in her mouth. She spat it out, and two or three strong words with it. A stagehand had substituted a quid of tobacco for the gum. Melba demanded that all the stagehands should be sacked, but she was probably less furious with them than with Caruso, who thought the incident was the best joke of the Covent Garden season.

John Hetherington, MELBA 1967

Miss Whiteley, governess to the Mitford sisters, had an aversion to snakes. Unity Mitford, who had a terrifying facility for laying bare adult weakness, entwined Enid, her pet grass snake, around the link chain of the toilet. Miss Whiteley emitted a terrified shriek and fell off the seat in a dead faint. A workman had to be called to prize the door off its hinges.

Peter Bushell, GREAT ECCENTRICS 1984

While playing at Swansea I rowed out with a realistic dummy as my companion. Then, in full view of the crowds on the beach, I seized the dummy and acted as if we were having a quarrel to the death. I could hear the cries from the shore. I lifted a scull and rammed it into the prostrate figure. The excitement became frantic. Boats began to put off. Standing erect I uttered a final bloodthirsty yell and emptied the six chambers of my revolver into the victim. It was a good stunt. When I stepped on to the stage that night I was received with cheers and loud cries of, "What have you done with the body, George?"

George Robey, LOOKING BACK ON LIFE 1933

Lord Rothermere became, in his late years, the prisoner of his own millions. Once when crossing on the *Empress of Britain* with an entourage the wireless went wrong for hours. A humorist, hoping the story would reach him, invented the yarn that a gang of financial crooks had jammed the wirelesses of the world while they worked a big Stock Exchange gamble. Suddenly Rothermere's closest intimate was summoned to the royal suite. Returning, he said, "He believes it! He's tearing his hair!"

Hannen Swaffer, World's Press News 5 *Dec* 1940

As vicar of St Mary Magdalene, Oxford, I found myself custodian of the Martyrs' Memorial which had been erected in what was then the churchyard as a counterblast to the teaching of the Oxford Movement. Generations of undergraduates had climbed it leaving an article of bedroom furniture on top as a record of their feat. During my incumbency some young men were caught having pulled a pinnacle or two down in their attempt and I had to discuss with the proctors what measure could be taken to protect the Memorial. I said, "Could not a referendum be taken in the university to find out the number of undergraduates who would like to see a jerry-pot on top, and if it proves a large number one could be cemented on." The Senior Proctor said reprovingly, "I sense a point of view coming on, Father Stephenson."

Colin Stephenson, MERRILY ON HIGH 1965

A favourite trick of James Thurber's, in his early newspaper days, was to draw small dogs on telephone pads, page after page of them. A reporter answering the phone would snatch at the phone-pad, tear off the dog picture seeking a clean page – then find dog picture after dog picture.

World's Press News 15 *Jul* 1937

Long runs made Beerbohm Tree so fidgety he would hand round a boiled lobster or a dead rabbit to stir things up on the stage. Once when playing Mephistopheles to Henry Ainley's Faust he had Faust's cup screwed to the table so that Ainley was forced to lap up his wine like a dog.

Madeline Bingham, THE GREAT LOVER: THE LIFE AND ART OF HERBERT BEERBOHM TREE

Henry Troy, one of New York's leading practical jokers once purloined from a club locker room the rubber overshoes of a typical absent-minded professor – one who habitually wore them if the weather even hinted rain. He painted them to resemble human feet, covered them with lampblack, and put them back. That afternoon the unsuspecting professor started home in the rain. He had walked no more than a block when the lampblack washed away. Such citizens as happened to be abroad were startled to see him sloshing along, so it appeared, in his bare feet.

H. Allen Smith, LIFE IN A PUTTY-KNIFE FACTORY 1945

Short entries in a date-book can sometimes pose a mystery. In Santa Monica, July 4, 1935, I scribbled "Leave for New York. Lend beach house to Joe." And then six weeks later a mystery comes to light. "Home from vacation. Find house in order except for FOOTPRINTS ON THE CEILING."

Only Hollywood could supply an answer to that mystery. Joe Schenck was an eminent film producer and in spite of his girth, advancing years and retreating hairline, he dearly loved to play. And I learned on investigation that those footprints had come about during a beach party Joe gave. It seemed that Johnny Weissmuller, the current Tarzan, had grabbed a starlet whose feet were smeared with sun-tan oil, and hoisted her, upside down, until she was walking on the ceiling.

Anita Loos, KISS HOLLYWOOD GOODBYE 1974

PRAYER

On transcontinental flights I would recite the Lord's Prayer to myself on take-off and landings. One day in May 1981 I found myself murmuring, "Our Father which art in Heaven, Hollywood be thy name," and realised it was time I got out.

Steven Bach, FINAL CUT 1985

Dean Inge was delighted with a letter he received from a lady who disagreed with one of his articles. "I am praying nightly for your death," she wrote. "It may interest you to know that in two previous cases I have had great success."

Alfred Noyes, TWO WORLDS FOR MEMORY 1953

Dame Madge Kendal could be terrifying at rehearsal. She once asked a manager to bring a kitchen chair to the middle of the stage. The company was summoned to gather round while she knelt down and said, "Oh Lord, we pray Thee out of Thy infinite mercy that Thou will cause some notion of the rudiments of acting be vouchsafed to this company, for Jesus Christ's sake, Amen." She got up and dusted her knees. "Well now, we'll see what that will do," she snapped.

James Harding, AGATE, A BIOGRAPHY 1986

Hesketh Pearson, Hugh Kingsmill and Malcolm Muggeridge walked great distances, chattered endlessly about Shakespeare, Dr Johnson, Frank Harris and English cathedrals. Above all, they laughed. They laughed in Westminster Abbey when they saw a notice which read, "Prayer, What is it for? And how is it done?" And Kingsmill said, "Considering all the money spent on this building they might have settled these elementary points by now."

John Mortimer, Sunday Times reviewing Ian Hunter, NOTHING TO REPENT: THE LIFE OF HESKETH PEARSON 1 *Feb* 1987

Driving somewhere along the Massachusetts North Shore in the early 1900s Bishop William Lawrence happened upon a driver swearing profusely as he struggled to pry a flat tyre from the rim. "Have you tried prayer, my good man?" gently inquired the bishop – upon which the poor fellow, in the desperation of his plight, fell on his knees, clasped his hands, and lifted his eyes heavenwards. He then picked up the iron, inserted it, and off popped the tyre.

"Well I'll be Goddamned," said the bishop.

Joseph Garland, BOSTON'S GOLDEN COAST 1981

PRISON

A prison visitor found Horatio Bottomley sewing mailbags. "Ah, Bottomley, sewing I see." "No," said Bottomley, "Reaping."

Julian Symons, HORATIO BOTTOMLEY

[Because he refused to take part in an attack on Le Havre in which 12,000 civilians were killed, William Douglas-Home was cashiered and sent to prison.]

I went to Wakefield and my Mama told me afterwards they went out from the gate at the prison to go back to York station and there was a taxi waiting outside. She got into it and my Pap started walking down the wall and she said, "Where are you going, Charlie? Here's our taxi." and he said, "I am just going to see the dear little governor and thank him for having our William here." And he went off and had tea with the man.

William Douglas-Home, quoted Mark Amory, Sunday Times Magazine 17 *Apr* 1977

In 1910 Smuts sent Gandhi to prison for leading a passive resistance campaign opposing discrimination against Indians in Transvaal.

From his gaol in Bloemfontein Gandhi sent Smuts a letter with his "sincere regards" and stating that "the prospect of uninterrupted study for at least a year fills me with joy".

E. Moore Ritchie, Western Morning News 16 *Dec* 1963

When the United States entered the war in 1917, Bertrand Russell wrote an article to the effect that the purpose of bringing American troops to Britain was to break strikes. For this he was sent very properly to prison for six months. He was given preferential treatment in prison, pens and paper, reading and writing materials, and while there he wrote one of his better books. It enabled him to concentrate better. When he read Lytton Strachey's *Eminent Victorians* it made him laugh so much that a warder had to remind him that prison was supposed to be a place of punishment.

A. L. Rowse, GLIMPSES OF THE GREAT 1985

I went into a prison one evening. Some of the younger women – on privilege – were singing round a piano. One, with the face of a Madonna and a well-trained voice was, singing *Ave Maria* – beautifully. Then I learned that she had been picked up in an empty house which she had been using as a brothel. I felt that the Blessed Master would want to weep – even as I did.

George Potter, FATHER POTTER OF PECKHAM 1955

Spotted in Wormwood Scrubs chapel, a grand piano donated by Ivor Novello. He served four weeks during the war for driving a Rolls Royce without a war transport licence, and conducted the prison choir during his incarceration.

The Times, Diary 25 *Jun* 1987

PRODIGY

When John Barbirolli was four, his grandfather Antonio began taking him to Empire ballet rehearsals. At home, wearing white gloves in the professional fashion of the day, he pretended to direct orchestras, beating time and singing at the top of his voice.

His habit of borrowing a family violin and wandering all over the flat while scraping it exasperated Antonio Barbirolli who one day took a hansom to a fiddle shop in Wardour Street and came back with a half-sized 'cello. "Play that instead," he told the boy." "You have to sit down to play the 'cello."

Observer, Profile 6 *Jul* 1947

When he was nine years old Edward Elgar was discovered sitting on the bank of a river with a pencil and a piece of paper whereon he had ruled five parallel lines. He was trying, he said, to write down what the reeds were singing.

Basil Maine, ELGAR: HIS LIFE AND WORKS 1933

In his flat off the Etoile, Maurice Goudeket, Cocteau's schoolmate, Colette's widower, in his seventies, newly remarried and the father of a small son whose godfather was Cocteau, was boasting to him of the child's precocity. "He's been walking since he was six months old." Cocteau's retort, "Where is he *now*?"

Francis Steegmuller, JEAN COCTEAU 1970

J.B. Haldane displayed signs of mental precocity almost from birth. At ten months he screamed so loudly that he induced a hernia. Two years later he had learned to read. Soon after that he accidentally cut himself. He contemplated the blood and then asked his mother, "Is it exyhaemoglobin or carboxyhaemoglobin?" By the age of four he was leaving notes about the house reading "I hate you" and at the age of eight he was helping his father in his laboratory.

Peter Bushell, GREAT ECCENTRICS 1984

Dame Nellie Melba remarked, on hearing the famous record of Ernest Lough singing *Hear My Prayer*, "I could murder that infant. He has all the qualities I worked for years to acquire; phrasing, breath control, diction, everything."

Percy Colson, MELBA 1932

When two years old Yehudi Menuhin asked for, and was given, his first violin and immediately smashed it because it was only a toy and would not "sing". His grandmother gave him a proper one, small size, and at four and a half he started taking violin lessons.

Donald Hodson, News Chronicle 6 May 1968

"Cartoonist, Actor, Poet – and only Ten". So ran a headline in a Wisconsin newspaper thirty-five years ago. It referred to a phenomenal child who could "talk like a cultured adult" at the age of two, made his stage debut at three, was a practised painter and magician at eight, and at ten created a small-town furore with a production of *Androcles and the Lion* in which he played both Androcles and the Lion. He was the young Orson Welles.

Lindsay Anderson, Radio Times 11 *Mar* 1960

For our return trip on the ocean, over Christmas, we felt bound to enquire, before booking on a United States line ship, the *President Harding,* whether it carried the agreeable fluids required on a Christmas voyage across the North Atlantic. We were informed, accurately, by the US Line's office in Washington that the Prohibition Laws permitted the carriage of all liquors, with one exception, as medical stores. The exception was beer, for which apparently no medical case could be made.

John Boyd-Carpenter, WAY OF LIFE 1980

When Frederick Lonsdale, the dramatist, was in America during the prohibition period, he asked for a whisky and soda. The bartender said, "All we can serve here is near-beer." "Right," said Freddie, "give me one." On tasting it, it was all he could do to contain himself on the contents. "What do you call this?" he asked the bartender. "Near-beer." "Well, all I can say is," said Freddie, "you Americans have no sense of distance."

Bertie Hollander, BEFORE I FORGET 1935

PROMISCUITY

Montgomery enjoyed recounting a story which dated from pre-war days when he was commanding a battalion of the Royal Warwickshire Regiment in Egypt. One of his younger officers was, in Monty's view, doing himself no good by being out too often with the girls. "So I gave him an order not to have another girl without my permission, though if I thought it necessary, I would give it." Some weeks later he was dining in Cairo with the Ambassador, Lord Killearn. During dinner the butler announced that there was a telephone call for Colonel Montgomery. The Ambassador said, "Ask who it is and what he wants." The butler returned and gravely announced, "It is Lieutenant X and he wants to know if he can have a woman." Permission was granted.

J.R. Henderson, MONTGOMERY AT CLOSE QUARTERS 1985

Baroness Rothschild had once been Mayor of Reux in Calvados, and a woman came every year to register the birth of an illegitimate child. The father, whose name had to be given too, was always the same. Finally the Baroness could not resist asking why, as she had borne him at least six children, she did not marry him. "Ah yes, Madame La Maire, it would certainly be the discreet thing to do, but you see, I do not love him."

Peter Coats, OF KINGS AND CABBAGES 1984

PRONUNCIATION

Jimmy Thomas, the railwayman's leader, had several comicalities of which one couldn't be sure whether they were intentional or not. His "h"s of course are celebrated, and I think he must have misplaced them with a conscious art. John Buchan told me of a reporter who asked him after a meeting what Mr Thomas could possibly have meant by the "Haddock Committee" as the subject of his speech hadn't been remotely connected with fish of any kind: and John had been able to tell him that what had been in question was an *ad hoc* committee.

Edward Marsh, A NUMBER OF PEOPLE 1939

There was a special pronunciation unit at the BBC consisting of two Scottish ladies whose job it was, not only to maintain a card index of difficult foreign names, but to sit beside the news reader, advising him whether to say *con*troversy or con*trov*ersy. One of their most difficult tasks came when the Koreans threw up a politician with the unfortunate name of Lee Bum Suk. The ladies, who were not without a sense of humour, suggested Boom Sook, an example I followed many years later when I had to interview a Vietnamese called Captain Phuc.

Gerald Priestland, SOMETHING UNDERSTOOD 1986

There was a well-known bishop who pronounced "o" as "u". On one occasion he visited a working girl's club in the East End of London and the weather being cold he was asked to partake of a cup of coffee.

"With pleasure," he said, "I am fund of a hut cup of coffee."

This elicited only a few repressed giggles. Not so, however, when proceeding to impress upon the members the necessity for arranging full occupation of their spare time, he said earnestly, "Above all, girls, try to cultivate a hubby."

Maud Royden, quoted Gerald Findler, HUMOUR FROM PULPIT AND PEW 1934

My efforts at learning Polish were not too successful. Having picked up such things as "Good morning" and "Good night" I sought to advance my knowledge through an English-speaking Polish officer.

"It is easy," he said, "every Polish word is pronounced exactly as it is spelt."

"Oh," I said, "then this town we are in, L-O-D-Z, I suppose is pronounced 'Loads'?"

"Ah no," he said, "it's 'Wootch'."

This proved too much, with words like Przemysl knocking around, so I confined myself to French and German.

H.B.T. Wakleham, HALF TIME 1938

PROPAGANDA

One day students started to march through Cairo carrying on a stretcher for all to see one of their colleagues who, they stated, had been killed by British soldiers. As the stretcher came past the spot where I was standing with some of my police I saw that one arm of the corpse was hanging down. Without anyone noticing I reached out my right hand with a lighted cigarette inside the curved palm and pressed the glowing end on the down-hanging hand of the corpse. With a yell to awaken the dead the false corpse leapt up from the bier to the amazement of the onlookers and the complete discomfiture of the student bearers. The death-like coating of flour fell off his face, and the defeated students faded quickly away, followed by the derisive laughter of the mob.

Russell Pasha, EGYPTIAN SERVICE 1949

PROPHECY

Richard Attenborough, who played Detective Sergeant Trotter in the first 700 performances of *The Mousetrap* recalls that when the play was tried out in Nottingham before coming to the West End the cast gathered in their hotel convinced that the second act wouldn't work. The conversation went on into the small hours, with the authoress quietly listening. Eventually she took her leave. "I should stop worrying and get off to bed," said Agatha Christie. "I think we might get quite a nice little run out of it."

Peter Waymark, The Times 22 *Nov* 1982.

When Lady Astor visited Russia in 1931 and talked to Stalin he asked her opinion of Winston Churchill. Lady Astor's eyes lit with triumph. About Winston Churchill she and the Communists shared a common opinion. She thought of the man in England pursuing a more and more solitary course, shunned by more and more of the politicians of his own party.

"Finished," she cried. She said that Stalin could forget about him, write him off. "I don't agree," Stalin said quietly. "You will send for the old war-horse yet, in the day of battle."

Geoffrey Bocca, Sunday Express 5 *Feb* 1956

The Sunday revivalist sessions of the little brown-skinned man who has called himself successively, The Messenger, Major J. Divine, Father

Divine and, finally, God, became so popular, so noisy with angelic shouts and song that one night the police carted God and 80 angels – 15 of whom were white – to jail. Convicted of maintaining a public nuisance Divine was fined 500 dollars and sentenced to a year in jail. On hearing his sentence he warned the judge, "You can't convict God. All who oppose me, I destroy." Four days later the judge was dead of a heart attack. Loudly, the Angels rejoiced at this punishment for opposing God's will. To make the incident more fantastic, the sentence was reversed on appeal and God went free. The story catapulted Father Divine from a small-time cult leader to national prominence.

Ollie Steward, Scribner's Commentator Jun 1940

When Stolypin tried to get rid of him, Rasputin prophesied, "This man wanted to do me harm. A bad look-out for him, and I foresee that he will be the victim of his own mistake." Sure enough, Stolypin was assassinated.

Raymond Poincaré, MEMOIRS 1928

PSYCHIATRY

On the outbreak of the Second World War, Lord Berners came close to a complete breakdown. At the beginning of 1940 he underwent psychoanalysis. "What was it like?" his friends would enquire. "They opened up my mind and found a dead bird."

Michael Ratcliffe, The Times 3 Sep 1983

A child's incessant weeping, at first attributed by her worried custodians to an incest-complex, a mother-fixation and a malfunctioning gland, was eventually traced (to the mother's surprise) to wearing shoes two sizes too small.

Peter Vansittart, PATHS FROM A WHITE HORSE 1985

The psychiatrist greeted his long-time patient with a smile. "I have good news for you," he said. "You have been completely cured of your delusions now. You won't need any more sessions with me." The patient sighed. "Disgusting," he said. "Yesterday I was Napoleon. Today I'm just nobody."

English Digest Mar 1965

PUBLICITY

When *Brighton Rock* was being launched in America the New York distributor wired frantically, ATTENBOROUGH'S NAME TOO BIG FOR BANNER. British to the core, the Boulting Brothers wired back, "Get bigger banners."

Richard Attenborough, Sunday Telegraph 22 *Aug* 1965

My TV interview with Brendan Behan is to me a memorable one because he was drunk and did not utter throughout it one single comprehensible word. For Behan the experience was decisive. The papers next day were full of him and, Miss Littlewood told me, several West End managements, hitherto uninterested in his play, telephoned offering to put it on.

So Behan learnt, and he was quick to learn – there was a crafty, calculating side to him – that one drunken, speechless television appearance brought more of the things he wanted, like money and notoriety and a neon glory about his head, than any number of hours with a pen in his hand.

Malcolm Muggeridge, Observer 26 *Jul* 1970

Brief ceremony at which Unilever present us with the famous Millais *Bubbles* on indefinite loan. A tiny child model called Christina – white socks and a fringe – patiently pirouettes before pressmen for half an hour, and then for photographers sits briefly on my knee while I make stilted conversation about Ribena. Nice to have the picture, but the PR circus takes the edge off the occasion, forcing everybody into artificial behaviour. Obediently we point, grin, shake hands, gravely consider, look thoughtful, point again – Christina, wise girl, shows signs of restlessness.

Hugh Casson, DIARY 18 *Feb* 1980

There were few propositions to which Salvador Dali did not agree. One of these involved an American business man who proposed buying the second letter of Dali's name so that he could open a chain of stores called Dalicatessens. Dali called him crazy and threw him out.

Meryle Secrest, SALVADOR DALI: THE SURREALIST JESTER 1986

After comedian Charlie Drake had been given his first seven-minute spot in a BBC radio show in 1946 he wrote himself eight hundred fan letters. He took the tube from Elephant and Castle, getting off at each stop to post a letter to the BBC. He thought that they'd be so overwhelmed that they would offer him his own show. A few days later his mum gave him a fat parcel. It contained all the letters, unopened. It was a rule of the BBC that they never opened personal mail.

Russell Twisk, Radio Times 7 *Dec* 1967

W.C. Fields was engaged to work at Fortescue's Pier, in Atlantic City, for ten dollars a week and cakes. There was no admission charge to the performances of Fields and his fellow artistes at Fortescue's. The management made its profit by selling sandwiches and beer. Fields, who was still in his teens, was engaged as a juggler and drowner. When business was good, he juggled. When it was bad he drowned. He would get into a bathing suit, wade out until the water was neck deep, and cry for help. Saved, he would be carried to Fortescue's and rolled on a barrel. Barkers urged beer and sandwiches on the excited people who had seen the rescue and come in to watch the stirring resuscitation act. Fields sometimes drowned three or four times a day, and sometimes juggled twenty times a day.

Alva Johnston, New Yorker, Profile 1935

Gilbert Frankau tells of a conversation he had with Sir Hall Caine on the value of publicity. "I often go to see my publishers about my publicity campaigns, quite openly," said Mr Frankau. "I used to do the same," said Sir Hall, "but I had to be very discreet about it. How lucky you are, Mr Frankau, to live in an age when an author does not have to be a gentleman."

John o' London's Weekly 31 *May* 1930

Lindbergh has an obsession about publicity and I agree with him. He told me that when Coolidge presented him with a medal after his Paris flight he had to do it three times over – once in his study, which was the real occasion, and twice on the lawn of the White House for the movie people. "The first time," he said, "I was kind of moved by the thing. After all I was more or less a kid at the time and it seemed sort of solemn to me to be given that thing by the President of the United States. But when we had to go through the whole thing on the lawn – me standing sideways to the President and looking an ass – I felt I couldn't stand for it. Coolidge didn't seem to care or notice. He repeated his speech twice over in the same words. It seemed a charade to me."

Harold Nicolson, letter to Vita Sackville-West 1 *Oct* 1934

Sir Thomas Lipton told me the story of Lipton's Bank Notes – almost the best piece of publicity that can have been invented. One of his chief slogans was "Lipton gives £1 value for 15/-". In order to spread this slogan all over England he had £1 notes printed with a note at the bottom saying goods to the value of £1 could be bought for 15/- at any Lipton's store. So beautifully were these notes engraved that occasionally they would be used by canny and dishonest persons in place of the real article. The authorities learned this and Lipton had to stop his notes. But not before several comedies occurred.

"D'you know," said Sir Thomas, "that a man in a hotel at Edinburgh actually gave me one of my own notes as part of my change. He was a clever fellow. I let him keep it. And I was travelling in the train once with two elders talking of the collection at the kirk the Sunday before. "Five pounds seventeen and elevenpence," said one. "Aye," said the other, "but three of the notes were Liptons."

Beverley Nichols, TWENTY-FIVE 1926

Publicity can be overdone and defeat its own ends. I organised a show for the *Daily Mail* at the Central Hall, Westminster. It was a tremendous success and on the second day there was a waiting queue half a mile long. A photograph of this was published. The following day there was no queue and very few visitors. The picture had frightened the public away.

Wareham Smith, SPILT INK 1932

Miles Thomas, chairman of BOAC, was a superb showman. I recall an occasion at Heathrow when Princess Margaret returned from an official visit overseas, and was met by the Queen, the Queen Mother, and by the Queen's two elder children, then quite small. After fairly elaborate formalities the royal party moved to the line of Rolls-Royces. The Queen said goodbye to the various dignitaries. She was about to get into the car when she turned round and said, "Where are the children?" They had apparently vanished. Then out on the tarmac, about half a mile away, we spotted the genial Chairman of BOAC with Prince Charles holding one of his hands and Princess Anne the other. He had taken them to have a look at the aircraft. As Thomas was well aware every camera swung on to this scene of kindly Uncle Miles amusing the children.

As the film was exposed he placed the group carefully in line with the BOAC markings on the aircraft, happily conscious of the thousands of pounds worth of free advertising his kidnapping initiative was obtaining. When it appeared that he was going to take his willing victims all round the interior of the aircraft an equerry departed at the double to the scene of the crime, and brought back two protesting children, together with a happily smiling chairman of BOAC.

John Boyd-Carpenter, WAY OF LIFE 1980

When airlines were young and people were wary of flying, a promotion man suggested to one of the lines that they permit wives of business men to accompany their husbands free, just to prove that flying was safe. The idea was adopted and a record kept of the names of those who accepted the proposition. In due time the airline sent a letter to those wives, asking how they enjoyed the trip. From 90 per cent of them came back a baffled cry, "*What* aeroplane trip?"

Marguerite Lyon, AND SO TO BEDLAM 1944

As surveyors responsible for the management of a number of buildings we are faced with the increasing irritation of "fly" posters pasted over any handy vertical surface and promoting anything from heavy-metal concerts to quasi-political meetings. At last we have found an effective cure. You simply paste a large "cancelled" notice across them and tell the organiser what you have done. Quite suddenly you find that your site is poster-free.

M.A. Wyldbore-Smith, letter to The Times 23 Jul 1987

PUBLIC SPEAKING

James Agate had accepted an invitation to speak at Cambridge University. It was as well his audience had not heard his conversation with his man Fred before he visited them.

Fred: I've put in two shirts, two collars, two white ties, both dirty, and two waistcoats, one of which looks all right. And you'll find yer speech in yer top pocket along o' yer 'ankercher.

JA: But I haven't written any speech.

Fred: I found some old ones in a drawer, and they'll do.

James Harding, AGATE, A BIOGRAPHY 1986

Horatio Bottomley attended an election meeting to speak on behalf of a young man making his maiden essay into politics.

"Ladies and gentlemen," he began, "I want to tell you how deeply I appreciate the honour of being able to introduce to you your next

Member of Parliament. I have known him ever since he was a child. I have dandled him upon my knee and watched his career with interest as I would watch a child of my own. The boy will be Chancellor of the Exchequer in the next Parliament – if not the next Prime Minister. It is your bounden duty to send him to Parliament so that your fellow citizens may have the value of his services. I have known him for twenty years and I can truthfully tell you he possesses the greatest brain in the country."

He sat down to thunderous applause. His labour was not in vain. The youthful candidate romped in with a majority of eight thousand.

Bottomley had never set eyes on him until that evening.

Sunday Express 28 *May* 1933

The Fairchild Tropical Garden Society, in Florida, invited me to give a lecture and be the guest of honour at their annual Garden Dinner. I concocted a suitable talk, which I was able to illustrate with my own photographs, made into slides. On the whole I felt it went well and there was a lot of applause at the end. I rather unwisely (I was new to the game) asked if anyone would like to ask a question. Dead silence. Until a nice-looking little woman held up her hand and said shyly that she did not have a question, rather a request. "Yes certainly, madam, if there is anything I can do, etc., etc." The request was could I please say the word "awfully" again, and I realised from then on that my English accent might prove a useful asset.

Peter Coats, OF KINGS AND CABBAGES 1984

When Major Gwilym Lloyd George was looking round for men to run his plan for the mines, known as "operational control", he assigned Mr Justic Evershed to Nottingham and South Derbyshire. For nearly two years he stayed in his native territory, holding the scales between owners and miners. After a long exhortation at one meeting an old miner came up to him and gave him the sage advice which lads are often given when first going down the pit. "Breath through tha' nose, Raymond, and keep tha' bloody mouth shut."

Observer 20 *Oct* 1947

At a lecture in New Jersey I tried out the notion that it helps a speaker to pick out one person in the audience to whom to address his remarks. In the second row I spotted a most gorgeously furred-up woman. I thought, "That's my audience. Look at those furs. She fairly drips furs." Through the whole talk I never let my eyes off her. She didn't budge an inch and I felt pretty set up. If a woman like that remained as intent as she had, my points had all gone over.

After the talk a friend of mine said, "We thought your talk was splendid, Morley, but why did you keep staring at the second row?" When I explained how I'd picked my woman, my friend nearly died. I suffer from near-sightedness and the person I'd picked out was the chair on which half the women in the audience had piled their coats.

Christopher Morley, quoted Whit Burnett, THE LITERARY LIFE AND THE HELL WITH IT 1943

In 1957, when A.E. Matthews was nearly 90 he was a guest at a luncheon to mark 50 years of film-making at Pinewood Studios. Sir Leonard Brockington was making a long, rambling speech. After 25 minutes he made a significant pause and some of the guests began to applaud. When it died down Sir Leonard resumed speaking. "My God," said Matthews, "doesn't he know I haven't got long to live?"

Leslie Halliwell, THE FILMGOERS BOOK OF QUOTES 1973

On the rare occasions when the portrait painter John Singer Sargent was called upon for a speech he would stand struggling with his nervousness, unable to utter. On one occasion, blurting out, "It's a damned shame," he subsided into his seat amid a tempest of applause.

Evan Charteris, JOHN SARGENT 1927

I accompanied Miss Alice Toklas and Miss Stein to Oxford to hear that gifted writer deliver her celebrated lecture under the auspices of my friend Harold Acton. I remember a certain commotion arising, and some accompanying laughter, when towards the middle of her discourse she remarked, "Everything is the same, and everything is different." Most undergraduates had come to the hall to amuse themselves after the lecture at the expense of a writer widely and angrily derided, her work dismissed as "the stutterings of a lunatic". But in the presence of this obviously distinguished woman, the wiser of them recognised there was nothing much to be done in this line. At the end two young gentlemen, not so easily discouraged, shot up to heckle her from positions widely apart in the audience, but they asked an identical question. "Miss Stein, if everything is the same, how can everything be different?" In a most genial, comforting manner, Miss Stein replied, "Well, look at you two dear boys."

Osbert Sitwell, LAUGHTER IN THE NEXT ROOM 1949

James Agate recalls meeting Marie Tempest shortly before her death. She had been to Drury Lane she told him, to rehearse. "Rehearse?" he echoed incredulously. "Yes," replied the octogenarian Dame. "I have to make a speech there tomorrow, and as I have never acted on the stage of that theatre I wanted to know exactly how to pitch my voice. So I went down to Drury Lane, walked to the place where I shall stand tomorrow and said to the charwomen cleaning the gallery, 'Ladies and gentlemen, can you hear me?' They said, 'Yes, Mum.' I said, 'Can you hear me perfectly?' and they said 'Yes, Mum,' so now I know I shall be all right."

James Harding, AGATE: A BIOGRAPHY 1986

PUBLISHING

At the publishers where I worked we had been waiting for months for Brendan Behan to deliver a manuscript. At the last moment he refused to hand it over. He disappeared and I was sent to find him. I traced him by the sound of his voice coming from a bar. The upshot was that, after an evening with him, I got the precious manuscript but was in such a daze that I left it in a tube train.

Rae Jeffs, quoted Robert Pitman, Sunday Express 5 *Jan* 1964

When G.K. Chesterton's first published book, *Greybeards at Play*, appeared in 1900, he told his future wife Frances that he felt a humbug. "To publish a book of my nonsense verses seems to me exactly like summoning the whole of the people of Kensington to watch me smoke a cigarette."

The Times Literary Supplement 17 *Apr* 1974

As a publisher T.S. Eliot is not only the firm's expert on poetry, but he is also a conscientious composer of blurbs for book jackets. He finds it an exacting task. "I don't know how to grow asparagus, or improve your lawn tennis, or the best diet for a six-month-old baby, but I have to write blurbs about them," he said.

Milton Shulman, Evening Standard 8 *Aug* 1950

Scott Fitzgerald's first notion for the title of *The Great Gatsby* was *Trimalchio in West Egg* and, when this was frowned on by his publishers, he suggested *The High-Bouncing Lover.* At the very last moment he cabled "Crazy about title 'Under the Red White and Blue'. What would delay be?" His publisher's one-word reply was, "Fatal".

Bennett Cerf, SHAKE WELL BEFORE USING 1948

PUNISHMENT

Midshipmen, although they may grow up into admirable officers, are apt to cause a good deal of trouble to their seniors in the growing-up process. One of them, lent to a destroyer, made himself such a nuisance that the captain suggested that his sub-lieutenant should administer suitable chastisement. Next morning he found the sub-lieutenant at breakfast.

"Good morning, Whitfield," he remarked, "I was glad to hear you chastising that young officer this morning." Whitfield looked up grimly from his eggs and bacon. "I hate beating these poor little devils," he remarked. "If I have to do it, I do it. I loathe having to do it. And what makes it worse, sir, is that there is no room in that ward-room to get a proper swing on the stick."

Vice-Admiral Humphrey Hugh Smith, AN ADMIRAL NEVER FORGETS 1938

Ordering the boy to be sent to an approved school for three years the chairman, Colonel F.G. Barker said, "What a dreadful commentary on modern education and religion. If he were at Eton he would be flogged out of his life."

The Star, quoted Michael Bateman, THIS ENGLAND

QUARREL

Winston Churchill's hostility to Stanley Baldwin, particularly over India, ended normal relations. Churchill found himself standing next to Baldwin in a neighbouring urinal in a lavatory at the House of Commons. As he did up his trousers to leave Baldwin remarked, "I am glad there is one common platform on which we can still meet."

H. Montgomery Hyde, BALDWIN 1973

I heard a noise, a big noise, as I was on my way to breakfast. It was my mother-in-law (Lady Ellerman) rowing with her husband, reputed to be the richest man in the world.

"How dare you," she raged, "I won't be chivvied. I won't have it. Do you hear me? I won't have any more of your planning your plans and ignoring mine." I managed to slip through the hall unseen. "Go back to your musty museum in London, but leave the management of my little cottage to myself." She relaxed, seeing Sir John cowed. She turned away haughtily. "There will no grouse served at my table this day. You can throw the filthy fowl away. Give it to the servants. You will content yourself with the fare I order. And mark me: if you wake me for one of your filthy runs this afternoon I shall go for you. Go ahead with your filthy letters. Business, business and never a thought for your family. Let those letters alone. Breakfast has been announced. You will not keep others waiting in my household any more than you permit us in your own."

Robert McAlmon, BEING GENIUSES TOGETHER 1938

I have been told by people who knew my father and mother when they were first married that their quarrels were so violent that after throwing every available throwable object in the room they would use the baby as a missile. I was the baby.

Daphne Fielding, MERCURY PRESIDES 1954

A dispute with Sir Eric Geddes in 1918 gave Beaverbrook an expected insight into Churchill's character. He gave an account of it many years later.

"Both Churchill and myself were greatly hampered by the stubborn attitude of Sir Eric Geddes. He controlled steel and was putting difficulties in the way of Churchill at the Ministry of Munitions. He was also witholding intelligence information from myself. We agreed the obstinacy of Geddes must be broken by a concerted attack. Imagine my astonishment when a few days later Churchill rang me up and asked me to lunch for the purpose of reconciling me with an old friend. The old friend was Geddes – the man he had agreed to attack. He had forgotten all about his anger and frustration. He was a man who 'carried anger as the flint bears fire'. He was incapable of rancour."

A.J.P. Taylor, BEAVERBROOK 1972

Unhappy about Dashiel Hammett's drinking, his ladies, my life with him, I remember an angry speech I made one night; it had to do with injustice, his carelessness, his insistence that he get his own way, his sharpness with men but not with himself. I was drunk, but he was drunker, and when my stride around the room carried me close to the chair where he was sitting I stared in disbelief at what I saw. He was grinding a burning cigarette into his cheek.

I said, "What are you doing?"

"Keeping myself from doing it to you," he said.

Lillian Hellman, AN UNFINISHED WOMAN 1965

Sir Edmund Gosse had pleasing stories about the rows in the house in Chelsea which was shared by Swinburne and Rossetti. Swinburne would throw himself on to the floor and scream in a horizontal position and Rossetti would remain stiffly upright, with his arms raised above his head, and scream in a vertical position. The rhythm of the two screamers was, apparently, flawlessly interwoven, the noise like that of an express train.

Edith Sitwell, TAKEN CARE OF 1965

QUOTATION

Isaac Foot possesses an astonishing repertory of quotations and a political opponent is liable to find himself suddenly transfixed by a shaft borrowed from Shakespeare, Cromwell, Junius or Macaulay. There was, for example, the unfortunate minister in the first Labour government who somewhat haughtily sought to dispose of a Parliamentary question by a reference to "the law's delay". "And," said Mr Foot, completing the quotation, "the insolence of office." And when, on a later occasion, someone asked him about the desirability of taxing the Channel Islands he at once recalled a line from Tennyson's *Ulysses* – "It may be we shall touch the happy isles."

Observer, Profile 23 *Mar* 1947

RADIO

Father Andrew was the BBC's adviser on Roman Catholic affairs. A producer who was planning programmes on the subject wrote asking how he could ascertain the official Roman Catholic view of heaven and hell. The answering memorandum contained just one word, "Die".

Paul Bussard, THE NEW CATHOLIC TREASURY OF WIT AND HUMOUR 1968

At a concert the BBC was broadcasting, Sir Thomas was to play the *Four Legends* of Sibelius. Only three, however, were at the moment available and the BBC insisted on a seven-minute filler. Beecham declared that this would unbalance the programme, but at last, to calm everyone, said "Leave it to me."

Just before playing the *Legends* he turned to the audience and started to explain the difficulty he was in of choosing an appropriate filler for "that august body, the BBC" fanatical about rigid timing. By the time he had cited several pieces he might have played and explained why each was unsuitable, and had chivvied the BBC a bit, it only remained to say, "Oh dear, I've been talking for seven minutes so there won't be any need for the piece, will there?"

Harold Atkins and Archie Newman, BEECHAM STORIES 1978

I'll never forget my first broadcast in 1924. I was playing the part of a sailor who had to sing a song while I pretended to row a boat. Suddenly the effects chap [Brian Michie] appeared between me and the mike with a basin of water and a spoon. He proceeded to splash the water about – the idea, as I discovered later, was to represent the sound of oars – and in no time had my score drenched. I sometimes wonder how I managed to finish the song.

Bruce Belfrage, Radio Times 11 *Jun* 1948

When E.M. Forster met a BBC executive who had just rejected a friend's script on the ground that it didn't give a general picture of China, Forster was quick to attack on the writer's behalf. "Give me a general picture of England," he asked the Head of the Third Programme.

Sylvia Clayton, Daily Telegraph 28 *Jun* 1985

In September 1924 I started my job with the BBC in Belfast. The technical aspect of radio still completely dominated the imagination, not only of the public, but of the BBC.

The head engineer had installed a fabulously scientific system of ventilation. A series of gold levers could be pulled, and gold arrows pointed to signs on gold dials, which purported to announce the temperature. This room was supposed to be filled with an especially invigorating ozone, which blew in through a golden grill. In fact, the temperature never changed. The room was perpetually cold, but at the same time, stuffy.

Some of us were silly enough to think there was also a very queer smell. The engineers laughed this idea to scorn and pointed out that it was an aroma of ozone, and infinitely healthy. Yet things were better when, from behind the golden grill, the controller removed the carcases of two dead rats.

Tyrone Guthrie, A LIFE IN THE THEATRE 1959

One evening before the war, after my late brother Alvar had read the news, a friend asked, "What was that about the Navy wanting more fish and chips?" My brother looked up the bulletin and found that in a Parliamentary report a speaker had said, "What the Navy needs is not more ships, but more efficient ships."

Y.P. Liddell, letter to the Observer 11 *Nov* 1984

I think it was Lionel Marson who quoted a Minister in the House of Commons as stating that he had been "completely mizzled" by another member of the House. The word, of course, was "misled" but it looks like "mizzled" when you are working under pressure. On another occasion when he was reading a speech from the Commons, Lionel quoted Churchill as saying, "It would be an utter impissobolity." And Stuart Hibberd it was who introduced a concert, "We are now taking you over to the Bathroom at Pump."

Another time I was introducing an early morning talk by Miss Monica Dickson on shopping and cooking. "Here," I said, "is Miss Monica Dickson to give you another talk on Cocking and Snooping – I beg your pardon – on Shocking and Cooping – er – I'm so sorry – Miss Monica Dickson."

Leslie Mitchell, LESLIE MITCHELL REPORTING 1981

I take part in the Brains Trust. Gilbert Harding is the Question Master, and the team consists in Violet Bonham Carter, Beverley Baxter, Julian Huxley and Frank O'Connor. The questions are, "Is knowledge better than wisdom?" "Should girls do national service as well as boys?" "Is the English sense of humour cynical?" "What existing legislation should be repealed?" (I say that covering sexual offences) "Is the telephone a boon or a bane?" "Is taste hereditary?" "Do beer and beef form national character?" "What event in history would you most have liked to witness?" They are silly about this. Of course we should have wanted to see the Crucifixion, but they say silly things like the first night of *Tristan and Isolde*.

Harold Nicolson, DIARY 24 *May* 1949

The broadcast commentary on King George VI's Coronation Ball was a hoax. As it was to be attended by crowned heads galore it was to be relayed by the Empire, and many foreign countries, including the United States.

When I got to the Albert Hall, five minutes before the broadcast which was due at 10.30 the huge ballroom was empty except for Bert Ambrose and his band and a few bored-looking waiters.

"What's happened?" I gasped to Tommy Woodrooffe.

"There's a State Banquet at the Palace. None of the bigwigs will be here until midnight."

But there *had* to be a broadcast. I tackled Ambrose.

"Bert, play as loud as you can, and get any of the boys who aren't actually blowing something to laugh."

Then I raced round the hall assembling as many of the waiters and attendants as possible.

"When I give the signal dance round as close to the microphone as you can, make as much noise with your feet as you can, and keep up a buzz of conversation."

Tommy Woodrooffe, now convulsed with laughter, signalled to me, the band launched into a fox-trot and while the waiters danced and chattered I launched into a frenzied description of all the gracious Princesses, bejewelled rajahs and noblemen who were thronging the mighty Ballroom on this night of nights.

So the world attended the Coronation Ball of 1937. Listeners told me afterwards. "It sounded marvellous. You made us feel as if we were really there."

Eric Maschwitz, News Chronicle 14 *Jan* 1940

I was interviewing a farmer. Halfway through I fired a question at him from the script which said "Now what can you tell me about sheep dipping?" Much to my horror he replied, "We 'aven't got there yet and tha's turned over two pages." I tried to laugh this off and said, "Now about this sheep dipping –" He replied, "Never mind about sheep dipping. I tell thee tha's turned over two pages."

The producer faded the progamme out and slowly faded it back again, hoping we should have righted the thing in the interval, but sure enough as he faded the programme in all he could hear was, "I'm telling thee tha's turned over two pages." What a nightmare – I *had* turned over two pages.

Wilfred Pickles, Radio Times 4 *Jun* 1948

After David Sarnoff, the overlord of the National Broadcasting Company, had completed a speech in which he had deified practically all of the inventors of radio, Clarence Buddington Kelland arose and remarked, "I regret that Mr Sarnoff has failed to mention the greatest genius of them all – the guy who invented the button that turns the damn thing off.

Frank Crowninshield, Vogue 15 *Mar* 1942

Raymond Gram Swing carries both a stopwatch and a wristwatch, and ordinarily, as soon as he arrives at the studio, he checks them with the studio clock, then places them on the table before which he sits as he broadcasts. "If one stops," he explains, "the other will still be going." Beside them he places two cups filled with water. "If one tips over," he says, "I still have the other." An engineer enters with what Swing calls his "cough-box" and Swing will say, "If I cough this will take care of it." No other commentator has a cough-box. Swing worried so much over possible bronchial interruptions to his broadcasts that radio engineers made this one especially for him. It is a wooden box and rests at his right hand on the table. If his throat tickles while he is broadcasting he presses a button on its top which cuts him off the air for just the instant he is coughing.

Richard O. Boyer, New Yorker 1942

On one of the first occasions when I went "street-interviewing" I stopped a very pleasant-looking couple who were walking arm in arm along the street. "Your name, Sir?" I enquired of the gentleman. He gave it and we talked for a minute. Then I made my fatal mistake. I turned to the lady at his side with the query, "Now, would your wife kindly say a few words?" The gentleman immediately seized me by the arm and, completely oblivious of the live microphone in my hand, whispered hurriedly, "Ssh, old boy! She's not my wife. Just a friend as a matter of fact. If my wife got to hear about this there'd be the deuce to pay."

Useless to warn him that at that moment his wife might be listening in.

There was only one thing to say – "Back to the studio."

Wynford Vaughan Thomas, Radio Times 6 *Aug* 1948

One night during our annual chase of the nightingale we felt certain of success. We were just about to invite listeners to join us in the depths of a Sussex wood when we heard strange whispers coming from one of the microphone points. We turned it up full strength and were shaken to the core. Under the tree from which our microphone hung a young couple had just sat down. In impassioned words never intended for the public ear, a love-lorn gentleman was pleading his case to his lady friend. Our engineer cut out at once and rushed down to the wood to explain to the couple. The gentleman was naturally indignant. "It comes to something when a man can't propose to his girl in a lonely wood without being overheard by the BBC!" But what if we had broadcast him, not on rehearsal, but on actual transmission?

Wynford Vaughan Thomas, Radio Times 5 *Mar* 1948

Not every BBC engineer gets the enthusiastic co-operation which we were accorded when one of our technicians went along to a big hall to discuss microphone positions with the manager. "Put your microphones where you like, old boy," beamed the manager. "Pull down that partition? Certainly. Build you a special stand? Nothing easier. Move the seating? But of course." At the end of the morning the hall was pretty well remodelled to suit the BBC. Our engineer was moved to shake the manager fervently by the hand as he left. "Never have I had such co-operation. How can I thank you?" "That's all right, old boy," said the manager. "This is my last day here. I've just been fired!"

Ibid.

It was in January 1930, the first world broadcast, when King George V, from the House of Commons, welcomed the delegates of the five great naval powers. Harold Vivian, the control operator, saw that a wire, transmitting the King's voice to early risers in America, had broken. With great presence of mind he picked up the severed strands and by holding them in his hands enabled the King's voice to pass through his body to millions of trans-Atlantic listeners.

Cesar Saerchinger, VOICE OF EUROPE 1938

When the US State Department appointed Alexander Kirk as Minister to Saudi Arabia and he was making his first visit last year from Cairo, an engineer from Standard Oil marked out landing lanes on the desert, not far from Riad, and sat down beside a field radio to guide the pilot in.

A crowd of Bedouin gathered, one of whom asked what the little box was saying. That in about an hour and a half a large bird would descend from the sky, carrying men, was the reply. When the plane appeared the engineer expected the Bedouin to regard radio and aeroplane as a sort of double miracle. Instead the Bedouin remarked critically that the plane was ten minutes early.

Noel F. Busch, Life magazine 31 *May* 1943

In the early days of radio the Head of Light Entertainment, or his equivalent, was holding auditions to attract talent from the music halls. He sat in his control box listening intently as one performer after another gave of his best. Then, after the announcement of the umpteenth name, there was a long silence, broken only by a faint rustling sound. Thinking something had gone wrong on the technical side the producer peered through the sound-proof window into the studio and saw his latest hopeful for top of the bill – juggling.

John Le Mesurier, A JOBBING ACTOR 1984

Toledo, Ohio. We have luncheon with a Women's Club. I sit next to a woman in purple silk. The inauguration of President Roosevelt was proceeding in Washington and a huge voice was braying out from the radio. "*And now,*" yelled the voice, "*the historic moment is about to arrive. I can see the President elect –*" "It is such a pity," twitters Mrs Scinahan beside me, "that you are only staying such a short time in Toledo, Mr Nicolson. I would wish to have you see our museum here. We have a peristyle of the purest white marble. A thing of utter simplicity but the purest beauty."

I strive to catch the historic words of Roosevelt.

"You see, Mr Nicolson," whispered Mrs Scinahan, "our peristyle is a dream in stone. I mean that literally. The architect Mr J.V. Kinhoff dreamt of that very peristyle and one day –"

"Mrs Scinahan," I say firmly, "do you realise that your new President has just proclaimed that he will, if need be, institute a dictatorship?"

"My," she said, "now isn't that interesting? Not that I care for the radio, Mr Nicolson. We have one at home of course, above the bathing pool. It sounds so much better out of doors."

Harold Nicolson, DIARY 4 *Mar* 1933

A dramatist employed to write stories from the Bible in radio form was astounded, at the end of the broadcast, to hear the announcer say, "Will Cain kill Abel? Tune in the same time tomorrow and find out."

Albert R. Perkins, Vogue 1943

RAILWAY

I was nearly mobbed by autograph hunters and other fans at Charing Cross station while waiting for a train. I did not want to leave the station and miss the train, nor could I seek refuge in a refreshment room. But the left luggage office was just behind me and close to the platform from which I was to start. I turned to the man in charge and demanded the right to book myself as a parcel. I paid my twopence and the man took me over the counter and I was saved. This method of retreat I confidently recommend to other picture stars in railway stations.

George Arliss, AUTOBIOGRAPHY 1940

In Brendan Behan's Dublin flat I saw his latest piece of prose. It was a letter to British Railways. He had claimed a refund on a ticket to Fishguard. But an official signing himself "for N.H. Briant" had written, "Before giving consideration to your claim for a refund I should be glad if you would be good enough to let me know the circumstances which prevented you from using it."

In Behan's typewriter I saw this reply, "Dear for N.H. Briant, I don't know that it matters, but we missed the train from Paddington and had to travel from Euston to Liverpool. If you do want to give me back my twelve quid, do so. If you need it, keep it. I am not depending on it. God help the poor traveller that was. I have more to do than be answering your silly letters. Send the money or don't. My time is valuable. I am usually paid more than twelve nicker for writing as much as this for Brendan Behan, BRENDAN BEHAN".

Robert Pitman, Sunday Express 12 *Oct* 1958

To identify himself with the masses of the poor, Gandhi would insist on travelling third class on his many journeys across India. The filthy third-class carriages with wooden seats and no cooling ventilation bulged with excess loads. Ragged people sat on top of each other, half out of the windows and perched on the foot-boards.

The British raj was rightly terrified of Gandhi travelling under such conditions; a special train was always laid on. It would have three third-class compartments, spotlessly clean. In the middle one sat Gandhi and his immediate disciples. In the compartments on either side the remainder of his retinue was housed. The wooden seats were a trifle uncomfortable, but nothing else was.

After the journey Gandhi would say, "Now find out how much the third-class fare is from Calcutta to Madras and send it to the Government. We must not be beholden to the British in any way." So, in return for the special train costing some £500 the railway authorities would receive a few rupees – the exact third-class fare for a normal train.

Ved Mehta, MAHATMA GANDHI AND HIS APOSTLES 1977

George Moore, when he and I were crossing the railway viaduct at Donabate, was reminded by the sunset of Nathaniel Hone, the landscape painter who lived nearby. He said, "I would give ten pounds to see how the sunset will imitate Hone." I tried to save him five pounds by pulling the communication cord, because the fine is only five pounds if you pull it wantonly. I knew that you could never explain to a railway guard that art is more important than an accident. He must have had artistic sympathies, though, because he "forgot" the incident for ten shillings.

Oliver St John Gogarty, IT ISN'T THIS TIME OF YEAR AT ALL 1954

An 18-year-old girl was found in a sailor's kit-bag at Herne Bay railway station yesterday. At Ramsgate she and the sailor were seen talking after the sailor had taken a ticket for Margate. As the girl was neither seen to enter the train nor leave the station railway officials telephoned the police at Herne Bay, who entered the carriage in which the sailor was seated and made him unlock the kitbag. The girl stepped out. Both stated at first that they had not enough money to pay the girl's fare, but later produced enough money to pay for a ticket to London and were allowed to proceed.

The Times 10 *Jan* 1945

The 18.22 and 18.36 trains from London's Liverpool Street to Bishops Stortford leave from almost adjacent platforms joined by a narrow bridge. At 18.40 one evening, when neither train had left, the guard on each assured his passengers that the other would be leaving first. The effect was electrifying. Both trains emptied and their occupants met in an inextricable jam on the bridge – from where they had an excellent view of both trains leaving together.

Oliver Weaver, letter to the Times 1981

The parcels traffic shipped from Windermere included regular consignments of mass-produced coffins. "They were made by Nicholson's, down at Bowness," Mr Mayor recalled, "and they were brought to the guard's van neatly stacked on platform barrows. I was on the footplate one day when a woman walked past and saw a pile parked beside the engine. She looked at them and turned such a funny colour I thought she was going to faint. 'Don't worry, love,' I called, 'they're only some instruments belonging to the Hallé Orchestra.' Next thing I heard, she was in the booking office pestering some poor clerk for a ticket to the concert."

Alexander Frater, Observer magazine, Stopping Train: Britain 28 *Feb* 1983

REBUKE

In the early days of the Labour Government Harold Laski wrote to Attlee suggesting that he should give way to Morrison. Rowan, Attlee's private secretary feeling unable to propose the usual draft reply himself, showed the letter to Attlee, who scribbled forthwith, "Thank you for your letter, the contents of which I have noted." A second letter arrived a week or two later, and was both lengthy and learned. To this Attlee replied with the oft-quoted words, "A period of silence from you would now be welcome."

Douglas Jay, CHANGE AND FORTUNE 1980

A.V. Alexander, at lunch today, lectured me on where I had gone wrong in my criticism of Esther McCracken's *Living Room.* When he had finished I said, "Would the First Lord like to hear my views on naval strategy?" Am bound to say he took it well.

James Agate, Ego 6 28 *Jul* 1943

An acquaintance who bored her once asked Margot Asquith to call her by her Christian name. "I couldn't," replied Margot. A moment later feeling she had perhaps been unnecessarily unresponsive, she continued, "Oh, all right then, Ermyntrude, or whatever your name is." The lady's name was not Ermyntrude.

Lord David Cecil, Observer, Staying With Margot 20 *Dec* 1981

A well-known American critic complained that Sir Thomas Beechan had wasted his gifts and time on second-rate stuff. Needless to say, there was a frightful row. He summoned a press conference and described the critic, to his face, as "a musical gunman from Chicago".

Lord Boothby, MY YESTERDAY, YOUR TOMORROW 1962

David Blunkett's handicap, blindness, has helped create a character both democratic and dictatorial, suffering no fools, yet quickly kind, and witty. His guide dog, Ted, is often used as an object for deflationary jokes, such as greeting the end of a long-winded committee bore's speech with the remark, "I'm afraid Ted's gone to sleep."

Colin Hughes, The Times 5 *Apr* 1984

Four years ago – in the middle of the Labour Party's leadership election – the *Sunday Times* asked the candidates in that election to give their opinion of past leaders. I described Jim Callaghan in language which was meant to keep just on the respectable side of idolatry. "Three quarters a great Prime Minister – very brave, very tough, very clever; but not quite ideological enough for my taste." The next day I received a handwritten note from the great man himself. Could I, it asked, help him to solve a constitutional dilemma? He had intended to support my candidature, but could he cast three-quarters of a vote? If not, he might have to reconsider his position.

Roy Hattersley, The Independent, reviewing James Callaghan, TIME AND CHANCE 13 *Apr* 1987

When I first met Mrs Patrick Campbell we were both guests at a country house where there was an immense marble swimming pool. On the first evening a very pretty girl appeared in a costume that left nothing to the imagination. Even in this sophisticated society people felt somewhat embarrassed.

Mrs Patrick Campbell took one look at her. Her deep voice rang out over the pool. "I hardly think you would appear like that before the man you loved."

It was an appalling, shattering remark. It seemed to freeze the waters. It was the remark of a queen, rebuking an errant subject. As such, there was no reply to it.

Beverley Nichols, Daily Sketch 17 *Apr* 1940

Clemenceau, visiting India in 1921, was shown the splendid stables of a native prince and asked whether the purdah system was observed among horses, too, and if the mares had to veil their faces when they went outdoors.

"No," replied the official who was showing him round.

"Then," said the Tiger, "in India mares are better treated than women."

Children's Newspaper 14 *Dec* 1929

Lord Curzon once summoned me and reprimanded me in true Curzonian fashion.

"I wanted to speak to you yesterday evening about Russia, but I need hardly say, you and your whole department had gone. May I enquire why?" "We did not leave until a quarter to eight, sir," I replied. "That is no explanation," said the Marquess. "I never saw such an office as this. You play golf all the morning. You think it necessary to have luncheon at one – whoever heard of anyone having lunch at one? And then in the evening you hurry away for some reason which I totally fail to fathom. Here I am, working sixteen hours a day – and you appear to have no consideration for me whatever."

J.D. Gregory, ON THE EDGE OF DIPLOMACY 1929

Four years at Kings, where he read history and economics, left Tam

Dalyell with a touching faith in academic wisdom. Not long ago a reporter entered the press gallery at the Commons to witness Dalyell, pale as a candle, shouting at an astonished William Waldegrave, a junior minister and a fellow of All Souls.

"What on earth did Tam say?" the reporter enquired. "He said," a colleague gravely reported, "'You are a disgrace to All Souls'."

Observer, Profile 26 *Aug* 1984

My mother, Mrs Dresel, had a liking for direct speech. She was once entertaining a young caller in her Blue Salon, in which she took quite a pride. "Would it incommode you if I smoked here?" he asked. "I really cannot tell you," she replied. "No one ever has."

Elizabeth, Lady Decies, TURN OF THE WORLD 1938

Gerald Du Maurier wrote Charles Laughton a glowing letter and sent him a present, a first edition of some book. Neither the letter nor the present were acknowledged. Later someone brought Laughton into the Garrick Club and introduced him to Du Maurier. "Ah yes," said Du Maurier, "Charles Laughton, a gentleman who can read but not write."

Michael Pertwee, NAME DROPPING

Father Hack, of Christ Church, Oxford, could be very sharp in rebuke and once stopped in the middle of a sermon and said to a woman who was fidgeting, "Either shut that handbag or leave the church."

Colin Stephenson, MERRILY ON HIGH 1965

A letter came to Victor Gollancz from Trinity College, Cambridge, in which the correspondent, having applauded his initiative, went on:

"It is because I strongly sympathise with your attitude that I think I ought to make what seems to me a serious criticism of your polemic. I shall, in what follows, be blunt in order to be clear. There are two ways of weakening and diluting an accusation. One is to couch it in half-hearted and ambiguous terms. This is not what you have done. But there is another way, which is to embellish a point which you have expressed forcefully by half a dozen subsidiary points which, even if they are not weak and dubious, draw the reader's attention from the main issue, and make the polemic ineffectual."

Victor's reply, in full:

"L. Wiltgenstein [sic] Esq, at Trinity College, Cambridge. Dear Sir, Thank you for your letter, which I am sure was well-intended. Yours truly, Victor Gollancz."

For the friend of Bertrand Russell, and the publisher of C.E.M. Joad to be so ignorant of the reclusive genius who had taken the trouble to write to him suggests a lack of intellectual awareness almost beyond belief.

Frederic Raphael, Sunday Times, reviewing Ruth Dudley Edwards, VICTOR GOLLANCZ 18 *Jan* 1987

With the German invasion of France imminent Peggy Guggenheim scurried round Paris buying up art on the cheap. The Parisians were delighted to sell everything and flee and Peggy stowed away in her packing cases works by Klee, Kandinsky, Miro, Brancusi, Dali, Magritte and others. Only Picasso refused to do business. When Peggy arrived at his studio with her shopping list he remarked laconically, "Lingerie is on the next floor."

Jacqueline Weld, PEGGY, THE WAYWARD GUGGENHEIM 1986

Much though I enjoy a good lunch with Enoch Powell I often feel I should go into training for it, lest a slip of grammar or sloppiness of thought should invite a withering attack. I recall one such when as we said farewell I asked him to remember me to his wife. He looked at me for some seconds and then said, "There is no need to remember you to Pam. She remembers you very well."

Patrick Cosgrave, The Times 14 *Jun* 1982

M. Roux, the distinguished surgeon, was a a man of remarkable character. A wealthy French lady had to have a delicate operation and the French surgeons, afraid to tackle it, recommended that Roux should be called in.

He came, the operation lasted two hours, and he was perspiring and exhausted by the complicated task. Before the patient came round the French doctors and surgeons said, "Now M. Roux, will you name your fee, as we have to get half." The distinguished surgeon, nettled and annoyed beyond words at this matter being raised at such a moment replied, "Well, gentlemen, my fee is twenty francs and a third-class ticket to and from Lausanne."

Sir Lionel Earle, TURN OVER THE PAGE 1934

Edith Sitwell had a letter from some silly woman saying, "Dear Dame Edith, As an admirer of your poems I am nevertheless greatly disturbed by a poem containing a line about the mating of tigers. I have a daughter of 19 – at that age when the brook runs into the river – and a son aged 10 who is very restless. I wish to entreat you, dear Dame Edith, when you write your poetry, to consider the disturbing effect that lines like those about the mating of tigers may have on the young." Edith wrote back, "Tell your dirty little brats to read King Lear."

Sir Stephen Spender, JOURNAL 18 *Dec* 1962

Igor Stravinsky came close to tears when his mother reproached him for not composing like Scriabin. "Now, now, Igor," said Mrs Stravinsky, "you haven't changed a bit. You were always contemptuous of your *betters.*"

George Antheil, BAD BOY OF MUSIC 1945

On the first occasion when I met H.G. Wells we neither of us liked each other very much, I think. I was anxious to play one of his characters on the stage, and asked him why he had not dramatised that one of his books. "I take no interest whatever in the stage," was his crushing reply.

Ernest Thesiger, PRACTICALLY TRUE 1927

RELAXATION

Kenneth Baker, the Education Secretary relaxes by blowing up an inflatable tulip. Yes, really. It seems he keeps this tulip in his office. It is green, with yellow flowers. Normally it flops quietly in a corner awaiting the moment when it is called into service. The last time his staff observed Mr Baker making use of his relaxation device was after a particularly stormy meeting about sex education. Once he was alone, Mr Baker was observed on his knees, blowing up the tulip; quite appropriately, given the topic under discussion, his astonished staff observed the tulip getting stiffer and stiffer.

Peter Hillmore, Observer 1 *Mar* 1987

Harold Macmillan was almost certainly the best-read British prime minister in living memory. He was addicted to Trollope and during the Suez crisis – so he confided in me – he had re-read the whole of

George Eliot. "It was the only thing that kept me from going barmy. I didn't mention this in my memoirs because I thought readers might have thought that a chancellor should be better employed."

Alistair Horne, Sunday Times 4 *Jan* 1987

RELIGION

Andrew Carnegie told a friend, "I have no religion to speak of. But on Sunday morning, when other people are going to church, I like to float about in my swimming pool while a Highlander in all his regalia plays sacred music on his pipes. And as I lie there in the water, thinking over my possessions, the conviction comes to me that if a commission were sent down from heaven to assess what I have I should be deprived of a great part of it."

Philip Morton, Sunday Express 2 *Oct* 1949

My grandfather, an ardent lay preacher, was concerned that he was speaking only to the converted. Then one day the Deacon rushed up to him after a service and announced, "Somebody has taken my new raincoat from the cloakroom." Grandfather raised his eyes heavenward and exclaimed with delight, "The Lord be praised. We're getting the sinners at last."

Mary Carter, Reader's Digest Nov 1977

Harold Macmillan used to tell with relish the story about Clementine Churchill reproaching Winston Churchill for non-churchgoing. "Ah, my dear Clemmy," replied Winston, "you are like a great pillar. You support the church from the inside. But I am a flying buttress. I support it from the outside."

Alistair Horne, Sunday Times 4 *Jan* 1987

A Welsh revivalist preacher swept to his conclusion by asking all the congregation who wished to go to heaven to raise their hands. They all did, except for Deacon Evans, sitting in the front row. "But, Mr Evans," the affronted shepherd said, "surely you want to go to heaven?" "Yes," said Deacon Evans. "But not by the excursion train."

Roy Jenkins, Observer 8 *Mar* 1987

When a preacher leaving Glamis Castle promised to send the Princess

Elizabeth, then a little girl of ten, a book, she thanked him but asked if it could be, "Not about God. I know everything about him."

Robert Lacey, MAJESTY 1977

During a survey expedition I visited the island of Tristan da Cunha. The islanders were delighted with the gifts brought by the expedition – except the Bibles. During the course of the years so many Bibles had been sent to the island that there was now an average of seven copies per inhabitant.

Francis K. Pearse, TO THE ENDS OF THE EARTH 1936

REMEDY

When I was practising in New York I was consulted by a woman whose son had been bitten on the arm by a dog. I untied the bandages and found that over each bite, held in place by adhesive tape, was a mass of dog's hair.

"Who put this dog's hair on these bites?" I asked.

"I did," said the mother. "You know the old proverb 'the hair of the dog that bit you will cure you' – but later I felt that I had better bring the child to see you."

The mother was a college graduate and a former school-teacher!

Dr William E.Aughinbaugh, I SWEAR BY APOLLO 1939

Andrew Carnegie's daughter was a delicate child and every day milk was brought specially from London for her, despite the fact that there was a dairy on the estate where the purest milk was produced.

One day the milk did not arrive from the South and, being afraid to tell her mistress, one of the servants gave the child milk from the dairy farm. Immediately there was a wonderful improvement in the child's condition, and from that time her health steadily advanced.

Sunday Referee 24 *Nov* 1936

My father was only sent to Harrow because it was quaintly thought at that time that he suffered from lung trouble and that Harrow-on-the-Hill would be better for him than Eton in fog. Lack of lung power has never been subsequently detected in my father, but perhaps it was indeed the climate of Harrow that rid him of this complaint.

Randolph Churchill, TWENTY-ONE 1964

I was put to bed at King's House [Kingston, Jamaica] with a fever that rapidly turned to malarial gastritis. The distressing feature connected with this complaint is that it is impossible to retain any nourishment whatever. The doctor tried half the drugs in the pharmacopoeia on me. The fever laughed at them all. He urged me to cancel my passage to England, but somebody told me that as soon as I felt the motion of a ship under me the persistent sickness would stop. I insisted on being carried down to the mail steamer and was put to bed. As long as we lay alongside the jetty in the smooth water of the harbour the distressing symptoms persisted at regular intervals, but no sooner had the ship cleared Port Royal and begun to lift to the very heavy seas outside than the sickness stopped as if by magic.

As the violent motion continued I was able to take as much food as I wanted with impunity, and the next day, the heavy seas tossing the *Port Kingston* about like a cork, I was up and about, perfectly well and able to eat "like a cormorant". I noticed, however, that the motion of the ship seemed to produce on most of the passengers an exactly opposite effect to what it did on myself.

Lord Frederic Hamilton, HERE, THERE AND EVERYWHERE 1921

While on a visit to Africa I had such a bad attack of malaria that I thought I was going to die. Fortunately some native women saved me by Spartan efforts. First they carried me out and dipped me in the icy waters of a creek nearby, then, wrapping me in blankets, laid me on a bed of well-heated stones. The contrast between the great cold of the water and the great heat of the stones set me into a perspiration as if I were in a Turkish bath, and although next day I was as weak as a bit of chewed string, I found that I was completely cured of the fever.

Francis K.Pearse, TO THE ENDS OF THE EARTH 1936

Albert Schweitzer found the long nights of medical study terribly exhausting. He asked his housekeeper to leave a basin of cold water in his room. She thought he applied this to his forehead. Months later she learned that he plunged his feet into the water and soaked them there when he felt sleepy.

George Marshall and David Poling, SCHWEITZER, A BIOGRAPHY 1971

Athene Seyler was appearing with me in the film *Doctor at Large*. She was no longer young and I took it upon myself to look after her. One day she called me over to where she was sitting.

"Donald dear, I don't want you to panic but I feel you should call a doctor. I think I've had a stroke. I was perfectly all right a few minutes ago, but now I can't move my neck."

Before going in search of help I thought I should make her comfortable by putting a cushion behind her head and in doing so discovered that she had caught her hairnet in the clasp of her necklace. I removed it.

"Oh Donald – how did you do that? I'm well again," she cried.

Donald Sinden, A TOUCH OF THE MEMOIRS 1982

RESEARCH

One day an incident occurred by which the greatness of Sir Alexander Fleming's mind was revealed. He was investigating the microbes of a cold from which he was suffering when a tear-drop happened to fall upon a culture plate. Next morning there was a clear space where the tear had dropped.

Instantly he made the right deduction. His prejudices fled with the winds. What all his previous experiments had seemed to prove to be impossible lay on the bench before his eyes – an antiseptic lethal to microbes, harmless to tissues.

When, years later, he saw a similar clear space around a contaminating mould he knew its import. His goal had been realised. Penicillin had been discovered.

Prof. C.A. Pannett, funeral address, St Pauls 18 *Mar* 1955

RETIREMENT

At the age of 23 I was a millionaire and retired. Two years later I came out of retirement. A man in his twenties who has known what it is to work can drink only so much champagne and paint the town red only so many times before he wakes up to realise that he is wasting time and energy on meaningless things.

J. Paul Getty, MY LIFE AND FORTUNES 1964

About 10 years ago in his own college, Balliol, Harold Macmillan, then eighty-two years old, was accosted by two unmannerly young dons who suggested that the time had come for him to retire. "Certainly," he said. "I should be only too glad to make way for an older man."

Kenneth Rose, Sunday Telegraph 22 *Jun* 1986

One of the original members of Fred Karno's company tells the story of his retirement. One night in Manchester, after a performance, the troupe complained that Karno's timing was off and that he had ruined the laughs. Karno, who had then accumulated £50,000 from his five shows said, "Well boys, if that's the way you feel, I'll quit." Then, taking off his wig, he dropped it on the dressing table, and grinned. "You can accept my resignation."

Charles Chaplin, MY AUTOBIOGRAPHY 1964

ROMANCE

Sir John and Lady Martin-Harvey took James Agate on a convalescent drive to Frinton, he in the back of the car with Lady Martin-Harvey while Sir John sat next to the driver. A desolate Essex village came into view, and the gentle knight said, "My dear Agate, do you mind sitting in the front? We are about to pass through the village where I proposed to my dear wife, and I should like to hold her hand."

James Harding, AGATE, A BIOGRAPHY 1986

ROUTINE

Monty's habits in the desert and thereafter were simple and regular. He would be called by his soldier servant, Corporal English, at 6.30 every morning with a cup of tea and would not come out of his caravan until 8, to walk across to the mess tent for breakfast. You could set your watch by his regular visit to the WC. He would retire to bed at 9.30 in the evening, no matter who was visiting headquarters. Even when George VI came he would say, "If you will excuse me, sir, we have a battle to win and I must go to bed."

J.R. Henderson, MONTGOMERY AT CLOSE QUARTERS 1985

ROYALTY

In all Princess Anne was in Eastbourne for 66 minutes. To make sure the Princess would be able to negotiate the narrow companionways, steep ladders and hatchways in a tight skirt, Lieutenant-Commander Stephen Emberton went through a special rehearsal – in drag.

Western Morning News

After a charity show at Alexandra Palace the Duke of Kent (then Prince George) walked on to the stage unannounced. Only Gracie Fields was completely unembarrased. Cool and smiling, she walked across the stage towards the Prince.

"Ee, I can see it now," she said. "Ee, I'd never 'ave believed it." She shook his hand.

"Lots of people 'ave told me," she said to no one in particular, "that 'e's just like our Tom."

Bert Aza, GRACIE FIELDS

Villa Mauresque, Cap Ferrat. I came down to the villa, had a bath, put on my best clothes. Because the late King of England was coming to dinner. Willie Maugham had prepared us carefully. He said the Duke gets cross if the Duchess is not treated with respect. With infinite tact he told a story of how recently some old friend of the Duchess had opened the conversation at luncheon by saying, "How lovely Wallis is looking, Sir." "Who?" snapped the Duke. In all innocence the poor old trout repeated, "I said, Sir, how lovely Wallis was looking." He turned his back on her and never spoke to her again throughout the meal. "Oh dear," said Sibyl Colefax "what then am I to call her?" "D-D-Duchess," said Willie. "I shan't," said Sibyl.

Harold Nicolson, letter to Vita Sackville-West 5 *Aug* 1938

I once accompanied Queen Mary, Princess Mary and her future husband, Lord Lascelles, as he then was, to a London art gallery. An American tourist was very excited at being in the same room as the Queen. Suddenly he took out a notebook and pen, and scribbled these words: "This certifies that Silas Wertheimer, Mrs Dilmot Wertheimer, and Junior have been in the – Art Galleries with the Queen of England, the Princess Mary and the Viscount Lascelles."

I saw no harm in signing it for him, and he wrote *Royal Detective* beneath my name.

Herbert Fitch, MEMOIRS OF A ROYAL DETECTIVE 1936

At a reception in Vancouver during the visit of the royal family to celebrate British Columbia's centenary, those to be presented were given a briefing on how to address the Queen, Prince Philip and Princess

Anne. When the time came for one of the ladies to be presented she executed a perfect curtsey, murmured something and then left. The royal guests looked at each other and burst out laughing. It turned out that she had quite rightly said, "Your Majesty" to the Queen and "Your Royal Highness" to Princess Anne. But when she got to Prince Philip she burst out, "You're Gorgeous."

Gwen Williams, Reader's Digest Jan 1974

RUDENESS

I went with Bill Lipscombe to the Ivy, and held the door open for a little, severe-looking man carefully dressed in a new grey suit who followed me in – Somerset Maugham. He walked in without a word of thanks, as if it was my privilege to pay attention to him. So I let the door go and said "Thank you" loudly to myself. I don't look like a commissionaire. I look like a *maître d'hôtel.*

Reginald Pound, THEIR MOODS AND MINE 1937

During the war [World War I] I was Director of Women's Service and had to go round speaking at meetings. At one town hall the chair was taken by a well-known politician. This important gentleman did not trouble to say how do you do to me, and had spoken for half an hour when someone called out, "We came to hear Mrs Peel," at which there was a little burst of clapping. My chairman glared angrily, looked at the agenda and remarked, "I see that Mrs – er-er – Peel is going to speak to you. I don't know who she is or why she is here. Perhaps she will tell you." He then sat down, crossed his legs, and appeared to go to sleep.

Mrs C.S. Peel, LIFE'S ENCHANTED CUP 1933

RUMOUR

Harley Granville-Barker was believed by many to be the natural son of Bernard Shaw though St John Ervine suggested, "The strongest refutal of it was GBS's refusal to boast about it, as he certainly would have done had it been true." On the other hand Shaw himself did not deny it, merely saying that "most people reject the hypothesis on the ground that I am physically incapable of parentage."

Eric Salmon, GRANVILLE-BARKER: A SECRET LIFE 1983

The dear *Daily Express*, which shall be nameless, said I'd been sauntering down the rue Royale in naval uniform. I heard Churchill had been annoyed by the report so I got a seat on the Cabinet plane to London and went to see him. I was furious that he'd believed it without checking.

I told him, "Next time you read that I'm your admiral and you're my cabin boy, don't believe it." He was perfectly livid. I later played six-pack bezique with him and knocked the living daylights out of him. It ended up with him owing me something enormous, like 17s 6d. "England can take it," he said.

Noel Coward, quoted Hunter Davies, Sunday Times 16 *Nov* 1969

In 1972 it was calculated by the Paris publication *France Dimanche* after analysis of the cuttings file on the British royal family that there had been published in France during the previous fourteen years sixty-three reports of Elizabeth II's abdication, seventy-seven reports of her divorce from Prince Philip, 115 reports of royal quarrels with Lord Snowdon, seventeen reports of rudeness to gossip-column monarchs like Princess Grace of Monaco and ninety-two reports of Elizabeth II being pregnant. Two of these last, however, did subsequently prove to be correct. *France Dimanche* figures in Queen Elizabeth's light reading and she has several times expressed genuine admiration of its writers' powers of imagination.

Robert Lacey, MAJESTY 1977

War hysteria quickly asserted itself in 1914. By September the story of the Russian armies in England had begun and I find Sacheverell, who wrote regularly to me from Renishaw every day, and who was unusually wise and cautious for his sixteen years, announcing the great news. "They saw the Russians pass through the station last night," he wrote, "and Miss Vasalt telephoned to Mother this afternoon and said trains in great number had passed through Grantham Station all day with the blinds down. So there must, I think, be some truth in it, don't you?"

Osbert Sitwell, GREAT MORNING 1951

A four-word Central News flash last Thursday sent reporters, camera men, newsreel crews hot-foot to Southend, Essex. "Quins born Southend today," said the message.

The news originated in a telegram, sent by Nurse Pirie, proprietor of a Southend nursing home, to her sister in London. "Betty had quins this morning," it stated simply. "Four boys, one girl. All doing well."

Somewhere between Southend and Barking, where Nurse Pirie's sister lives, there had been a leak. Central News got in touch with their Southend correspondent who telephoned the nursing home and checked the story.

London also telephoned and a girl in the nursing home confirmed the fact that quins had been born there. She also gave the times at which the five had been born. Asked for the parents' names she said she was sorry, but she could give no further information.

When the combined strength of Fleet Street and Wardour Street arrived in Southend, however, the awful truth was revealed. Quins, certainly – but Betty was an Alsatian.

World's Press News 23 *Apr* 1936

RUSSIAN REVOLUTION

To my paper, the *New York World*, I had sent a lengthy cable on The Red Terror, using the phrase for the first time. Within a few hours of it being printed the phrase "Red Terror in Russia" was being cabled everywhere. This fact, and the name of the man who had cabled the news out of Russia, was also cabled back to Russia, but it had not occurred to me it would get back so quickly.

Unsuspectingly, in Moscow, I was being bumped along in an old *ishvaskik* when near the picturesque gate to the old Tartar city I stopped the *ishvaskik* to get down and speak to a Russian acquaintance who was at the Allied secret service. At that moment a covered black van with only one small barred window was passing and beside it was riding a soldier with a stern Mongolian face. In his hand, hanging down, he was holding a large-sized automatic.

"If you don't want to have a ride in that," the secret agent said to me, "get out of Moscow. The Bolsheviks are looking for you."

I speedily left for Finland.

Arno Dosch-Fleurot, THROUGH WAR TO REVOLUTION 1931

At Kiev the carrying out of tortures was entrusted mainly to a young Bolshevik Jewish girl known as Rosa. She would cause a captured soldier to be tied to nails driven into a wall, and would then sit a few feet away from him with a revolver in her hand. She would treat him to a little talk about the proletariat, punctuating her remarks every ten minutes by shooting at and smashing his main joints one after the other.

John Ernest Hodgson, WITH DENIKIN'S ARMIES 1932

During the war I was Vice-Consul at Baku. The Tsar made a tour of the Caucasus front and the wives of foreign consuls were invited to meet him. When my wife returned I placed her right-hand glove in an envelope on which I light-heartedly wrote, "The glove that shook the Emperor by the hand."

Later, after my belongings had been "nationalised" the Bolsheviks arranged a little exhibition of confiscated horrors to impress the workers to the detriment of the bourgeoisie; among other exhibits was the glove; under my inscription was written in red ink, "The glove that was clasped by the hand of the slayer of our comrades. A treasure of the British Vice-Consul."

Ronald MacDonald, AND NOTHING LONG 1938

Only three weeks had passed since the beginning of the revolution but it seemed like years. Every day the Emperor, in exile, came into the garden with the children and, under the supervision of many guards, cut the ice and cleared the snow. The place for this performance was usually chosen near the fence of the park, and the inhabitants of Tsarskoie-Selo, especially those of the lower classes, gathered on the other side to stare and jeer. Remarks, always rude and sometimes obscene, flew about, while the Emperor continued his modest work, very calmly, as though he heard nothing.

The Grand Duchess Marie, THINGS I REMEMBER 1931

Life was a day-to-day hazard and I decided to conceal what valuable possessions I could. I had, for instance, a diadem in an old setting consisting of diamond rays strung on wire. I bought a large bottle of office ink and emptied it out, then, having unstrung the rays, I dropped them to the bottom of the bottle and poured paraffin over them. The last step was to pour back the ink. Since a large label surrounded the bottle it was all but impossible to make out its contents. It stood for months on my desk in full sight of everybody.

Other things we fastened in home-made paperweights; still others in empty cocoa tins; dipped afterwards in wax and provided with a wick they appeared to be the ends of church candles. We adorned them before ikons to divert the attention of the servants.

Ibid.

Chaliapin's fortune, more than £1,000,000, was lost in the Russian Revolution. For one of his concerts in Russia he was paid – six months afterwards – by 10lbs of flour, one ham, 51lbs of sugar and a selection of weird potatoes. But even the revolution and the changing of the economic order did not end the fascination his voice held over the people. He was made the Artist of the People by the Bolsheviks. He was paid in food.

Sydney Morrell, Sunday Express 5 *May* 1935

SALVATION

"Are you lost, or eternally saved?" This was on a sandwich board being carried in Regent Street by a young man. I frowned at it because it isn't really right to ask such intimate questions in public. The young man smiled. "It's all right," he said, "it ain't meant for you."

J.R. Ackerley, Diary 11 *Oct* 1950

SANITATION

At his famous boat-yard at Cowes, Isle of Wight, Uffa Fox installed an open-plan, two-seater lavatory in the cellar, being of the opinion that the art of conversation was being lost through the selfish act of one man shutting himself up in the smallest room.

June Dixon, UFFA FOX 1978

In Spain, Orson Welles was preparing a film from the Shakespeare King Henry IV histories. The castle of Cardona stands high on a hill near Andorra. It was built a very, very long time ago before the niceties of sanitation were resolved. Certain basic problems present themselves when filming goes on from sun-up to dusk. It was not discussed, but tacitly understood that when nature trumpeted the crew had claim to the disused dungeons and the extras to the thorn patch below the crumbling wall.

Actors more discreetly found their own comfort stations among the still flowering gorse and quietly removed themselves. It was always a jolly sight to see Sir John Gielgud, robed as the king in scarlet velvet, disappearing tactfully through a gap in the hedge, his crown glittering in the sun. Once he returned in dismay. "I found four nuns squatting there."

Keith Baxter, The Times 2 *Aug* 1980

The *Surrey-Hants Star* newspaper has a story about a clean-up campaign on Surrey Heath, headlined, "Dog Dirt Menace. Council Steps In".

Sunday Telegraph 23 *Mar* 1986

SARCASM

During the making of a film Sam Goldwyn had a habit of phoning his associates whenever an idea came to him, regardless of the hour. Richard Nash, who was writing the screenplay for *Porgy and Bess*, was the unfortunate recipient of such a call at three o'clock in the morning. "Do you know what time it is?" he snapped. Goldwyn paused for a moment, then turned to his wife. "Frances," he said, "Mr Nash wants to know what time it is."

Norman Zierold, MOGULS 1969

While Arthur Ransome, now a favourite children's author, but then a correspondent for the *Daily Mail* was in Russia, Mrs Pankhurst, the suffragette leader arrived. She said she had come to teach the women of Russia their duty in whetting the men's almost blunted purpose of victory.

Ransome, who had been in Russia for many dreary months and had had time to realise the people's utter exhaustion and war-weariness, asked ironically "Mrs Pankhurst, how long have you been in Russia?"

The sturdy little lady, impervious to sarcasm, answered innocently, "We arrived last night. Our train was two hours late."

Alex M. Thompson, HERE I LIE 1957

In Enniskillen, Northern Ireland, they tell of Tyrone the lorry driver who drove his 14-foot high vehicle under a 14-foot bridge with noisy results. Jammed tighter than a boot in an Irish bog, Tyrone tried reversing his lorry. The only result was smoking rubber. Bystanders tried shoving, to no avail. Finally a police constable came along on his bicycle. He stared at the 600-yard traffic jam and frowned at Tyrone. "Are you stuck, then?" asked the officer. "Not a bit of it," seethed Tyrone. "I was delivering this damned bridge, but I lost the address."

Herb Shannon, Reader's Digest Jun 1987

SCHOOL

When Stanley Baldwin – who went to Harrow – was Prime Minister, his Home Secretary was Mr Bridgeman – who went to Eton. One day Baldwin produced some quip in the Eton-Harrow context which Bridgeman did not judge to be up to standard. He bided his time. One morning at Cabinet the Prime Minister congratulated the Home Secretary on the rapid ending to a riot at one of HM's prisons. "How did you do it, Home Secretary?" he asked. "Oh, Prime Minister, it was easy. I just told the Governor to order the prison band to play *Forty Years On* (the Harrow School song) and the prisoners stood to attention and quietly returned to their cells."

Lord Home, THE WAY THE WIND BLOWS 1976

Cecil Beaton began his education at a day-school in Hampstead. On his first day there the bullies "growling like wire-haired terriers" descended on him. They were led by a boy half the size of themselves, who wore green knickerbockers and who promptly picked out Cecil as the obvious lamb for slaughter.

Beaton writes in *The Wandering Years*, "He then stood on his toes and thrust his face, with a diabolical stare, closer and closer to mine, ever closer until the eyes converged into one enormous Cyclops nightmare. . . . By the time the physical onslaught began fright had mercifully made me only half conscious. That the tortures were devilish in their invention I can be fairly certain, since they were conducted under such expert leadership."

The Hampstead boy in green knickerbockers had a name that became better known later. It was Evelyn Waugh.

Percy Howard, Sunday Express 16 *Jul* 1961

When Max Beerbohm was a schoolboy at Charterhouse his mother came to visit him on a day of school festivities. His housemaster's wife wore a fine new pearl necklace. "Do you see that?" Max asked his mother. "Every pearl represents a boy's empty stomach."

Lord David Cecil, MAX, A BIOGRAPHY 1965

When Gerald Gardiner's [afterwards Baron Gardiner of Kittisford QC] father visited him at Harrow he noticed a copy of the *Nation*, later incorporated into the *New Statesman*, lying around and yelled that no other son of his would attend a school where such publications were openly displayed. He was as good as his word, and Gerald's brothers were sent to Eton.

Muriel Box, REBEL ADVOCATE 1963

At Eton each boy from the start had a room of his own, small but undeniably his territory, into which nobody – not even his House Master – could come without knocking. Years later I took the wife of the President of Pakistan to see a typical boy's room at Eton. She was sure that it must be the clothes cupboard.

Lord Home, THE WAY THE WIND BLOWS 1976

I was sent to school at Wantage. It was small and select and generally utterly unsuited for a child of my regrettable proclivities. When I attempted to argue during the Scripture lesson – that put the lid on it. I tied my box up with a length of clothes-line which I found in the garden. I drove in a milk cart to the nearest station and took the train to Chichester, where my mother was living. The milkman was young and must have been touched with romance, for he helped me with my box and drove me all the way to the station for nothing, only saying darkly, "If so be as anyone asks questions they get no answer 'ere."

When I arrived home my mother said, "Good gracious, what are you doing here?" I told her and she shrugged her shoulders and said, "I don't know that I approve, but after all, well, you didn't like it, so you didn't." As an after-thought she added, "You must send the clothes-line back at once."

Naomi Jacob, ME: A CHRONICLE ABOUT OTHER PEOPLE 1933

A letter written to a teacher ran as follows: "Dear Miss, Jim was off school because he caught a chill and had terrible diarrhoea through a hole in his wellies."

Mrs J. Cowrie, letter to Woman 24 Mar 1982

A schoolteacher friend told me how he always managed to make a good impression when his class was "inspected". He told his pupils beforehand that when he asked a question in front of the inspector those who knew the answer were to raise their right hands, those who didn't, their left.

North Devon Journal-Herald 17 *May* 1984

SCHOOLMASTER

My tutor at Eton, C.M. Wells, was a scholar whose normal conversation with a lower boy was just the word "Refused".

"Can I go out to lunch on Sunday with my aunt sir, please sir?"

"Refused."

He never vouchsafed the explanation that it was against the rules for any boy to go out to Sunday lunch with anybody other than his parents. He left one to find that out for oneself.

There is a story that after his retirement from Eton he was returning up Bond Street towards his St John's Wood home, having dined with a friend at a St James's Street club. As he strode along, swinging an invisible gown, one of the women of the town, sheltering in a shop doorway on a draughty corner said, "Chèri – come home with me." "Refused," said Mr Wells.

William Douglas-Home, HALF TERM REPORT 1954

My housemaster at Eton in 1917, A.W. Whitworth, disliked having to punish, and would invariably use one argument, which was almost naive, but so devastatingly logical, that it deterred us from the worst. I recall the first occasion on which he used it. One of us had poured a jug of water over the stairs and the contents had landed on his head. "H'm," he said, "suppose the whole House had done that?"

Lord Home, THE WAY THE WIND BLOWS 1976

C.H.K. Marten was the first of my teachers to make me realise that characters of history had once been human beings like us. Marten had a raven which used to sit on the back bench of the Division. If anyone was inattentive or slow, at a signal from him, the bird would nip the offender's ear. There were not many laggards in that class.

Ibid.

As a boy in Swansea Harry Secombe's English teacher had high hopes for him, deciding that he had the makings of a fine journalist, and gave him every encouragement. Secombe left school with every intention of fulfulling his teacher's dream. But the war intervened. Secombe joined the Army. When he finally returned to civvy street he found himself not a journalist but an entertainer. Years later the famous Sir Harry returned to Swansea in his Rolls Royce and decided to pay his old teacher a visit. He parked the limousine outside the house, knocked on the door, and moments later pupil and teacher were regarding each other for the first time in decades. "Harry boy," said the old man, shaking his head sadly. "What went wrong?"

Linda Hawkins, TV Times 18 *Oct* 1986

SCULPTURE

John Mason Brown was studying a large sculpture by Jean Arp that was supposed to depict a female form. Peering through a large hole in the middle of the piece he commented, "Ah, a womb with a view."

Cass Canfield, UP AND DOWN AND AROUND 1971

A figure of Ariel sculpted by Eric Gill in the late 1920s for the facade of the BBC building had a peculiar and almost embarrassing history. Lord Reith, then head of the BBC complained that the sculptor had emphasised Ariel's reproductive organ beyond necessity. Gill refused to make any changes. It was decided to submit the matter to arbitration; Sir Israel Gollancz, the noted Shakespearian scholar and editor, and Israel Zangwill, the novelist, were among the Shakespearians deputed to investigate. After concluding that Ariel's approximate age should be thirteen they called in a doctor, who agreed with Lord Reith that for such a boy the genitals were over-emphasised. The necessary surgery was performed and the statue of Ariel put into the place it still occupies on the building.

Louis Marder, HIS EXITS AND HIS ENTRANCES

Bernard Shaw was sitting to Rodin, in his studio, and proceeded to criticise Rodin's sculpture The Thinker. He backed his criticism with a demonstration, by undressing and showing how a thinker should look. Alvin Langdon Coburn, the photographer, was present and snapped Shaw in this position. He claimed the photograph made a finer composition than the statue, the body being quite as well trained as the mind of the dramatist.

Cecil Roberts, HALF WAY 1931

On the day in 1939 that George Bernard Shaw finished writing *Good King Charles's Golden Days* I was invited to lunch.

In the drawing room Mrs Shaw gathered guests at a bronze bust of Shaw, standing on a pedestal, while we had coffee. "This side," she said, "shows Shaw the philosopher. Now come round here." We shifted a few paces and were joined by the great man, who stood listening, smiling and approving. "From this angle," Mrs Shaw explained, "you see Bernard the humorist. You will notice the mouth turns up at the corner; while from this side –" we all shuffled back to our first position "– the corner of the mouth turns down. The Philosopher!" We inclined our heads gravely.

Sir Alec Guinness, BLESSINGS IN DISGUISE 1985

SEA

My ship was proceeding inside the Great Barrier Reef in dense fog when I suddenly smelt the most delicious scent. I told the officer of the watch to go full speed astern and to let go the anchor for, in addition to the scent, I could hear sea-birds which were evidently on the reef immediately ahead of us, but invisible owing to the thick fog. Some of my officers went away in a boat to reconnoitre, and soon came back with the report that the reef was close to. What I had smelt was the powerful sweet scent of lilies on the mainland, and thus my nose had saved us from what might easily have been a disaster.

Admiral Sir Frederic William Fisher, NAVAL REMINISCENCES 1938

Everyone must have heard of the little girl who got her first glimpse of the sea on a Sunday School excursion. The child seemed terribly disappointed at something, and in answer to her teacher's question said that she liked the sea, "but please where are the tindamies?" Pressed for an explanation the little girl quoted, "In six days the Lord made heaven and earth, the sea and all the tindamies." Tindamies is quite a convenient word for starfish, crabs, cuttle-fish and other flotsam and jetsam of the beach.

Lord Frederic Hamilton, HERE, THERE AND EVERYWHERE 1921

In Samoa I went shark fishing with a man who used his hand for bait. We paddled just outside a barrier reef. The chief put his hand in the water and trailed it slowly. Soon a shark drifted up and moved as gradually after his hand. As the fish moved alongside the canoe a noose was dropped gently between it and the hand; the shark, unheeding, followed through. When the rope had passed behind the first fin it was gently pulled tight. If it were to slip over the tail the shark would struggle and the boat might be upset.

The moment the noose was taut Fau Mui Na withdrew his fingers. "It's all in knowing how," he said. "If you move your hand slowly the shark will also move slowly. If you move it quickly, off will come your hand."

Dr Victor Heiser, A DOCTOR'S ODYSSEY 1936

I was diving at Aden and was hampered by sharks scraping past my head. Finally, seeing one come towards me, I opened the front tap of my helmet and shot a jet of air into his face. The effect was so startling, for me as well as for him, that I wanted to laugh out loud. He dashed off as though tearing away from some terrifying disaster. I had found out now how to scare away the most dangerous of all sharks. It was done with ammunition no more deadly than air bubbles.

Thomas F. Milne, THIS WORLD AND THAT 1934

I once knew a diver who went to sleep at the bottom of the sea. He stayed down so long that I descended to see what was wrong. I found him apparently lifeless, so proceeded to have him hauled up. To lighten the task of hauling I closed the man's outlet valve, and as his dress gradually inflated he came to a standing position. Then it was that the astounding thing happened. The "dead" sprang into life and aimed a blow at me with a hammer. The bang on my helmet sounded like the last crack of doom. He let go the hammer and his hand shot up to the outlet valve. Before he could close it he was jerked off his feet and I had the vision of a pair of legs disappearing upwards as they hauled him to the surface. The rum ration he had had before going down had sent him to sleep, and waking up suddenly he had lashed out in panic.

Ibid.

One pitch-black night, when I was Second Officer of the *Avondale Castle* we were hugging the South African coast when I was joined on the bridge by the captain. I had just reported that all was well when through the night air we heard the distant crow of a cockerel, followed by a chorus of others.

"Good God!" yelled the old man, "we're nearly ashore. Hard a-port!"

She immediately answered her helm and stood out to sea.

"What's the matter, sir?" I asked, amazed.

"Matter! Matter!" he spluttered. "Heavens, man we're ashore. Can't you hear those damned chickens crowing?"

"Yes sir," I answered, shaking with silent laughter. "They're on the poop deck. We took them on at Algoa Bay for Durban this morning."

Captain G.T. Whitfield, FIFTY THRILLING YEARS AT SEA 1934

See also **SHIPWRECK**

SEANCE

Groucho Marx, who loathed pretension and could not abide the occult, was once coaxed into attending a seance. He sat, quiet and respectful, as the Swami stared into a crystal ball, called up departed souls from the beyond and answered queries from his guests in an eerie monotone. After a long spell of omniscience the sorcerer intoned, "My medium is growing tired. There is time for one more question." Groucho asked it. "What is the capital of North Dakota?"

Leo Rosten, I KNEW GROUCHO MARX 1982

Strindberg's interest in spiritualism caused Julien Leclerq and me to play a trick on him. I asked them both to my room one evening and after dinner we had a seance of table-rapping. The lights were turned down and we joined hands round a small table. After ten minutes of ominous silence the table began to rock and Leclerq asked what message it had for us. The first letter rapped out was M, and with each letter Strindberg's interest and excitement seemed to increase, until the momentous word MERDE had been spelled out in its entirety. I do not think he ever quite forgave us for this.

Frederick Delius, quoted Philip Heseltine, FREDERICK DELIUS 1923

SECURITY

One afternoon not long after my arrival in the Treasury I was summoned to lunch with the top brass of ICI, just down the road on Millbank. I said I would take my bike. As I was about to leave the Treasury courtyard I was accosted by the security guard, who required my pass. I had left it in my office. I would go back and fetch it. "Hold on," he said, "I recognise you. You're one of the messengers, aren't you?" "Well, no." I explained I was one of the Ministers. "Oh well, I knew your face." I sometimes felt in the months ahead he'd got it right anyway.

Jock Bruce-Gardyne, MINISTERS AND MANDARINS; INSIDE THE WHITEHALL VILLAGE 1986

Dion Clayton Calthorp had a strong sense of atmosphere and liked to be in tune with his surroundings. During the war [World War I] he served with a Naval Intelligence department and wrapped himself in a good deal of mystery. One day his brother Donald called for him at the Admiralty. Side by side they walked up Whitehall. Then he said, "Drop your gloves, and when you pick them up, see if anyone is following us."

Donald did so and remarked "There are a lot people coming our way."

"Hmm, one wondered whether they would have."

In Trafalgar Square he made Donald wait, and hastened back to the Admiralty. He returned a quarter of an hour later. Donald asked what he had forgotten.

"To burn my blotting paper," was the significant reply.

Ronald Pertwee, MASTER OF NONE 1940

I've been learning some of the problems of ministerial responsibility. This started at Banbury station where we were met by the station-master, and all the other people were looking at us and saying, "Why does this confounded fellow need a whole compartment to himself?"

The security people have laid it down that if we are to open our red boxes and read our documents in the train this can only be done in a reserved compartment; a reserved seat will not be sufficient. However, having made a big fuss to George Wigg, whose job as Paymaster-General included oversight of the security services, I have decided to be extremely careful in everything I do personally so I have had scramblers and big safes installed in London as well as down at Prescote, and I have agreed to reserve a whole compartment despite the fury of the commuters.

Richard Crossman, DIARY 2 Nov 1964

No secret of the war [World War I] was better kept than the departure of the British Mission to America in April 1917. Or would so have been kept, but for the indiscretion of the Chief of the Mission himself. It happened in the Station Hotel at Dumfries where the 25 members of the party waited until some activities of the U-boats off the north coast of Ireland should subside.

After 24 hours word came to entrain once more and as the special train moved off Sir Eric Drummond said to Lord Balfour, "Thank goodness we are off without anyone finding out that you were here." "Except the lift-boy," said Balfour. "But how on earth –?" "Well, he brought me his autograph book, so of course I signed it."

Blanche E.A. Dugdale, LIFE OF LORD BALFOUR 1936

I went to the Ministry of Foreign Affairs in Moscow to protest that I was being followed, and was told by the secretary not to worry.

"I'm followed; everybody's followed in Russia," he said, "If the Czar went out, he'd be followed, too. It's a sort of mania. I did not know you were being shadowed. Probably the police are doing it, but it may be you are being shadowed just because you are a foreigner. You know the police get so used to shadowing people that they do it out of habit. If you have recognised your shadowers invite them for a glass of tea. They would probably appreciate it."

Arno Dosch-Fleurot, THROUGH WAR TO REVOLUTION 1931

Accompanied by Sir Pierson Dixon, then British ambassador in France, the Queen Mother requested an informal evening in a typical French bistro. Sir Pierson suggested there was a possibility she might be recognised but Her Majesty insisted that could not possibly be the case.

The ambassador had a tactful word with the local *préfet* and on the evening of the royal visit the small working-class cafe was filled, wall-to-wall with gendarmes and their wives, all dressed like French peasants, all studiously taking no notice of the cosy little English lady who turned up with a party of friends. She had a wonderful time. It only went to prove, she told the ambassador afterwards, how easy it was, if she wanted to, to go abroad incognito.

Robert Lacey, GOD BLESS HER, QUEEN ELIZABETH, THE QUEEN MOTHER 1987

J.L. Garvin, editor of the *Observer* was repeatedly given secret information by "Jacky" Fisher when he was First Sea Lord. Just after Garvin had taken over the editorship Fisher showed him in advance naval estimates for 1908-9. Complaints were naturally made of this highly confidential information being divulged to a newspaper.

Lord Tweedsmuir instructed Fisher to discover the source of the leak. A farcical public correspondence then took place between Fisher, demanding who had inspired the articles and what documents had been used, and Garvin, protesting with feigned indignation that no outsider had briefed him or shown him any document whatever.

Alfred M. Gollin, THE OBSERVER AND J.L. GARVIN 1908-1914 1960

I was on duty near Westminster Abbey for the wedding of Princess Patricia of Connaught to Captain Ramsay in 1919. I was standing by the great doors as they emerged, amid thunderous cheering. I saw a burly man nearby slip his hand into his overcoat pocket and withdraw it again, holding something as if about to throw. I gripped his arm, but he opened his hand and grinned cheerfully at me.

Crunched in the palm lay a four-leaved clover – the only one I had ever seen. I let him throw it in the path of the smiling bride.

Herbert Fitch, MEMOIRS OF A ROYAL DETECTIVE 1936

Lord Lichfield, the talented royal photographer has been telling of an unnerving experience recently while he was in Delhi photographing Rajiv Gandhi. As he waited, surrounded by security men, in the lobby of the Taj Mahal Hotel his young assistant called out, "Hey, guv, what time are we shooting the Prime Minister?" The security men stiffened, Lichfield blanched, but, I'm told, the results of the session are excellent.

Daily Telegraph 7 *Aug* 1985

My cameraman and I were in Athens and went to interview President Pangales. He worked in a small room with hardly any windows, so that when Chris let off his flashlight there was a terrific bang that seemed to shake the whole building. The next instant the door burst open with an awful crash – and we were ordered to "stick 'em up" by the taut and effective method of having a couple of bayonets pointed at our chests.

Bert Garai, I GET MY PICTURE 1935

It was a glorious evening at Chevening, the official residence of Sir Geoffrey Howe, the Foreign Secretary. The old house basked in sunshine. Bees buzzed drowsily. Wood pigeons cooed in the distance. The world of war and terrorism seemed a thousand miles away. Suddenly a shot rang out. Security men rushed furiously into action. Then they relaxed. It was only Howe opening a bottle of Bollinger on the lawn.

Atticus, Sunday Times 2 *Aug* 1987

When Roy Jenkins was Home Secretary he was dining with a friend in a Soho restaurant. "Where are all these detectives you are supposed to have?" the friend asked. "They're somewhere about the place." "But they're not in the restaurant?" "No, but they'll be perfectly all right. They live off the land."

Alan Watkins, Observer 15 *Jun* 1980

It had taken me days to get a visa to Baghdad, and when I arrived at the airport they tried to confiscate my typewriter on the grounds that I might use it to circulate subversive propaganda. When I pointed out that it did not even type Arabic they admitted it only on condition that it be granted its own visa, which they inscribed in the space labelled, "Accompanied by his wife". For months afterwards immigration officers were demanding to see "Mrs Olivetti Priestland."

Gerald Priestland, SOMETHING UNDERSTOOD 1986

When the Special Branch raided the Scottish offices of the BBC over the Zircon affair it worked out a very simple selection process. Anything with the word "secret" in it was promptly taken away for inspection. This included a tape of *The Secret Servant*, a spy thriller by Gavin Lyall.

Peter Hillmore, Observer 22 Feb 1987

A gardener who applied for a job at Hampton Court was asked to sign form E 74 of the Official Secrets Act, in case he gave away information about watering the begonias.

Clement Freud, Speech, House of Commons 19 *Jan* 1979

SERMON

Complaining that modern sermons tended to be secular in tone, Margot Asquith remarked, "It would be as surprising to hear God mentioned in one of them as to find a fox in a bus."

Lord David Cecil, Observer, Staying with Margot 20 *Dec* 1981

On Sunday President Coolidge attended church without his wife. When he returned to the White House she asked him the subject of the sermon. "Adultery," said the President. "What did he say about it?" she persisted. Coolidge thought for a moment. "He was against it," he reported finally.

Bennett Cerf, TRY AND STOP ME 1947

At a rehearsal for the coronation of Edward VII the late Lord Salisbury was asked if he would impersonate the King. He consented, curled himself up in the Chair of State and, head in hand, apparently went to sleep. Presently the Dean announced, "The Rev. – will now preach the sermon." The Rev. – came forward and said, "My Lords, we will take the sermon as read." Upon which Lord Salisbury suddenly sat bolt upright, and clasping his hands together said, "By Jove! That's the best parson I have ever met. We'll make him a bishop tomorrow," and quietly curled himself up in the Chair again.

Lord Ormathwaite, WHEN I WAS AT COURT 1937

SERVANT

To the end of her life Nancy Mitford remained appalled at the prospect of cooking herself so much as a plate of porridge for dinner on her maid's night off. Her ideal was the one she described in *The Blessing*; servants to change the mimosa three times a day.

Hilary Spurling. Observer, reviewing Selina Hastings, NANCY MITFORD 13 Oct 1985

SHIPWRECK

I was one of the survivors from *Anglo-India* which went on to the rocks off Formosa, then notorious for its piratical inhabitants. I attempted to swim ashore with a rope. I was hurled forward by a gigantic wave and then – blackness. I hit my head on a submerged rock and lost consciousness. A racking pain in the third finger of my left hand brought me to, and it seemed as if I had opened my eyes on a coffee-coloured world.

A woman was sprawled across my chest and she was biting my finger just above my gold ring. She was trying to chew through the bone so that she could take off the ring, which would not pass over the knuckle.

Thomas F. Milne, THIS WORLD AND THAT 1934

In Cleveland Bay, Queensland, four companions and I were returning from shore when our boat capsized. We spent nine hours clinging to the side in the shark-infested water before being rescued by a steamer. Later we read in the Townsville *Gazette* that our timely rescue was only due to a chance remark let fall by a passenger on the steamer to the chief officer who was passing by. "Look, chief. Five crows sitting on a plank. I've never seen those birds at sea before." The chief levelled his glasses. "Crows! My God! It's five men's heads!"

Captain G.J. Whitfield, FIFTY THRILLING YEARS AT SEA 1934

SHOOTING

The captain of a gunboat journeying up the Yangtze called on a local Chinese governor and was invited for a day's shooting. He suggested bringing with him two dogs he had with him on the gunboat, but the governor told him not to bother. When he went on to tell his visitor he had two cats which would do the retrieving as well as the best-trained dogs the captain of the gunboat quite naturally thought his host was jesting, but in due time he found out that the governor had every reason to be serious, for his two tabby cats retrieved so marvellously that his guest offered him £50 for them. The offer was refused.

Admiral Sir Frederic William Fisher, NAVAL REMINISCENCES 1938

Immediately after the Munich crisis a journalist asked Lord Halifax if he was not worn out by all the late nights. The Foreign Secretary replied, "Not exactly. But it spoils one's eye for the high birds."

Paul Johnson, THE OXFORD BOOK OF POLITICAL JOKES 1986

To a complaint that one of the churchyards on his estate was disgracefully overgrown the 3rd Earl of Leicester replied, "Nonsense. Best breeding ground for partridges in England."

Kenneth Rose, KINGS, QUEENS AND COURTIERS 1985

SHOPPING

In search of ideas, I spent yesterday morning in walking about, and went to the stores and bought things in four departments. A wonderful way of spending time and money. Better than most theatres. I think this sort of activity does stimulate ideas.

Arnold Bennett, Journals 1911–1921

My father said he would buy me a hat from Mrs White's shop in Jermyn Street. We looked at the hats through the window and went in. Settling himself in a chair father bade Mrs White "Good afternoon, ma'am". He asked if the blue bonnet in the window would suit a lady of 40.

"Admirably," Mrs White answered.

"Then it will not do for my daughter aged 17. Good afternoon, Madam."

Mrs J.D. Bailey, The Times 26 Jul 1963

Herbert Marshall had a blinding headache. He walked into what he took to be the nearest chemist's, and demanded aspirins. In fact the shop sold only surgical appliances and contraceptives.

"I'm extremely sorry, Mr Marshall," said the assistant, "but we only deal in the *lighter* side of pharmacy."

Michael Pertwee, NAME DROPPING

At Marks and Spencers in Oxford Street an Arab told a salesgirl, "I'll take that rack of nightdresses." When she pointed out that they were all different sizes, he said, "So are my wives."

Maureen and Timothy Green, Reader's Digest Aug 1979

SHYNESS

A wealthy American woman tried to get in touch with Sir James Barrie but he eluded her. In desperation she went to H.G. Wells and asked him for a letter of introduction. "It would be more than my life is worth," said Wells. "But I'll tell you what. Go and sit on his doorstep and make a noise like a crying child. That will fetch him down." The woman, it is reported, followed Wells's joking instructions, and the trick worked.

Leo Condon, Sunday Referee 20 Jun 1939

Very ordinary transactions were inclined to make Asquith quite unreasonably shy. The act, for instance, of giving money to his children was performed with a painfully guilty expression of countenance, and an averted eye, and often followed by a hurried flight from the room.

J.A. Spender and Cyril Asquith, LIFE OF LORD OXFORD AND ASQUITH 1932

I invited Ronald Firbank to tea. Anxious to entertain him properly I bought a monumental bunch of grapes and a glutinous chocolate cake. Insuperably shy, he sat with eyes averted from me and my well-meaning repast. His most rational response to my efforts to draw him out about literature and art was "I adore italics, don't you?" His cup of tea remained untasted, and he quailed when I drew attention to my large and cosy pile of crumpets. As a gesture of politeness he slowly absorbed a single grape.

Siegfried Sassoon, SIEGFRIED'S JOURNEY 1916–1920 1945

Because of his shyness George VI found it practically impossible to say goodbye. This could be very hard on his visitors since, according to etiquette, they could not leave until they had been dismissed – though George Bernard Shaw speeded up the process when he took his gold watch ostentatiously from his pocket and gave it a long, cool look.

Robert Lacey, MAJESTY 1977

My husband is a shy man and whenever he brings me flowers he always conceals them under his bowler hat. As a result they have to be little flowers, like violets or anemones, and tend to smell of brilliantine. Surely there must be some way in which shy men deal with this problem?

Letter to Today, quoted Denys Parsons, FUNNY HA HA, FUNNY PECULIAR 1965

SINGING

I won a prize at Eton for singing "Rose in the Bud" and Roger Quilter's setting of "Now Sleeps the Crimson Petal". As I finished the latter – "slip into my bosom and be lost in me" – I heard one of the masters whisper, "What a very inadequate bosom to slip into." I didn't like that at all.

Lord Boothby, MY YESTERDAY, YOUR TOMORROW 1962

Once when I heard Maria Callas singing *Norma* in Paris she broke on a high note as I have never heard a professional singer break in public. The house fell into an uproar, half the audience booing, half cheering. She raised her hand. There was silence. She motioned to the conductor to start the aria again and this time she did not break – and there was pandemonium. I went back stage to her dressing room afterwards and I did not know whether to refer to this episode or not – it's like a woman wearing a very low-cut dress, you're not sure whether it's more rude to look, or not to look. I decided not to mention it, and she never mentioned it either.

Rudolf Bing, The Times 14 *Oct* 1972

Towards the end of Gracie Fields' first year at school in Rochdale came the big day for parents and pupils alike, the annual school concert.

"Every girl," said the headmistress, "must be given the chance to do her bit on the platform."

The music mistress, who was to pick the most promising performers, arranged a preliminary audition. Gracie's turn came. Without a trace of nerves she put all she had into it, flinging her small personality across the place where the footlights would have been if the school platform had had any. It was a very different performance from the other girls, who had sung in small genteel voices; so different that the music mistress raised her eyes to heaven, and spoke just two words.

"Oh, shocking," she cried, and turned Gracie down.

So Gracie never sang in the school concert. Bitterly disappointed, she asked her teacher some days later, "What went wrong with my little song?"

"You sang too loud," said the music mistress.

Bert Aza, Sunday Chronicle 23 *Jul* 1939

Playing at the Albert Hall, Tetrazzini was so nervous that she missed a top note, greatly to her agitation and distress. She came running off the platform, literally wringing her hands – stopped – then without a word she rushed back and sang just that one missing note, greatly to the delight of the audience.

Mathilde Verne, CHORDS OF REMEMBRANCE 1936

SLEEP

Throughout his life Robert Baden-Powell never slept more than four or five hours a night; on active service two were enough. Only his secretary, who found a huge pile of work (and sometimes a few trout as well) on her doorstep with the morning milk, knew how many hours of toil he put in while most people were asleep.

Jack Cox, Radio Times 22 *Feb* 1957

Exhausted socially and mentally I slept for two hours this afternoon in the Library of the House of Commons. A deep House of Commons sleep. There is no sleep to compare with it – rich, deep and guilty.

Sir Henry Channon, DIARY 15 *Jul* 1937

"Once in a while I have a bad night," wrote Paul Gallico, "but it really doesn't matter because I am off my feet and comfortable. So I decide to stay awake and work out a story. My brain, in horror and indignation at being asked to work overtime, goes numb and I fall asleep."

James Bender, HOW TO SLEEP

It is alleged by a friend of my family that I used to suffer from insomnia at the age of four, and that she asked me how I managed to occupy my time at night. I answered, "I lie awake and think about the past."

Ronald Knox, LITERARY DISTRACTIONS 1941

Scientists at the University of Chicago decided to test the theory that coffee is a sleep preventative. The subjects of the experiment were given coffee one night, and then the next night, at the same hour, they were given milk. All went to sleep faster the second night. They were positive that the coffee the first night had kept them awake. They weren't told that the milk had been spiked with three times as much caffeine as was in the coffee.

Leonard Lyons, Reader's Digest Sep 1946

SMOKING

Do send me, from the stores, every twenty (or perhaps eighteen) days a box of cigars. I can live, as I am doing, on bully beef. I can drink, as I am doing, cocoa and tea. But I cannot, and I will not, as long as my bank will honour my cheques, wash them down, so to speak, with nothing but a pipe. I can smoke two pipes a day and no more, which leaves me with a necessity for five cigars or say seven (two for a friend) and honestly the support of my system requires this. This is most important and quite serious. Tell the Stores not to print any indication that the boxes are cigars. Have printed yourself some gummed labels as follows: ARMY TEMPERANCE SOCIETY. PUBLICATION SERIES 9, and put these and nothing else on the outside. These precautions are very necessary as cigars are always stolen by the men if they escape the officers.

F.E. Smith (Lord Birkenhead), letter from the Western Front to his wife 21 *Oct* 1914

General de Gaulle has always been a heavy smoker. One day at Colombey he and Andre Malraux were discussing the tobacco habit.

"It's not so hard to give up," Malraux said. "When the Nazis had me in jail I found it quite easy." De Gaulle scoffed. "All right, I'll prove it," said Malraux, who is a chain smoker. "I'll give it up for a month."

When Malraux came back to Colombey and reported that he had kept his tobacco fast, as promised, de Gaulle eyed him respectfully. "If you can do it, I can," he said. He has never smoked since.

Alden Hatch, Sunday Express 15 *Jan* 1961

After the Easter Rebellion of 1916 Eamonn de Valera was sentenced to penal servitude. En route to prison he took out his pipe and was about to light it when he stopped suddenly and said, "I will not let them deprive me of this pleasure in jail." He immediately threw away the pipe and from that day never smoked again.

John Gunther, PROCESSION 1965

When Chiang Kai-Shek saw a small boy smoking in the street he demanded to be taken to the parents. They were sharply reprimanded for allowing such a shocking thing to happen.

Brian Crozier, THE MAN WHO LOST CHINA 1970

One woman gave up smoking when her parrot developed a persistent cough. A vet gave the bird a check-up and found that it didn't have pneumonia or psittacosis. The final diagnosis was that it had been imitating the cough of its cigarette-smoking owner.

Neil Morgan, San Diego Tribune 1973

SMUGGLING

When an airport officer asked a young couple why they were going to Pakistan the man said he hoped to find work there. But according to his passport he was a barman – an unlikely occupation in a country where alcohol is forbidden. A few weeks later Customs men were waiting for the couple to return. They were carrying a £1000 worth of morphine.

Anthony Brown, Reader's Digest Jul 1980

Drug smuggling is one of the evils that the British official in Sinai has to fight. A policeman examining a camel caravan was struck by the fine quality of the white wool that adorned a certain camel's hump and said casually that he would like some to make an *agal* (head rope). The merchant in charge protested so vigorously that the policeman's suspicions were aroused; he rode after the camel, gripped a handful of the wool, gave a tug, and away came a large quantity, on the inner side of which was stuck a large slab of hashish.

The rest of the caravan was promptly examined and it was found that on every camel six holes had been cut in the wool by hair-clippers; on to the bare skin was stuck, by means of glue, a slab of hashish and the wool had then been affixed to the other side of the slab by the same method, the hair being carefully combed together afterwards.

Major C.S. Jarvis, THREE DESERTS

SNOBBERY

During the war [World War I] I commanded a battery of the Royal Horse Artillery in Egypt. There I found what may be described as a certain coolness between the English and the Australians towards whom our people were, I am afraid, a little apt to adopt a slightly superior attitude. I remember at one juncture a certain Staff Officer refused to let his Mess join in with the Australian Staff Mess because the latter did not have dinner, but "high tea".

Eliot Crawshaw-Williams, SIMPLE STORY 1935

A fabulously wealthy lady demanded Fritz Kreisler's services and would not be deterred when he quoted a fee of 3000 dollars just for playing a few little pieces. So he accepted the engagement. The lady then told him she did not wish him to mix with the guests, many of whom would be very prominent people. "In that case, madam, my fee will be only 2000 dollars."

Donald Brook, VIOLINISTS OF TODAY

On one of T.E. Lawrence's spells in the ranks he was assigned as a batman to an officer of the class who used to be known in the War as "temporary gentleman". Lawrence hated him at sight, and on the first evening, when he was unpacking his kit, looked round and said, "I beg your pardon, sir, but I can only find one of your razors." "I've only got one razor." "Indeed, sir? I thought most gentlemen had a razor for every day of the week." After a moment he looked round again, "Sir, I can't find your left-handed nail scissors." The poor man rushed out of the tent and applied for a less exacting batman.

Edward Marsh, A NUMBER OF PEOPLE 1939

Edith Wharton, author of *Ethan Frome*, was what some people would call a first-rate snob. She explained that "only eight people in New

York are worth dining with", and therefore had only eight chairs in her dining room.

Bennett Cerf, TRY AND STOP ME 1947

The Abbey Club meets the needs of those who have hitherto been deterred from joining a naturist club by the fear that they might find as fellow-members some humble employee, the butler, baker, broker and insurance man. Not that there is anything snobbish about the club.

Naturist, quoted Michael Bateman, THIS ENGLAND

SNUB

Mr Astor, having built a new patio for his house with tiles brought from Segovia proudly showed it to Mrs Stuyvesant Fish. In the centre of the patio was a large fountain. With an air of pride he waited for her to express admiration.

"Beautiful," said Mrs Fish, her head on one side. "Beautiful! Just the sort of watering-trough you might put up for a favourite horse."

Elizabeth, Lady Decies, TURN OF THE WORLD 1938

I once ventured to compliment Sir Thomas Beecham at a dinner party on his interpretation of Mozart. Sir Thomas thereupon turned to a woman guest and remarked, "I discuss music only with musicians."

Jacques-Emile Blanche, MORE PORTRAITS OF A LIFETIME 1939

When F.E. Smith [afterwards Lord Birkenhead], opening a case before Mr Justice Ridley, rose to address the jury, the judge most injudiciously observed, "Well, Mr Smith, I have read the pleadings and I do not think much of your case." Smith replied quickly, "Indeed, I am sorry to hear that, m'Lud, but your lordship will find that the more you hear of it, the more it will grow on you." He could use either the rapier or the bludgeon with devastating effect.

2nd Lord Birkenhead, LIFE OF LORD BIRKENHEAD 1933

Mrs Patrick Campbell took the lead in a stage version of a then very popular novel by Hall Caine, the prolific and best-selling novelist whose books were read by millions. At rehearsal he ventured to suggest a few stage moves. "You don't mind, do you?" he asked politely. "Oh dear, no, Mr Caine," Mrs Campbell sweetly answered.

"My greatest desire is to achieve success for *your* sake. By the way, have you ever written anything else?"

James Harding, AGATE, A BIOGRAPHY 1986

Winston Churchill gave a delicious snub to the budding Oswald Mosley, who was thought to get on his legs unduly often. "I can well understand the hon. member speaking for practice, which he badly needs."

Edward Marsh, A NUMBER OF PEOPLE 1939

Noel Coward was in New York with Claudette Colbert after Arthur Miller's autobiographical play *After the Fall*. She could see an indiscretion coming on and sought to put as many playgoers as possible between them. This only made it worse as Coward had to shout, "I preferred *This Is Your Life* when it was a television programme."

Ned Sherrin, A SMALL THING LIKE AN EARTHQUAKE 1983

Relations between T.S. Eliot and W.B. Yeats were marked by their long, languid incompatibility. Among their mild collisions none was more defined than the dinner at Wellesley College when Yeats, seated next to Eliot but oblivious of him, conversed with the guest on the other side until late in the meal. He then turned and said, "My friend here and I have been discussing the defects of T.S. Eliot's poetry. What do you think of that poetry?"

Eliot held up his place card to excuse himself from the jury.

Richard Ellmann, EMINENT DOMAIN 1967

When, in December 1916, Lloyd George had become the new prime minister he sent a request to Lord Northcliffe to visit No. 10 Downing Street. The reply was, "Lord Northcliffe sees no advantage in any interview between him and the prime minister at this juncture."

Lord Beaverbrook, POLITICIANS AND THE WAR VOL II 1932

At an international conference in Geneva in 1956 our then Foreign Secretary, Harold Macmillan, asked Lord Gladwyn to lend some of the magnificent silver from the British Embassy in Paris, so that he could welcome his fellow ministers in style. Sitting next to dour Molotov at Macmillan's dinner party, Gladwyn asked him whether he did not admire the silver plate, the huge salvers along the wall and the great candelabra by which the room was lit.

"In Moscow," Molotov replied, "we have *electric* light."

Kenneth Rose, Sunday Telegraph 16 *Nov* 1986

Bill Moyers, President Johnson's press secretary, was saying grace at lunch one day. "Speak up, Bill," shouted Johnson. "I can't hear a damn thing." "I wasn't addressing you, Mr President," said Moyers quietly.

Bill Adler, THE WASHINGTON WITS

Bernard Shaw detests music with his meals – and rightly so. Once he called to the leader of a Tzigane band, which was making the usual deafening and distracting noises in a restaurant. "Could you play something if I asked you to?" "But certainly Monsieur." "Well would you either play poker or dominoes – whichever you like – until I have finished my dinner."

Mrs Claude Beddington, ALL THAT I HAVE MET 1929

When American actress Cornelia Otis Skinner appeared on Broadway in his play *Candida,* Bernard Shaw sent her a cable, "Excellent. Greatest." She cabled back, "Undeserving such praise." "Meant the play," returned Shaw. Bristling, the actress answered, "So did I."

Newsweek 1981

When Dame Edith Evans and Dame Sybil Thorndike appeared in the same play the theatre's management was faced with a delicate exercise in diplomacy. Who should be given the Number One dressing room? The choice was in no way eased by the fact that the lavish amenities of Number One were matched by those of Number Two, situated a couple of steps up the back staircase. In despair the stage manager approached Dame Sybil and explained the situation.

"There's no problem at all," she told him. "Let Edith have Number One. I can climb stairs."

David Crane, Reader's Digest Aug 1978

As Oscar Wilde put it, "a snob is a person who knows the price of everything and the value of nothing". I once sat next to a person at a dinner who would most certainly have described herself as a lady, but who had evidently not read Wilde. Practically every remark she made was designed to impress the rest of the guests with her affluence. She met her match, however, when she turned to a distinguished portrait painter who was also a guest and demanded how much he would charge her for a full-length portrait. The exasperated painter mentioned a sum which would have shaken even Jackie Onassis. Recovering her breath the lady then asked how much a half-length portrait would cost. "It depends which half," said the painter sweetly, while all the guests gave him a silent cheer.

Douglas Sutherland, THE ENGLISH GENTLEMAN'S WIFE 1979

SOUVENIR

At a semi-summit meeting of Foreign Secretaries in the fifties Ernest Bevin, Khrushchev and Georges Bidault had been relaxing over a drink, when Bevin took a watch out of his pocket and consulted it. It was a grand affair in gold and engraved on the back, "To Ernest Bevin in memory of forty years devoted to the Docker's Union." Georges Bidault, not to be outdone, then showed his watch, which was inscribed "Pour Georges, de la part de ses parents, à l'occasion de sa majorité, 1920."

Khrushchev looked embarrassed, but the others insisted that he, too, show his watch. It turned out to be a slim Cartier, one of great elegance; he twirled it on its chain while the others insisted on examining it closer, and he had to hand it over. The inscription read, "To His Imperial Highness, The Grand Duke Constantine, from his fellow members at the Hurlingham Polo Club 1913."

Peter Coats, OF KINGS AND CABBAGES 1984

I was browsing round the treasures in John Pierpoint Morgan's library when I suddenly saw, under a glass case, a thrilling object. It was a little lock of hair bound together with a piece of ribbon, and underneath was a label which read, "A lock of the hair of Keats. Given to Shelley by Keats' friend –", and then there was a description of the time and place at which the lock had been given.

This object so excited me that I could not drag myself away from it. Jack Morgan came up. "What are you looking at?" he said. "Keats' hair? Like to hold if for a minute?"

He produced a key from his pocket, undid the case and put the precious thing in my hand. I felt an almost schoolboy emotion at the thought that this hair had grown from the head in which the *Ode to a Grecian Urn* had been conceived.

Suddenly Morgan said, "Give it to me for a minute." Reluctantly I handed it over and then, marvel of marvels, he extracted a single hair from the lock – a long curly one – put it on a piece of paper, dropped a spot of sealing wax on it, and then wrote, as a sort of testimony, "Keats' hair, from a lock in my possession. J. P. Morgan."

This hair he gave to me and, as all writers of autobiographies as constantly assert, "it is one of my most treasured possessions".

Beverly Nichols, TWENTY-FIVE 1926

Thursday 21 Jan 1915. Many of the Indian troops are fine, tall, well-built men and physically command great respect from the English soldier, but their tastes have too much of savagery about them to win favour. A Territorial was very proud of a piece of shell which had burst near him, and of the spike and badge from a German helmet. A Pathan listened gravely while these were being shown. "Souvenir!" he said scornfully, "No good. Here right souvenir." He put his hand into the voluminous folds of the shawl wrapped round his breast and produced a cord on which he had strung the ears of all the Germans he counted himself to have slain. These he was keeping carefully to take back to India to his wife.

Rev Andrew Clark, ECHOES OF THE GREAT WAR 1914–19 1985

STAMMERING

Everyone knows that Arnold Bennett was afflicted with a very bad stammer; it was painful sometimes to watch the struggle to get the words out. What to most men was as easy as breathing was to him a constant strain. It tore his nerves to pieces. Few knew the humiliation it exposed him to, the ridicule it excited in many, the impatience it aroused, the awkwardness of feeling that it made people find him tiresome; and the minor exasperation of thinking of a good, amusing or apt remark and not venturing to say it in case the stammer ruined it. Few knew the distressing sense it gave rise to of a bar to complete contact with other men. It may be that but for the stammer, which forced him to introspection, Arnold would not have become a writer.

Somerset Maugham, John o' London's Weekly 24 Jun 1933

My OC was a charming Irishman named Cusack, who possessed a

vigorous stutter. On one occasion he was promulgating the proceedings of a court martial in which a second lieutenant had been found guilty of improper conduct with a WAAC. He was making heavy weather of it, and the expression on the faces of the officers attending the parade threatened imminent laughter. Coming to a definition of the actual offence, Cusack stumbled and fluffed badly.

"They were f-f-f-found in a f-f-f-field and he was – he was – he was –."

The laughter exploded and swept the room.

"You're a d-d-d-dirty lot of d-d-d-devils," said Cusack, "He was – he was k-k-kissing her."

Roland Pertwee, MASTER OF NONE 1940

The famous war correspondent George Kingswell was renowned for his picturesque flow of language, and his stutter. On one occasion he met Sir George Grey, then High Commissioner of the Cape. He, too, stuttered and said "Are you G-G-George K-K-Kingswell?"

"Yes," said Kingswell, "a-a-and are you G-G-George Grey?"

Thinking that Kingswell was imitating him, Grey hit him in the face.

With a roar Kingswell leapt at him. "W-w-what the hell is the m-m-matter with you? And what in the name of Satan d-d-do you think you are doing?"

"W-w-what!" said Grey. "D-d-do you st-st-stutter too?"

The pair shook hands and both roared with laughter.

Elma Kingswell, KINGSWELL; WAR CORRESPONDENT 1938

SUEZ

When ships which had been loaded for so many weeks eventually off-loaded their cargoes at Port Said there were some unexpected surprises. At the fishing harbour a senior staff officer one day noticed a 3-ton lorry, so overladen that its rear springs were all but concave and stuck fast on the ramp. "Who the bloody hell are you?" he enquired kindly, "and what are you doing?" "I, sir," responded a voice of much dignity, "am the mess-sergeant of Her Majesty's Life Guards, and I have with me the officers' mess silver and champagne."

Roy Fullick and Geoffrey Powell, SUEZ: THE DOUBLE WAR 1979

We were to mop up the opposition around Navy House, but the order did not get through in time. As darkness fell the battalion pulled out of Port Said to a beach where the richer inhabitants had chalets and we settled down for the night.

I unrolled my sleeping bag on a bed in a particularly luxurious hut, and awoke to find that I had become a battleground myself. Armies of bed bugs were advancing over my body. The only defence was to abandon my sleeping bag. I had just decided I was too tired to move when the Egyptians intervened with a salvo of mortar bombs which exploded among our chalets. I jumped out of the chalet into the sand. The last official shots in the Suez campaign had routed my bed bugs.

Sir Philip Goodheart, Sunday Times 2 *Nov* 1986

SUFFRAGETTE

When my father was going to unveil Sir Henry Campbell-Bannerman's memorial at Stirling, we were in an open car. Detectives were behind and before but they were no good, and suddenly our car was brought to a stop by two suffragettes who leaped out from the hedges, lying on the road in front of it so that we could only advance over their bodies. Meanwhile a posse of others sprang upon each step of the car and lashed us over the head with dog whips and shook enormous pepper pots in our faces, such as you would see in a pantomime. However we were unscathed because he had on a top hat, which was very good protective covering, and I probably had on one of those vast hats which protect one to some extent. Those sort of experiences were unpleasant.

Lady Asquith of Yarnbury (Violet Bonham-Carter), The Times, interviewed by Norman St John Stevas 22 *Nov* 1968

On another occasion we were assaulted on Lossiemouth golf course. Two or three ran up to him (Asquith) and tried to tear his clothes off his back. He stood clinging to the lapels of his coat. I tore first one and then another off him. Though a weedy athlete, rage made me strong until the detectives came up. I took the precaution of throwing away my putter, since I should have been tempted. These experiences were common and accentuated my father's prejudice.

Ibid.

Diana and I used to be taken for a daily morning airing in Green Park in a double pram; this must have been just before the war. There were people called suffragettes who wanted to get votes for women, which, I later discovered, was a proposal to which my father and Mr Asquith were strongly opposed; so the suffragettes tried to kidnap me in the park. I have a fugitive memory of being pulled out of the pram, and of the nursery maid catching hold of me and pulling me back. More strongly etched on my memory is the detective who thereafter discreetly accompanied us on our morning airings.

Randolph Churchill, TWENTY-ONE 1964

At the 1913 Derby we all took our shots and got away quickly after the finish of the race. On the way back to London we saw a placard "Suffragette Killed at Epsom".

We stopped to buy a paper to see what had happened. None of us had seen the incident when Emily Davison had flung herself to her death at Tattenham Corner in front of the King's horse. But when Peat developed his plates he found that he had shot at the psychological moment, just before the horses trampled her. Peat had got one of the scoops of the century without knowing it.

James Jarche, PEOPLE I HAVE SHOT 1934

I was never more than a hard-working member of the rank and file, with a love of playing jokes that never got me anywhere. I went to ask if I might go to prison for the suffrage cause. I was interviewed by Christabel Pankhurst. She wore a red tam-o-shanter and her hair was inclined to be wispy. She listened, and tapped on her desk with a pencil all the time I was talking. When I'd finished she said, "No, you can't go?" I said, "Why can't I?" "Because you'd make a joke of it all, and play the fool."

Naomi Jacob, ME, A CHRONICLE ABOUT OTHER PEOPLE 1933

Christabel Pankhurst was particularly smart at quick-fire retorts. "My question, Mrs Pankhurst," said a weedy-looking individual at one meeting which I attended, "is this, and will you answer it honestly if you can? At the bottom of your heart, really, don't you think you would like to be a man?"

Christabel looked at him, and wagged her head in that way she had when she was going to cope with anyone.

"Quite honestly, my friend, I don't know," she said. "But don't you wish that you were?"

Naomi Jacob, ME, A CHRONICLE ABOUT OTHER PEOPLE 1933

SUICIDE

It is against the tradition of the Foreign Office to show emotion in any emergency. Private secretaries are almost unapproachable persons. One of these was Henry Foley, who on one occasion received the visit of a desperate consul, monomaniacally bent on obtaining a particular post. When Foley was obliged to tell him that he could not have it, the poor fellow there and then drew a revolver from his pocket and blew his brains out. Foley at once rang the bell, whereupon the office keeper appeared, and maintaining an impassive silence, mopped up the blood on the carpet with official blotting paper.

J. D. Gregory, ON THE EDGE OF DIPLOMACY 1929

As I went towards company headquarters to wake the officers I saw a man lying on his face in a machine-gun shelter. I stopped and said, "Stand-to there." I flashed my torch on him and saw that his foot was bare. The machine-gunner beside him said, "No good talking to him, sir." I said, "What's wrong? What's he taken his boot and sock off for?" I was ready for anything odd in the trenches. "Look for yourself, sir," he said. I shook the man by the arm and noticed suddenly that the back of his head was blown out. The first corpse that I saw in France was this suicide. He had taken off his boot and sock to pull the trigger of his rifle with his toe; the muzzle was in his mouth.

Robert Graves, GOODBYE TO ALL THAT 1929

I tried to commit suicide by gas. It is a lovely sensation, just like taking anaesthetic, so I shan't be sorry any more for schoolmistresses who are found dead in that way, but just in the middle of it I thought that Romie (Drury-Lowe) who I was staying with might have a miscarriage, which would be disappointing for her so I got back to bed and was sick.

Nancy Mitford, letter to Mark Ogilvie-Grant, 4 *Feb* 1931, *quoted Harold Acton,* NANCY MITFORD, A MEMOIR 1975

I have just had the most awful shock. Virginia [Woolf] has killed herself. It is not in the papers but I have got letters from Leonard [Woolf] and Vanessa [Bell] telling me. It was last Friday. Leonard came home to find a note saying she was going to commit suicide, and they think she has drowned herself, as he found her stick floating on the river. He said she had not been well for the last few weeks and was terrified of going mad again. He says, "It was, I suppose, the strain of the war and finishing her book, and she could not rest or eat."

I simple cannot take it in. That lovely mind. That lovely spirit.

Vita Sackville-West, letter to Harold Nicolson 31 *Mar* 1941

Paris. A young man survived a suicide attempt yesterday, but in the process killed two, injured thirteen, and partly demolished a five-storey apartment building when he turned on gas jets in his kitchen but then decided to have a last cigarette.

The Independent 11 *Nov* 1986

One of the gentleman's most treasured possessions is his game book, in which he keeps a meticulous tally of everything he shoots or catches. This habit was so ingrained with one gentleman that when he decided to take his own life he was careful to enter himself in the game book under "Various" before pressing the trigger.

Douglas Sutherland, THE ENGLISH GENTLEMAN 1978

An elderly German decided to commit suicide, took a lot of sleeping pills, tied a briefcase full of stones round his neck, rowed out into the middle of the Rhine – and was found sound asleep in his boat.

Buffalo News, quoted Denys Parsons FUNNY HA HA, FUNNY PECULIAR 1965

SUPERSTITION

Caruso's life was ruled by superstitions. Never on a Friday would he travel or wear a new suit – and before putting one on for the first time he would slip a coin into the right-hand pocket.

Charles Neilson Gatty, THE ELEPHANT THAT SWALLOWED A NIGHTINGALE 1981

Although Caruso smoked up to sixty cigarettes a day he was convinced his health would not suffer so long as he kept a dried anchovy suspended over his chest by a chain from his neck.

Ibid.

On tour with *The Rape of Lucretia* his librettist, Ronald Duncan, found Benjamin Britten (then thirty-three years old) in a hotel corridor in Edinburgh, hobbling along as if crippled. "What I am trying to do," Britten explained, "is walk down the corridor and back without touching any of the red lines on the carpet."

Duncan asked what he hoped to achieve by that.

"If I can get up and down the corridor without touching the lines," said Britten, "it will mean that I am a composer."

Norman Lebrecht, THE BOOK OF MUSICAL ANECDOTES 1985

V.S. Naipaul practised magic – superstitious, propitiatory. He always used stolen BBC "no-rustle" paper ("it seemed less likely to attract failure"). He never numbered his pages ("for fear of not getting to the end"). And on the typescript of his first four books he never wrote his name ("Such anxiety – Such ambition"). Such modest voodoo.

Martin Amis, Observer 6 Jul 1984

A dove entered the mausoleum at Frogmore as the royal party knelt at prayer on the anniversary of Queen Victoria's death. "That's mama's spirit," they murmured. "We are sure of it." "No I am sure it is not," said Princess Louise. "Dear mama's spirit would never have ruined Beatrice's hat."

Philip Ziegler, DIANA COOPER 1981

SURREALISM

In 1936 Salvador Dali inadvertently caused more sensation than he had intended at the International Surrealist Exhibition at the New Burlington Galleries. On a hot summer's day he made a dramatic entrance for a lecture he was due to give, holding in one hand two Russian wolfhounds on a leash and in the other a billiard cue. On his head was a diving helmet. He strode on to the stage and tried to remove the helmet but it had been bolted down. The audience waited, unaware that Dali was suffocating. He was finally rescued and practically dead when released. The audience applauded what it thought was a humorous pantomime.

Penny McGuire. Observer Magazine, Surreal Life Legend 20 *Nov* 1985

TACT

Queen Alexandra, inspecting an office group of VADs during World War I paused before a typewriter and said to the typist, "Ah, a sewing machine, I see. How useful." "Yes, ma'am," the girl replied tactfully.

Dame Katherine Furse, HEARTS AND POMEGRANATES 1940

Marlene Dietrich stormed at her photographer for producing unflattering close-ups, "What's wrong with you? Eight years ago you used to make me look marvellous." "I know," he said, "but I was much younger then."

Leslie Halliwell, THE FILMGOER'S BOOK OF QUOTES 1973

Sir Oswyn Murray, Secretary of the Admiralty for nearly twenty years from 1917, once intervened diplomatically to prevent what might have been a serious quarrel between Sir Eric Geddes and Douglas Brownrigg, the Chief Naval Censor. Sir Eric had written a fierce letter to Sir Douglas, and the difficulty was to get him to accept it without taking offence. So Murray and Edward Packe, Sir Douglas's private secretary, agreed that the note should be delivered when Sir Douglas was in Murray's room. Its effect was exactly what had been anticipated. Flinging the note on the table with the demand that they should "read that" Sir Douglas declared that he would never darken the doors of the Admiralty again.

"Oh, but you're *quite* wrong," insisted his friends after reading the note, "you don't understand the First Lord; this is positively gracious, coming from him, you should see his usual style; compared to that it is almost abject."

The strategy had the desired effect and Sir Douglas was pacified.

Lady Murray, THE MAKING OF A CIVIL SERVANT 1940

An official of the Imperial Court was once asked, "How do you manage to keep the Kaiser in such a good temper?"

The official replied, "His Majesty delights in explaining mechanical contrivances, such as a clock, or a compass, or a barometer. I keep a special barometer, and whenever the Emperor comes in I ask him to explain how it works, telling him I have forgotten what he told me last time. He gives an admirable exposition; this puts him in an excellent temper, and he signs the documents I put before him."

Lord d'Abernon, AN AMBASSADOR OF PEACE 1929

TACTLESSNESS

Mrs Patrick Campbell said to a friend of mine, "Norah, were your eyes *always* as far apart as that?" She received the reply, "No Stella, didn't you know? They had to be *dragged* apart."

Osbert Sitwell, LAUGHTER IN THE NEXT ROOM 1949

When I was playing Hamlet in New York I asked my director to invite Mrs Patrick Campbell to the party after the performance and she behaved with appalling tactlessness. She went up to Judith Anderson, who was playing the Queen and said, "Why do you sit on the bed? Only housemaids sit on the bed."

John Gielgud, AN ACTOR AND HIS TIME 1979

Gielgud once had lunch with a writer called Edward Knoblock. "Do you see that man just coming in?" Gielgud said to Knoblock in one of those glorious, unmalicious boobs when the rushing stress of his thought breaks its banks. "He's the biggest bore in London – second only to Edward Knoblock." And then, in a terrible attempt to put matters right, he added hopelessly, "Not *you* of course. I mean the *other* Edward Knoblock."

John Mortimer, IN CHARACTER 1983

When I had a heart attack in Leeds I was helpless in my Jensen at one o'clock in the morning and the only living being around me was this man who'd been in the Territorial Army. He drove my £7000 motor car like a tank for miles. Then he had to wake someone at the hospital. Finally as they wheeled me into intensive care I saw him bending over me. He whispered in my ear, "Can I have your autograph before you go?"

Eric Morecambe, quoted John Mortimer, IN CHARACTER 1983

TEA

Not only is Tony Benn a teetotaller, he is a total tea drinker, consuming at least eighteen pints a day. I once asked a doctor about the effects of drinking such huge amounts of caffeine, tannin, and tiny black leaves. He reeled off an alarming catalogue of ailments adding, "And if Mr Benn was a racehorse he would foam at the mouth."

Peter Hillmore, Observer 27 *Feb* 1983

After Nasser's funeral, a hot and hectic occasion, Sir Alec Douglas-Home regained his plane at the cocktail hour. But when the steward asked him what he wanted with his ice he replied by asking what time it was in London. "Four o'clock," said the steward. "Very well then," said Sir Alec, "I'll have a cup of tea."

Hugo Young, Sunday Times 3 *Oct* 1971

Lanspance Montecchi, a 22-year old Italian, accused of crashing his car and doing £1000 worth of damage, explained in court at St Helier, Jersey, that he had drunk a lot of English tea, which sent him to sleep while he was at the wheel.

Daily Express, quoted Denys Parsons, FUNNY HA HA, FUNNY PECULIAR 1965

TEETH

Sophie Brzeska had gold fillings in her teeth and when she went to see friends or people she wished to impress she smiled a lot in order to show the gold, but when speaking to prospective landladies she took great care to keep her mouth closed so that they should not suspect a millionairess and raise their prices.

H.S. Ede, SAVAGE MESSIAH 1931

TELEGRAM

An ever-ready pitfall for the sub-editor is the cryptic telegram, boiled down to its bare bones, which skeleton he must re-clothe with words and turn into sensible English. One such message which arrived at an Australian newspaper ran as follows: "Dean Swift Ob Icy Mountains."

An easy one, the sub thought. "Ob" was obviously "obit" or dead, and padding out the rest was a matter of minutes. So his paper went to bed with the rather belated news that "Dean Swift, author of the well-known hymn from Greenlands Icy Mountains has died in England."

What the message really meant was that Dean Swift, Ob and Icy Mountains were the first three horses in an important race.

Hamilton Fyffe, SIXTY YEARS IN FLEET STREET 1949

TELEPATHY

When I was soldiering in India I had an attack of cholera. When I was at the worst stage the doctor gave me some hydrate of chloral, then a new medicine; in my agony I clutched at the glass; at the same time my mother, who was in Ireland awoke from her sleep and said to my father, "Surely our son is ill, for I have seen him sitting up in bed clutching a medicine glass." The hour was found to coincide, allowance being made for the difference in time.

Lord Rathcreedan, MEMOIRS OF A LONG LIFE 1931

A famous music hall turn were the Zanzigs, who amazed everybody with their "thought transference" act. After the show one night Mr Zanzig explained, "It is simply dis, dat at any hour or place, whatever I gaze on, whatever I place my hand on, Madame can see very clearly."

Then said my colleague Arthur Binstead of the *Sporting Times,* with the gravity of one appreciating to the full the dangers of a new situation, "I only hope for your own sake you possess the power to – er – to ring off Madam occasionally."

J.B. Booth, LIFE, LAUGHTER AND BRASS HATS 1939

TELEPHONE

Much nervous strain in my home life arose from the newly installed telephone. Whenever Papa was at home he had it switched through to his room, and as he intercepted every call, naturally he got bored by being charged with messages for all the other inmates of the house. For instance one morning when he was feverishly anxious to consult his stockbroker, to whom he had just got through, he was cut off by a strange woman's voice. "Who's that speaking?" he barked. "Hold on, my man, while I get a pencil and paper," a voice imperiously charged him, "and then tell me where Mr Horniblower goes for his teeth." (Mr Horniblower was Alfred, the footman.)

Cynthia Asquith, REMEMBER AND BE GLAD 1952

When Leslie Banks was in New York he was awakened by the hotel operator with the message, "Ada Clark, Mr Banks, and thank you." Banks was not expecting any Ada Clark and wondered who she might be. He got up, put on a dressing gown, and waited for his visitor to appear, presuming she was an early bird among publicity or newspaper women. As she did not arrive, he asked the telephone girl why. She said, coldly, "I said 'Eight o'clock, Mr Banks, thank you'."

Reginald Pound, POUND NOTES 1940

Maurice Baring had a good way of spelling his name on the telephone. "B for Beastly, A for Apple, R for Rotten, I for England, N for Nothing, G for Gee", all rattled off at top speed.

Edward Marsh, A NUMBER OF PEOPLE 1939

When I arrived at Lord Beaverbrook's apartment in Arlington House he was bawling into the telephone, "No. No. No. No. No. No. No." He replaced the handset and walked slowly across the room, his hands on his hips. He then returned to the instrument, picked up the handset and as he jumped six inches into the air he delivered one final thunderous "No!"

Hugh Cudlipp, WALKING ON THE WATER 1976

Once, at Kedleston, Lord Curzon was summoned by his butler to the telephone. His private secretary at the Foreign Office, Robert Vansittart, wished to tell him that a certain foreign statesman had died suddenly. Curzon said, "Do you realise that to convey to me this trivial piece of information you have forced me a walk the length of a mansion not far removed from the dimensions of Windsor Castle?"

Paul Johnson, THE OXFORD BOOK OF POLITICAL ANECDOTES 1986

By nature Edgar Dégas was conservative. His friend the etcher Jean-Louis Forain believed in progress. Forain had recently installed that new-fangled invention, the telephone. Arranging to have a friend phone him during the meal, he invited Dégas to dinner. The phone rang, Forain rushed to answer it, then he returned beaming with pride. Dégas said, "So that's the telephone. It rings – you run."

Roy McMullen, DEGAS, HIS LIFE, TIMES AND WORK 1984

After breakfast King George V would telephone his sister, Princess Victoria. The phone call came through to her daily about half-past nine. "Hello, you old fool," she would greet her brother. "Beg pardon, Your Royal Highness," the Buckingham Palace operator had to interject on one occasion, "His Majesty is not yet on the line."

John Gore, KING GEORGE V, A PERSONAL MEMOIR 1941

Not long after the death of Swinburne, Sir Edmund Gosse was engaged on the Bonchurch collected edition of the poet's works. On one of the crowded Sunday afternoons at 17 Hanover Terrace, a telephone message was misunderstood by the parlourmaid who took it. Knowing nothing of the death of the poet she stood in the doorway and announced, "Mr Swinburne to speak to you on the telephone, sir."

Greatly as he appreciated Swinburne, it was an opportunity not to be missed by Gosse. In the breathless hush that naturally followed the rather appalling announcement all eyes were fixed on his glittering spectacles as he exclaimed, "Mr Swinburne to speak to me on the telephone? I shall certainly not speak to Mr Swinburne. I don't know *where* he may be speaking from."

Alfred Noyes, TWO WORLDS FOR MEMORY 1953

The conductor Robert Kajanus, one of Sibelius's most intimate friends, sought to excuse himself from a dinner party in Helsinki and take his departure as he was due to conduct a concert in Petrograd. The others present protested that the occasion was not one to be sacrificed to such sordid material considerations and pressed Kajanus to telephone to Petrograd and cancel the engagement. Seeming to comply with the suggestion Kajanus left the table, but went to the station, took a train to Petrograd, conducted the concert and returned to Helsinki where, on re-entering the restaurant, he found the company still seated at the same table, engaged in the same animated discussion. On seeing him Sibelius mildly expostulated with him saying, "That was surely a very long telephone call of yours, Kajanus?"

Cecil Gray, MUSICAL CHAIRS 1948

I went to see Harold Macmillan immediately after his resignation in 1963. He had one complaint, he said. Within twenty-four hours of his ceasing to be Prime Minister, the Post Office had taken out his line at Number Ten. Now he was having to pay a penny-halfpenny a call. So please would I call him, rather than wait for him to call me?

Sir Harold Evans, DOWNING STREET DIARY 1981

My telephone rang in Beverly Hills. Rosten, "Hello?" Voice, "Do I have the honour of addressing the world-famed proctologist, Marmaduke Montague?" Rosten, "You have the wrong number." Voice, "Then why did you answer? For years I've been calling this number and getting Professor Marmaduke Montague. What have you done with the body? I am going to call the police. What I'll call them is none of your business. What number is this, anyway?" Rosten, "Crestview 829." Voice, "Aha, so you admit it! Why, if you were a man you'd come over and knock my teeth out." Rosten "I – " Voice, "And if you were half a man you'd knock half my teeth out." Rosten, "Who – ?" "And if you were a woman we could dance the night away in wild abandon."

It was many minutes before I could get Groucho Marx down from the high, demented plane he loved to inhabit. Then he revealed the purpose of his call. "Free for lunch? Fine. Twelve thirty. I'll have a rose clenched between my teeth."

Leo Rosten, I REMEMBER GROUCHO 1982

I was in Harold Ross's office one hot day in the middle of August 1928 when the phone rang, and he turned to it impatiently and said sourly, "Yeah? Ah, Aleck. Just a second." He capped the transmitter with his hand and said, "It's Woollcott. He wants to tell me about the wedding of Charlie MacArthur and Helen Hayes . . . OK, Aleck. Go ahead."

Alexander Woollcott began talking in the fluent, practical, almost compulsive way he had of telling a story. Ross promptly put the receiver down, gently, on the top of his desk, got up, walked across the room and began alternately staring out the window and scowling at the jabbering receiver. An unintelligible babble came out of it, a little like the sound track of a Donald Duck cartoon. Against this dim and distant monologue, wasted on the office air, Ross set up a counterpoint of disdainful comment. "Listen to that glib son-of-a-bitch," he said. "He thinks he's holding me spellbound."

James Thurber, THE YEARS WITH ROSS 1959

TELEVISION

An American television crew arrived and tried to lure Max Beerbohm in front of the cameras. No persuasion, financial or otherwise, would induce him to yield. All he had to do, he was told, was to smile and say, "Good evening, I am happy to be with you." "But that wouldn't be true," Max sweetly riposted.

Malcolm Muggeridge, TREAD SOFTLY FOR YOU TREAD ON MY JOKES 1966

During one of my *Dinner Party* shows both I and the cameras resolutely ignored one of the guests, a newspaper editor who had turned up absolutely sloshed with gin. All the viewers saw of him was some mysterious cigarette smoke drifting across the screen, though occasionally the discussion was punctuated by a disembodied voice asking, "I say, chaps, what are we talking about?"

Lord Boothby, RECOLLECTIONS OF A REBEL 1975

My uncle Jack Cockburn was devoted to television which he always watched with the sound off, claiming that words ruined everything. "Saw ye on the television the other night," he would tell me. "What did you think of what I said?" I would ask. "Och, I said I *saw* ye. I didn't *hear* ye. I dinna bother with that blether."

Gerald Priestland, SOMETHING UNDERSTOOD 1986

When the evening spent in front of the TV has been a pleasant one for President de Gaulle and nothing has gone wrong with the news commentary he says "*My* television." If he is not satisfied with the commentator's tone, if he is annoyed or bored he says "*The* television". If he feels he or his regime have been made to look ridiculous he summons the Minister of Information next morning and greets him by saying, "I watched *your* television last night –."

Pierre Vinnsson-Ponte, THE KING AND HIS COURT

Before television's first party political broadcast it was impressed on McDonald Hobley that there must not be the slightest hint of political bias when he introduced it. Hobley concentrated hard, then announced to viewers that they would now hear, "Sir Stifford Crapps". He was severely carpeted.

The Times Aug 1987

On *You Bet Your Life*, Groucho Marx's popular television show, he created a kind of host never seen before. I was backstage one night when one of the contestants turned out to be from a country area. Let's call him Floyd.

Groucho, "How did you meet your wife?" Floyd, "Well, I drive a truck." Groucho, "You ran over her?" Floyd, "No, she was in the barn." Groucho, "You drove your truck into a *barn*?" Floyd, "No, no. Her family had been missing some chickens." Groucho, "They were lonely for *chickens*?" "No, they had been *missing*, so they turned on a light in the barnyard, and I'm driving up to get some turkeys, and her father hollers 'the turkeys are in the barn'." Groucho, "You married a *turkey*?" Floyd, "*No*! As I go to the barn a big skunk starts for the chicken house, and a girl yells, 'Get that skunk.' So I jumped on it and she fell on it, too – and we both smelled so bad –." Groucho, "That's the most romantic story I ever heard."

Leo Rosten, I REMEMBER GROUCHO 1982

In the early days of television the decision was made that as a performance was continuous and alive the medium was more akin to the theatre than the cinema – where actors were only required to sustain dialogue for a few seconds at a time. Thus stage actors were employed and expected to perform in a mechanical medium. New techniques had to be learned – sometimes to disguise a deficiency. When one actor forgot his lines he continued to move his lips. This caused the control box to start twiddling knobs in panic, as they assumed the sound equipment had broken down.

Donald Sinden, A TOUCH OF THE MEMOIRS 1982

One interviewer in particular must remember with some embarrassment questioning Mother Teresa on television as to how she came to be doing such remarkable work. "Jesus" was the simple and uncompromising reply. The interviewer, who had evidently been expecting a considerably more prolonged and involved reply was left floundering among his notes for the next question.

Kathryn Spink, FOR THE BROTHERHOOD OF MAN UNDER THE FATHERHOOD OF GOD 1981

THEATRE

Tallulah Bankhead's role in *Conchita* was that of a dark-skinned Cuban dancer; she wore a dark wig over her golden bob, and carried on her arm a tiny monkey. On opening night the monkey panicked, grabbed Tallulah's wig, pulled it off, darted to the footlights, whirling the wig above its head like a lariat. The audience started to titter. Tallulah, for want of anything better to do, threw a cartwheel. The audience roared with laughter and approval.

Brendan Gill, TALLULAH 1973

During the desperate twelve-hour dress rehearsal for the first performance of *Peter Pan* in a fog-bound theatre I was with J.M. Barrie in the stalls at about 4 o'clock in the morning when Pauline Chase entered in tears and an Eskimo costume.

"Oh please, Mr Barrie, I can't go on like this," she wailed. "My hair is too long and my boots are too big."

JMB, stroking his head, observed, "Well, put some of your hair in your boots." Exit Pauline Chase, smiling through tears, and the fog slowly dispersed.

William Nicholson, Sunday Referee 5 *Dec* 1931

Sir James Barrie was taken to the theatre by a lady with whom he had dined. She told him what theatre she had chosen. He asked what the play was. She didn't know. He asked if she admired the principal actor and actress. She had no idea who they were. "Then why," he asked, "did you pick this theatre to go to?" She explained gravely that "it was a nice quiet street for the horses".

Hamilton Fyffe, John o' London's Weekly 2 *Jul* 1937

I understudied Sir George Alexander in *The Admirable Crichton,* in 1914. At the first rehearsal I looked in vain for Sir James Barrie, the author. A little man, wearing an overcoat, bowler hat and muffler came up to borrow a match. I asked him if Barrie came to rehearsals. The little man said he did, and added that he himself helped Barrie to write the plays.

"Well, if you help Barrie to write the plays why doesn't your name appear on the programme?" I asked with a laugh.

"It does," he said, "Ssh, not a word to a soul."

He waddled off. A little later I discovered that he had taken my box of matches with him. And later still I learnt that he was Sir James Barrie.

Hesketh Pearson, THINKING IT OVER 1938

I once notified the manager of the theatre at, I think, Kings Lynn, where *Tristan* was being put on, what scenery was needed. For the second act a tower was required. I had no time before the performance to inspect the scenery and you may judge of my astonishment, when the curtain rose, to discover none other than our old friend from the second act of *Iolanthe* with Big Ben in the background.

Sir Thomas Beecham, A MINGLED CHIME 1979

Spent today auditioning boys at her Majesty's [for *Forty Years On*]. In the afternoon, when we had been going for about an hour, there was a quavering voice from the Upper Circle. "Could you tell me when you are going to start, please?" It was an old lady who had come for the matinee of *Fiddler on the Roof* on the wrong day.

Alan Bennett, DIARY 9 *Jul* 1968

Frank Benson suffered wonderful lapses of memory. As Caliban one of his effects was to swing by his ankles on suspended ropes while he beat his chest, Tarzan fashion. Madge Compton, as Miranda, was waiting to make her entrance when she noticed Benson's dresser trying to attract his attention as he looped across the stage. When Benson looked towards the wings Madge could see that apart from his whole body covered in his half-fish, half-animal make-up, he still had his pince-nez perched on his nose.

Donald Sinden, A TOUCH OF THE MEMOIRS 1982

If last Thursday the public paid £600, and this Thursday they have paid only £580 we are "down £20 on last week". If it was the other way – £620 today – we should be "£20 up" and all would be smiling. But we are "£20 down" and there are grave debates. The only time I met Gertrude Lawrence she told a delightful tale about Lillian Braithwaite.

The Dame had a long run in *Arsenic and Old Lace*. They kept going even when the doodle-bugs appeared, though I found that difficult to believe – to go on acting when those terrifying falterers and stoppers were about. The Dame lived in some penthouse in Mayfair, and used to spend the noisy nights in the bathroom. One morning – it may have been the night that I myself, on duty on the river, counted eighty-five of the obscene machines – the secretary, maid or someone found the Dame cold and half asleep in her dressing gown, woke her and said, "Oh Dame, did you have a terrible night?" The old lady drew herself up and said, "No indeed. We were £30 up."

A.P. Herbert, APH, HIS LIFE AND TIMES 1970

The first time Jack Buchanan appeared on the music-hall stage he "got the bird". The audience threw things at him and the curtain was rung down so suddenly that it hit him on the head and sent him staggering.

The crowd's hoots turned to sympathetic laughter, and the manager paid Jack £1 a week to go through the routine twice nightly.

Leslie Mallory, News Chronicle 21 *Oct* 1957

Once Mrs Campbell objected to he-men with pink chins; she thought they ought to be blue chins, though we secretly feared that the effect might be what is known among actors as "a dirty shave". However we all came on with blue chins. I never heard exactly what happened, but I believe Mrs Pat's manager came round to the front of the house and told her she appeared to be surrounded by burglars, and that she had turned a drawing room comedy into a crook play. Anyway, we were told that we needn't do it any more.

George Arliss, ON THE STAGE 1927

My wife, Gladys Cooper, was playing at Leeds with Seymour Hicks and I went up unexpectedly to see them. I found them in the middle of a railway-station scene. Borrowing a hat much too small for me from the stage manager I walked across the stage to Seymour. "Could you tell me, sir, what time the next train leaves for London?" I thought he would be taken aback, as he didn't even know I was in Leeds, but he showed not the slightest surprise. "No, I couldn't," he snapped, at the same time reaching for a bun from the tea wagon. With an unerring shot he threw it at me as I walked off – a beautiful shot that knocked my little green hat flying into the wings. The Leeds audience screamed with delight, and thought it was part of the play.

Herbert Buckmaster, BUCK'S BOOK 1933

I asked Noel Coward whether, faced by failure, as he sometimes has been, he'd ever despaired. For good measure I threw in the name *Sirocco* which was booed off the stage as few plays have been since.

"Well, if I'm going to have a flop," he replied, "I like it to be a rouser. I didn't despair at all. What made it much more interesting was that my mother, who is slightly deaf, thought the booing was cheering. Incredibly Basil Dean, the producer of the play, made the same mistake. He was ringing the curtain up and down with a *beaming* smile. I said, "Wipe that smile off your face, dear – this is it."

John Heilpern, Observer 14 *Dec* 1969

The last thing an author in his senses does is to go near his leading lady just before a First Night. She is fairly sure to say, "I feel terrible. I have forgotten all my lines and I think I am going to be sick." But on the first night of *Mother of Pearl* C.B. Cochran gave me some message to deliver to Alice Delysia and through the pass-door I went. I knocked at her door and heard a hearty "Come in."

"How are you feeling Alice?" I said. She smote her bosom, rather in the George Robey style and said, "I am feeling fine. I am going out there to show them what I can do." And she did. This utterance must be a theatrical record.

A.P. Herbert, APH: HIS LIFE AND TIMES 1970

A playwright, having had a plot accepted, asked George Edwardes for an advance so that he could go down to the seaside and finish the job. Edwardes offered him fifty pounds.

"Fifty isn't enough," protested the author. "I can't possibly go away on fifty. It means shutting up the flat in town, and what with my wife, the two children, my wife's maid and the nurse – what about two hundred?"

"Very well, very well," growled Edwardes. Then, turning to his assistant, "Arthur, in future see that all my librettists are bachelors."

J.B. Booth, LIFE, LAUGHTER AND BRASS HATS 1939

In one of the scenes in *Walk This Way* Gracie Fields was a maid waiting on a smart family at meals. She was ready for her cue to enter when she spotted a messenger boy parking his bicycle near the stage entrance. She just had time to rush and grab the bike and make her entrance on it. Round the table she pedalled, throwing the knives and forks on to it without missing a single one. It wasn't only the audience that roared. The cast were simply rolling in their chairs. They laughed so much it was quite some time before they could get on with the show.

Bert Aza, Sunday Chronicle 13 *Aug* 1929

When I was waiting to be demobbed at the end of the war I formed a touring company to keep the troops entertained. By the time I got back to camp I found I'd been demobbed two weeks before. "Well," my CO said, "well, Fraser, what are you going to do in civvy street?" I told him, the theatre. "Oh dear, dear. They've blown up all the piers, haven't they?"

A lovely line. I've always cherished it.

Bill Fraser, Radio Times 24 *Jan* 1974

The audiences at the Vic were very lively. There was an old lady called Miss Pilgrim who had been a fan of the Old Vic for years. She always sat in the gallery and at the end of the performance she would sing "God Save the King" in a very loud cracked voice. She had a wall eye. We all knew her by sight, and she used to write letters to us. A year or two after I left when Tyrone Guthrie took over the direction, stars like Charles Laughton, Athene Seyler, Flora Robson and James Mason were in the company. Miss Pilgrim went to the stage door one night and asked everyone to sign their autographs for her as they came out of the theatre. The next day they found that the paper had been folded over and on the other side she had written a demand to the Governors that Tyrone Guthrie should be sacked.

John Gielgud, AN ACTOR AND HIS TIME 1979

In the first act of my play *Nana* a man is breaking away from his mistress of whom he is tired. He keeps repeating, "I can't go on. You bore me stiff. Clear out."

I had offered the part of the mistress to a well-known old actress. When the first act was read to her she all but threw me out. "It's bad enough," she said, "that you should write a play about my private life but to think that you should dare to ask me to play in it! Really you must be out of your mind."

Sacha Guitry, IF I REMEMBER RIGHT 1935

On one occasion I gave a quavering, senile performance as the old man in a Spanish play called *A Hundred Years Old* – a performance only marred by an unfortunate incident arising from a change of costume which I made between the dress rehearsal and the actual show. The frock coat provided by the academy being too small I borrowed another from my great uncle Charles Lambton. This coat had not been in use for some forty years, but it fitted admirably. Unfortunately I forgot to transfer from the rejected coat a letter which, in the dress rehearsal, I had drawn from my inner pocket and then read. When the moment for my letter-reading came on the night of the performance I put my hand inside my pocket, felt the welcome pressure of my fingers on the letter (as I thought) and then drew forth a sheaf of toilet paper which, in joyous freedom for the first time since the century began, flew skittishly about the stage.

William Douglas-Home, HALF TERM REPORT 1957

As the Doge of Venice I secured the biggest laugh of my theatrical career. A keen and enthusiastic student had made me up, with total accuracy in the likeness of the Doge in Bellini's portrait of that name. Discovered on the stage, I conducted the Trial Scene with dignity and grace, and then retired. Unfortunately my lovely golden robe had burst open down the back and the audience were treated to the exit of a Doge of Venice, wearing flannel trousers and a cricket shirt.

Ibid.

In the theatre one of the all-time great Upmen is Wilfrid Hyde-White. When I was a young actor in a play with him I had a long and terribly difficult speech which he knew I always had trouble remembering. So every night he'd wait until I'd just managed to get through to the end of it and then he'd say, "I'm awfully sorry, I must be a little hard of hearing. Would you mind just saying that again?"

Richard Briers, Radio Times 6 *Nov* 1976

The audience for last Thursday's performance of Eugene Ionesco's *Journeys Among the Dead*, at the Riverside Studio in West London, included an old Frenchman in the front row who talked all the way through the first act. He left, still muttering, before the interval. It was Ionesco himself.

The director told the cast that Ionesco had muttered to him afterwards, "Oh my God, I have written an awful play. I have let a lot of people down. My life is worthless."

Two days later Ionesco gave the play another chance, but again created quite a disturbance. One actor asked, through the director, if it was possible for the playwright to pipe down a bit. Ionesco had apparently not seen the play before and came over for that purpose. He is now presumed to have gone back to France, bearing thoughts that lie too deep for tears.

Francis Wheen, The Independent 27 Jan 1987

Irving was intending to use, for a new production, a cage of "property" birds who, when a button was pressed, would burst into song. He came down, looked at the cage, and nodded.

"Very nice – very pretty – beautiful property. But – er – too clean eh? Birds will be birds – you can't get away from – er – nature. Craven!" Hawes-Craven arrived. "Can you do anything to make this look more – er – natural, Craven?"

Craven thought that he could, and brought a pot of white paint. Irving wandered down to begin rehearsing. Craven began splashing with the paint to get the effect he needed. Suddenly Irving turned round and stared.

"Craven," he said at last, "they're canaries and linnets, not eagles, my boy."

Naomi Jacob, ME, A CHRONICLE ABOUT OTHER PEOPLE 1933

Ruth Gordon was telling George Kaufman about her latest play. "In the first scene I'm on the left side of the stage," she explained, "and the audience has to imagine I'm eating dinner in a crowded restaurant. Then in the second scene I run over to the right side of the stage and the audience imagines I am in my own drawing room."

Kaufman was unimpressed. "And the second night," he said, "*you* have to imagine there's an audience in front."

Robert Drennan, WIT'S END 1973

George Kaufman looked in at the theatre while William Gaxton was starring in *Of Thee I Sing,* in which Kaufman had collaborated with George Gershwin, to make sure all was running smoothly. He was appalled at the liberties Gaxton was taking with the script. In the intermission Kaufman hurried out and sent Gaxton a wire. "Am sitting in the last row. Wish you were here!

Oscar Levant, THE UNIMPORTANCE OF BEING OSCAR 1968

George C. Tyler commissioned George Kaufman to adapt Jacques Duval's French farce *Someone in the House.* George did a good job, but a weak cast, plus a city-wide epidemic of influenza, shortened its life. Tyler reluctantly turned down George's suggestion for an advertising slogan for the faltering play: "Avoid crowds. See *Someone in the House* at the Knickerbocker Theatre."

Marcus Connelly, VOICES OFF STAGE 1968

Dinsdale Landon told today a wonderful story of his days as an assistant stage manager at Worthing. He was a walk-on when Wolfit was there as a guest star, playing Othello, but was not told what to do until the dress rehearsal, at which the great man said it would be a very good idea for Othello to have a page who followed him everywhere. He handed Dinsdale a loin-cloth, told him to black up, and said he'd got the part. Dinsdale did not know the play, and just went wherever Wolfit went, the completely dutiful page, always in attendance. But at one point he found himself in a scene in which he felt rather ill at ease, he had an instinct about it. Suddenly he heard the great man roaring, "Not in Desdemona's bedroom!"

Peter Hall, DIARIES 1 *May* 1978

Marie Lloyd, given her first and only job as principal girl at Drury Lane, knelt down and said her prayers before climbing into bed, in one scene, to dream of an imaginary lover, but then got so tired of lying there during a long tableau that it got on her nerves, she felt that she must do something. So she yawned, stretched herself, got out of bed, knelt down and searched underneath it for an obvious article not usually mentioned in polite society.

The effect was instantaneous. Roars of laughter greeted her action. Mothers with their children hastily got up and left the theatre. The criticisms next morning described the pantomime as coarse and vulgar, and the result was disastrous.

Horace Collins, MY BEST RICHES 1941

A theatre owned by David N. Morton in Brisbane was invaded by flying ants and he received a telegram stating, "Show stopped by flying ants." He is supposed to have replied by cable, "Book them for a further week."

Michael Bentine, THE LONG BANANA SKIN 1975

Edward My Son began its run at His Majesty's on May 30, 1947. It was written by Robert Morley and Noel Langley. Morley played the part of Lord Holt. On the night before the opening there was an interminable lighting and dress rehearsal. Robert ducked the third act altogether and took his place beside Henry Sherek, who was presenting the play, in the dress circle. He had removed all his make-up.

"What are you doing?" Henry asked.

"Going home," Robert told him. "I have a first night tomorrow."

Margaret Morley, LARGER THAN LIFE 1979

Robert Morley, starring in the Broadway production of *Edward My Son,* was approached by a small group of theatre producers from all over America and asked the best way to raise funds for putting on a new play.

Said Morley, "Just go to the richest man in your town and tell him it's the only way to fight Communism."

News Review 2 *Dec* 1948

We opened in Auckland, New Zealand, with *Hamlet* and one of the stage hands offered the opinion that it was a play "that would live". I said that it had lived a few hundred years.

"There you are," he said. "That just bears out what I say. We 'ad another piece 'ere by the same author larse autumn. Midsummer's Nice Dream, it was called. That was good too, though calling one of the characters Bottom was a bit near the knuckle."

Roland Pertwee, MASTER OF NONE 1940

Arthur Roberts, given the speechless part of a manservant in a gala performance of *Money* at Drury Lane was so annoyed that when George Alexander, in the leading part, asked, "Who will lend me £10 for my old nurse?" Roberts stepped to the centre of the stage, shouted, "I will – I got the girl into trouble. I'll see her through," bolted from the stage door and ran down the Strand.

Horace Collins, MY BEST RICHES 1941

When Stella Roman was playing Tosca in Puccini's opera she was supposed to leap to her death from a prison parapet and land safely off-stage on a mattress. Roman, feeling insecure one night, demanded two extra mattresses. She leaped, and the mattresses bounced her back on stage. She had to kill herself all over again.

Robert Merrill and Robert Saffron, BETWEEN ACTS 1978

Last week, in Scarborough, they were playing Peter Shaffer's *Black Comedy*, which shows what happens when the lights go out in a Kensington flat. "I don't know," said an old Yorkshire voice in the audience at the end. "Two bloody hours to mend a fuse!"

Ian Jack, Sunday Times 30 *Jun* 1974

I saw Edmund Teale in *The Three Musketeers* at the Grand Theatre, Leeds. When the beautiful queen, standing well down to the footlights, declared her love for Buckingham, taking us, the gallery, into her confidence, Richelieu walked down the wide stairs, listening.

A Leeds lad, gallant and much moved by the queen's recital, shouted "Shoot oop, missus. T'ould bastard's behind you."

Naomi Jacob, ME, A CHRONICLE ABOUT OTHER PEOPLE 1933

Recently I heard two men at the National Theatre discussing a forthcoming play at the Haymarket. "It's bound to be good," said one, an incredible optimist. "It's by the man who writes Mrs Thatcher's speeches."

Ned Sherrin, A SMALL THING LIKE AN EARTHQUAKE 1983

When Beerbohm Tree was rehearsing the dramatised version of *The Eternal City* Sir Hall Caine wanted him to drag Constance Collier, who was playing the part of Roma, round the stage by the hair and bang her head on the floor. "Very effective," said Tree, "but I seem to remember that identical incident in another famous drama."

Sir Hall, deeply interested, asked what it was. "Punch and Judy," replied Tree with a chuckle.

John o' London's Weekly, 31 *May* 1930

When I was living in Brighton I often used to go up to London to see a play. On one occasion I wanted to go up to see Tree in *Hamlet*, but knew that the curtain was not likely to descend before eleven forty-five. This would mean leaving before the last scene, so I sent Tree a wire. "Can you play *Hamlet* in a businesslike manner next Thursday night, so as to enable me to catch the midnight train from Victoria?" He wired back,

"Cannot alter my conception of the part to fit midnight train, but will cut a scene if you will run to Victoria." He kept his promise and omitted a scene in which Hamlet did not appear.

Hesketh Pearson, THINKING IT OVER 1938

Beerbohm Tree always seemed to have heard the lines of the other performers for the first time and even to be taken a little aback by them. Let me give you an extreme instance of this. In *Pygmalion* the heroine, in a rage, throws the hero's slippers in his face. When we rehearsed this for the first time I had taken care to have a very soft pair of velvet slippers provided, for I knew Mrs Patrick Campbell was very dexterous, very strong and a deadly shot. Sure enough, Tree got the slippers well and truly delivered, bang in the face.

The effect was appalling. He had totally forgotten there was any such incident in the play, and it seemed to him that Mrs Campbell, giving way to an impulse of diabolical wrath, had committed an unprovoked and brutal attack upon him. The physical impact was nothing; but the wound to his feelings was terrible. He collapsed in tears on the nearest chair, and left me staring in amazement, while the entire personnel of the theatre crowded round him solicitously, explaining that the incident was part of the play, and even exhibiting the prompt book to prove their words.

But his *morale* was so shattered that it took quite a long time, and a good deal of rallying and coaxing from Mrs Campbell, before he was in a condition to continue the rehearsal. The worst of it was that it was quite evident that he would be just as surprised and wounded every time. Mrs Campbell took care that the slippers should never hit him again and the incident was consequently one of the least convincing in the performance.

George Bernard Shaw, quoted Hesketh Pearson, BERNARD SHAW 1942

During a rehearsal for *Macbeth* at Her Majesty's, Sir Herbert Beerbohm Tree found himself interrupted in full flow by an uncued clap of thunder. Shading his eyes with his hands he peered into the auditorium. In a frosty voice he said, "When I require the assistance of our sound-effects department you may be sure I shall ask for it." After a moment's pause a disembodied voice replied, "I think you will find that was real thunder, Sir Herbert." "Ah," Tree replied pensively, "I thought it wasn't as good as ours."

Peter Bushell, GREAT ECCENTRICS 1984

During the intensely dramatic scene in *The Ghost Train*, when the leading lady, Marie Clare, was describing the terrible train accident, everyone was silent. The atmosphere was tense. "And the train went into the valley below – crash!" said Marie Clare. "Bang, Wallop!" cried a young man in the gallery. The tense, dramatic situation was ruined, both audience and players had to laugh, and it was quite two minutes before the actors could regain control of themselves and re-establish the minds of the audience. Later the author, Arnold Ridley, took the interrupter to task and asked him why he did it. He said he didn't know – it simply slipped out, and he was sorry for it immediately afterwards.

"Galleryite", GALLERY UNRESERVED 1932

A lead comic at Collins Music Hall, grumbling about the awful week he had endured, with small audiences, elicited from the manager the bleak response, "Well, what do you expect when there's polo at Hurlingham?"

John Le Mesurier, A JOBBING ACTOR 1984

Occasionally front rows talk animatedly, just as they might in their living rooms in front of Parkinson or Robin Day. At the end of one of David Kerman's more lyrical songs in *Side by Side by Sondheim,* one which he delivered with considerable quiet charm, I saw an old lady nudge her neighbour as the last lovely notes died away. She was pointing at his trouser legs with some animation. "Look," she said in a bright, clear voice, "turn-ups are coming back."

Ned Sherrin, A SMALL THING LIKE AN EARTHQUAKE 1983

At the interval of Stephen Sondheim's *Company* at Her Majesty's, a Knightsbridge blue-rinse lady approached the barmaid urgently. "How long does the second act last?" she enquired. "About an hour, madam." "Oh," she considered the prospect. "I think I'd rather go home and watch the King of Denmark's funeral."

Ibid.

THRIFT

Arnold Bennett never quite grew accustomed to the appurtenances of wealth. Once he said to me, "If you've ever been poor you remain poor at heart all your life. I've often walked when I could well afford to take a taxi because I simply couldn't bring myself to waste the shilling it would cost." He both admired and disapproved of extravagance.

Somerset Maugham, John o' London's Weekly 24 *Jun* 1933

John Christie, while lavish about some things, was remarkably mean about others. He would spend £30,000 on an opera production, but travel in a third-class carriage and carry his own luggage so as not to have to tip a porter.

Rudolf Bing, 5000 NIGHTS AT THE OPERA 1972

During a visit to Marienbad I accompanied King Edward VII to luncheon with the daughter of an old friend. The lady was charming, but careful with her money. When the King came to the table he found that the decorations consisted of four little vases of artificial flowers torn from the lady's old hats. He pulled out a spray of lilac and said, "Surely my dear, with the wealth of flowers being sold on every street corner in the town I am worth more than these old castaways?" "I quite agree, Sir," was the reply, "but I thought by decorating your table with immortal flowers I could better testify to my eternal devotion to Your Majesty."

Lord Ormathwaite, WHEN I WAS AT COURT 1937

Paul Getty's meanness was legendary and in my opinion mythical. He was a man who hated waste of any kind, and this quality can be mistaken for meanness. During the rationing period after the war Getty had invited three guests to dinner at the Caprice. It was fairly late, 9.45, and they were all feeling hungry. As they neared the restaurant Getty said "Let's walk around for a bit before we go in."

"Walk around?" said one of his friends. "I'm hungry."

"Let's walk. It's not 10 yet." Then added, "There's a cover charge of five shillings a head, and after 10 p.m, they take it off the bill. I don't want to pay an extra pound for fifteen minutes."

Charles Forte, AUTOBIOGRAPHY 1986

John D. Rockefeller was concerned little, if at all about clothes. One suit had a big patch on the coat, and a bright shine on the pants. "What's wrong with the suit?" he asked crankily when a friend urged him to discard it. "Everything," said his friend. "Your father would be ashamed of you. You know how neatly he used to dress."

"But," protested Rockefeller triumphantly, "I am wearing a suit of my father's right now."

Bennett Cerf, TRY AND STOP ME 1947

To get funds for his hospital in Lambarene Albert Schweitzer went back to Europe in 1934, lecturing. When asked why he travelled third class on trains he replied, "Because there is no fourth."

Gerald MacKnight, VERDICT ON SCHWEITZER 1964

In a speech to the Press Club William Blackwood replied to a jocular proposal by Hannen Swaffer that in order to curb the growing Scottish invasion of Fleet Street a trough of poisoned porridge, labelled "Free" should be placed on the arrival platform at Euston. Willie declared, however, that the scheme would surely miscarry, because all Scotsmen arrived at King's Cross, the fare by the East coast route being a penny cheaper.

Newspaper World 20 *Dec* 1950

When, after GEC took over rival AEI Lord Weinstock first went into the new company on his usual meticulous search to cut costs he demanded, "Why do we need two copies of the *Financial Times*?"

The Independent, Profile, Lord Weinstock 20 *Dec* 1986

TIPPING

Tommy Cooper once got out of a taxi and, slipping something papery into the driver's breast pocket said, "Have a drink on me." It was a tea bag.

Observer 11 *Sep* 1976

Somerset Maugham, towards the end of his life persisted in tipping in French hotels as though pre-war currency still existed, so that when he offered the head waiter the equivalent of less than a shilling his secretary, Alan Searle, had always to be on the watch, supplementary purse in hand.

Alan Pryce-Jones, THE BONUS OF LAUGHTER 1987

When Paderewski was in Boston he was approached by a boot-black who called "Shine?" The great pianist looked down at the youth, whose face was streaked with grime and said, "No, my lad, but if you will wash your face I will give you a quarter." The boy ran to a nearby fountain and made his ablutions. When he returned Paderewski held out the quarter. The boy took it and then returned it gravely, saying, "Keep it, mister, and get yourself a haircut."

Edmund Fuller, ANECDOTES 1942

Ladies, however practical, can have peculiar ideas of rewards and prizes. At the Coronation of our present Majesty it was necessary, on account of the great number of Peeresses who were by right invited to the Coronation Ceremony, to erect an immensely dignified and comfortable convenience adjacent to the Abbey – a sort of aristocratic lean-to.

One of the first to use it was a well-known Marchioness who unfortunately, on entering had the misfortune to knock her tiara against the lintel, precipitating it into the water closet. Unable to retrieve it by her own efforts and unwilling to appear before her new sovereign inadequately decorated, she was lucky enough to enlist one of the Gold Staff Officers who managed to retrieve it with the use of his ceremonial sword.

Being a Marchioness, unaccustomed to carrying money, she rewarded her saviour with one of her Horlicks tablets with which she had equipped herself to sustain her throughout the long ceremonial which was to follow.

Douglas Sutherland, THE ENGLISH GENTLEMAN'S WIFE 1979

TRADE UNION

One day (in about 1920) Aneurin Bevan went to Golders Green to hear Jimmy Thomas, the railwaymen's leader, explain to a great meeting why the union had capitulated in a clash with the government. Afterwards he heard Thomas remark to an aide, "When the buggers are giving you trouble, give 'em a mass meeting. It gets it out of their system."

Michael Foot, LIFE OF ANEURIN BEVAN 1962

During a miners' strike, Herbert Smith, who was president of the men's union, and Frank Hodges, the secretary, were invited to spend the weekend at Chequers to discuss the position with Lloyd George.

"It's all these 'ere ums," complained 'Erb Smith. "First there was the referendum, then the maximum, then the minimum, now it's the datum, and what I say is buggerum."

A.J. Sylvester, THE REAL LLOYD GEORGE

TRANSLATION

Peter Page, a journalist who wrote the "Mr Gossip" column in the *Daily Sketch* told James Agate, "I remember going to the theatre in Athens and seeing a play called *The Sister of the Mother of Karlos.* It was an hour before I found out that the play was a Greek version of *Charley's Aunt.*

James Harding, AGATE, A BIOGRAPHY 1986

Winston replies to the debate on war power. He is in terrific form. Authentic, reasonable, conciliatory, and amusing. In the course of his speech he uses the phrase *primus inter pares.* Labour people cry out, "Translate". Winston, without a moment's hesitation goes on, "Certainly I will," – then he pauses and turns to his right – "for the benefit of any Old Etonians who may be present." [Churchill went to Harrow.]

Harold Nicolson, DIARY 22 *Jan* 1941

I once found myself in Petrograd and I was excessively bored. I hardly understood Russian at all, but I decided that the only way to cheer myself up was to go to the theatre, choosing the largest and cleanest I could find, and sat down to watch the play.

It was a comedy, and so far as I could judge the audience found it amusing. It did not amuse me in the least because I could not understand a single word of what it was about. But towards the ends of the first act it seemed to me that there was something vaguely familiar about the situation on the stage. I had a sense of listening to something I had heard in a dream. I looked down at the programme to discover who had written it. The author's name was Mum, and the name of the play was *Jack Straw* [by Somerset Maugham, first produced in 1908].

Somerset Maugham, quoted Beverley Nichols, TWENTY-FIVE 1926

When waiting for my train at Waterloo I ran into one of the French correspondents in London. He asked me where I was off to. I said I was going down to Windsor to study the archives. He asked whether he might enquire what was the subject of my new book. "*Une biographie,*" I answered, "*de Georges Cinque.*" He expressed surprise that there should be documents at Windsor about such a person. Rather puzzled, I replied that there was a whole room full of papers. "*Quelle étrange personne,*" he said, "*avec cette passion presque nymphomane pour les hommes.*"

I was much startled by this, and then found he thought I had said George Sand.

Harold Nicolson, DIARY 3 *Feb* 1950

TRAVEL

The Balfour Mission to America set forth on board the *Olympic* on Saturday April 14, 1917, and encountered a storm that forced the escort of destroyers to turn back almost as soon as the liner came out of the Forth. A life-preserving suit of india-rubber was placed in Lord Balfour's cabin, but after inspecting it for a moment he said that on the whole he would prefer to drown in his nightshirt.

Blanche E.C. Dugdale, LIFE OF LORD BALFOUR 1936

When crossing the Jabel Shamar in Central Arabia Gertrude Bell donned a tea-gown for her evening meal. After spending the night on the summit of Finsteraarhorn she would come down to lunch in a lovely Liberty dress of mauve velvet decorated with a wide collar of *broderie anglaise.*

Elizabeth Burgoyne, GERTRUDE BELL 1968

Gordon Bennett, the American newspaper proprietor cruising in his steam yacht *Lysistrata* arrived at Madeira with the intention of staying a few days, but suddenly changed his mind and bade the captain make for Palm Beach without a stop. "But we shan't be able to carry enough coal in the bunkers," said the captain. "Then pile what you want on the deck," was Bennett's answer. The ladies protested about the unsightly mess, which threatened to ruin their dainty summer attire. "That will be attended to," remarked the sea-dog apologetically. "I will have the coal whitewashed." And he was as good as his word.

Bernard Falk, FIVE YEARS DEAD 1937

Mrs Alice Brayton was an expert in lifemanship. When the father she had tended not very willingly for nearly three-quarters of a century died, leaving her a rich spinster, her friends encouraged her to visit Europe for the first time. Reluctantly she agreed and took a cabin in the *United States*. She came on board early. She settled in a deck chair.

Then a succession of stewards came into action. Flowers for Miss Brayton. A hamper for Miss Brayton. A parcel of books. She became a centre of attention for all on board, and immediately was claimed for the Captain's table. She did not say that she had sent the flowers and the books and the hamper to herself as a means of gaining notice among the passengers.

Alan Pryce-Jones, THE BONUS OF LAUGHTER 1987

On the first morning out from Bombay my cabin-mate and I woke up early and began to chat cheerfully to each other. From the opposite cabin came a peevish cry of "Stop that damned noise". We naturally decided to investigate. Scowling at us from a lower bunk was a very youthful person clad in a beautiful pair of pink pyjamas. Smart and I said nothing; but we each took hold of a foot. Whilst he voyaged up and down the cook's galley on his back we realised that our victim, though his language would have done no credit to a present-day BBC announcer, was a born orator. And he was; for his name was Winston Churchill.

Colonel H.A. Irvine, LANDS OF NO REGRETS 1938

The *Daily Express* was hounding Noel Coward. A reporter kept following him about, asking "Mr Coward, why are you going to Switzerland?" They were trying to make him say, "To avoid tax." On the last day they followed him to the steps of his Montreux flat. Noel turned and said, "I *adore* chocolates."

Eric Ambler, quoted Caroline Moorehead, The Times 12 *Jun* 1985

Noel Coward travels abroad to meet people rather than to see sights. He was once staying round the corner from the Taj Mahal and refused to go to see it. He said, "I've seen it on biscuit boxes and I didn't want to spoil the illusion."

John Heilpern, Observer 14 *Dec* 1969

When I was climbing the Blue Mountain peak in Jamaica the wind was very strong and when I stopped to be photographed my hat blew off and disappeared down a precipice. Realising that it would be impossible to recover it, we started the return journey and towards evening, when we halted at a coffee estate, I was amazed to see a turkey buzzard about to settle on the roof of a house with my hat in its claws. Upon being frightened by us the bird dropped the hat, which I immediately recovered.

Admiral Sir Frederic William Fisher, NAVAL REMINISCENCES 1938

With a friend, I was on a train from Bangkok to Penang. During a stop at a station the only other occupant of the compartment, a Chinese, bought a durian and proceeded to cut it in half. Almost overpowered by the smell, we called the guard and asked him to persuade our travelling companion to eat his durian on the platform, which he obligingly did.

We had just begun to eat our ham sandwiches when he returned and started to make gestures of repulsion, shook his head and ejaculated "Whew! Whew! Whew!" as though he was overcome with disgust. Then he, too, called the guard to whom he spoke in Malay. The guard turned to us and asked if we would mind stepping outside to eat our lunch. Since the Chinese had been so polite in acceding to our request we felt we could do no less than return the favour. To a final "Whew!" we also left. When we had finished our innocent sandwiches and returned the jocular Chinese looked up with a broad grin on his face.

Dr Victor Heiser, A DOCTOR'S ODYSSEY 1936

Aldous Huxley is the only man I ever heard of (my informant was his brother Julian so I assume the story to be well founded) who, on setting out to go round the world, caused a special packing case to be made for his *Encyclopedia Britannica*.

Frank Swinnerton, THE GEORGIAN LITERARY SCENE 1935

The eccentric Professor Kasner (1878–1955) liked to take his summer vacations in Brussels, where he had become especially attached to a particular chair in a certain outdoor cafe. He maintained that he liked Brussels because it was a convenient base from which to organise mountain-climbing expeditions to the highest point in Belgium. "How high is that?" he was asked. "Twelve feet above sea level," he replied.

Clifton Fadiman, THE MATHEMATICAL MAGPIE 1962

"The Prof", F.A. Lindemann, later Lord Cherwell, was devoted to foreign travel. He would set out on leisurely voyages of exploration in a Rolls-Royce or a Mercedes driven by his chauffeur, and often accompanied by his friend and protégé, Bolton King. He travelled in patrician comfort, his progress resembling that of some English milord of the eighteenth century. He complained in the Common Room that there was no second class on the Golden Arrow. An astonished chorus of voices protested. "Oh, but Prof you surely never travel second class?" "No, but I mean that one has to have one's servant with one."

Earl of Birkenhead, THE PROF IN TWO WORLDS 1961

At Hurstmonceaux friends brought an American woman to lunch. On being asked about her yachting trip around the Greek Islands she said she had gone as far as Constantinople and even into the Black Sea. "So you saw the Dardanelles?" "No," she replied, "They were away."

Peter Coats, OF KINGS AND CABBAGES 1984

Among the tourists gazing into the Grand Canyon was Mr Ed La Gambina. He was impressed. But even more impressed was a nearby gentleman who turned to Mr Gambina to say, "Gosh! I wonder what happened?"

Walter Davenport, Colliers Magazine 27 Jun 1963

In the Colombia jungle, during Expedition Darien, Major Blashford–Snell's splendid bay horse Cromwell was so badly bitten by vampire bats that a sapper made him a voluminous dress and bonnet from a pink parachute, to protect his wounds. One night Cromwell broke loose and wandered into the jungle, where he was seen by Indians returning from an all-night drinking party. They fled in terror, believing the pink apparition to be an ancestor reproving them for drunkenness. Next morning Cromwell – disrobed – was given to the Indians in the interests of good relations.

Geoffrey Lucy, Reader's Digest Jan 1974

"We must go to Stratford-on-Avon tomorrow," said a tourist to her friend. "What's the point of that?" was the reply. "We can buy Stratford postcards right here in London." "But one travels for more than to send postcards. I want to write my name on Shakespeare's tomb."

Neal O'Hara, New York Post 1939

We were on our way to the Lupa River in Tanganyika and I had cycled ahead of my companions, looking for a camping site. My rifle was slung beneath the crossbar. The path dipped sharply over a loose bamboo bridge, up a short hill, and on to the flat again. Free-wheeling down the hill. I crossed the bridge with a loud rattle of rifle against cycle-iron and bamboo poles shaking against their supports.

Looking up, I saw something lying asleep in the road. It looked like a large brown dog. But it was a lion. I was so busy watching it that I omitted to look where I was going and crashed into a thicket.

The bicycle landed noisily on the path, the rifle came unstuck and scraped between the wheels, a tyre burst and the general din disturbed a flock of squawking birds. Picking myself up from the thicket I jumped for the gun. But the lion had gone. A hundred yards away I saw him. In a cloud of dust the King of Beasts was running with his tail between his legs.

Rex Tremlett, EASY GOING 1940

One drawback of having been to Iraq was that I now could not get into Kuwait. The Iraqis had decided that Kuwait really belonged to them and the sight of an Iraqi visa in one's passport was a mortal affront to the Kuwaitis. Not for the last time I defaced Her Majesty's property by covering the offending page with Lebanese excise stamps, overprinted smudgily with a rubber stamp marked *Urgent* and finished off with an illegible signature. No one ever asked what it was, and I got into Kuwait in time for a state visit by the King of Saudi Arabia.

Gerald Priestland, SOMETHING UNDERSTOOD 1986

UNDERTAKER

My uncle Billy, an undertaker's assistant, came into a pub, ready to stand drinks all round with a bright sovereign. "Where did t'a get that, lad?" "In the mouth of this Jewish bugger we just coffined." "But that's to pay his fare across the River Jordan." Billy pocketed his change and said, "Bugger'll have to swim."

Anthony Burgess, LITTLE WILSON AND BIG GOD 1986

Preparing a baldheaded body for its coffin, Uncle Billy had been told by the widow that her poor husband was to be buried with his wig on. He found difficulty in affixing it. He called up to his employer, "Mr Clegg, have you got a bit of glue?" And then, "Never mind. I've found a nail."

Ibid.

UNIVERSITY

When Gerald Gardiner (later Baron Gardiner of Kittisford QC) was up at Magdalene in the summer of 1924 he published a pamphlet on pink paper which resulted in his being sent down. A woman undergraduate had suffered the same fate a few days previously for climbing into Somerville after a dance. Gardiner, characteristically, rushed to her defence and the Vice-Chancellor, Farnell, notoriously out of touch with the post-war generation, asked Gardiner to leave at the intolerable hour of 6 a.m. in the morning; any later hour, Farnell knew, would have meant a sympathetic funeral procession several hundred strong.

The name of the girl to whose defence Gardiner had so gallantly flown has since become well known to readers of the *Sunday Times*; it was Dilys Powell.

Godfrey Smith, Sunday Times 5 *Apr* 1984

At the end of every term a terrible ordeal takes place known as "collections", or more colloquially, "collecers" which consists of an examination of work done during the term.

When Sacheverell Sitwell came up for his viva voce he was greeted with black faces and remarks of that strange and curdled quality which, in academicians, passes for sarcasm.

"As it is obviously superfluous to comment on your knowledge which is non-existent – we are only left with your style, Mr Sitwell" said one of the examiners. "You appear to write very much in the style of Ouida."

"That," remarked Sacheverell calmly, "is my aim."

Beverley Nichols, TWENTY-FIVE 1926

VANITY

It was at the Council of Europe that Boothby and Churchill dined together for the last time. "I was wearing my Legion of Honour in my buttonhole," says Boothby. "He glared at it. 'What is that?' he said. I told him I'd received it for my wartime services in France. He scowled again. Then went upstairs and came down again with the Medaille Militaire in *his* buttonhole. 'That's better than yours,' he said."

Susan Barnes, Sunday Times Magazine 1 *Apr* 1973

Asked whether he had ever been wrong Foster Dulles considered the question a long time before replying. "Yes," he admitted, "once, many, many years ago. I thought I had made a wrong decision. Of course, it turned out I had been right all along. But I was wrong to have *thought* I was wrong."

Henri Temuanka, FACING THE MUSIC 1973

"I love my hands," Ronald Firbank crooned, holding them out before him. "They are too beautiful. Don't you love my hands?" He minced and draped them one way, and then another. "When I am alone I am never lonely, because my hands are beautiful."

Robert McAlmon, BEING GENIUSES TOGETHER 1938

Dame Nellie Melba was in the great tradition of prima donnas. Commanded to sing at Windsor Castle with Mary Garden, the reigning diva of the Opéra Comique, she confided to the Lord Chamberlain in a penetrating whisper, "What a dreadful concert this would have been if I hadn't come."

Joseph Wechsberg, RED PLUSH AND BLACK VELVET 1962

I took Nye Bevan's young nephew, Vincent Stafford, to lunch at the House of Lords. Field Marshal Montgomery sat down at our table and spoke to Vincent. Picking up the menu card, the cover of which was a photograph of the Queen opening parliament with himself as sword-bearer, he pointed to himself with a fork and said, "That's me."

Mervyn Stockwood, CHANCTONBURY RING 1982

Lord Northcliffe once told me I must see Napoleon's hat at Fontainbleau, and said in all seriousness, "I have had it on. It fits me."

Tom Clarke, MY NORTHCLIFFE DIARY 1931

At a function in Tripoli Qaddafi had to walk up some steps to a podium. He did so with some difficulty and appeared to be limping.

"Look at his leg," said one diplomat. "He's had a stroke."

"Look at his shoes," replied an Italian colleague.

Qaddafi was teetering, like a girl at her first dance, on huge Cuban heels.

David Blundy and Andrew Lycett, QADDAFI AND THE LIBYAN REVOLUTION 1987

Arnold Schoenberg went to Venice in September 1925 to conduct his Serenade Op. 24, the first concert piece to apply an organised method of composition with twelve notes, at the International Society for Contemporary Music festival. He over-ran his rehearsal time and was interrupted by Edward J. Dent, the society's president, asking him to make way for the next performer. Schoenberg ignored him.

"Herr Schoenberg," insisted Dent, "you are not the only composer here."

"I think I am," said Schoenberg.

Norman Lebrecht, THE BOOK OF MUSICAL ANECDOTES 1985

There was a streak of vanity in C.P. Scott [editor of the *Manchester Guardian*] on which Lloyd George was not slow to play. Whenever Lloyd George spoke in Manchester, CP must always be given a seat on the platform close to him, and Lloyd George would never miss referring to his presence as that of "the world's greatest living journalist". During the final somersaults of the Coalition in 1922 he was hard put to it to find a saving word for Lloyd George and I remember H.W. Massingham, editor of *The Nation*, saying at lunch one day, "To me there are few spectacles more melancholy than that of dear old C.P. Scott wearily dredging in a foul pond for the soul of C.P. Scott."

Vivian Philips, MY DAYS AND WAYS 1943

VEGETARIAN

I delivered myself of an unbounded denunciation of Theosophy. Mrs Annie Besant listened to me with complete and genuine amusement and then said she had become a vegetarian (as I was) and that perhaps it had enfeebled her mind.

G.B. Shaw, Daily Telegraph, Annie Besant obituary 21 *Sep* 1933

Once, when Wilfred Scawen Blunt was bent on seducing a vegetarian peeress she did not turn up, and he had to eat a solitary dinner of spinach, cauliflower and sago pudding by himself in his Mount Street flat.

Anthony Powell, Daily Telegraph 12 *Jul* 1979

I dined with a curious collection of guests including Sir Stafford Cripps who has charming manners and is honest, if demented. He ate three scraped carrots, some salad and an orange, nothing cooked. He only drank orange juice.

Sir Henry Channon, DIARY 8 *Mar* 1944

A young friend of Gandhi's who had abandoned the customs of his people and taken to meat-eating, persuaded Gandhi that he had only to eat meat in order to be as brave as an Englishman. The two friends then sought out a lonely spot by the river and there Gandhi tasted meat for the first time. The result was a night of horror during which "every time I dropped off to sleep it would seem as though a live goat were bleating inside me and I would jump up in remorse."

He abandoned meat-eating.

Robert Lynd, News Chronicle 24 *Oct* 1930

George Bernard Shaw is a noted vegetarian. At a dinner he had before him on his plate the special concoction that was always provided for him, consisting of some greens with a mixture of salad oils. Sir James Barrie, his neighbour at the table, bent over him and asked, "Have you eaten that – or are you just going to?"

Edmund Fuller, ANECDOTES 1942

A young Warwickshire couple specially asked for "Sheep may safely graze" to be played at their wedding. When the vicar asked them why, the bride replied, "Because we are both vegetarians."

Peterborough, Daily Telegraph 19 *Jun* 1985

VIETNAM WAR

Peace talks were proceeding in Paris and the US Military Command wanted a North Vietnamese soldier taken prisoner to prove allegations that Hanoi was breaking truce terms by sending troops into the demilitarised area.

It was around midnight when Colonel Oliver North told his squad quietly, "We are going to take a prisoner."

With no quarry to be found in the demilitarised zone North – who prided himself that he never failed to carry out any mission – spotted a dozing enemy across the border.

Unhesitatingly he silently signalled one of his men to follow him across the border. He wounded and subdued the North Vietnamese sentry, then carried him back to headquarters like a sack of potatoes.

Randall Herrod, who helped North carry the prisoner back, said, "No superior ever asked where we got the prisoner, and North just told us that this was something that we had to keep our mouths shut about."

Ross Mark, Sunday Express 12 *Jul* 1987

VIOLENCE

Just before the war a *clochard* to whom Samuel Beckett had refused money stabbed him in the street. The wound put him in hospital with a perforated lung. Discharged from hospital, Beckett went to see his assailant in gaol. He asked the tramp why he had done what he did. The unhappy *clochard* said he didn't know.

One could make much of this. When, in 1945, Beckett started writing again, in French, he was to write much about tramps and dead-beat characters of every kind. It might be thought he was trying to identify with the man who had stabbed him, and whose only answer was, "*Je ne sais pas, monsieur.*"

Observer, Profile 9 *Nov* 1958

WEALTH

After losing his fortune in the Russian Revolution Chaliapin built up another. He is the simplest and most humorous philosopher in the world. Four years ago he bought a great bar of gold and put it in a safe in his cellar in Paris.

"People in Britain think that governments cannot collapse," he said. "They think banknotes are money; banks are impregnable. But I have had everything I made in twenty-five years stripped from me. I was reduced to singing for tea in which there was sawdust, and bread in which there was wood. With my bar of gold and a penknife I shall never go hungry.

Sydney Morrell, Sunday Express 5 *May* 1935

Visiting a newly rich friend in the country, Wolcott Gibbs refused to be impressed by tennis courts, swimming pools, stables and other forms of luxury. Finally, returning to the house, the owner pointed to a magnificent elm, growing just outside the library window and boasted, "That tree stood for years on top of the hill. I had it moved down so that on pleasant mornings I can do my work in its shade." Said Gibbs, "That just goes to show what God could do if he had money."

Frank Case, DO NOT DISTURB 1945

Amadeo Peter Giannini, a Californian banker, asked a distinguished looking grey-haired man to get him a taxi. When the man came back with the vehicle Giannini gave him a twenty-five cent piece. The recipient was obviously embarrassed. He explained that he was the head of the Los Angeles Bank of America. Giannini apologised, took back the quarter and gave him a dollar.

J.K. Galbraith, A LIFE IN OUR TIME 1981

When William Randolph Hearst's *New York Journal* was locked in a gigantic circulation battle with Joseph Pulitzer's *World* and Hearst was pouring his resources into the struggle someone observed to his mother that he was losing a million dollars a year. Mrs Hearst was unmoved. "Is he?" she said. "Then he will only last about thirty years."

Pauline Kael, THE CITIZEN KANE BOOK 1971

John D. Rockefeller conducts his affairs in a very comfortable but modest office. A visitor, disappointed, asked, "How can you hope to impress anybody in an office life this?" Mr Rockefeller answered, "Who do I have to impress?"

Bennett Cerf, SHAKE WELL BEFORE USING 1948

WEDDING

On the day of her wedding to Tom Lewis, Elizabeth Arden continued to work until four o'clock, taking only enough time off to have one of her girls give her a quick facial and for the Ogilvies to run a hot curling iron through her hair. When the clock struck she said she was taking an hour off, but nothing about why or where she was going.

She returned precisely at five. She announced, "Well, I've done it," and went back to work until eight, when she went to join Tommy for their wedding supper.

Constance Woodworth and Alfred Allan Lewis, ELIZABETH ARDEN, AN UNRETOUCHED PORTRAIT 1972

At the wedding of actress Dorothy Hyson and Robert Douglas the clergyman summoning bride and bridegroom to the altar and addressing them inaudibly and interminably, a fellow actor, Bobbie Andrews was heard to whisper, "I think he's trying to sell them a play."

James Agate, DIARY 21 *May* 1936

It became understood between Sir John Ellerman and Esther de Sole that they would marry. It was a strange wedding for a multimillionaire. A few hours before the ceremony the bridegroom rang up half a dozen close friends and relatives. "Esther and I are getting married in the morning," he said. "Would you like to come?"

"But where is it to be?" asked the bewildered guests.

"That I can't tell you," he replied. "But if you want to come I'll send a car to fetch you."

And not another word would he say. They were married at Chertsey Register Office.

Leo Condon, Sunday Referee 4 *Oct* 1936

Port Maria, in the parish of St Mary, is a crumbling slice of old Jamaica. It was here, on 24 March 1952, that Ian Fleming's carefully maintained bachelor life went for good, when he married

Lady Rothermere, née Anne Charteris. Noel Coward was one of the witnesses.

In Jamaica the wedding breakfast is called a brekinge. Fleming had arranged it at Goldeneye and it was a hilarious occasion. "We all crouched round that horrid table," says Coward, "and Violet brought in an enormous wedding cake gleaming with green icing. Then as a special treat for the Commander there was black crab. It can be wonderful, but that month can't have been a good time for crab, and it was like eating cigarette ash out of a pink tin."

When it was all over the bridegroom gathered together the remains of the green wedding cake and buried them carefully in the garden.

John Pearson, LIFE OF IAN FLEMING 1966

The *Irish Times* reported at the weekend that at a recent wedding in Ireland the father of the bride discovered that £1000 was lifted from his pocket during a reception at a local hotel. So short of cash did this leave him that he is having to re-mortgage his house to pay for the party.

A week later, when a video recording of the event was played to a family gathering, the bridegoom was seen rifling his father-in-law's jacket. "The happy couple are on honeymoon," reports the newspaper. "They are due back next weekend. A very different reception awaits them."

Daily Telegraph 27 *Aug* 1986

WILL

Ivy Mabel Blackhurst, of Beauchief, Sheffield, left £20,000 to her cat Blackie. For three years, until her death in 1978 at the age of eighteen, Blackie lived on in Mrs Blackhurst's detached house, waited on by a full-time housekeeper.

Catherine Caufield, THE EMPEROR OF THE UNITED STATES OF AMERICA AND OTHER MAGNIFICENT BRITISH ECCENTRICS 1981

During the 1914–18 war Lord Lascelles, then a colonel in the Grenadier Guards, was home on leave from the trenches, and was taken by a friend to a club to dine. He saw the Marquis of Clanricarde sitting alone and said, "I must speak to Uncle. I haven't seen him for years."

The Marquis looked up in surprise when the smart Guardsman greeted him. They talked about the war. Clanricarde listened intently to his nephew's stories. Lord Lascelles went back to Ypres and the battle. Lord Clanricarde went home and altered his will.

In 200 words he made the man who had spoken to him on an impulse the heir to the Clanricarde fortune of two and a half million pounds. His housekeeper and butler witnessed the altered will.

Two months later Clanricarde died. Lord Lascelles, still in the trenches, was offered a staff appointment. His comrades pressed him to take it, saying it would give him a better chance to live to enjoy his inheritance. But Lord Lascelles, a DSO and twice wounded, refused to leave his men. He remained in command of his battalion until the armistice.

John L. Garbutt, Sunday Express 31 *July* 1949

Ernest Digweed, a retired schoolmaster from Portsmouth, who died in 1976, left £26,000 in the care of the Public Trustee with the following instructions, "If during the next 80 years the Lord Jesus Christ shall come to reign on earth, then the Public Trustee upon obtaining proof which shall satisfy him of His identity shall pay to the Lord Jesus Christ all the property he holds on His behalf." If by 2056 the Lord has not appeared to claim his bequest the whole amount will revert to the State.

Catherine Caufield, THE EMPEROR OF THE UNITED STATES OF AMERICA AND OTHER MAGNIFICENT BRITISH ECCENTRICS 1981

The late Douglas Fairbanks senior, famed among his friends as a practical joker, couldn't resist keeping up his reputation even after his death. Four of his best friends, who had been given to understand that they would be remembered by him in his will were surprised when that document made no mention of them. However, an envelope not to be opened until 60 days later was placed in the custody of Douglas Fairbanks junior and when the friends had long given up any thought of an inheritance Douglas had his joke. The envelope contained a supplementary will leaving then 60,000 dollars apiece.

Peggy McEvoy, Reader's Digest Jun 1940

I have often thought that man betrays his friendships in his will. So there is a clause in mine in which I name all the people I have loved or who have been nice to me. And to each of them I leave a little thing – either an object or a little money. I tried to remember them all. When I made my will my lawyer looked at me in dismay. "Mr Menotti," he said, "this is not a will. This is a jumble sale."

Gian-Carlo Menotti, quoted John Gruen, MENOTTI, A BIOGRAPHY 1978

WORLD WAR I

In 1913 Raymond Gram Swing got himself appointed Berlin correspondent of the *Chicago Daily News.* When the First World War began the twenty-seven-year-old reporter went direct to Theobald von Bethmann-Hollweg, the German Chancellor and explained the moral questions involved in waging war. Bethmann-Hollweg answered that Germany had no intention of annexing Belgium or any other territory. Swing asked if he could convey that statement to Sir Edward Grey, the British Foreign Secretary. Bethmann-Hollweg granted this permission, adding, however, that if the Allies agreed to a peace they would have to pay an indemnity. Swing got the impression, though, that this would not be insisted upon if he could actually make peace. He embarked for England where he was immediately received by Grey. Upon hearing the proposal of an indemnity Grey began what Swing described as "a magnificent tirade".

It was so magnificent that Swing forgot to add that he thought the indemnity might not be insisted upon. Swing occasionally wonders, even now, whether his lapse of memory changed the world. He sometimes feels that if the First World War had ended in 1914 there might never have been a Bolshevik Revolution or a Treaty of Versailles, and that Fascism and the present World War might never have occured.

Richard O. Boyer, New Yorker 1942

On August 4, 1914, I went to Edinburgh where accommodation had been taken for all ranks in the Yeomanry. I was awoken at midnight by someone who informed me that German destroyers were in the mouth of the Firth of Forth. The Lothians and Border Horse paraded at a very early hour near the North British Hotel and the majority supposed that we were to fight against the Germans that very same day. Lord Binning, being well aware of all the drawbacks, had chartered a two-wheeled dog cart to convey the ammunition to our destination at Haddington.

When we reached Haddington officers and men went in search of the ammunition. The chartered dog cart was seen approaching with the huge horse stepping out like a prize trotter. The horse was pulled up and Lord Edward Hay's civilian servant sprang from the seat. With one voice four squadron leaders and their sergeant majors asked "Where's the ammunition?"

"Oh," he said, "was that what was in those heavy boxes? I didn't know that and I left them on the pavement in Prince's Street, otherwise there wouldn't have been enough room for Lord Edward's luggage."

Lt-Col. Lord George Scott, THE FLEETING OPPORTUNITY 1940

On the outbreak of war I became a special constable. I had occasion one night, whilst on my beat, to enter the house of a professional man in Harley Street whose house, in defiance of the Lighting Orders, was blazing like the Eddystone Lighthouse. I gave the doctor a severe lecture and pointed out that he was rendering himself liable to a heavy fine. I trust that as a policeman I blended severity with sympathy.

He promised to amend his ways and then added hospitably, "As perhaps you have been out some time, constable, you might be glad of some sandwiches and a glass of beer. If you will go down into the kitchen I will tell cook to get you some."

John Leech's pictures from *Punch* have been familiar to me from my earliest days – some of his most stereotyped jokes revolved round the unauthorised presence of policemen in kitchens, but in my wildest dreams it had never occurred to me that I, myself, could find myself in a policeman's uniform, in a London kitchen, being regaled on beer and sandwiches by a corpulent cook, and making polite conversation to her.

Lord Frederic Hamilton, HERE, THERE AND EVERYWHERE 1921

When the question was raised as to what was the smallest number of troops the British Government could usefully send to France there was a flash of Foch's genial wit. He gesticulated, held up one finger and said, "One soldier. I will see that he is killed at once, and then the whole British Empire will come to avenge him."

Major-General Sir George Ashton, BIOGRAPHY OF THE LATE MARSHAL FOCH 1929

Asked by the chairman of the tribunal, at his examination as a conscientious objector, "I understand, Mr Strachey, that you have a conscientious objection to all war?" Lytton Strachey replied, in his curious falsetto voice, "Oh no, not at all. Only to *this war*."

Robert Graves, GOODBYE TO ALL THAT 1929

I was in Belgium at the outbreak of War and rushed in a taxi to Louvain encountering the flying country folk at every turn. Then suddenly a single horseman rode around the corner into the Rue de Bruxelles. He was in a dust-grey uniform and carried a lance. Close behind him came another grey-uniformed soldier on a bicycle, a carbine slung over his handlebars.

For ten seconds I stood in the middle of the road and stared at them before I realised that they were German soldiers. They were the vanguard of many more. Then I heard the high note of a motor horn and a long grey German war automobile came racing towards me. Over it, reaching from the ground in front to the back of the tonneau, were two long, sharp, scythe-like knives bent convexly. They were merely wire-cutters fitted on the cars of the invading army to cut any wires the civilian population might have strung across the road, but they gave the car a sinister air. A general staff officer, very erect in his pearl-grey cape, stared straight ahead through his monocle.

Arno Dosch-Fleurot, THROUGH WAR TO REVOLUTION 1931

Yesterday, for the first time, and at my suggestion, we had no bread on the table at dinner. People who want it must ask for it from the sideboard. Wells gave me this tip. The value of these dodges is mainly disciplinary. If the whole of the well-to-do classes practised them the wheat problem would be trifling.

Arnold Bennett, JOURNAL 1917

On 31 August 1914 Lord Castlerosse was hit by a sniper, the bullet breaking bones in his lower and upper arm. It was several hours later, when he was lying on the ground in considerable pain, that a German came along, kicking all the corpses that he passed. When he kicked Castlerosse, Castlerosse swore. He was immediately loaded on to a cart and transported to a crossroads, where he was laid beside several other wounded prisoners.

A German soldier came along and, to amuse his comrades, started pricking him in the leg with his bayonet until Castlerosse raved and swore. Presently an officer came along and ordered the man away and spoke to him. Before he left he wrote his name in Castlerosse's notebook and said, "Remember, if you get back into the war, that we looked after you prisoners and restrained our fanatics."

His name was Von Cramm and he was the father of a famous tennis champion of the twenties and thirties.

Leonard Mosley, CASTLEROSSE 1956

Dear Whelk. Probably if anyone had said to me on the evening of July 2, 1914, "Will you bet me £500 that on this day twelvemonth you are not riding a fawn-coloured mule through the streets of a place called Poperinghe with a bottle of Bordeaux in each pocket and an assortment of vegetables round your neck?" I should have closed with him and lost my money.

Alan Lascelles, letter to his sister, END OF AN ERA: LETTERS AND JOURNALS 29 *Jul* 1915

Dear Whelk. I had two days leave in Paris last week. I found a fly in my soup at Voisin's, which is a sign of the times.

Ibid., 3 *Sep* 1915

Dear Father, I forget if I told you that when Benning, our squadron leader, took a party up to Fricourt to bury the dead last week he found a live cat with five kittens in the same dugout as five dead Huns; and in the middle of No Man's Land, surrounded with shell holes, a lark's nest with not an egg broken. The bird, however, had deemed it prudent to abandon then.

Ibid., letter to his father 16 Jul 1916

The large church [at Richebourg] and the almost rococo churchyard astonished everybody. They had been bombarded into that state of demi-ruin which discovers the strongest fascination. Men went to stare into the very popular tombs all round, whose vaults gaped open unroofed. Greenish water stood in some of these pits; bones and skulls and decayed garments there attracted frequent soldiers past the "No loitering" notice boards. I remember these remarks; "How long till dinner, Alf?" "Half an hour, chum." "Well, I'll go and 'ave a squint at the churchyard."

Edmund Blunden, UNDERTONES OF WAR 1928

One night Aglionby, the adjutant, and I dined together in a pigsty with a sheet of elephant iron over it. This was at Fonquevilliers, which was being shelled heavily. The mess waiter was a bit shaky and spilt some of the soup over my tunic. Aglionby asked him what was the matter. Said the mess waiter, "They're shelling the crossroads something shocking." Aglionby cocked an ear. "Why, so they are," he said, "but unless you can suggest a way of stopping them we would rather eat our soup than have it poured over us."

That was before the German retreat to the Hindenburg Line in March 1917.

Roland Pertwee, MASTER OF NONE 1940

During the second battle of Arras we were seldom more than a day or two in the same place. Orders would come through and away we wallowed to take up more advanced positions. One night I found a dugout in which five men were sleeping. There was an empty bunk and I climbed into it gratefully. But presently I fell to wondering why my fellows were so silent and, lighting a match, held it to the face of the nearest. He was dead. They were all dead.

Ibid.

I am in the trenches and have been for three or four days now. I won't labour the point, as they are exactly like what you read about them in the ½d press. So far they are more uncomfortable and less dangerous than I had been led to expect. Waders are essential as the mud and water are well above the knee and the cold is intense. An unpleasant feature is the vast number of rats which gnaw the dead bodies and then run about on one's face, making obscene noises and gestures.

Raymond Asquith, letter to Lady Diana Nanners 19 *Nov* 1915

We have a parson attached to us now – a Cambridge don – who wanted to hold a service today in our battalion mess room; but the walls have been thickly papered with French pictures of naked women. He had to confess the site inappropriate for a holy purpose.

Raymond Asquith, letter to his wife 28 *May* 1916

On the occasion when, during an air raid, a bomb fell in Piccadilly, a man was horrified to see a woman's head rolling towards him. It came to a stop almost at his feet when he discovered it to be the head from one of the dummies in Swann and Edgar's window.

Mrs C.S. Peel, LIFE'S ENCHANTED CUP 1933

Asquith, then Prime Minister, sent for General Sir Henry Wilson to come to Downing Street and asked him, somewhat anxiously, what would happen if we lost the war. Leaning forward in his chair and tapping the Premier significantly on the knee Wilson replied genially, "They'll hang you."

Valentine Williams, THE WORLD OF ACTION 1938

You can imagine that, with trenches so close, we potted at each other all day and night. One chap, a German, was digging his particular part of the trench deeper, and every time he raised his head to shovel the soil out we greeted him with a volley, and he then put his spade up and signalled "miss". It takes something to be humorous when you've been 72 hours up to your waist in clay and water, 51 hours of which it has rained.

The Times, quoting letter from a private with the Liverpool Scottish 5 *Feb* 1915

During the East African campaign hostilities were not carried out as ruthlessly as they were in other parts of the world. A sergeant was taking three German prisoners back to base when they came upon some eland. The sergeant halted his party and took several shots, but he missed badly. One of the prisoners, forgetting his position for a moment, asked if he could have a shot. The sergeant promptly gave him the rifle and the prisoner succeeded in bringing down an eland at a distance of about five hundred yards – a feat which called forth much applause from the entire party. He gave the sergeant his rifle back and the party marched on.

Gordon Makepeace, SAFARI SAM 1933

Delius returned to England from France in 1918 with a new orchestral work for the promenade concert. When he reached my house with his wife he proceeded to unbutton his waistcoat, shirt and top trouser buttons and to my astonishment pulled out sheet after sheet of manuscript which proved to be his new work *Once Upon a Time.* "What a relief to get it to London," he murmured and subsided into a chair. "I, too, am relieved," whispered Madame Delius. "I was so afraid they might search him and commandeer it." They had feared arrest throughout the journey, alarmed by rumours that a conductor in America had been transmitting coded war secrets to Germany in the guise of musical compositions.

Sir Henry Wood, MY LIFE IN MUSIC 1938

I asked Clemenceau how he heard that Germany was soliciting a armistice. "By telegram," he said. "What did you say?" I asked. "Nothing." "What did you do?"

He looked at me, hesitated, and did me the honour of telling me.

"I took my head in my hand – like this – and I wept."

Elbows on the desk he let his heavy, rough-hewn head fall into his hands.

Sacha Guitry, IF I REMEMBER RIGHT 1935

As the hour of eleven approached on 11 November 1918 the soldiers I was with kept their eyes on their wrist-watches. From the direction of Verdun the fog-muffled rumble of the cannonade gradually died away. In our sector there had been occasional rat-tat-tats from machine guns. Now they ceased.

Eleven o'clock! The war had ended!

It would make a better story if I could tell of men cheering, yelling, laughing, weeping with joy, throwing their tin hats in the air, embracing each other, dancing with delight. But they didn't. Nothing happened. The war just ended.

Webb Miller, I FOUND NO PEACE 1937

WORLD WAR II

What ghastly hours. If only you were not in London. It makes me physically sick to think of air raids. I was rung up in the middle of luncheon and asked if the Buick would take an eight-foot stretcher "or only sitting cases and corpses".

Vita Sackville-West, letter to Harold Nicolson 24 *Aug* 1939

I take a deck chair and sit at the door of South Cottage so that I can hear the telephone if it rings. Vita comes along the path walking quietly. "It has begun," she says. It seems that last night Forzter, Nazi Gauleiter in Danzig, with Hitler's approval, announced the incorporation of Danzig in the Reich, and that hostilities between Germany and Poland have already begun. The House has been summoned for 6 o'clock tonight. It is exactly 10.45 that I get this news. Miss Macmillan, my secretary, appears with my gasmask in a box.

Motor up to London. There are few signs of any undue activity beyond a few khaki figures at Staplehurst and some schoolboys filling sandbags at Maidstone. When we get near London we see a row of balloons hanging like black spots in the air.

Harold Nicolson, DIARY 1 *Sep* 1939

On the day Hitler invaded Poland I was in the Long Room at Lords. There were balloons in the sky, but although a game was being played there were no spectators in the stands.

As I watched the ghostly movements of the players outside, a beautifully preserved member of Lords, with spats and rolled umbrella, stood near me inspecting the game. He did not speak, of course; we had not been introduced. Suddenly two workmen entered the Long Room in green aprons and carrying a bag. They took down the bust of W.G. Grace, put it in the bag and departed with it. The noble lord by my side watched their every move, then he turned to me. "Did you see that, sir?" he asked. I told him I had seen. "That means war," he said.

Neville Cardus, A CARDUS FOR ALL SEASONS.

In the kitchen my grandmother mixed the Yorkshire pudding and my mother and father sat at each side of the wireless, which had a fretwork and canvas front, listening to Mr Chamberlain. While he was speaking my grandmother stopped her mixing, and stared at the wireless. When he had finished speaking she turned back to her bowl and said, "Bugger Hitler!" My father said, "Mother! It's Sunday!"

Russell Harty, Observer 28 *Jan* 1979

I was in the Cabinet Room at 11 o'clock on September 3 when our ultimatum to Germany expired. Ten minutes later the Prime Minister told me to inform the Service Departments that they might consider themselves at war. I went into the adjoining room and telephoned Gladwyn Jebb, who by arrangement was to be the link. This was the action which set the war in motion.

Lord Butler, THE ART OF THE POSSIBLE 1971

Edwards had volunteered Glyndebourne as an evacuation centre. The day the buses arrived from London some three hundred children and seventy-two adults were dumped on the Glyndebourne lawn. There were not enough rooms for so many, of course, and nowhere near enough bathrooms. I raced to Woolworths in Lewes and asked the assistant, "Do you keep chamber-pots?" She said the store did have them available and I said, "Give me six dozen, please." It made quite a sensation.

Rudolf Bing, 5000 NIGHTS AT THE OPERA 1972

A tiresome letter has just come, saying that the Kelvedon gates are to be requisitioned. They were expensive and I shall regret them. All iron is being collected and the first drive is to be made in Essex. The gates are very fine. Black, with gilded wreaths and fasces and my monogram on the shield. Damn.

Sir Henry Channon, DIARY 13 *Jan* 1942

Sibyl Colefax comes to stay. She minds so much the complete destruction of London social life. Poor Sibyl, in the evenings she goes back to her house at 19 Lord North Street, Westminster, which is so cold since all the windows have been broken. And then she creeps round to her shelter under the Institute for the Blind and goes to sleep on her palliasse. But all this leaves her perfectly serene. We who have withstood the siege of London will emerge as Lucknow veterans, and have annual dinners.

Harold Nicolson, DIARY 26 *Jan* 1941

During the occupation but before his imprisonment King Christian X of Denmark noticed a Nazi flag flying over a public building. He immediately called the German commandant, demanding that the flag be taken down at once. The commandant refused to comply with the King's request. "Then a soldier will go and take it down," said the King. "He will be shot," said the commandant. "I think not," said the King, "for I shall be the soldier." The flag was taken down.

Kenneth Edwards, MORE THINGS I WISH I'D SAID 1978

On a June evening in 1940 a group of retired French officers sat in a little house in a Breton village. In the house was a white-haired old lady who had fled from Paris.

They watched the first German motorcyclists ride up the cobbled village street. Then down this street among the cyclists ran the village priest, his robes flapping. He pounded on the door and burst into the room. His eyes were shining with excitement and hope.

"I have just heard the most wonderful thing on the radio," he said. "A

French general in London says France is not finished. That the war will go on from our empire and the whole world. The flame of her resistance will never die."

The old men looked up, hope fighting scepticism in their eyes.

"Who is this general?" one of them asked.

The priest said, "His name is General de Gaulle."

The old lady rushed at him and pulled at his robe. In a voice that soared exultantly over the enemy engines she shouted, "That is my son! That is my son!"

Alden Hatch, Sunday Express 8 *Jan* 1961

Speculation is rife about the "invasion". Wherever one goes one sees pillboxes and road barriers and field obstacles. In the towns one is struck with the number of women and girls in the population of the streets. The Budget has come and the complaint is that it is not drastic enough. From the richest it takes about 15/- in the pound. From my sort it takes 10/-, but who would dream about complaining?

Thomas Jones, letter to Abraham Flexner 14 *Jul* 1940

Within hours of the French capitulation Louis Spears invited me to lunch to meet what he called "a French brigadier whom I have just brought from Bordeaux". The brigadier was de Gaulle. When Spears took him to see Churchill the latter said, "Why have you brought this lanky, gloomy brigadier?" Spears replied, "Because no one else would come."

Lord Boothby, RECOLLECTIONS OF A REBEL 1978

Most of the Nazis I found struggling out of their parachutes on English soil were arrogant and surly. One Luftwaffe ace, Wertain, was captured by a farmer armed with a pitchfork. He gave the countryman one of the numerous medals that adorned his tunic and told me in good English that the brown lounge suit he wore underneath had been cut for him in Saville Row some months before the war started. He always wore it when he flew over England, he told me in the farm kitchen where the farmer's wife gave him a cup of tea, so that he would look "nice and smart" when he was finally run to earth and interned.

Edward J. Dean, LUCKY DEAN, REMINISCENCES OF A PRESS PHOTOGRAPHER 1944

A Nazi who showed some foresight in parachuting into the grounds of a hospital lost his parachute almost as soon as he got out of it. It was missing when the military escort arrived and its disappearance remained a mystery until it was learned that the nurses at the hospital had feloniously acquired it and cut it into several abbreviated undergarments for their own use. The authorities, always anxious that everything that came down with enemy airmen should be handed over to them, dropped their enquiries when this piece of news reached them.

Ibid.

During an air raid on Dover several bombs fell on our hotel. Chaotic though the results were, few of us failed to notice that the hotel parrot, stripped of every single feather he possessed, and in no way ashamed, kept whistling the noise of a falling bomb.

Ibid.

A lot of Ian Fleming's ideas, when he was personal assistant to the Director of Naval Intelligence, were just plain crazy. One had to accept this element of wildness in all his thinking. But a lot of his far-fetched ideas had just that glimmer of possibility in them that made you think twice before throwing them into the wastepaper basket. Just before the Dieppe raid, for instance, he had the idea of sinking a great block of concrete with men inside it in the English Channel to keep watch on the harbour through periscopes. We never did it, of course, but it *might* have worked.

Admiral Denning, quoted John Pearson, THE LIFE OF IAN FLEMING 1966

At Tonbridge, where we change trains, there are two German prisoners. Tiny little boys of 20, they are, handcuffed together and guarded by three soldiers with fixed bayonets. They shuffle along sadly, one being without his boots, shuffling in thick grey socks. One of them looks broken-down and saturnine; the other has a superior half-smile on his face as if thinking, "My Fuhrer will pay them out for this." The people on the platform are extraordinarily decent. They just glance at them, then turn their heads away, not wishing to stare.

Harold Nicolson, DIARY 7 *Sep* 1940

The bombardment began again at 9.15. I have to walk back to the Ministry through a deserted London. I have no tin hat and do not enjoy it. When things get very bad I crouch in a doorway. In one of them I find a prostitute. "I have been drinking," she says. "I am frightened. Please take care of me." Poor little trull.

Ibid., 12 *Sep* 1940

Go round to see Julian Huxley, secretary of the Zoological Society, at the Zoo. He is in an awkward position since he is responsible for the non-escape of his animals. He assures me that the carnivores are pretty safe, although a zebra got out the other day when its cage had been bombed, and bolted as far as Marylebone.

Ibid., 8 *Oct* 1940

Weeks ago we were all given green cards and white armlets with "Press" on so that we could get past the police. Generally the police have been helpful, although H.R.S. Phillpott found himself in trouble the other day in the East End. Someone saw him go into a telephone box and consult the book without dialling a number. This was regarded with such suspicion that a policeman came up and demanded his business.

Phillpott produced his credentials – NUJ card, a green identity card, a blue card and his passes for the House of Lords and House of Commons. This proved too much. "Only a spy would have all those," thought the policeman.

"I must take you to the station," he said. "I'll drive you," said Phillpott. He did. It was all right then. But you must not have too much proof.

Hannen Swaffer, World's Press News 19 *Sep* 1940

After a severe air raid Queen Elizabeth ordered 10 suites of furniture from Windsor Castle – including pieces dating back to Victoria's reign – sent to damaged homes in London's poorer districts. Many blitz victims received anonymous gifts of rugs, bedding, linen and clothes. Some are wearing the Queen's dresses, hats and shoes today – and don't know it. They have not been told lest they keep them as souvenirs instead of using them.

Claud J. Rolo, The Rotarian Sep 1943

No one in Buckingham Palace may bathe in more than five inches of water. The King has had a blue line painted in every bathtub at the five inch mark. To save coal no central heating is used at the Palace and fires in any bedroom are forbidden except on doctor's orders. Only one light is permitted in each bedroom and bathroom.

Ibid.

What impressed people and gave them heart in the Second World War was that the Queen refused to send her children to a place of safety, such as Canada. She said, "The Princesses would never leave without me, and I would never leave without the King – and of course the King will never leave."

David Sinclair, QUEEN AND COUNTRY 1980

The King and Queen paid a visit to Lancashire during the war, when I was Chief Constable. Food was very short at the time and when the King and Queen went in to lunch they were somewhat taken aback to see an enormous Lancashire spread laid out before them.

The Queen was not amused and in an acid voice she said to the Mayor, "You know, Mr Mayor, while food is so short in this country we don't have any more food on the table at Buckingham Palace than is allowed to the ordinary householder according to the rations for the week."

"Ah well," the Mayor replied, quite unabashed, "then thou'll be glad of a bit of a do like this."

Sir Eric St Johnston, ONE POLICEMAN'S STORY 1978

My pleasantest memory is of the time, during the war, when George VI and his Queen decided to test the Buckingham Palace alarm system, ready for use in case of an enemy parachute drop. They pressed the button. Nothing happened. Enquiries revealed that the officer of the guard, alerted by the alarm, had been quickly reassured by the police sergeant on duty. No raid could be impending, "as he had heard nothing about it".

Sir John Wheeler-Bennett, FRIENDS, ENEMIES AND SOVEREIGNS

I boast of being the only man in London who has been bombed off a lavatory seat while reading Jane Austen. She went into the bath; I went through the door.

Kingsley Martin, New Statesman 1940

Nobody who saw Lady Astor, as I did, when Plymouth was being bombed almost out of existence, could feel anything but profound and affectionate admiration. I remember in 1942 walking with her through the streets after a bad blitz. She dashed here, there and everywhere, encouraging, scolding, making little jokes. In the sitting room of one pathetic house, the roof and kitchen of which had been demolished, she ordered a pale young man to take the cigarette out of his mouth, told him he would ruin his lungs and morals with nicotine, slapped him on the back, and on we went.

Noel Coward, FUTURE INDEFINITE 1954

During the terrible bombing that left the centre of Plymouth a devastated wreck it was Nancy Astor's idea to start public dancing on the Hoe. She herself led off the dance, with the Prime Minister of Australia. Soldiers, sailors, airmen, townsfolk all joined in, evening after evening.

A.L. Rowse, The Times 6 *May* 1964

During the war my father was a meter reader. The odd thing about him was that he looked like Hitler – the same lock of hair, the same little moustache. When he was reading a meter one day the woman in the house pushed him in a cupboard and locked the door, then rang up the police and said she'd captured Hitler.

Eileen Atkins, quoted Philip Oakes, Sunday Times 15 *Mar* 1970

My arrival at RADA coincided with the building being bombed. We spent days sweeping up broken glass and pulverised brick, all of us aware that, as a result of the incident, our careers might not get off the ground; not at any rate from that particular runway. We waited in the hall while the Council conferred, and then a door opened and George Bernard Shaw appeared at the head of the stairs. He danced down them, his lean legs crossing like knitting kneedles. "We're going to open, children," he cried. "We're going to open."

Richard Attenborough, Sunday Telegraph 15 *Aug* 1965

A recent survey of London schoolchildren shows that youngsters between the ages of five and seven have forgotten, or have never known, many of the attributes of peace-time living. When questioned about such things as street lights and bananas they stared suspiciously and indicated plainly that they did not believe that such things existed. . . . When one teacher brought a seashell to school and asked her pupils to name it none of them could do it. "It's a shell," she explained finally. "That's no shell," a little boy replied heatedly. "Shells come out of guns."

Tania Long, New York Times 1942

Walking home from the theatre one night during the blitz, John Gielgud happened to glance up at the moonlit barrage balloons. "Oh dear," he murmured to his companion, "our poor boys must be very lonely up there."

John Mortimer, IN CHARACTER 1983

The Battle of Britain was in full swing. I was posted to Dover. Hitler's invasion was expected at any moment, and we lived on the alert. An officer was kept on duty day and night awaiting the code signal "Cromwell". When this ominous name came down the telephone the officer knew that invasion was on the way. At 3 o'clock one morning it was my turn to be on duty. The telephone rang. I picked up the receiver. "This is High Command QE2X," came from a rather cissy voice a long way off. "I say old, boy, sorry to tell you – Oliver Cromwell." "What?" I screamed, my heart in my boots. "Are you sure? Are you absolutely sure?" I had no reason for questioning the man's words, beyond the absolute horror of the announcement.

"Well, I may have got it wrong," the voice said affectedly. "Then for dear Christ's sake," I pleaded, "do get it right." There was a pause, during which I had my finger on the special telephone to the colonel's bedroom, as it were on the pulse of England.

"Sorry old chap," the voice came back. "It's only Wat Tyler. I get so confused with these historical blokes."

James Lees–Milne, ANOTHER SELF 1970

Diana Cooper, wearing amber slacks, met me in her little car. She looks a dream of golden beauty and is now obsessed by farming. Still in London clothes I helped her drive pigs and feed rabbits. She showed me her poultry and the swill for her pigs, of which she is very proud.

The world's most beautiful woman, showing off her swill. She was, as always, beautiful, delicious, simple and affectionate. As we talked we heard aeroplanes roaring overhead.

Sir Henry Channon, DIARY 23 *Apr* 1942

I was appearing at the old Holborn Empire with Max Miller and Florence Desmond. When I turned up for the matinee the road was blocked off. A time bomb had fallen nearby. But before we could get into the theatre it got a direct hit from a bomb. So the show was moved over to the Palladium.

Vera Lynn, TV Times 6 *Dec* 1986

There were holes in the road the morning I had to get to the Decca studios in West Hampstead to make a record. I got as far as Aldgate and there was smoking rubble everywhere and firemen's hoses all over the road. I kept being diverted but each time landed back in the same place. Eventually I had to go all round London and arrived at the studio with just ten minutes of the three-hour session left. I was all bleary-eyed from the smoke and covered in smuts from the fires. I was familiar with the songs and we were able to record the two sides in the 10 minutes we had left. Then I had to get to the theatre.

Ibid.

I was in digs in Sheffield when I was bombed out for the first time. It was three o'clock in the morning when I heard the sirens. I tried to get into the shelter but I was too late – they were full. So I just went back and sat in my room waiting for the inevitable to happen.

When it did I was surprisingly calm, in spite of what I looked like. My face was jet black and all my hair and eyelashes had burned off in the explosion. I gathered what possessions I could and walked up the road to the nearest hotel where I guessed the rest of the cast would be.

Out of the 300 houses in the street where I lived only six were left standing. You felt good to be alive.

Beryl Reid, quoted Barbara Young, TV Times 8 *Nov* 1980

I was twelve when war broke out. I simply wasn't old enough to realise the tragedy of it all. The real high spot for me was going out into the street and watching the bombers pass overhead. I was immensely proud of my souvenir collection, gathered mainly from the rubble of abandoned bomb sites. Once I found a glove with someone's hand still in it. I threw it back on the smouldering rubble because I didn't think my parents would appreciate me bringing it home.

Jimmy Saville, ibid.

The Blitz became a sort of apocalyptic *son et lumière*. Many repaired to the nearest Underground station, where they bedded down on the platforms and along the draughty corridors. Then, surfacing at dawn, a strange sight – grey, dishevelled figures carrying blankets, sometimes draped in them, emerging in the pale light from below ground, like a Brueghel painting of Resurrection Day – predestined souls rising from their graves. Long after the blitz was over the nightly underground habitués continued to sleep there preferring these public beds to private ones. Finally they had to be dislodged by force, otherwise they might be sleeping there yet.

Malcolm Muggeridge, THE INFERNAL GROVE 1973

Andreas Mayor and I made our way to the Temple on foot, treading on firemen's hoses, and ducking when things fell about us, though he, noticing a fire bomb fall near us, was liable to murmur in a disappointed voice, "Oh, it missed us!" Just as someone, looking out of a window and seeing the postman pass without a rat-at-tat at the door murmurs, "Nothing for us!"

The Inner Temple was a smouldering ruin, the Round Church largely gone, but we managed to get into the Library, awash with water. The two of us alone there, the sodden shelves at our disposal, a trolley of books ready loaded for distribution, but never to be distributed. Andreas mourned for the books, tenderly picking up one or two to see if the damage was reparable.

Ibid.

Aneurin Bevan was on his way to join Jennie at George Strauss's house in Kensington Palace Gardens while London was being blitzed and was nearly hit by an explosion in Oxford Street. He saved himself from splinters by the miner's habit of falling to the ground in the presence of danger. When he arrived, still brushing the glass from his shoulders, he remarked, "I could have loved London tonight."

Michael Foot, LIFE OF ANEURIN BEVAN 1962

In Paris Samuel Beckett, who was living with Suzanne Deschevaux-Dumesnil, was recruited into a Resistance cell organised by Jeanine

Picabia. On one of her missions she picked up a kitten with a broken leg and took it back home to nurse it back to health. Shortly after, she was called to London for a briefing and had to be prepared to meet a pick-up plane outside Paris at a moment's notice. She asked Beckett to keep the cat while she was away. In the meantime Suzanne was given an assignment to carry a message to two elderly sisters. When she arrived she found them sitting in a room filled with German soldiers who were hoping to trap unsuspecting agents. The chief interrogator asked Suzanne what she wanted. She replied calmly that she had come to tell the ladies that her husband had set the cat's leg and it was recovering nicely.

The interrogator suggested she take them to see the cat. She agreed with trepidation, afraid they would discover Beckett had no neutral alien papers. Fortunately he was out. Even more fortunately Beckett had been studying *Mein Kampf* and making detailed notes to help with his propaganda work. When the Germans saw the well-thumbed, heavily underlined book they began to trust Suzanne.

"I'm sorry. I must go to the station to meet my mother," she told the Germans. "Her train arrives shortly from Troyes." When Madame Deschevaux-Dumesnil stepped from the train she saw Suzanne waiting for her surrounded by three burly German soldiers! At this point, since everything Suzanne had told them had proved true, they clicked their heels and left.

Deirdre Bair, SAMUEL BECKETT 1978

In February 1942 a cable ordered me to fly to Miami. A tender took me from Key West 22 miles out to the *Queen Mary* which I was to take over. On board were 8398 US troops, the first to be sent to Australia.

My instructions about saving life at sea were explicit. I was never to stop the ship to save life, not even to put out a boat to save a man who fell overboard. A hundred miles north of Bermuda we sighted five lifeboats loaded with men near a capsized boat. I made a signal with a powerful morse lamp that I would report their position by radio and reluctantly left them. Jerry was probably lurking around for just such a rescue as I might be tempted to make. I refused the bait, but broke radio silence as promised.

In New York I was thanked by the US Navy for my action. The men had been picked up next day. Our purser's son was among them!

Commodore Sir James Bisset, Sunday Express 20 *Sep* 1947

After the sinking of the *Hood* we had to get the *Bismarck*; the nation expected it. One admiral said his ship hadn't enough oil to get him there and back again. I sent the telegram, "You get there and we'll get you back."

Winston Churchill, quoted A.L. Rowse, MEMORIES OF MEN AND WOMEN 1980

The Stalingrad battlefield is dead, and as only a dead battlefield can be, it is sordid and horrifying. A Russian soldier brought something to show me that he had just caught amid the wrecked machinery and rubble. And as he stood for a moment with his back to Stalingrad, and told me tales of Stalingrad, he played tenderly with a mouse until it had lost its fear and began to nibble crumbs on the ground.

The Times 10 *Feb* 1943

Round the corner of an orange grove in Italy Eric Ambler came face to face with a soldier pointing a rifle straight at him. It is one of those things he does not like to remember. The soldier was dead, frozen in an attitude by a cadaveric spasm.

Observer 3 *Jan* 1970

General Mihailovitch, Yugoslav guerilla leader, has made a deal to exchange Italian prisoners for fuel. He has worked out the following scale of values: one Italian soldier for one can of gasoline; one Italian officer up to the rank of colonel, four cans; one Italian colonel, 50 cans. The Italian command complained that these demands were unreasonable, but finally accepted.

Reader's Digest, Jul 1942

Life following the Allies into Germany as a Red Cross nurse was certainly tough, but it had its lighter side. Sharing a bench with matron in a field latrine was not something any of us relished. Not wanting to perform next to her we'd try to leave when she arrived, but she'd always misunderstand and say, "Do sit down. You don't have to stand on ceremony here."

Brenda McBryde, A Nurse's War 1986

General Patton received a message from headquarters ordering him to by-pass Triers as it would take four divisions to capture the city. But when the message arrived the city had already fallen. Patton replied, "Have taken Triers with two divisions. Do you want me to give it back?"

Brooks B.Mills, Reader's Digest Aug 1945

During the advance through Southern Holland a German one-man submarine was found washed up on the beach at Walcheren. Ralph Izzard inspected it and then excitedly telephoned Admiral Bertram Ramsay, Naval Commander-in-Chief of the Allied Expeditionary Force. "Nonsense," said Ramsay, "there is no such thing as a one-man submarine."

"Very well, sir," said Izzard, "I'll have it sent round to your headquarters immediately." And he had the submarine loaded on to a tank transporter and shipped off like a tiny tin whale. It arrived as the Admiral was finishing breakfast. He was still unimpressed. "The thing's a toy," he said.

"I suggest, sir," said Izzard, that you have a look down the periscope."

The Admiral did so, and staring at him from the other end was the still open eye of the dead German submariner who had been killed when his vessel foundered.

John Pearson, LIFE OF IAN FLEMING 1966

I ended the war as an air-gunner cameraman, having trained for my AG's brevet in Northern Ireland. It would be nice to think that some of the footage I shot was used in subsequent documentaries, but I have my doubts. At the time I was too air-sick to know or care. On average the raids over Germany took us between seven and eight hours. In our plane they were measured not by the clock but by the number of times I thundered to and from the Elsan as we cruised over the North Sea.

Richard Attenborough, Sunday Telegraph 22 Aug 1965

When General Wavell rightly decided to evacuate Somaliland, and carried out a brilliant retreat, Churchill complained that his casualties had been too light. Wavell sent him a telegram, "Butchery is not the mark of a good tactician," and that was the end of him.

Lord Boothby, RECOLLECTIONS OF A REBEL 1978

General Wingate was directing a reconnaissance patrol to a jungle area called Tamanthi. I said to him, "Sir, I have discussed at length the Tamanthi area with the Forest Officer who used to be in charge of it, and he assures me it is impenetrable." He rolled a cold eye upon me and added to the orders he was dictating, "No patrol will report an area impenetrable until it has penetrated it."

Bernard Fergusson

In the smoking room Churchill was much amused by a story of an American chaplain who, when a German major complained of the lack of organisation in the prisoners' cages replied, "It's no use complaining to me. I came out here to bury you guys."

Harold Nicolson, DIARY 8 *Jun* 1943

Nilgata, in Japan, was one of the worst prison camps. Our food got so bad that the officers – who had slightly less work than the men – formed a volunteer patrol to search for weeds along a railway embankment. Anything to put some food value into the two daily cups of warm water which was called soup.

But we knew things were getting bad for the Japanese when we noticed that the local civilians were getting to the weeds on the embankment first. By this time we were beginning to notice various signs and portents when something really special happened. A few men were kicking a stone around like a football and it smashed a window – the property of the Emperor. But the man who kicked it was not beaten to a pulp by the guards. When that happened we knew the war had ended.

Douglas Ford, quoted Robert Pitman, Sunday Express 16 *Jun* 1961

Lady Cunard was a guest at one of the first balls to be given in London after World War II had ended. Encouraged by limitless champagne, patricians of English high society danced away the night in elegant surroundings. A fellow guest, the diarist Sir Henry Channon, gestured towards the glittering throng and said, "*This* is what we fought the war for." "Oh, do you mean they are all Poles?" enquired Lady Cunard.

Harold Acton, NANCY MITFORD, A MEMOIR 1975

Index

D

E

M